LONG SHOT

LONG SHOT

My Life As a Sniper in
the Fight Against ISIS

AZAD CUDI

WEIDENFELD & NICOLSON

First published in Great Britain in 2019 by Weidenfeld & Nicolson
This paperback published in 2020 by Weidenfeld & Nicolson
an imprint of The Orion Publishing Group Ltd
Carmelite House, 50 Victoria Embankment
London EC4Y 0DZ

An Hachette UK Company

1 3 5 7 9 10 8 6 4 2

A CIP catalogue record for this book is
available from the British Library.

ISBN (Mass Market Paperback) 978 1 4746 0979 1
ISBN (eBook) 978 1 4746 0980 7

Typeset by Input Data Services Ltd, Somerset

Printed and bound in Great Britain by Clays Ltd, Elcograf S.p.A.

www.orionbooks.co.uk
www.weidenfeldandnicolson.co.uk

Azad Cudi is a British national from a Kurdish background. He grew up in eastern Kurdistan, where he was conscripted into the Iranian army and escaped to the UK aged just 19. He was granted asylum and citizenship, learnt English and began working as a journalist for the Kurdish diaspora media. In 2011, he was working for a television station in Stockholm when the Syrian civil war broke out and the Kurds established their autonomous enclave of Rojava. Azad's response was to fly out to Syria and work as a provincial administrator, but as the civil war expanded he became a fighter in the volunteer army, the YPG, part of the anti-ISIS coalition of more than 60 countries, deploying as a sniper in the victorious battle to save Kobani. He now lives in the UK.

*For all freedom's martyrs who came before us,
and for the thousands who fell in Kobani*

Contents

Author's Note

My account of the 2013–2016 war against ISIS and, in particular, the five months of resistance in Kobani from late 2014 to early 2015 is based on my personal experience. I made extensive notes during the year I spent in Kobani immediately after my part in the fighting was over. Since then, I have consulted my comrades for their recollections, made free use of what records were kept by the YPG and YPJ, sought out official records from the US Department of Defense, interviewed historians, activists and journalists, and cross-referenced everything with media reports from the time. Any errors that remain are my own.

I am aware, of course, that while the essential facts of when and where ISIS' advance across the Middle East was halted and reversed are well known, the story of how it happened on the ground is one hitherto untold. That is largely because so many of those who took part in those events did not survive them. It is my fallen comrades, above all, who have been my guide in these pages.

Leeds
February 2019

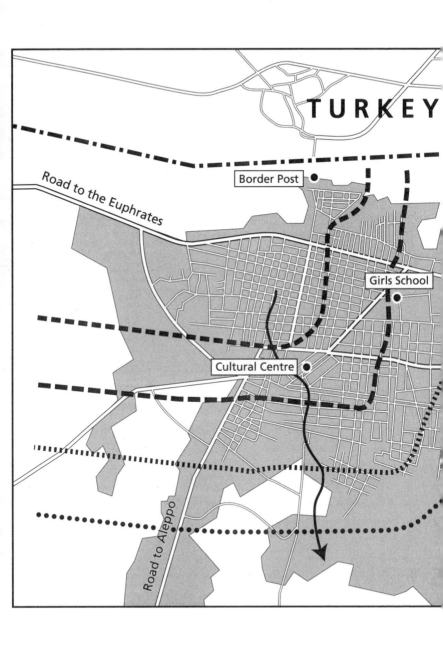

TURKEY

Road to the Euphrates

Border Post

Girls School

Cultural Centre

Road to Aleppo

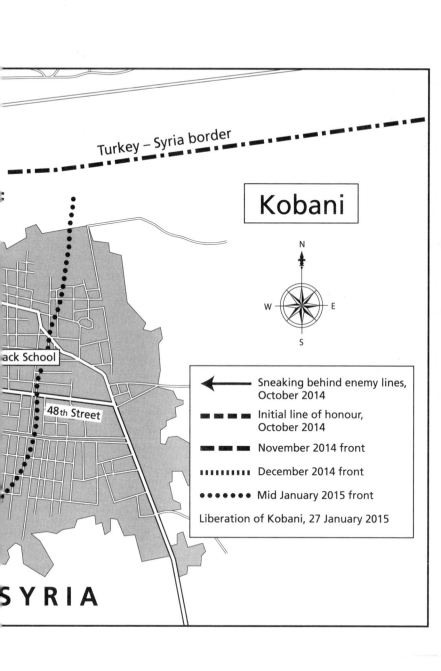

Turkey – Syria border

Kobani

N
W E
S

ack School

48th Street

	Sneaking behind enemy lines, October 2014
	Initial line of honour, October 2014
	November 2014 front
	December 2014 front
	Mid January 2015 front

Liberation of Kobani, 27 January 2015

SYRIA

ONE

Outside Sarrin, southern Rojava,
April 2015

I have had many names – Sora as a boy in Kurdistan, Darren in my British passport – but as a sniper I went by Azad, which means 'free' or 'freedom' in Kurdish. During the war, my name would remind me of a Kurdish saying: that the tree of freedom is watered with blood. It's a proverb about righteous sacrifice, about how liberty is never easily given but requires long and painful struggle. And perhaps one day enough of our women and men will have fought and died that we will live in a world of peace, equality and dignity, drinking water from the mountain spring and eating mulberries from the trees. But Kobani was not that world. In Kobani, we lost thousands and we killed thousands – and it was like that, feeding the earth of our homeland, drop by drop, that we nursed and raised our freedom.

I had been fighting for sixteen months in Kurdish territory in northern Syria by the day in April 2015 when I was asked to leave my position on the eastern front, close to the Turkish border, and join an advance on our southwestern one. We had recaptured Kobani in January. In the battles since, we had pushed the jihadis back far enough in every direction that crossing our territory was no longer a short dash through the streets but a five-hour drive across open country. As we set off, to the north across the Turkish border, I could make out the snowy peaks where they say Noah beached his ark. Below them, rolling towards us, were the wide, grassy valleys and pine forests of Mesopotamia, the land between the Euphrates and the Tigris where our people have lived for fifteen thousand years. As we drove further south, the slopes eased into prairie farms and bare-earth hills that rose and fell like the swell on a big sea. When the sun began to dip, I watched the late afternoon light play on the last of the apricot blossom and the red and yellow poppies by the side of the road.

Soon it was dark. The old farmer's pickup in which I was travelling was in a terrible condition – no suspension nor lights nor much tread on its tyres – and the roads were rutted and slippery. I am not sure we managed more than twenty miles an hour the entire journey. At one point, we came across a group of our women comrades sitting around a fire and stopped for a glass of black tea. Finally, at 11 p.m., long after I was numb with bruises, we arrived at a small settlement of fifty mud-walled houses, some of them bearing the familiar signs of invasion: bullet holes, RPG splashes and the jihadis' black graffiti. There I was asked to a briefing with the commanding officer, General Medya.

Medya was in her thirties and a veteran of more than a decade of fighting. She went into battle with her long black hair tied back in a ponytail and a green headscarf tugged down above her one working blue eye. One thing that outsiders always find surprising about the Kurdish resistance movement is our insistence that women and men are equal in all things, including war. In our People's Protection Units, a volunteer has to be eighteen to pick up a gun but otherwise all that matters

2

to us is whether you are sharp and useful, not where you are from and certainly not the accident of your gender. Men and women fight alongside each other in separate entities: the YPJ, or Yekîneyên Parastina Jin (pronounced *yek-een-ayen para-steena jin*), for women; and the YPG, or Yekîneyên Parastina Gel (pronounced *yek-een-ayen para-steena ghel*), for men. And the women fight, kill and die as hard as the men, as ISIS can attest. We often talked about how confused the Islamists must have been to find a woman standing over them in their last moments. If they left this earth in doubt, then it made us doubly sure that we were the perfect army to defeat them.

Medya began by saying that the day of our liberation was at hand. The moment we took back the last yard of our homeland would be the one in which we saved our people. It would also be the day that civilisation and progress triumphed over the medieval backwardness of the jihadis. Though they would never admit it, we would be achieving what the great nations of Europe and the Americas could not. We would even be saving our oppressors in Turkey, Syria, Iraq and Iran. And with our victory, we would finally bring due attention and support to our cause of an autonomous Kurdistan.

For that great day to arrive, said Medya, these last advances had to succeed. Our next immediate objective was a fortified ISIS base on a hill outside the northern Syrian city of Sarrin. Taking it would be best done at night, and that would require a sniper with a thermal scope to lead the attack. 'The hill you are to capture is about two kilometres in this direction,' Medya told me, pointing to the south. 'To take it, you must first climb another one next to it from where you can fire across at them. There might be fifty of them. We think there are only a handful. Arrive, assess the situation and proceed.'

Medya led me over to meet the small team I would be

taking. Leaning up against a wall holding his Kalashnikov was Xabat, perhaps twenty-one, who spoke clearly and with great enthusiasm and who had scouted the hills we were to attack earlier that day. There was a second man with a Kalashnikov, dark and skinny, who said nothing. There was a short, strong woman with a round face called Havin, who carried an RPG launcher. She had a loader, a nineteen-year-old man who carried her spare rockets and radio. Completing the squad was an older guy, Shiro, maybe twenty-eight or twenty-nine, skinny, tall, unshaven, with thinning long hair, who carried the BKC, a 7.62-calibre machine gun.

It felt like a good team. When I walked towards them, they turned to me. When I regarded them, they looked back at me with clear and steady eyes. We introduced ourselves and shook hands. I checked my kit – one spare night-scope battery, two grenades in my vest, five M16 mags filled with thirty cartridges each – and we set off.

For a daytime assault, a sniper picks a high place like a building or a hill and covers the advancing soldiers from behind. At night, however, a sniper with night vision leads the attack because only he can see the target. That night, the moon was just a thin crescent. Everyone in the team would be blind except me.

To advance to the first hill, we followed an established procedure. I walked ahead two or three hundred metres, checked it was clear and, after finding cover, said 'Now!' into the radio, which was the signal for the others to join me. We repeated this manoeuvre seven or eight times and were around five hundred metres from the first hill when we came under fire. I could hear the sharp, hollow sound of gunshots in the distance, then *fzzz fzzz*, like the sound of a honeybee, as the bullets passed overhead. Though the incoming fire forced us to drop to a crawl, in other ways it was useful. We had been quiet on our approach, which meant ISIS had to have night vision to have been alerted to our advance. If their bullets were passing over our heads, however, that suggested that the jihadis didn't have night scopes on their weapons, only a pair of binoculars. The sound of the fire also indicated only a handful of men, ten at the most, which meant we were evenly matched.

At 1.30 a.m., still under fire, we reached the top of the first hill. I could see there was a cairn at the summit where the farmers had stacked the stones they cleared from their fields. I stopped about fifty or sixty metres before the rock pile and called Xabat to join me. 'It's probably booby-trapped,' he said as he crawled up to me. As Xabat spoke, there was another burst from the ISIS positions and more *fzzz* sounds over our heads. We were getting closer.

Leaving the team behind a boulder, I stood up quite openly and, in full view of the ISIS fighters, walked briskly towards the cairn. When I reached it, I stopped for a moment to make sure they had seen me. Then I dropped down as though I was taking cover and crawled back the way I had come. Back behind a rock, I waited. If ISIS had mined the cairn, they would wait for all six of us to assemble next to it before they detonated it. In the end, the jihadis waited seven full minutes.

An explosion up close initially feels like your inner ears are being peeled. A split second later, you suffer a mini blackout as the blast wave hits your brain. You must keep your mouth open to allow the pressure to travel through you. If the detonation is truly close, you will probably reboot to discover that you are rag-dolling through the air, your nose, eyes and mouth filled with dust. If you are further away, it will be the earth that you feel bouncing. Next comes a shower of pebbles. Through all of it, there is nothing to be done but close your eyes and trust your luck. If you are going to die, it will be quick, as you are caught by the blast or hit by debris or smashed up against a wall or a rock. If you find yourself conscious and hugging the ground, unless something heavy lands on you, you're going to live. I remember the earth flexing, rocks shooting past our heads and pebbles raining down on us. We jammed our eyes and mouths into our elbows.

As the air cleared, my radio shrieked. 'Are you OK? Are you OK?'

It was General Medya.

'Fine,' I replied. 'Remote-control mine. They didn't get us.'

Through the dust, I could see Xabat grinning. 'I told you it was a booby-trap,' he said.

'Now,' I said into the radio. The team came up behind me and, as one, all six of us moved forward to what was left of the cairn.

At our new position, I told the others to place a few stones in front of them for cover. I took three rocks, arranged them under my rifle and pulled my scarf tightly around my head to hide the light from the night scope. Once I was satisfied I was concealed, I turned it on.

I saw them immediately. Through the thermal, I could make out a rock-walled base on a slope near the top of the hill opposite us, about five hundred and fifty metres away. As I scanned the area, I could see a skinny figure standing a few metres below the base, his heat image shining like a moon in the night. Three more men – one tall, one medium in height and a stocky man dressed in a long flowing shirt – were grouped together a few feet away. The skinny man was talking. The other three were listening. All four were out in the open.

The skinny one is the commander, I thought. *He is giving instructions. He is in charge.*

Five hundred and fifty metres is close range for a sniper. There was no need to adjust for wind. With a bullet travelling at seven hundred and sixty-two metres per second, the round would hit Skinny three quarters of a second after it left my barrel. The trigger on an M16 is also very quick. You just tense and it fires. I went for Skinny's head.

The stock punched my shoulder. Through my scope, I saw Skinny's head jerk away from me and his legs fall open. Then, as though he were a burst balloon, he deflated, slumping limply against a rock, his head on his chest.

I turned to the three other jihadis. Tall was trying to take cover behind some stones to the right. Medium Size and Long Shirt were running back up the hill towards the base. Medium Size stopped for a second. I aimed for his chest and tensed. Another kick. Medium Size was down.

Long Shirt was still running away up the hill. I followed him in my sights. When he stopped to pick up a large machine gun, I aimed for his body. Punch. Punch. The sound of my shots echoed off the rocks as Long Shirt went down.

I looked for Tall. He was over to the right, jumping from one boulder to another. He fired back at me but his aim was wild – just spray and pray. Behind the rocks, I could see part of his head and chest and one of his legs. I went for the leg. Punch. Tall fell to the ground, then started dragging himself to cover.

Now I could see a fifth man, short and fat, inside the base. Every now and then Fat Man would peek out over the wall, his round head appearing for a second, then he would disappear. I shot at him twice but he kept vanishing. He would show himself, fire a burst, disappear, then reappear at another place and fire once more.

I moved back to Tall. He was crawling in the dirt. He might have been trying to flank us. I told Havin, our RPG gunner, to move forward so she had a clear line of fire down the hill should he try to come up at us. I waited several minutes until Tall's head appeared between two rocks, then fired. His head tore away from me, pulling his body into a somersault and flipping him on his back. Tall was finished.

To the left, I could see Long Shirt was moving again, trying to hide behind a boulder. I switched my M16 to rapid fire to scare him into the open. I fired a burst, then another, then a third. But when I went to shoot a fourth time, my weapon jammed.

I removed the magazine, took my cleaning rod from my pack, lowered it into the gun, pushed the bullet out, put the mag back in and pulled the mechanism back to a firing position. Once again, it failed to load.

I turned off the scope, sat back on my knees, took off my headscarf and smoothed the material on the ground in front of me. Then I closed my eyes and exhaled. Keeping my eyes closed as we had been trained, I picked up the gun, removed the magazine, detached the stock, trigger and pistol grip from the barrel, then separated the charging handle and finally the bolt carrier. I laid everything in order on the scarf. Then I reversed the order – bolt carrier, charging handle, pistol grip, trigger and stock – until I had put the gun back together again. As I was finishing, Fat Man seemed to see me. He began shooting, his rounds slapping the rocks around me, sending burning needles of stone into my left leg.

The disassembly and reassembly took me two minutes. I opened my eyes and pulled back the release. There was nothing wrong with this gun. I put the magazine back in, and through the noise of Fat Man's assault heard the faint twang of a loose wire coil. *That* was the problem. If the magazine's internal spring had come loose, it wouldn't be pushing cartridges into the breech. I released the faulty mag, put it to one side, picked up a fresh one, slid it in and pulled back the release. *Shtick.* The exquisite sound of a round being securely chambered.

My pause had given Fat Man and Long Shirt time to breathe. Their bullets were coming in regularly now. A rocket grenade roared over our heads and exploded just behind us, the blast rinsing us with dirt and shingle. Xabat stood up and returned fire. Shiro started firing the BKC. I shrouded myself with my scarf once more and turned my scope back on.

Long Shirt had moved twenty to thirty metres down the hill. I fired the moment I saw him. He went down clutching his head and crying out '*Allahu Akbar! Allahu Akbar!*' This was their battle cry. But Long Shirt's voice was weak and I guessed he was bleeding out. Havin ululated back at him. 'Tilililiiiiii-Tilililiiiiii!' she sang, using her hand. 'Tilililiiiiii! *Biji reber Apo!* [Long live leader Apo!]'

To the left, I saw some movement from Skinny. He was on his back. One leg was lying flat on the ground but the other was moving up and down. I fired at the still leg. The other one kept moving, then dropped abruptly to the ground. Skinny was finished.

We had been in combat for fifty minutes. Four enemy were down. Only Fat Man remained. I asked Havin to fire at the walls behind which he was sheltering. With her first rocket, she hit the corner. The next went over. The third just below. I told Shiro to advance fifty metres down the hill and open fire. Then Fat Man would return fire, and show himself, and I would have him.

Shiro did as I asked, Fat Man stood up and I fired – but again he was too quick, ducking back down before I could get off my shot. Fat Man was defending himself well. He fascinated me, in a way. His comrades were all dead. But he was not leaving his position.

Xabat suggested that he and Shiro crawl around behind the base and attack it with grenades. It took them twenty minutes to reach the bottom of the hill. I kept firing so that Fat Man stayed low and did not spot them. But he guessed anyway. When Xabat and Shiro were a hundred metres in front of him, he detonated another mine. From my position, the explosion appeared to go off underneath them. But when the smoke cleared, I could see them crawling uphill, still unharmed.

'How's it progressing?' came Medya's voice on the radio.

'Nearly there,' I said.

When our men began circling around behind him, Fat Man heard them. It sent him into a panic. He kept sprinting outside, trying to spot them in the dark, then running back. I was following him and harassing him with short bursts, trying to make it impossible for him to shoot. When Xabat and Shiro were less than thirty metres behind the base, they called me.

'Fire more, please.'

As I shot several bursts, Xabat and Shiro ran towards the base and threw two grenades inside. There were two explosions. We waited for a minute. Silence.

I picked up my rifle, walked down the hill and up to the ISIS positions. Skinny, whom I had taken to be the commander, turned out to be the youngest. I had shot him in the head and the leg. Tall, Medium Size and Long Shirt were all in their late thirties. I had hit Tall three times in the leg and once in the head. Medium Size had bullet wounds in his shoulder, kidney,

10

stomach and knee. I had hit Long Shirt in the head and neck. What remained of Fat Man after two grenades suggested he was the oldest, perhaps fifty, and probably in charge. He had died a captain's death, going down with his men.

Medya released me from duty and I walked alone back over the hills, through the boulders and thorn scrub that filled the valleys, until I arrived back at the village where I had left the pick-up. I packed up my gear and we drove the five hours back to the eastern front. The sky was brightening and through the morning fog I could see Sarrin in the distance. In the still of the dawn, with the battle ebbing in my veins, there was a tranquillity to the way these southern flatlands rolled gently down to the Euphrates. The houses were modest and purposeful: plain stone walls, a roof, windows and small wire chicken pens to the side. As the car descended into the valleys, kicking up pale dust as soft as flour, I have a memory of small clutches of pink and blue daisies appearing on either side of us.

In our movement, we trust each other to do the right thing. I knew it was my duty to fight on. I also knew my experience was needed. Over the last year, fighting had become so easy for me. All that time, I had kept just two questions in my mind. How are we going to attack them? And: how are they going to attack us? I squeezed all my past, present and future into answering them. Night after night, day after day, month after month, I had lain behind my rifle. Through scorching summers, chilling autumns, endless winters and wet, numbing springs, I had kept the enemy in my crosshairs. I had burned my eyes with looking. I had survived other snipers, gun attacks, suicide bombers, tanks, mortars, rocket grenades, booby-traps, trip-wires, stray air strikes, artillery strikes, heavy machine guns and remote-control mines. On a diet of scavenged cheese, jam, the occasional yoghurt and biscuits, I had wasted away to the weight of a thirteen-year-old boy. Without sleep, I lurked in the abyss between adrenalin and exhaustion. So many of my friends had died that I had acquired a new, unwanted duty: to survive in order to keep their memories alive. Observing, waiting, shooting – I packed all of life into that tight existence. If you had seen me back then, carrying my trigger finger through the sharp edges of war as though it were a baby, you would have understood that human beings can survive almost anything if they have purpose.

But lately I had begun to think that I had nothing left. I felt as though I had used up thirty or forty years of life in months. I was losing the ability to feel the passing of days. One misjudgement, one push too far, and the lone candle that remained in my soul would blow out and the darkness would eat me. Climbing up to the ISIS base outside Sarrin, I had felt myself falling asleep on my feet. The mud had sucked at me, drawing me into the earth's infinite embrace. Twice my team had called over to me as I drifted off to the side. At one point, Xabat had challenged me with his gun raised, suspicious of this wandering figure way off among the stones.

I had been back in my old position on the eastern front for a few days when General Tolin came to visit. 'It's good that you are here,' she told me. 'We need you here. How are you doing?'

'Coping,' I said.

Tolin nodded and sucked at her teeth. She looked off to the horizon. After a while, she said, 'Coping's not enough, Azad.'

I tried to reassure her. 'I can stay here,' I said. 'Here is OK for me.'

Tolin regarded me for a moment. She had made up her mind.

'You go back to Kobani,' she said. 'I will see you there.'

And like that my war was over.

TWO

Kobani,

December 2013 to April 2015

When the Islamic State of Iraq and Syria (ISIS) advanced into Kurdistan in December 2013, they might have expected to overrun us in days. Formed seven years earlier by a handful of inmates inside the crucibles of torture and humiliation that were the American prisoner-of-war camps in Iraq, ISIS was an evolution from al-Qaeda, established as an alternative for those who found Osama bin Laden's original group too tame.

The world hardly welcomed this new model of jihadi. But its retreat before ISIS suggested it largely accepted the Islamists' central contention: that no force on earth could match their vengeful, suicidal pathology. By the time ISIS invaded northern Syria, they were an army of tens of thousands on an unstoppable march across Iraq, Libya and Yemen, advancing in Afghanistan and Pakistan, and mushrooming in the Philippines, Algeria, Mali, Nigeria and Somalia. Even in places where the group had minimal presence, governments were spending billions trying to prevent attacks by its disciples, all the while resigning themselves to picking up the bodies after their failure.

For ISIS was no billionaire's plaything, no bomb-and-hide

operation run from a walled villa by a man who couldn't find the safety on a Kalashnikov. It was a sophisticated, proficient and well-resourced army. It borrowed skills, personnel and materiel from Saddam Hussein's old regime. It bankrolled itself to the tune of several billion dollars through taxes, donations, confiscations of businesses and the sale of pillaged oil and artefacts. It used its wealth to build a military stronger than many national armies, equipped with artillery, mortars, tanks and heavy machine guns, mobile battle kitchens and surgeries, even social media managers and investment specialists. And rather than al-Qaeda's few hundred members, ISIS was reinforced by thousands of foreign volunteers who flocked to it from Marseilles to Melbourne.

Of all the obstacles that stood in the jihadis' way, the tiny enclave that we had built around Kobani from the wreckage of the Syrian civil war was perhaps the least significant. Kobani was a small town of forty thousand people that you could cross on foot in thirty minutes. The area around it, which we called Rojava, was a thin, five-hundred-kilometre-long strip of bare-walled towns and mudbrick goat and wheat farms sitting below the border with Turkey. When civil war engulfed Syria in 2011, it was here that the Kurds had first risen up. In July 2012, after the forces of Bashar al-Assad withdrew, it was here that they declared the creation of Rojava, an autonomous and democratic province of Syria. Yet while we had our own frontiers and civil administrators, our defences were all but non-existent. We possessed just a few thousand young men and women volunteers. We had almost no money and lacked the most basic equipment, right down to binoculars and radios. What guns we had were generally older than we were.

But in Kobani, between September 2014 and January 2015, around two thousand of our men and women stopped ISIS' twelve thousand. Six months later, we pushed all the jihadis out of Rojava. Our defeat of ISIS set in motion their collapse. By early 2017, the jihadis' dream of a new caliphate had been squeezed to a few pinheads on a map and almost all of ISIS' foreign volunteers were either dead or fleeing the Middle East in their thousands.

How did we do it? When you hear that Nasrin shot two hundred jihadis, I shot two hundred and fifty, Hayri three hundred and fifty, and Yildiz and Herdem five hundred each – meaning the five of us took down a sixth of the army ISIS sent against us – you might think you have your answer. But, in truth, that was just one part of it.

The town where we made our stand, Kobani, wasn't much to look at. A collection of bare-brick houses clustered around a few dusty bazaars, it sat in a shallow valley surrounded by fields of dry, grey soil and pebbly semi-desert. In the late nineteenth century, Kobani had been a stop on the railway between Berlin and Baghdad. After the Allies redrew the map of the Middle East in 1916, the track was replaced with guard posts, fences and minefields – and what had once been a link between nations became an instrument of division. In the twentieth century, Kobani had eked out an existence as a small border town on the trade route between Arabia and Europe. Few of its people became rich, but no one starved, and most lived their whole lives there, learning in its schools, shopping in its markets and celebrating the spring festival, Newroz, in its squares.

Kobani's real significance was in its history. At its centre, archaeologists had found evidence of a dried-up oasis that once served herders moving their flocks between the Euphrates and the Tigris. Among them, supposedly, was Abraham, his wife Sarah and their son Isaac, who had lived for many years at Haran, a day's walk to the east, around 2,000 BCE. The archaeologists' digs showed that long before even that time, Kobani had been at the centre of the vast prairie of Mesopotamia. There, around thirteen thousand years ago, our ancestors had been among the first people on earth to give up wandering the land for food and, by domesticating sheep and goats and sowing wheat and barley, invent farming. Around Kobani, they established a homeland of grass-roof villages, and a mythology based around Nature and fertility. Historians called the area the Fertile Crescent. The Torah, the Bible and the Koran called it Eden.

In the year I spent in Kobani after General Tolin sent me back from the front, I came to realise that these terms were less descriptions of the land than a tribute to the people who had conjured forth a verdant paradise from the desert. The way Kobani sprang back to life after the war was astonishing. Each morning, the vegetable and fruit growers in the bazaars would construct displays so over-abundant as to suggest a lingering anxiety over whether this new-fangled idea called cultivation was going to work. Stalls would be piled high with lemons, prickly pears, pomegranates, black grapes and oranges, while small rockfalls of watermelons sat to the side. The next row would be a mosaic of turnips, potatoes, beetroots, carrots and white-and-fuchsia radishes. In another alley were the market's true giants: tomatoes the size of small pumpkins, and cucumbers, red and green peppers and shiny black aubergines the length of my forearm. These would be penned in by walls of lettuces, cabbages and cauliflowers and armfuls of coriander, spinach, mint, dill, rosemary and parsley. Yet another alley would be lined with buckets of green and black olives stuffed with chillies and garlic, great sacks of peanuts, walnuts, pistachios and hazelnuts, and spice stalls heaped with miniature hills of dried chilli, scarlet paprika and golden turmeric.

As I wandered the markets, I inhaled the smell of sweet black tea, cigarette smoke, lamb stuffed with apricots and, my favourite, partridge roasted with honey and cinnamon. In the end, I came to see Kobani as a gigantic village. My alarm each morning was the sound of a cockerel. My view was a row of houses made of home-sawn wood and corrugated iron. Every backyard seemed to contain a cow or a goat.

When I think of how we withstood the Islamists, I think of Kobani's stubborn farmers. What anchored us all, fighters and farmers, was a connection to our land. With careful shepherding and untiring care, we had nurtured a rich and varied life from this meagre earth. The diversity was reflected in the city's population, a mongrel mix of Kurds, Armenians, Assyrians and Arabs, and a large population of Christians living alongside Sunni, Shia and Sufi Muslims, small communities of Sephardi and Musta'arabi Jews and even Zoroastrians.

Such a mosaic of humanity had often proved to be a recipe for division and conflict in the Middle East. Our intention, guided by the writings of our leader Abdullah Öcalan (also known as Apo), was to embrace it. By celebrating difference, and using tolerance to create community, we would break the cycle of tribe against tribe, and tyrant succeeding tyrant, and all the centuries of bloody murder and revenge that had scarred the region. Our plan was for an egalitarian, democratic society built on respect for all races, religions, communities, genders and nature. We rejected the patronising platitude, so common among Western commentators, that democracy and peace were alien to our land. We rejected, too, the notion that all freedom fighters were doomed to follow the same sorry path of liberating their people, only to turn around and oppress them.

17

And our ambition extended far beyond Rojava or Syria. The reason the Middle East was beset by continual war and crisis, we argued, was because it lacked an example of a peaceful, stable, free and fair society. Rojava was to be that beacon. Once we had planted the seed of liberty in every man and woman, our hope was that they would scatter it across the region and the world, just as they had sown the first grain in the first fields all those millennia ago.

To foreign observers used to labelling Middle Eastern movements with terms like 'religious', 'ethnic', 'socialist' or 'nationalist', we were, I think, a puzzle. Dogmatically broadminded. Inflexibly anti-sectarian. Freedom fighters who eschewed power. Most confusingly, Middle Eastern *and* feminist. At the core of our philosophy was the conviction that all tribalism, injustice and inequality stemmed from an original act of oppression when man, the hunter-gatherer, abused his brute strength to violently subjugate his equal partner, woman. In a region where women had been enslaved by governments, culture and religion since time immemorial, in Rojava they were to be equal partners with men in marriage, faith, politics, law, business, the arts and the military. Some outside observers drew parallels to the Spanish revolution of the 1930s, which also united anarchists, communists, republicans and a vanguard of *mujeres libres* against fascism. We understood the comparison was intended as a compliment. But to us it underestimated what we were attempting: to end prejudice, free the downtrodden and allow the Middle East to escape the carnage that had gripped it for so long.

This was one reason why Kobani was about more than the achievements of a small band of snipers. Another reason was the courage and sacrifice of two thousand other men and women who fought there, many of whom I never met. All of them have their own tale of heroism. The stories of Herdem, Hayri, Yildiz, Nasrin and me are merely five in a library. To think of our use of sniping as some kind of brilliant tactic, or even a choice, would be misguided. If all you have is forty-year-old Kalashnikovs, a handful of hunting rifles and handmade grenades, your only option is to kill your enemy one by one.

But if you had seen me back then, lying out alone in the freezing ruins of Kobani, starved half to death, waiting days to take a single shot at a single man in an advancing army, I think you would have understood. This was about freedom and never giving up. The jihadis talked about commitment but their resolve was the swarm of the mob, a great wave smashing anything in its path. Ours was the grit of the barnacle, the wit and dexterity of David against Goliath. A good sniper understands craft and patience but great ones are masters of destinies, both their own and those of every person on the battlefield. Alone, you watch, decide and act. Alone, you end the other man. There are few purer expressions of free will in this world.

This unbreakable bond with liberty reflected the principles for which we fought and for which we were prepared to die. It also gave us a mental agility that was key to outwitting the automatons of ISIS. Rather than rely on some external code to guide our behaviour, we trusted in personal responsibility and self-discipline. Inside our military wings, there were no ranks, only operational leaders, and no orders, only suggestions. Nor did we see war as about heroes or glory or purifying fire, or even winning or losing, as ISIS did. War is the darkness in humankind's nature and the profanity in our imagination. It is a violation and an abomination. Only the malevolent or deranged would seek a war.

But with ISIS, malevolent and deranged were often what we faced. In many ways, the jihadis denoted the darkness in humanity. If we believed in human possibility, they took a more pessimistic view, regarding people as inherently corrupt and man-made progress as conceptually impossible. And since they reckoned that people couldn't be trusted to run their own affairs, ISIS had taken it upon themselves to keep them in line using the only language that sinners understood: repression. The jihadis imagined the otherworldly holiness of their cause excused them of any earthly morality. Democracy, equality, rights, tolerance, feminism, freedom – these were the pretty words Satan used to spread his corruption. The way to free people was, paradoxically, to make them servants to Allah and Islam. Likewise, if the first Muslims had been pure and the fourteen centuries since had been a corrosion, then the answer to humankind's arrogant, sinful advancement was a corrective, cleansing reverse.

These, then, were the stakes of our fight. Progress or regression. Light or dark. Life or death. Perhaps it was the way we held up a mirror to their craziness that persuaded the jihadis they had to crush us. For our part, though we would have settled for ISIS' withdrawal, we understood that there could be no accommodation with men who had given such free rein to their inner beasts.

And in Kobani, as perhaps nowhere else, we had a slim chance to stop them. ISIS had captured hundreds of towns, some of them with only a handful of men. That it had sent twelve thousand to attack this one town, and that we had deployed hundreds of men and women to defend it, reflected Kobani's strategic importance. If ISIS captured it, they would cut Rojava in two and take over a ninety-kilometre stretch of the Turkish border over which thousands more foreign jihadis could cross. They would also crush our dream of building a new democratic and free society in the Middle East.

But by committing so many men to Kobani, the jihadis unwittingly gave us an opportunity to defeat them. And as Vasily Zaytsev had shown in Stalingrad in 1942, when the enemy enters the city, a single unblinking sharp-shooter can keep an entire army in the dirt and change the course of a war. In Kobani there were five of us who could hit a man from a mile away. It was a moment that would never be repeated. In the months after Kobani, Hayri was killed, then Herdem, and as I write now it has been years since I have seen Yildiz and Nasrin. I alone am here to tell the story of how we stood our ground, took back our homeland street by street and house by house and, man by man, shot the jihadis to pieces.

THREE

Kobani,

September–October 2014

I first saw Kobani on an evening in September 2014. The sun was setting, the first hints of an autumn chill were stealing into the air and before me, about a mile away, ISIS was laying siege to the town with columns of fighters in pickup trucks, supported by heavy machine guns and tanks.

In the previous few days, ISIS had taken the three hundred and fifty villages that surrounded the town and advanced deep into its streets. Hundreds of our men and women were already dead. Some had made extraordinary sacrifices. One team commander called Cudi, facing a mass of advancing jihadis on a position called Sûsan Hill outside the city, had refused his general's suggestion to pull back. 'I can see the houses of Kobani from here,' he said over the radio. 'How can I leave? Their tanks will have to go over my body.' Minutes later, his commanders observed that, after wounding him, the jihadis did exactly as Cudi had predicted.

Arin Mikan, a platoon commander from the YPJ, the women's militia, made another extraordinary last stand. As ISIS advanced to her position on Mistenur Hill, the gateway to

Kobani, Arin told the women of her platoon to pull back. Then she strapped as many grenades and explosives as she could to her body, tied them to a single trigger and ran down the hill towards the jihadis. The Islamists tried to shoot her. Despite being hit several times, she kept running, crashed through their lines and pulled the detonator. Arin took ten jihadis with her when she died.

But ISIS had pressed on. Within days, they had pushed our surviving volunteers into a thin crescent of territory along the Turkish frontier that ran for several kilometres but was only about a dozen blocks from north to south at its widest point. Encircled as our forces were, the only way to join them was from Turkey. I followed the road to the border, eventually reaching an abandoned Syrian immigration checkpoint that consisted of a guardhouse and a pair of bruised and bullet-scarred gates, seemingly bent back by the maelstrom beyond. Squeezing between them and stepping out into the dusk, I found myself slipping and rolling on a carpet of bullet casings and unexploded mortars. I also came immediately under fire. I stumbled for cover and ran into the debris of collapsed walls, flattened houses and three-storey buildings that had vomited their insides into the street. Everywhere there was broken glass, splintered doors, burned earth, torched cars and soiled clothes. It was like a dark mirror of existence. The accessories of living were all around, yet life itself was absent. I stumbled on until I found my way to a basement in which a small group of our fighters were sheltering.

Kobani, I knew, was built on one of the oldest settlements on earth. It was astonishing how one week of war had erased so much history. Some of that was our doing. Talking to my comrades, I learned that since enemy snipers now had our entire territory within range, moving in the streets had become impossible. Instead our men and women were busy smashing through the walls of houses and shops and ancient bazaars to create a network of hidden, covered passageways. They were living and fighting in these tunnels, scurrying from a kitchen stacked with crockery and pots of rotting rice through a hole in a wall into a garden, then ducking back into the living room of a neighbouring house where a sofa might still sit in front of the television, a small bowl of dusty, shrivelled grapes to the side.

I became used to so much in the five months we fought in Kobani but I don't think I ever made peace with the way we robbed and vandalised these homes. We paved our passageways with prized carpets and precious mattresses so we could run without tripping over concrete and debris. Anything red we laid on top to conceal the blood that spilled from our wounded as they were dragged back from the front. I would desecrate children's brightly coloured bedrooms by smashing holes in their walls to make an aperture through which to fire. I would demolish kitchens, tables and wardrobes to find flat pieces of wood or marble on which I could lie behind my gun.

As I found my way through my new surroundings, I realised the war was suffocating all the colour in Kobani. Our green uniforms were covered in dirt. ISIS dressed in black. Everything else – the shops, the cars, the trees, the photographs of children on the walls, the tablecloths and bedspreads, the skirts and shirts on the washing lines – was being subsumed under a blanket of sticky yellow filth. With little to guide me through this monochrome wasteland, I found my way by smell as much as sight. The dull stink of unwashed bodies meant I was near the frontline. The sharp reek of bloating corpses told me that I was on it.

The only calm was what you could create in your mind. At night, I would lie out on the rooftops, listening to the flapping of the giant curtains that our volunteers stitched together out of sheets and prized rugs raided from closets and sitting rooms and hung across the streets to block ISIS' line of sight. The sound was like patchwork sails in a storm, and as I lay there, I would imagine I was a sailor out on deck, adrift on an ocean far away.

We all knew Kobani would be bloody. The jihadis had set the tone of the war from its first days in January 2014. They advanced by blitzkrieg, arriving in an overwhelming horde, subjecting us to an onslaught of artillery, tanks and mortars, then moving into the ruins to mop up survivors. In one early battle in eastern Rojava, in a place called Tel Hamees, ISIS pretended they were retreating to lure two hundred and fifty of our men and women into an open field that they had surrounded, then opened fire, tossed in hand grenades and finally waded through the bodies with swords, decapitating at will. Days later, when my comrades pushed ISIS out again, they found their friends' heads stacked up in piles like pomegranates on a street stall.

By the summer we had learned that such battlefield massacres were often just the start of ISIS' atrocities. Even against the dark record of fellow Islamists around the world, the jihadis distinguished themselves with their depravity and childlike simplicity. Here were grown men who roasted prisoners over fires and sold sex slaves with notes of provenance tied around their necks while carrying spoons into battle because of a fairytale they had been told about the feasts with the Prophet that awaited them in paradise. Their fighters made videos showing themselves executing hundreds of prisoners at a time by herding them into pits and opening fire. They filmed themselves beheading journalists, crucifying prisoners and throwing homosexuals from rooftops. They executed moderate imams and Christians for 'sorcery'. They sawed the heads off grand-fathers just for daring to stay put in their homes when they invaded. They left hundreds of corpses piled high in central squares or hanging from lamp-posts. They paraded whole families through the streets, then gathered crowds to watch as they shot fathers in front of sons, sons in front of mothers, mothers in front of daughters and daughters in front of the bloody heap that had once been their families – and all this they broadcast on giant outdoor screens. They liked to say they would behead their enemies so swiftly that the first they would know of it was when their heads were on the ground and their eyes were looking back at their own feet.

That summer of 2014, the jihadis had attempted to escalate their butchery into a genocide. The Yazidis were Kurds, though with their own distinct origin, religion and culture, whose an-cestral land in Iraq was just across the border from where I was initially stationed in eastern Rojava. From my sniper's nest in the town of Al-Yarubiyah, I could see across the frontier to the great edifice of Mount Shengal (Sinjiar in Arabic), to where the Yazidis had always retreated in times of trouble and where jihadis had surrounded tens or even hundreds of thousands of them with the intent of exterminating them.

Yazidis fleeing into our territory told us that ISIS had sig-nalled the start of the massacre by issuing proclamations declaring them to be godless half-humans, a pollution on God's earth and undeserving of life. That was a cue for the jihadis to wipe out whole families and entire villages in an onslaught of blood and fire. If they took prisoners, it was only to extend their suffering. They demanded the men convert. If their captives refused, or sometimes even if they obeyed, they beheaded them or lined them up and shot them en masse. In one massacre, the jihadis led a group of elderly men into an ancient Yazidi temple, only to blow it up with the old men inside. Just having hair under their arms was enough to condemn Yazidi boys to the same fate. The jihadis seemed to take particular pride in the ingenuity of their cruelty. Some men they led in chains to roundabouts, tied them to a stake and left them in the heat so they died of thirst in view of passing traffic. Others they herded into steel cages where they were burned alive or left to starve, or lowered into rivers to drown.

Some of the women were spared. A few were put to work as cleaners. But mainly these men of God took the women and girls as objects to be raped and passed around fighters. Gang-rape was routine. After the fighters were done, they would execute the women for licentiousness or sell them in the market as sex slaves. A few virgins were reserved for ISIS' business managers, who would sell them to rich Arabs for up to ten thousand dollars each.

Lest anyone imagine they were barbarians, ISIS had regulations for their trade in sex slaves. Some Yazidis brought us copies of an ISIS pamphlet entitled 'Questions and Answers On Taking Captives and Slaves'. It was permissible to have sex with a pre-pubescent girl, ISIS' leaders decreed, 'if she is fit for intercourse'. It was also legal to 'buy, sell or give' Yazidi females since, as unbelievers and sub-humans, 'they are merely property, which can be disposed of'. This also seemed to apply to the children that inevitably resulted from the jihadis' industrial-scale raping. These were taken away from their mothers as infants to be trained as Kurdish-looking suicide bombers who could infiltrate their own people.

One problem the jihadis encountered was that there were simply too many Yazidi women and girls for them to be able to rape or sell them all. The jihadis solved this conundrum by liquidating the excess. In the late summer of 2014 we heard about one massacre when ISIS, with an apparent eye on conserving labour and ammunition, buried alive hundreds of mothers with their children.

If there was a strategy behind this savagery, it was to persuade their enemies to flee. We did not. When ISIS advanced on Shengal, twelve of our volunteers set up on its summit and kept thousands of ISIS fighters at bay for days before they succumbed, allowing many hundreds of Yazidi families to escape. In the end, a total of five hundred thousand Yazidis fled to our territory or to Turkey. Still, the death and destruction were grotesque. ISIS killed around five thousand Yazidi men and abducted seven thousand women and children, most of whom remain missing to this day. Hundreds of Yazidi children died of thirst and starvation as they fled.

The Yazidis told us that scores of their women and girls had leapt to their death from the cliffs of Mount Shengal rather than let themselves be captured. As the jihadis switched the full force of their fury to us across the border in Syria, we soon had similar stories of our own. Arriving one afternoon in August 2014 in the town of Jazaa, not far from the Iraqi border, I found everyone talking about how three weeks before, when Jazaa had fallen to ISIS for the second time before being recaptured once again, a group of twelve young YPJ women defending a position on the rooftop of a two-storey building had fought to the end rather than let themselves be taken prisoner. When it became clear they were surrounded, they had gathered in a circle and pulled the pins on the grenades that each had kept for the purpose.

The story stunned me. Like many comrades, I carried three bullets in my breast pocket, one for each calibre of rifle, so that I would always be able to take my own life rather than be taken prisoner. We called these rounds our 'saviour bullets'. They gave us a sense of indomitable will. We alone would decide how we lived and how we died. I had already come across the bodies of comrades who had used their saviour bullets. One man was sitting down, his finger still on the trigger. One woman had tied her hand to her rifle. But saviour bullets were neat and precise and left a body for comrades to bury and a grave for relatives to visit. Grenades disintegrated you. It would be like you never existed.

I walked into the ground floor of the building where the women had died to find piles of clothes – soft fabrics in cheerful pinks, purples and greens – drenched in blood on the floor. There was a guard on duty. He told me the women had died on the second-floor roof terrace. I would have to go up there alone. 'I can't look at that again,' he said.

I climbed the stairs. The entire terrace was covered in a thick film of blood, some dry, some still wet, like the floor of an abattoir. All around were pieces of flesh and clumps of hair. There was a black ponytail, its tie still around it. On the walls was more hair, and on the parapet a few scattered wisps trembling in the wind. These young women would have known their fate if they were captured by ISIS. The story went that they decided they couldn't allow the jihadis to use their bodies in any way, not even allowing them the fleeting pleasure of a glimpse of their beauty.

I was still on the roof, trying to digest the power of what I was seeing, when General Qahraman, commander of our eastern front, climbed up and gingerly moved to a corner to get a signal on his phone. All week Qahraman had been calling

Kobani. That day, as Qahraman listened to the voice on his phone, his shoulders slumped. When he hung up, he said the latest information was that our forces were down to their last few hundred yards and ISIS was hours from capturing Kobani.

I looked around the rooftop. It wasn't that anyone wanted to die. But war had been thrust upon us and suicidal defiance often seemed the only response we had. We all knew we would face injury, horror and death – and we set our minds to sharing these things with our comrades. Using a Kurdish saying, we said we embraced the moment with 'wild flowers and mint'.

I also knew I would be useful in Kobani. In eight months, I had shot around fifty ISIS fighters: fifteen kills I had confirmed with my own eyes and around thirty-five probables. I hated the body counts. Only a weak man would measure himself in kills and only a fool would try to describe all the hate, loss, sacrifice and love in war with a number. But like the women of Jazaa, I knew there were times when extreme actions were necessary. I told Qahraman I would go to Kobani to assist the resistance.

He nodded. 'Try not to get killed in the first three days,' he said.

As I made my home in the ruins of Kobani, I was happy to come across a familiar face. But whereas General Tolin had been warm and positive when I first met her months earlier in eastern Rojava, now, at a briefing for new arrivals, her face was tight and focused. She went around our small group, asking each man and woman their names and skills. Then she summarised the situation. There were three fronts – east, south and west. All of them were backed up against the Turkish border to the north and barely three hundred metres at their widest. 'We have run out of space to retreat,' she said. 'Our frontline is now a line of honour. We hold it or we die fighting. This will be our legacy to our fellow Kurds.'

Tolin said each front was defended by around one hundred and fifty men and women, broken down into three platoons of fifty, each of those made up of four or five squads or teams. Ideally, each team would have a heavy machine gun, an RPG, a medic and a sniper as well as four or five fighters with Kalashnikovs. But after so many casualties, most were several bodies short, with barely enough guns to go around. Tolin assigned the new volunteers to fill the gaps as best she could. When she came to me, she asked me to stay behind.

After the others had left, Tolin said she was dispatching a special operation of seventy men and women to cross secretly over our front and into enemy territory. There, in the villages and fields deep behind their lines, we were to run sabotage operations to create confusion and paranoia among the jihadis by showing we could live fearlessly among them, killing them at will. Though Tolin didn't say it, we both knew it was potentially a suicide mission. If ISIS found or captured us – if any of us made one small noise or movement at the wrong moment – it would be over for all of us.

The mission required two snipers to back up the main force, which would be divided into small teams of three to seven people. I suggested I go with another experienced marksman from Jazaa. When I went to retrieve a rifle for each of us, however, all I could find were two badly damaged Kalashnikovs. I was about to query Tolin when she interrupted me. 'Ah, Azad,' she said. 'I see you found your weapon.'

I looked at the battered gun in my hands. 'I can't use this,' I said. 'I couldn't even kill myself with this.'

Tolin pulled a ball-shaped object from her waistband and gave it to me. In my hand I held a mass of nails taped to a stick of dynamite, with a string fuse hanging to the side. Tolin took my free hand and slapped a plastic lighter into it. 'Welcome to Kobani, comrade,' she said.

FOUR

Britain and Sweden, *2004–2013*
Rojava, *September–December 2013*

It was almost exactly a year since I had arrived in Rojava as a volunteer civil administrator. To return to the Middle East a decade after fleeing as a twenty-year-old Iranian army deserter and political dissident might make little sense to some. After all, my family had borrowed everything they could to smuggle me to Europe. In Britain, I had found asylum. In Leeds, and later Stockholm, I had found a new home and a new, free life. But in my time away I had become convinced that I couldn't live in comfort while my brothers and sisters tried to build a new homeland. In particular, I had been deeply affected by the writings of the leader of the Kurdish Workers Party, or PKK, Abdullah Öcalan.

Apo, as we called him, using the ward for 'uncle' in Kurdish, had first emerged as a leftist student leader in Turkey in the 1970s. Initially, he proposed that the Kurds should violently overthrow centuries of repression by the Turks before going on to reunite their homeland, which lay divided between Turkey, Iran, Iraq and Syria. He had remained a radical until his early fifties, leading the Kurdish struggle from exile. But in February

1999, he was in Kenya en route to South Africa at the invitation of Nelson Mandela when he was kidnapped with the assistance of the American, Israeli and Turkish intelligence agencies and handed back to Turkey.

Kurds erupted in outraged protest around the world. American, Israeli, Turkish and European embassies and political party offices were picketed and occupied. Around ninety demonstrators set themselves on fire, several dying of their injuries. In Turkey, Kurds rioted across the country, battling police and petrol-bombing vehicles, and more than a thousand were arrested.

The Turks, like the apartheid authorities in South Africa, viewed revolution as a virus. Just as the white supremacists tried to hinder its transmission by quarantining Mandela and other African National Congress leaders on Robben Island off Cape Town, so the Turks transported Apo to the tiny island of Imrali off Istanbul where they built him a prison in which he was the sole inmate, guarded by hundreds of soldiers who were forbidden to talk to him.

But the Turks underestimated Apo. After his lawyers won him the right to read and write to prepare his appeal against his imprisonment, Apo built himself a prison library in which he dedicated himself to study and thought, and the preparation of a grand defence that took in thousands of years of history and philosophy. He was said to have read more than three thousand books. He set out the case for his defence in eleven books and pamphlets of his own.

What emerged, by the spring of 2004, the year I arrived in Britain, was a new Kurdish political philosophy that reflected profound changes in Apo's thinking. Like Mandela, Apo had entered prison a firebrand. Like him, he had found the isolation of a cell conducive to reflection. Apo's view completely transformed in the way he saw conflict. So did his demand for an independent Kurdistan, replaced by a more modest proposal for a borderless, democratic confederation that reunited the four parts of Kurdistan: northern Kurdistan in Turkey, western in Syria, southern in Iraq and eastern in Iran. And in place of Apo's earlier attachment to Marxist-Leninism was a new philosophy that borrowed from socialism but also environmentalism, feminism, anarchism, communalism, social justice and self-determination.

Apo now argued that capitalism and repressive occupying states need not necessarily be overthrown. Instead, he put forward a more reasoned analysis. Any perceptive person could see that capitalism was leading humanity towards intermittent economic crisis and ecological disaster, he wrote. His new proposal was to change the system from within. The driving dynamic of capitalism – selfishness – was to be replaced with something more noble: public interest instead of self-interest; collaboration over competition; public responsibility ahead of personal reward; social good over the mere consumption of goods and services.

The emphasis was on common good and common sense, and a revitalisation of consensus and cooperation. Apo wrote that everywhere humanity was paralysed by division that, over time, had become entrenched in hierarchies: man over woman, humankind over nature, rich over poor, white over black, old over young. To base a society on exclusion in this way was a recipe for conflict and suffering, and ultimately unsustainable. Western social democracy was, in that sense, a mere halfway house on the path out of feudalism. Completing the journey required private profit to be replaced with social profit. In practical terms, that meant embracing almost all forms of progressiveness, from organic agriculture to feminism to municipal decentralisation. What's more, wrote Apo, the time was right. He was convinced the world was on the brink of a historic transformation. 'Let the guns be silenced and politics dominate,' he wrote. 'A new door is being opened from the process of armed conflict to democratisation and democratic politics. It's not the end. It's the start of a new era.'*

In prison, Apo wrote five interconnected manifestos. Two of them were extracted in booklets called *The Sociology of Freedom* and *Liberating Life: Woman's Revolution*, which were especially influential. One of Apo's sayings was: 'A country can't be free unless the women are free.' In *Liberating Life*, he went further. 'The five-thousand-year-old history of civilisation is essentially the history of the enslavement of women,' he wrote. What most men called progress, said Apo, was actually a story of humanity's gradual loss of freedom. In Neolithic times, society was matricentric, organised around mothers as 'the central life-element that both gives birth and sustains life through nurturing'. It was that system, wrote Apo, that gave us farming, villages, trade, tribes based on family and a collective social consciousness characterised by equality and freedom.

All the inequality, hierarchy, autocracy and militarism since then stemmed from the moment when man used his physical strength to usurp and denigrate woman. Man violently replaced notions of collective welfare and common ownership with private enterprise and exclusive property. Shamans and religious leaders entrenched this misogyny with faiths based on divinely ordained male dominance. Soon, all religion was based around a single male God, all states were structured around a male-dominated hierarchy, and all economies were built on

---

* https://peaceinkurdistancampaign.com/2013/03/24/ocalans-historic-newroz-2013-statement/

men's ability to earn. Sexism and power, at least as humanity had known it for five thousand years, had been more or less the same thing. What Apo called 'housewifisation' was, he said, the oldest form of slavery and 'the vilest counter-revolution ever carried out'. For the same reason, 'the solutions for all social problems in the Middle East should have women's position as focus'.*

These were the ideas that I and thousands of others devoured in our exile. They were what my comrades tried to put into practice in Rojava when Syria fell apart in civil war in 2011. I felt I had to join them. And after flying to Silemani (known as Suleimaniyah in Arabic) in northern Iraq in September 2013, then crossing into Syria, I was made the administrator of a poor neighbourhood of the city of Qamishli called Heleliyah, home to around one thousand four hundred people.

My remit was broad: to deal with people's needs. And Heleliyah needed everything: water, electricity, schools, jobs, health clinics and sanitation. We set up new direct-democratic town administrations which included Kurds, Christians, Assyrians, Arabs, Turkmens, Chechens and Armenians. We handed over the supply of water, electricity and healthcare to engineers and doctors who had not fled the war. Higher education we gave to students forced to abandon their studies in Homs, Aleppo or Damascus: they soon opened the University of Rojava, where they taught each other. We gave control of agricultural machinery to farmers. Though the anti-Kurd prejudices of the Syrian education system ensured that we lacked much

---

* http://ocalan-books.com/#/book/liberating-life-womans-revolution

professional expertise, our greatest strength, I soon discovered, was the eagerness of the people. They were delighted to volunteer to build Rojava and to run their own affairs rather than be ruled by an Arab authority from the distant south. It gave them a sense of honour and dignity.

Equally noticeable was a flowering of Kurdish culture. After centuries of hiding our songs and stories in the dark, Kurds were bursting into the street with all the colour and noise they could muster. Cultural centres sprang up all over. In every neighbourhood you would find men and women practising traditional dances and songs or giving recitals of Kurdish poems, or holding language classes where people, often for the first time in their life, could learn to read and write in their native tongue. On every street corner and in every park, everyone was talking politics with the abandon of a people arriving at a river after a long walk through the desert.

Perhaps the most dramatic change was the transformation in women's lives. Previously our women had been largely restricted to the home. Now they created women's councils, women's schools, safe-houses for women who wished to live alone, even women's driving schools and a women-only police force to investigate violence against women. All our offices were at least forty per cent staffed by women. Every leadership position was jointly held by men and women. We created new schools in which women could be educated for free. We began work on a new justice system under which child marriage was outlawed, polygamy was banned and women and men were equal in all matters.

Most significant was the creation of the women's militia, the YPJ. All over the world, soldiering was still largely men's work. The YPJ showed what folly that was. Here were self-assured, fearless, powerful women like Tolin and Medya who felt no need to abandon their femininity. Just as brotherhood described the bond between male fighters, so sisterhood expressed the loyalty between women. The YPJ showed that qualities such as endurance, courage and sacrifice could be coloured, textured and enhanced by womanliness just as well as manliness. The only difference we allowed between men and women was at the level of command. Because of men's baleful history of ordering women around, female commanders only were permitted to instruct both men and women.

I had been in my job for a few months and was closing up our community centre for lunch one day when a woman approached me barefoot and in great distress, her skin dry and lifeless, her eyes darting around the street. I showed her inside. After briefly scanning the room, the woman announced that she wanted to join the YPJ. When I asked what she knew about the YPJ and their aims, she grew suspicious. Not wishing to unnerve her further, I suggested she talk to a woman colleague of mine who worked ten minutes away.

'I can't wait that long,' said the woman. 'My family are after me. I told them I wanted to join the YPJ. They refused and instead they asked me to marry a man in exchange for my brother marrying the man's sister. I don't want to marry this man. I don't want to marry *at all*. My brother is furious. He starves me and beats me. Today he pointed a gun at my head and told me that he was going to kill me. But I still want to join the YPJ.'

I persuaded the woman to wait for my colleague, who arrived and ushered her away. I let a week pass, until I was sure the woman was no longer in Qamishli. Then I visited her family.

Her mother and brother welcomed me into a small home where garlic hung on the walls to keep scorpions away. I addressed myself to both, telling them their daughter had joined the YPJ and would not be coming home. 'It is what she wanted,' I said. 'She did not want to get married.'

There was a silence. The brother stared unhappily at the floor. After a while, the mother spoke up. 'I am happy,' she announced. 'She will be safe with them.'

I remember thinking that this was how we would build our new nation. Though everyone liked the sound of freedom, few men wanted to give up their traditional authority. But here, right in front of me, in the remaking of the relationship between a mother and a son, and a brother and a sister, was all the promise of our revolution. We were building something new, and that was difficult. If we were to succeed, it would require sitting down with families, and bosses and workers, and respectfully suggesting a path out of patriarchy and enslavement. I believed people were inherently good and that the triumph of progress over backwardness was as inevitable as time. Rojava offered proof that I might be right. To live there for those brief few months was to experience an exhilarating explosion of hope. Once the rest of humanity noticed what was happening in Rojava, I was sure we would change the world.

I still believe that now. One day, we will have a free, progressive and enlightened Kurdistan and millions around the world will follow our example, ringing the bell of liberty so loudly that it will echo through the ages. Of course, it was precisely that prospect that the jihadis wanted to destroy.

After advancing unseen to the outskirts of Qamishli in December 2013, the jihadis fired several mortars into the city one morning. I heard the impact from my office, like the sound of a giant overladen table collapsing. Running the few blocks to see the strike, I found a house had been hit. Half of it was gone and half was still standing upright, oblivious. It was a state I would come to recognise in fatally wounded people in the years to come.

Even before the Islamists attacked, people had been preparing themselves. Some families had packed up what they could and left for Turkey. Most had decided to stay, emptying the market of rice and flour and tins of oil. A few whose work required them to move in and out of the jihadis' territory – doctors and traders, mainly – could be seen in the cafés and the streets practising Islamic verses, in case they were stopped at a checkpoint.

The same day the jihadis attacked, seven of us civil administrators presented ourselves to the YPG and the YPJ for military service. We were assessed by a veteran commander of the women's militia, General Tolin. When it came to my turn, I told her that I had served in the Iranian army. She suggested the sniper unit. Because we were pressed for time, I would have just twenty-one days of basic training before being deployed to the front.

FIVE

Qamishli,

December 2013 to June 2014

Any competent soldier can learn the basics of sniping in an hour. The scope of a standard sniper rifle has a crosshair in the centre and, to the left, a curved graph with distance on the vertical axis and a flat line representing the ground on the horizontal one. You pick an average-sized man, line up his feet with the horizontal line and the top of his head with the curve, then read off the distance on the vertical axis: '2' for two hundred metres, '4' for four hundred, and so on. That's your range. To 'zero' the scope on your target, you twist a dial on the top of the scope until it is set to the required distance, between a hundred and a thousand metres. For targets more than a kilometre away, you turn the dial to a thousand metres, then use the chevrons below the crosshairs to account for gravity's pull. The top chevron is for a thousand metres, the second for a thousand one hundred, the third for a thousand two hundred, and the fourth for a thousand three hundred. You can still make shots at greater distances, but you will, to some extent, be guessing.

The marks on the horizontal crosshair are for wind. We carried pocket tables into battle on which we could read off how

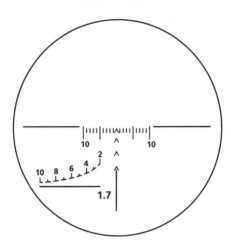

far to shoot to the left or right according to the wind's strength, its angle and the range. In the diagram, a perfect shot, taken at a range of one thousand two hundred metres in a brisk wind blowing directly from left to right, would hit the target 1.9 seconds after it was fired if the scope was zeroed to one thousand metres and the number '6' was directly over the man's head.

Every rifle has its own character and power and a sniper must learn each one's temperament. Different tools are also suited for different tasks. M16s, for which we had a handful of thermal scopes, were for night-time and close-quarters fighting. Dragunovs were for daytime and longer distances. Barrett rifles, or Zagros rifles as we called them, which were as tall as a man and mostly built from spare parts, were for day shots of a kilometre away or more.

You also need to know each gun's different firing mechanism. Any weapon can jam, and since turning on a light is a good way to get shot, we were taught to take apart and reassemble each gun in the dark. Practising with rifle parts, disassembling the mechanism and putting it together again over and over, has the added advantage of teaching you why touch is a sniper's most important sense after sight. It is through your trigger finger that you communicate with your rifle. Through it, too, you learn the different action of each weapon. The trigger of an M16 fires quickly. A Dragunov has two parts to its pull – a slow, long draw to the firing position, then a short final squeeze. A Barrett has a hair trigger. The importance of the trigger finger is why snipers go to such lengths to keep their forefingers shrouded and unbruised and why so many cut the finger off a glove to better connect with their weapon. After a while, I learned to recognise other snipers by their whiter, cleaner, smoother forefingers.

Since each gun takes a different calibre of round, a sniper needs to be familiar with their different impacts. Because M16 rounds, at 5.56mm in diameter, are much smaller, they often pass right through a target without much immediate effect. Days later, however, an M16 round can prove to be the deadliest of all since a tight, narrow bullet hole is hardest to clean. For the same reasons, the larger 7.62mm Dragunov bullet is often fatal on impact but if a target survives, their chances of recovery are often better. Barretts fire 13mm-calibre rounds the size of a fountain pen, known as 0.50-cal because they are half an inch in diameter, which can pass through several walls and still kill you. If you are hit by a .50, survival is unlikely and is generally achieved only after the amputation of an arm or leg. Snipers generally consider Barretts and Dragunovs more honourable weapons than the M16. The first two are designed for clean kills. The M16 is designed to wound and trap the enemy in an impossible dilemma: rescue a fallen soldier and risk being shot himself or stay hidden and let his friend bleed out.

*

I honed my craft in eastern Rojava. For eight months I shot long-distance, alternating between a Dragunov and a Barrett. We had two frontlines, one facing south of Qamishli, the other confronting the east and the border with Iraq. On both fronts, the fighting was sporadic and conducted across open no-man's-land. Initially I was stationed at Al-Yarubiyah, the name we gave our eastern front, in the stony desert and dried-up riverbeds that lay in the shadow of Mount Shengal. We were billeted in a new five-storey administrative building. I built a hide in a toilet on the roof, hanging my Barrett from the ceiling by a strap so that it was suspended in the air and pointed through the window at the ISIS positions about a kilometre and a half away.

During my first few days on the front, the constant *fzzz* of bullets overhead made me tense up and blink. Every now and then ISIS would start up a mortar barrage and I would grab my rifle and run down a floor inside the building. Even when I had time to fire, I mostly missed. If I was startled during my shot, as often happened, the bullet would veer wide to the left. A rushed shot meant it skewed right.

I soon learned not to blink or flinch. But mastering my breathing took longer. As you prepare to shoot, your breaths must be almost like meditation. You start with a chest full of air. You breathe out half of it as you line up your sights on your target. At that point, you pause for up to six seconds. Too much air and you'll shoot high. Too little and you'll tip forward and the bullet will go low. The idea is to slow your heart and blood so that nothing, not even your pulse, shakes your aim. For the same reason, you hold the rifle to your bones, not your flesh. Through those five or six long, deep, calm seconds, you stay focused on the target, squeezing your trigger. You fire almost without realising. The slower and stiller you are, the truer the bullet leaves the barrel.

I started hitting the enemy after a week or so. From my position on the roof I could see a hospital building inside Iraq where ISIS had placed a tripod-mounted Dushka heavy machine gun. A Dushka could shoot through several buildings and still kill one of ours. If my enduring mission was to stop the ISIS attacks, my daily preoccupation was taking down the Dushka operator. Each morning I would wait for the Dushka to open up, after which I would return fire and shut him down. I fired at that gun for weeks. I must have hit more than a dozen men behind it.

I had other targets, too. One time, during an ISIS advance, I fired more than twenty times at an ISIS pickup that was dashing back and forth along a road more than a kilometre away, only for an American jet to sweep in, fire a rocket and send the vehicle flying through the air as though it were a stone skipping across a pond. That was the first I knew that the US was supporting us with air attacks. I remember being amazed by how quiet that distant scene was.

As I became more experienced, I realised that sniping was as much about human observation as shooting skill. Through the scope, I learned to be able to size up my enemy at a glance: the way he held himself, the way he walked, whether he was confident with his rifle, whether he was careful with his approach, how long his beard was. If I caught a glimpse of someone walking loosely, with his hands hanging down by his knees and his shoulders collapsed – someone who was weak and without purpose or hope – I knew that was someone who was going to make a mistake, and that our advancing team should direct their initial attack at his position. On the other hand, a jihadi who had real purpose, who moved like a mouse, popping up and down, and checking all around himself, was going to be much harder to shoot. But he was also more likely to be someone of stature, and therefore a more important target.

When I was going after a truly high-value target such as another sniper or a high-ranking officer, I would try to create a portrait of my target: who he was, how he behaved, how old he was, what time he woke up, whether he preferred the cold of the morning or the heat of the day. From these studies, it was possible to make some predictions about where and when my enemy would show himself and how to position myself to take advantage. It required total concentration. I had to observe all the information I could, analyse it in an instant, and draw a conclusion about where to target and when.

My enemies, who knew I was watching them, often tried to frustrate my observations. They would stay hidden, erect curtains and build corridors through houses, firing through holes in the walls. It was like boxing. You sized up your opponent, tried to hold for your opportunity, and eventually took your shot. Many times I had to go by what I heard, not what I could see. On more than one occasion my target looked right at me and even waved at me. Some played games, running into view, then stopping for a split second, then running on again. Once, for days, I tried to shoot a motorbiker who was crossing a street in front of me about seven hundred metres away. I could hear him coming from the sound of his revving engine, then he would burst across the street and I would fire – once, twice – and he'd be gone, tooting his horn as if to say: 'You missed! I am still alive!'

Often the idea behind these games was to tempt me into giving away my position by firing. They weren't without risk for the players: I once hit a man running across a street from eight hundred metres away. Another ISIS tactic was to try to spook us by enforcing a silence. At those times, every sound – the wind blowing through my firing hole, shaking the corrugated roof and the clothes on a washing line – would become so loud. The idea was to give us too much time to think. What were they doing? How come I couldn't hear them? Were they going to attack?

Since our enemy was also watching us, we practised our own manipulations and deceptions. We dug holes in walls through which to shoot, then dug new ones in less likely positions – close to the ceiling or hidden by a shadow – to fool ISIS into targeting the unmanned ones. We dampened our holes with water so that our shots didn't kick up dust and reveal our positions. We switched lights on and off in places we didn't use. We left signs of movement in corridors through which we never passed. We even used mannequins to confuse the enemy. Often I found I had most success in lining up a shot, then persuading my enemy to walk into it by pretending I was somewhere else. I'd take down one man, then wait for his friend to run out, too.

After a few months, I found that my instincts had augmented and sharpened. I acquired the ability to judge distances to within a few metres without the aid of a scope. I learned to distinguish the different sounds, sights and trajectories of different bullets. I found enemies with my eyes, my ears and even my nose. I also developed my own technique for scanning an area, standing square on to the range and closing my eyes, then opening them again, then closing, then opening. Repeated three or four times, I found this camera-shutter technique would print an image on my mind which I could then examine at leisure for anything unusual, almost as though I was looking at a picture in my hands.

As my technique improved and my knowledge expanded, I felt something swell inside me. Not quite confidence, nor hope, nor will, though it contained shades of all three. Mostly I felt I was uncovering a long-buried instinct for survival. Somehow, I knew I possessed the ability to endure and overcome. It was there in how I tuned in to the moment, how I learned to listen to my intuition. It was about accepting the battle as inescapable and entering it with the calm trust that you will somehow sense what to do and how to react. This is the peace in war.

To be a good sniper, of course, you need to come to terms with the idea of taking human life. When I thought of blood and killing, my mind always went back to my village in East Kurdistan and my mother showing me how to dispatch a chicken as a boy. It was a mess. Once I began shooting, I was surprised how clean it could be. Soldiers on the ground have to confront the hot intimacy of death. Snipers dispatch in cold blood, often silently and without sensation.

After five months of taking long shots and watching distant guns fall silent, the day finally came when I saw it all. I was hiding with an attack team in a village house on the eastern front, watching a second village less than two kilometres away where ISIS had a position. We could see them moving around their base, positioning sandbags and moving rocks for cover.

'They're using a bulldozer,' said one of my team, looking through binoculars at a plume of black smoke coming from the village. 'They're breaking down houses and turning the rubble into fortifications.'

That was the signal for the team to start shooting. It was unlikely that they would hit much at that range but at least they could harass the enemy. As they did so, I crept forward on my elbows, sweating in the summer heat, until I guessed I was within range. Dragging my Barrett into position, I checked the distance through the scope: one thousand and five metres.

I zeroed the scope to a thousand metres and settled in to watch. I could see two ISIS fighters, one skinny and one big. They were heaving the three legs of a heavy Dushka into position to fire at us. I couldn't allow that. The bigger fighter walked away, apparently to retrieve something. When he turned around and walked back towards me, I thought to myself: *This is my guy. I might miss the skinny one. This bigger man is the guy.*

I followed him through the scope, my crosshairs on his chest. He had a rifle with him. At one point, he bent over the Dushka, manoeuvring it to target us.

I exhaled.

One . . .

Two . . .

I didn't hear the shot. I barely noticed the kick. But as if I were watching a silent movie, I saw that big man knocked right into the air, then fly four or five metres back, all the way into the backyard of a house behind him. I saw the whole thing. I still see it now.

SIX

Kobani,

October 2014

The night after my briefing from Tolin, we set out to cross the ISIS frontline. For five hours we crawled silently on the ground and ducked between the houses, following a guide who was equipped with one of our few night-vision scopes. As we approached ISIS' positions, we could hear them in houses on either side of us. We tried to move slowly and carefully to avoid making noise but we also had to cross before the sun came up and revealed us to the enemy. Twice we had to back-track after nearly walking into a jihadi base. Several times we had to wait for their sentries to pass. Finally, we passed the last house on the outskirts of town and sprinted for cover in the fields beyond.

Just before dawn, we found an abandoned village on a hill twelve kilometres inside ISIS territory in which we hoped to hide ourselves without being discovered. Below us, about six hundred metres away, was the main road from Kobani to Aleppo. All day we watched the jihadis drive up and down in their pickups and motorbikes, so close I could distinguish them by the length of their beards. But attacking them when they were together would have meant a very quick death. Our mission was to stay concealed and send out small teams of two or three on sabotage and assassination missions several kilometres away from where we were hiding.

For two weeks, we crawled in the dirt, sweating through the day and freezing all night. Within a few days, everyone was sick with flu and fever. But we also had success. A de-mining team that was part of our group rewired an old device, then detonated it under one of their pickups. When the jihadis arrived to investigate, we killed all four of them, then hid their bodies to confuse the Islamists further. We shot another two on a motorbike, then stowed their bodies and their bike under a bridge. We would hear the shouts of confusion as their friends arrived to find them dead so far from the frontline.

One day, all seventy of us were hiding in the village when a BMW camouflaged with mud sped in from the countryside and skidded to a halt under a large mulberry tree perhaps five metres in front of us. Inside were two ISIS fighters, dressed in black with long beards. They stepped out of the car and began scanning the sky. Overhead, we could hear one of the two American fighter jets which had begun patrolling the skies above Kobani in the past week.

The way we were positioned, we were already surrounding the car. We were deliberating whether or not to shoot, and give away our position, when a shot rang out from one of our units – and after that, we all opened up. One of the jihadis died instantly: he turned out to be a general with valuable information on a memory stick in his pocket. The driver, a tiny man, scurried behind a small stone wall, then ran into a house behind it shouting, 'Surrender if you want to live!' There were seventeen volunteers inside that house waiting for him, their guns levelled at the door. That tiny man flew back out of the house and landed in the garden.

After two weeks of harassing, sabotaging and killing as deep as twenty kilometres behind ISIS' frontline, our last mission was to inflict a final humiliation on the Islamists by heading back to Kobani and, coordinating with comrades inside the town, attacking them from behind as our other forces harassed them from the front. We moved silently in three teams – one to my left, one to my right and my team in the centre – radioing ahead to our forces inside Kobani to fire so as to distract the jihadis, allowing us to surprise them from behind.

After four hours, shortly after 1 a.m. we found ourselves walking by moonlight through the olive farms and farmhouses below Mistenur Hill. This was the strategic gateway to Kobani. As we rounded a cluster of boulders on its lower slopes, we could see the entire town before us. Descending into the streets again felt like stepping out into the ocean. The sound of gunfire up ahead – Kalashnikovs, Dushkas, RPGs – became constant. Bullets began splitting the air over our heads. Black smoke soon enveloped us, choking us but covering our advance. Deeper and deeper we marched. On the right, one of our units came across a house of jihadis and killed six of them. On the left, there was another firefight, with the same result. All of a sudden the Islamists seemed to realise they were being encircled. We heard shouts of '*Allahu Akbar*'. For a few minutes, they fought intensely. Three of our volunteers were injured but we returned fire and killed five of them. After that, the remaining Islamists seemed to lose heart. The gunfire stopped. As we walked on, moving house to house, we found empty buildings and abandoned trenches.

Shortly before dawn, we crossed back over our lines. In the first position we came to, we found two YPJ fighters facing us.

These two women were holed up together in a house, alone, almost out of ammunition, their radio dead and their eyes red from exhaustion. They said they had been there for four days, part of a thin line holding out against attacks that could last seven hours at a time. Of our original force of four hundred and fifty, the two women said scores, possibly more than a hundred, had died in the days we had been away. On either side of them, they knew of only seven survivors. We relieved them, pulling desks and refrigerators across the doors and mining the front garden. And almost without anyone noticing, the smoke lifted and the light of morning broke over Kobani.

Before us lay our new frontline, one block further south than when I had arrived. I was free to walk north through the streets. Everywhere my comrades were preparing new defences, digging trenches, filling sandbags and pillows, knocking new firing holes in the houses. It was hard not to feel a small sense of triumph. A few days earlier, Turkish President Recep Tayyip Erdoğan had predicted that Kobani would fall to ISIS within hours. We had proved him wrong. Though we had gained just one street, we had stopped them and turned them around. Possibility rippled through our people like a wind through grass. If we had done it once, we could do it again.

All the time I was behind enemy lines, I had been without a sniper's rifle. The morning I crossed back over, I tried to find my way to the snipers' base to equip myself. That was when I met the others.

The first I encountered was Herdem. I was in the street talking with Tolin when he strode up and interrupted. 'Walk out of the back of that building,' he said to me, pointing to a ruined house across the street, 'turn to the right and there is a burned-out black van parked in front of a house. That's where we have our headquarters. I'll see you there.' That was Herdem's way of saying hello.

I had heard of Herdem before I arrived. He had been in Kobani since the start of the war and had become something of a legend. In the months ahead, a Turkish photographer from a French news agency would take a series of portraits of him crouching in the ruins of the city, his black beanie pulled down low over his forehead, his black Dragunov slung across his back. The images would become famous, turning Herdem into a latter-day Che Guevara, a symbol of freedom to millions. The pictures captured Herdem as I knew him: sharp, intense, silent and alone. In the years since, other photographs have emerged of a younger man laughing in a meadow of flowers, shaking the hand of a general or playing a lyre on a rooftop, his Dragunov lying next to him on the tiles. I'd like to have met that other Herdem. The one I knew fought every hour of every day.

I followed Herdem's directions to the snipers' base, which turned out to be an equipment store for the sharp-shooters of both the YPG and YPJ. There I met a broad-shouldered woman with her black hair tied in a ponytail and a pronounced cow-lick that was turning grey. She introduced herself as Yildiz, commander of the YPJ's snipers. If Herdem was gruff and monosyllabic, Yildiz was the opposite. She immediately engaged me in a discussion on the tactics of building bases, arguing that when we were advancing there wasn't always time to sandbag a nest. 'Just throw a few empty sandbags on yourself and hide in the rubble,' she said. 'It's much smarter. People get stuck into one way of doing things and we need to remember always to be flexible.'

As the leaders of our snipers, Herdem and Yildiz made a

point of visiting their shooters on the frontline. Herdem would generally stick to issuing commands. Yildiz always seemed like she was dropping in for a chat. One day she found me only a few hundred metres from the enemy, reached up to me with a glass of hot black tea and suddenly started talking about the art of making infusions, how there were different teas with different tastes and strengths and colours, and how it made such a difference whether you used an electric kettle or a smoky wood fire and whether the water was from a tap or fresh from a spring. I used to relish these monologues – about tea or the value of a good pair of combat trousers or the beauty and peace of a morning fog. They were diverting and refreshing and, for the briefest of moments, I was transported to another time and place. But with Yildiz, there was always a lesson for the present. When I laughed and complimented her on how much she knew about tea, Yildiz replied that the point was that the harder and more creatively you worked for it, the better the tea. It was the same with defending Kobani, she said. The more care you took, the more effort you made, the better the result.

I understood that Yildiz's chatter was also her attempt to distract us. There were a number of subjects no sniper would ever discuss. We never talked about the fragility of our endeavour, for instance. Eight months of fighting had taught us all that there was no meritocracy in war. On the days when death came and snatched a life to the left of you and another few to the right, it was tempting to imagine it was working to a scheme, the way a sculptor whittles away the extraneous and leaves only the fine and necessary. But that was a delusion. I had seen the best warriors fall in the first shots of battle. I had seen the least experienced pass through the fiercest fights unscathed. Death could be a brave sacrifice or a lowly accident. Alexander the Great conquered most of the world only to be bitten by a malarial mosquito. A day's drive west of Rojava was the Saleph river in which Holy Roman Emperor Frederick Barbarossa died, an old man who had won innumerable battles dragged under the water by the weight of his own chain mail. There was no predictability to war, no logic to death, and no arguing with any of it. Death took, tirelessly and carelessly. You couldn't explain it, and to discuss it was pointless. You could only accept it.

The war required us to live with unpredictability. Faced with chaos, the only real plan is to have no plan. Fear is what you don't know, whether it's war or ISIS or death, and by Kobani we were acquainted well enough with all three not to be surprised by any of them. Practising, learning, adapting, the craft of life and death – that was how you found purpose and focus.

Maybe our facility for calm concentration was one reason why the five of us – Hayri, Herdem, Yildiz, Nasrin and I – had survived long enough to find ourselves in the same place at the same time. It was certainly true that when we were together there was a peace to our group. We couldn't afford a noisy mind. By the nature of the work, we were quiet loners. Others confronted the enemy face to face. We floated above, moving from unit to unit and commander to commander. They fired as they had to. We fired when we chose to. We depended almost entirely on ourselves – and the experience set us apart. We didn't share. It was months before I learned that Yildiz was originally from North Kurdistan and had been in the movement for years. So at home did Herdem seem in Kobani that it was only years later that I read that he didn't come from the city but a small village high up in the mountains on the border between Iran and Turkey.

As for Nasrin, I never learned anything about her life before the war. Nasrin was blue-eyed, pale-skinned and short, with a round face marked by sharp wrinkles around her eyes. She always wore a red *keffiyeh* – a headscarf – blue jeans and a bulky military sweater. Other than that, there was just her commitment and the unspoken measure we had of each other, a bond somehow stronger because we exchanged so few words. She would never talk about what happened at the front or what she had seen or the three times she was wounded, and I never once heard her mention her kills. Those who did speak about killing were generally looking for acceptance or credit. I preferred Nasrin's silent capability. You could see she had the will. Anything she did, even offering you a cup of tea so the handle faced you, she did with decency and care.

We had two snipers with us who were not fit to fight, one so depressed he couldn't talk, another, an eighteen-year-old, who complained all the time that he was never sent to the front. I had no time for either. But Nasrin would listen to them like a mother. When I was with her, the two of us often sat in silence, content to be in the company of a comrade who understood. If we spoke, it was to swap tactics or techniques or tips for equipment maintenance. For months, the most I heard her say was that first day at the base when I selected a Dragunov from the rack and she complimented me on my choice, saying the weapon was a favourite of hers as the scope was extremely precise. Everything else – the shots we had made, the expression on an enemy's face as you pulled the trigger, the youth of some of those we had to take down – we left unsaid.

Perhaps the gentlest among us was Hayri. Hayri had arrived in Kobani with Nasrin and like Yildiz he was from North Kurdistan, though I never knew precisely where. He had a black-and-white scarf which he always wore. I had a similar one in my pack, and Hayri's way of introducing himself was to take the loose threads hanging from mine and say, 'You're knotting these up wrong. You need to make them thinner. Then they'll look better.' Then, to show me, he began twisting the threads around each other and tying them.

'It's quicker my way,' I said.

'But not as pretty,' he replied, smiling.

Other people would tell me Hayri was a great sniper, a person of discipline and character. Like Nasrin, he never talked about the war or how he handled it. If anyone asked, Hayri would just smile and stare off into the distance. I think, like all of us, he thought killing was abhorrent. But faced with the choice we all faced, us or them, Hayri had made his peace with it. He didn't need to explain or justify. He took responsibility for what he was doing. And if there was death and dying all around, to Hayri that made it even more important that two comrades who were alive and well greeted each other and shared a moment in each other's company. Don't let death consume you, he was saying. Remember life.

SEVEN

Sardasht,
1983–1997

I was born in the autumn of 1983 in Sardasht, a small town
next to a hill spring in northern Iran, below the mountains
where the borders of Iran, Iraq and Turkey converge. My
father, mother, two sisters and I lived in the upper part of town,
on a road leading out into the fields and towards the peaks.
The walls of our house were made of stone and mud, the floors
were cement and our roof was tin. We had a toilet, a bathroom and a kitchen downstairs and, upstairs, two bedrooms,
one for my parents, and one for me and my sisters. We slept
on the floor under blankets made by my mother. We ate rice,
tomatoes, aubergines, soup, bread, salad and fried potatoes
and, once a week, chicken or goat or trout from the river. My
mother's pride was an oil-heated hot-water tank, big enough
for a shower. Still, when the snow came in winter we would
freeze, while in summer the house was like an oven. Then we
would stretch out on the roof at night and fall asleep watching
the stars in the cool breeze.

   Most of the families in our street traced their origins back
thousands of years to the people who first settled the lush

valleys at the foot of the Zagros mountains. For centuries, they had tended mountain vineyards producing Sardasht's famous black grapes, which they ate fresh or turned furtively into strong, sweet wine. By the time I was born, several thousand families had abandoned the fields for the town, where the men found work as shopkeepers, bureaucrats or book-keepers, and the women worked as nurses, seamstresses or teachers.

My father was a trader, travelling to and from Iraq, returning with cheap Chinese tea sets, European car parts and American military-surplus jackets. He liked to keep up with technology. We were among the first people we knew to have a telephone. I remember my sisters and I waiting in the kitchen for it to ring, arguing over who was going to pick up – though, of course, since almost no one else had a phone, we sometimes waited for weeks. We were also the first in our street to have a television. My mother, who made traditional clothes and wedding dresses for the neighbourhood, stitched a cotton shawl to hang over the screen to keep the dust at bay. At weekends, the entire street would crowd into our house and watch black-and-white images of Iranian newsreaders and Japanese cartoons. My favourite show was *The Wonderful Adventures of Nils*, about a miniature boy brought up on a farm who hitches a ride on the back of a white goose and is taken on a grand tour of Sweden. What I loved about it was how at first Nils is punished for his naughtiness but, in the end, his pure spirit is celebrated.

Even in the city, the families stayed close to the land. Before he became a trader, my father had been a vegetable grower. He still kept a plot outside town and in our backyard, like most of our neighbours, we grew lilies and flame nettles and towering elephant ears and sharp, spiky mother-in-law's tongue. In spring, everyone would sandbag their doors against the flash floods which would roar down from the mountains and funnel through the streets, ripping up the asphalt and burying it under avalanches of mud. In the summer, people would head out to the fields, where they would pick fruit and vegetables and lay them on rugs for a picnic. One of my earliest memories is of my mother's friends taking me out to the countryside on their backs and passing me around, fussing over whether I was chubby enough.

As a young boy, the countryside was my playground. In the winter, the rivers would freeze and my friends and I would skate, using shoes whose rubber soles we made as smooth as river pebbles by rubbing them on our mothers' iron stoves. In spring I would hunt for tiny birds which I would knock off their perches with a catapult I made from the tongue of a shoe tied to a pair of washing-up gloves, then hurry over to my aunt's, who would fry them whole, ten to a pan. I became quite the shot. Later, of course, my marksmanship would prove useful. But as a boy my mother was always scolding me for breaking neighbours' windows and climbing onto their roofs. Come the long weekends of summer, however, she and my father were happy for my friends and I to head off into the country, where we walked for hours through vineyards and orchards of figs, pears and plums, on through a deep, cool oak forest until we reached a waterfall at whose edge we would sit and eat watermelon. Sometimes we would jump in. Sometimes we would fish. I loved sinking my feet into the cold, clear water. It washed away the city. It felt like freedom.

When I look back now, though my childhood was mostly one of idyllic innocence, I think I was always aware of a looming malevolence that might crush us all at any moment. I probably have Saddam Hussein to thank for that. Sardasht was only four hours' walk from the Iraqi border. From the day Iran began shelling Kurdish villages over the frontier in 1980 in response to an Iraqi invasion further south, my father had been expecting the Iraqis to retaliate. He carved out a shelter deep in the rock beneath our front yard. Some of the neighbours laughed at this barely literate man and his bunker. They laughed harder still when, during the times that he sensed trouble, he herded us underground with a small oil torch and a pile of towels which he would dip in a bucket of water and hand to my sisters and I to hold over our mouths and noses.

But on 28 June 1987, when I was three, the sirens sounded, the gas fell and that evening my father, mother, two sisters and I emerged from our shelter to discover that in and around the bazaar one hundred and thirty people had died screaming and vomiting, six hundred and fifty had lost their faces or entire sides of their bodies and eight thousand were poisoned, including my uncle Fouad, who wheezed like a harmonica for the rest of his life. To the world, the Iranian government made much of the attack, demonising Saddam, forcing the last of his Western friends to desert him and making him pay Tehran billions of barrels of oil in compensation. But in Sardasht, we never saw any of it. The regime in Iran, we figured, hated Kurds as much as their neighbours in Iraq, Turkey or Syria.

The story of my people is filled with bitter ironies like these. The Kurds are one of the world's oldest peoples and, as pioneers of agriculture, were once among its most advanced. Though the rest of humanity now largely overlooks how it was Kurds who were among the first to create a civilisation, the evidence is there. In 1995, German archaeologists excavated a temple discovered by a Kurdish shepherd at Göbekli Tepe in northern Kurdistan. They found a structure flanked by twenty-ton stone pillars carved with bulls, foxes and cranes, which they dated to 11,000 BCE. At the end of the last Ice Age, when most human beings were still wearing furs and living in caves, and a full eight and a half thousand years before the erection of Stonehenge or the pyramids at Giza, my ancestors were living together as shamans, artists, farmers and engineers.

That our ancestors picked this spot to cultivate always struck me as bull-headed. To live in the mountains was to risk your animals freezing in winter and your crops being washed away by the spring floods, while to live on the plains was to invite them to wither and die in summer droughts. But if the great strength of the Kurds was their resilience, their great blight has been the greed and laziness of others who, as far back as anyone can remember, wanted our farms and markets for themselves.

For the last few millennia, our people have been conquered by a succession of outsiders. First Persians, then Seleucids, Romans, Daylamites, Islamists, Turks, Mongols, Safavids, Afsharids, Zands, Qajars, Ottomans, then finally the British and the French. The first Kurdish uprising happened in 838. There have been twenty-six since. Despite possessing our own language and culture and a population of forty-five million – ranking us alongside Spain, Argentina and Uganda as the thirtieth most populous nation in the world – today our people and our nation still pass unrecognised as either, split between what others call southern Turkey, northern Syria, northern Iraq and northwestern Iran. In each of these misnamed, amputated limbs Kurds are repressed. Intermittent bans outlaw our language, dress, folklore, our names and, in Turkey, even the words 'Kurd', 'Kurdistan' and 'Kurdish' (we are, instead, 'mountain Turks'). Our struggle has also been alternately embraced and betrayed by the wider world. The Allies promised to create Kurdistan after the end of World War I and the dissolution of the Ottoman Empire, only to allow Turkey to block it.

Britain backed the Kurds when we declared the independence of the Republic of Ararat in eastern Turkey in 1927, then let the Turks reconquer it in 1930. When Kurds in Turkey formed the militant Kurdish Workers Party (PKK) in 1978, Turkey persuaded the world to classify it as a terrorist group. After the end of the Gulf War in 1991, the US and others urged the Kurds to rise up against Saddam (who had killed one hundred and eighty-two thousand Kurds in the 1980s), then abandoned us when we did so and let twenty thousand refugees who fled die of cold and exhaustion. Two years later, the world stood by when Turkish death squads killed a further three thousand two hundred Kurds and Assyrians.

With our obstinate farmers' blood, we have never given up. When I was young, my mother would tell me the legend of Kawa, the blacksmith, who was said to have come from a small nameless town tucked into the folds of the Zagros mountains. Above the town was an enormous castle with tall turrets cut out of the mountain rock and gates carved in the shape of winged warriors. There lived a cruel Assyrian king, Dehak, who had been possessed by an evil spirit, Ahriman. Until Dehak's time, people had only eaten bread, herbs, fruit and nuts. But Ahriman, who had disguised himself as a cook, fed the king the flesh of animals.

One day, Ahriman kissed Dehak on his shoulders, there was a flash of light and two giant black snakes sprouted above his arms. The only way Dehak could assuage the snakes' hunger was feeding them the brains of young boys and girls. From then on, the townspeople were forced to make regular sacrifices of their children, killing them two at a time and delivering their brains to the castle in a walnut-wood bucket.

With the advent of this great evil, darkness fell on the land. Crops, trees and flowers withered. Peacocks, partridges and eagles left. None felt the pain of Dehak's rule more than Kawa and his wife, who gave up sixteen of their children. When Kawa and his wife were told to give up their seventeenth and last, Kawa sent his surviving daughter to a valley far away and delivered instead the brain of a sheep to Dehak. The king didn't notice the deception, the other townsfolk copied Kawa, and soon there were hundreds of children living secretly in the mountains. Eventually, Kawa led the children in a rebellion, they stormed Dehak's castle and Kawa killed Dehak with his blacksmith's hammer. Dehak, Ahriman and the possessive serpents of greed were gone. The next day, the sun rose once more, flowers bloomed, trees blossomed and the animals returned. To this day every spring equinox, Kurds celebrate Newroz, or 'New Day', and the destiny that it promises: that after a long, dark night of repression, the bright day of freedom will dawn.

Of course, a key element of that story – that the first fighter in Kawa's army was a girl – is *haram* (forbidden by Islamic law) in much of the present-day Middle East. In Iran's case, when Ayatollah Khomeini seized power in Tehran in 1979, his regime enshrined misogyny in law. God was a man, as was the Prophet, and that, said our new leaders, gave men a divine right to subjugate women. Men could have up to four wives and marry girls as young as nine. But women couldn't work, bear witness, divorce or, should a man divorce them, expect custody of their children. These laws were enforced by a male-only religious order and a male-only judiciary, both of which equated feminism and femininity with indecency.

The Kurds have women like my mother to thank that such bone-headedness never conquered our people. She was kind and honest, and a caring and loving mother. But as a wife, she refused to submit to my father or defer to his will, as the Iranian state and traditional patriarchy demanded. My parents fought constantly. My father insisted that my mother recognise him as the head of the family and herself as family property. My mother insisted she was an independent woman who required no man's permission to do what she wanted, go where she liked and say what she thought. Her honour and integrity were inseparable from her freedom, she said. These were not qualities to be found in meekly obeying a husband or taking note of neighbours' gossip. More than once, the two of them came to blows.

A few men in Sardasht despised my mother for her independence. Many others, and almost all the women, admired her for what, under Iranian law, was close to revolutionary courage. People would talk about how clean her spirit was and how she carried herself with dignity. She was a huge influence on anyone who knew her including, eventually, my father. As her son, I hated it when my parents fought. But I also understood that my mother was holding fast to her beliefs and self-respect. Today I can see that the life I chose had everything to do with the tenacity and dignity she showed me as a boy.

I had my own battles at school. At seven, I was suddenly in a world where even the most basic things such as bread or water or home had a new Farsi name. I often couldn't understand a word that my Iranian teachers said. Nor could I read the new Arabic alphabet. Even my people's ancient story was replaced with the eleven-year footnote of history that was the story of Iran since the 1979 revolution. To me, school felt like a conspiracy designed to favour the Iranian boys and girls, who were forever one step ahead, and to guarantee the disappointment of my father, who had bought me new shoes and clothes for my classes. The injustice of it gave me a headache. I spent my days praying for snowstorms to close the school. My mother, who was illiterate, valued education but shared my suspicion of Iran's version of it, and her example gave me the strength to endure the unfairness of it. On weekends or during the holidays I began disappearing to the villages outside the city. Unsurprisingly, I was made to repeat my first year. Even today I have trouble with basic mathematics and spelling.

Outside school, my mother took a fierce interest in every aspect of my development. If she didn't like the look of a neighbour's family, she would ban me from seeing their children. One day, when I was eleven, I got into a fight at school with a boy called Shina who was two years older than me. When I arrived home with a bleeding nose, my mother asked me what had happened, then marched me round to the boy's house to confront his mother. When the woman emerged, however, it turned out she and my mother were old friends from the same village and had played together as girls. I was impressed when the other woman slapped Shina across the mouth, splitting his lip. Then, to our mutual disgust, Shina and I were made to hug each other. Much to our surprise, we quickly became good friends.

One of the things Shina and I agreed on was how much we hated the religious leaders who even we boys could see were using faith to terrorise people. My family was especially sceptical of Iran's theocracy. When the weather was fine, my father and his friends would take me for barbecues. The men would build a big fire and cook chicken and fish and drink wine. One time, as a young teenager, I was fasting for Ramadan and my uncles, who saw no connection between holiness and hunger, were having another feast. 'Eat!' they told me. When I declined,

73

they held me down and, laughing, forced a piece of chicken into my mouth. After that, they gave me a glass of 'grape juice'.

In time, Ramadan barbecues became a family ritual. Pious neighbours objected, which was their right, but we felt they were missing the point. It wasn't that we didn't believe in anything. We believed in our land. We were inspired by Nature's gifts and celebrated what it gave us. We were happy in our place. That was our faith. We would say that you could betray your land or even leave it, but it would never betray or leave you.

Matters came to a head for me around the age of fourteen. The older I became, the clearer I could see the discrimination and injustice around me. I started taking notice of how many soldiers the Iranian regime had stationed in our streets. Why did our own government feel the need constantly to check our identity? Why did they require tanks to face us? Why did they plaster Sardasht with photographs of dead Iranian soldiers, killed as they tried to crush our people's dissent? I wasn't sleeping well and getting into fights. Despite my agnosticism, my mother told me that she had heard that there were some verses in the Koran that calmed the nerves and she suggested I take up prayer. So I learned one *hadith* and practised it over and over every night before I went to bed. Unfortunately, the exercise only deepened my distress. *I'm saying my prayers in Arabic,* I thought. *But I'm Kurdish. Why should I denounce my language? What God is this, if he can only understand Arabic? If this God doesn't like Kurdish, then this Kurd doesn't like this God.*

Doubt about the state was one thing. But to deny God was a huge leap. For two months I was caught between my anger and a suspicion that I would burn in hell. I felt there was something inside me – not the devil exactly, but a restlessness, an undeniable sense of self-determination. For weeks, I felt torn. I was just a small boy from a small mountain city and I was blaspheming before the Almighty. Why hadn't I thought it through?

Then one day, hiking in the mountains, all my doubts vanished. *There is no God*, I heard myself say. *Religion is illusion. The mountains and the trees, the eagles and the rivers – they are the real peace and harmony. Why look for anything more?*

It's probably no coincidence that around the same age I started showing an interest in politics. Shina, who was sixteen by then, was already a member of an underground left-wing Kurdish nationalist party called Komala. He would spend his free time distributing socialist pamphlets critical of the regime. I began to read the articles, which were about social injustice, colonisation and Kurdish culture and how we were third-class citizens in our homeland, starved by an invader state of jobs, electricity, hospitals and roads. Often the pamphlets contained wrenching memorials to Kurds who had died in prison or been hanged.

The words had a profound effect on me. I began joining Shina on his subversive newspaper round every month, venturing out after dark with the new issue, throwing it over walls into people's gardens and tucking it inside their doors. To be caught handing out anti-state publications would mean a lengthy spell in prison or worse, so Shina devised a system whereby he was the only party member I knew and he was the only person who knew of me. With my experience now, I can see that what he created was an archetypal dissident cell.

At the time, Komala's influence was spreading and the authorities were beginning to feel it. One day, we were all ushered into Sardasht's central square and told we had been gathered to witness a hanging. Officially, the condemned man was said to have killed his friend in an accident, dropping something on his head when they were drinking. The truth, people whispered, was that he was a Komala activist like Shina and me.

The guy was young, maybe twenty-eight or so, and they had him stand on a small table in front of a crowd of thousands. I saw his mother, begging the authorities and being restrained by the guards. When they put the rope around his neck, the woman broke free and ran to her son, trying to save him, but they threw her to the ground and held her there. She screamed. Her voice was still echoing around the mountains when they pushed her son off the table. He struggled, then went quiet. But when they took him down, he was still alive. Twice more they strung him back up. Twice more they brought him down again only to find he was still breathing. Finally, they just left him hanging there.

It seems so clear now that the authorities' purpose was to terrify us. At the time, all I could feel was disgust. It was a show, a filthy circus. They had brought us together to watch somebody's death, and we had stood there and seen it. It was sickening. And somehow, just by watching, they made us complicit.

I can still feel the anger and shame that grew in me as I walked home. Nobody had the right to take somebody's life to demonstrate the power of the state. Why did we have to fear them? Why punish a man for calling for his freedom? How could these people call themselves pious? How could they demand our respect and obedience when they did something so vile and sordid? The Iranian regime had managed to provoke a reaction in me that was the precise opposite of what they intended. And I have pursued my freedom ever since.

EIGHT

Kobani,

October 2014

The day after I met Herdem, he returned to the snipers' base to find me. 'We're going to the southern front, close to where you crossed back into Kobani,' he announced. 'I hear you've been shooting long-range.' He handed me a Barrett. 'Be careful,' he said. 'There's only one. We had to make the scope ourselves from parts.'

I jumped into Herdem's small van and we drove south for a few blocks. Autumn was now upon us, it was freezing, and Herdem was wearing a black woollen beanie. As we turned a corner, Herdem started bobbing his head up and down, looking sharply left and right. He reminded me of a character in a film I had seen once.

'You look like a car thief,' I laughed.

Herdem regarded me seriously. 'You can get shot here,' he said. 'A bullet can come from anywhere. Positions change. Buildings disappear. You go for a piss, come back and everything's different. You have no idea where you are or where the enemy is.'

I should have paid more attention.

*

Herdem dropped me at a three-storey house on our southern frontline, one of ten buildings we held there. Unlike the built-up areas that formed most of our territory, buildings in the southern part of Kobani were spread out, with open space between them. Our front formed a slow curve from east to west, strung between the buildings we held. The house I now entered was in the middle of a street, with a garden in front and a clear view of the enemy's lines which could be as close as the house across the street or as much as a mile away. Inside my new base were seven comrades led by a YPJ commander called Viyan. I made my introductions, then headed for the roof.

In the distance, I could see a small village on the edge of the city occupied by ISIS. Next to it was a graveyard. To its right was the main road to Aleppo. To its left was Mistenur Hill. It was a cold and sunny day, clear enough that I could see that some of the village houses had gardens. One was bordered by a wall that looked strange, as though it were somehow too long. I studied it through my scope. Eventually I realised that the enemy had extended the wall by adding a beige curtain. It was just within range but it was hard to see what I would be shooting at.

There were other problems with my position. I was the only sniper on this part of the front, covering one hundred and fifty people, but from my vantage I could only fire across about a third of our line. The whole set-up was frustrating. When Herdem came back after two days, I told him I needed coffee, and action. 'It's boring,' I told him. 'There's some movement. Maybe a guy running from time to time. But it's too far away to shoot at. I'm just watching.'

On my third day, I was relieved to receive a radio call asking me to move position. Some comrades on another part of the front thought they had spotted an ISIS fighter. They sent a teenager from the neighbourhood to guide me through the streets to their position. Once there, I installed myself behind a pile of rubble on a slight slope and waited. After an hour and a half I saw a figure moving behind a mechanical digger, freezing for a few seconds, then moving again, then freezing once more. I waited for the next freeze, then fired once, twice, and a third time. There was no more movement.

It seemed unlikely that another jihadi would risk using the same route, so I decided to return to my first position. But as I walked back through the tunnels and curtains, focusing on keeping my shadow from falling anywhere a sniper might see, it dawned on me that I was lost. From the distance I had walked, I should have arrived already. But I didn't recognise anything. I ran across the street. To my left, I could see a curtain and some holes in the walls. I walked towards the curtain. But as I approached it, a voice behind me called out, using our word for 'comrade': '*Heval! Heval!*'

I looked around. There was no one. I continued towards the curtain. *Fzzz! Fzzz!* Bullets hit the ground around my feet. I stopped and looked behind me. *Fzzz!* came another round. Then a hand appeared from a hole in the wall of a house I had just passed, beckoning me. '*Heval*, come back!' came a shout. 'Come back! You are walking towards ISIS!'

Apparently, the curtain I had chosen belonged to the enemy. I ran to the side of the street, leapt through a broken window into what had once been a small shop, kept running, burst through the back door into the street behind, and doubled back so that I was running in the direction of the comrade who had saved me. I arrived a minute later, breathless.

'I saw you,' my fellow fighter said. 'I watched you for a while because I wasn't sure who you were. You didn't stop so I had to fire.'

I tried to push my mistake from my mind. I had walked into ISIS territory alone, which could have been catastrophic. But I hadn't died, and there was no point dwelling on it. When Herdem came to see me again six days later, I was half-expecting Viyan to embarrass me. By sending me to the southern front, Herdem had been testing me. So far I had taken out a single ISIS fighter and nearly got myself killed. But instead of reprimanding me, Viyan declared: 'This guy's a real sniper. He made his base up on the roof and he's been there almost ever since, watching, waiting, day and night, never leaving his post.'

She smiled at me. I tried to look impassive. Herdem considered his reply.

'There is a front in the east that's very hard,' he said. 'The range is very close. It's very intense fighting. It's our most difficult position. But if you want to volunteer, it would be useful.'

With Viyan's assistance, I had passed Herdem's test. Now he was asking me to insert myself into the most important battle we faced.

'Of course,' I nodded. 'Let's go.'

Driving east, the wide-open spaces of southern Kobani were replaced by a maze of concrete canyons, all narrow streets and high buildings. As we approached the front, we had to leave the van and proceed on foot through buildings and tunnels. It was hard going. Many of the houses had collapsed. Every window had been shattered in the force of the onslaught. Chests of drawers, cupboards, satellite dishes, water tanks and railings had been blown into the streets. Peering through cratered buildings and fallen walls, I could see clear through to their back gardens, where plants were dying of thirst and clothes were still flapping on the line. Roofs had fallen in on themselves. Clustered in the craters, I saw jumbles of beds, mattresses, blankets and sheets, brought down from the terraces where the families who had lived there had been seeing out the last of the summer heat. Mixed in with them were glass bowls of tomatoes, grinders and glass jars. Evidently, ISIS attacked on a day when the mothers of Kobani had been making tomato paste.

As we neared the front, the sounds of gunshots, mortars and RPGs became ever louder. I tried to clear my mind. Here the war would be all-consuming. We wouldn't be taking territory block by block. Here we would be fighting room by room.

When we arrived, we asked to meet the two commanders on the eastern front: Haqi, who was leading the YPG, and Zahra, who was in charge of the YPJ. We found Haqi first, in his base up a set of stairs in a ruined building close to where I was dropped. Haqi was in his mid-forties. Short and skinny, with the tan and wrinkles of the farmer he was, I realised when I saw him that I'd met him years before in our territory in the mountains. We'd taken a long hike through the snow to reach some camps high up in the hills and at one point I had wondered whether we would make it. At the time Haqi had been painfully thin, convalescing from a wound sustained in an air strike. Haqi often had a pained expression which strangers mistook for frustration and melancholy but which, after watching him tackle the snow, I understood as what happened when unbreakable will confronts a cold, hard life. I could see he was fitter than before and I congratulated him on how well he looked. Haqi nodded. Then, since Herdem would be leaving, he gave me someone to show me around.

The comrade could not have been more different from Haqi. He looked broken and brought to mind a saying I once heard

81

in the mountains: that if you lose hope, you may find it again, but if your hope dies, all is lost. I followed the man through the corridors, ducking through holes in walls and behind giant curtains stitched together and strung across the streets, up to five stories high. All of them were peppered with hundreds of bullet holes. As the wind blew, it inflated these giant canvases and whistled through their battle scars.

My guide led me to Zahra, who I found making tea in a ruined kitchen. As we introduced ourselves, I watched Zahra place some tissue in a small pot of oil and light it as a candle. Then she took a piece of hard cheese, softened it in water that she warmed over the flame and laid some of it on the seat of a chair. I could see Zahra was not hungry. Still, she wanted to be a good host and make me comfortable, and to encourage me to eat she took small pieces of the cheese as we sipped our tea.

Zahra had been on the eastern front so long that the building in which she based herself was known simply as the 'Zahra building'. It had four floors and stood on the western edge of a roundabout that connected two main roads, one running directly west to east, the other running northeast to southwest. On either side of her building were rows of houses. This was our frontline. In every second or third house we had a unit of five comrades, each of them with their own code name. This meant there were gaps in our line – we didn't have enough people to fill every building – so one of my jobs would be to stop the jihadis sneaking between our positions.

Zahra showed me the garden in front of her building in which the comrades had built two sandbagged bases, one converted from an old garage, the other sheltered behind a wall in which our fighters had dug firing holes. 'They've tried three or four times to take over my building,' said Zahra. I peered over the wall. The bodies of three ISIS fighters lay just on the other side. There were four more out in the street. One man next to the wall had died with his mouth locked open. 'Still trying to catch his breath,' said Zahra.

We mounted the staircase. On each floor I could see the city through large holes made by RPG strikes on the building. On the top floor, the fourth, a base had been fashioned out of oil drums filled with mud and stones. From there, about two hundred metres away across the roundabout and slightly to the south, I had a clear view of a long two-storey building with a flat roof and open ground in front of it. This was Kobani's old cultural centre and it was ISIS' main command post.

Every battle we fought in the city, there would be a building that would become the focus of our nightmares. The cultural centre was such a place. If we could take it over, we calculated we would control a quarter of Kobani. Huge, solid, with a white-and-yellow face, and providing good cover against mortars and heavy weapons, even from a distance I could see the centre would make an ideal sniper base, commanding a view of the entire street below, and an observation point from which to monitor the ISIS-controlled houses in the street opposite and another running perpendicular to it. From the roof, Zahra pointed out the enemy positions on either side of the building. Their main one was the centre itself, said Zahra. 'There's constant movement there,' she said. 'Last night, our sniper killed two of them. You're going to have your work cut out for you.'

My best position was on the roof of Zahra's building. But because the top floor was taking steady fire, I decided I would shoot from the third floor, which had better cover. Due to all the RPG holes in the walls, it was far from safe. Still, I had an idea for protecting myself that I had been wanting to try for a while.

I took a ball of wool that I had been saving, wound it around a sharp edge in an RPG blast hole that looked directly out at the ISIS positions and, keeping it tight, stretched it to the back of the room. I marked the spot on the wall, then, taking a hammer, went around behind it and knocked a hole in it about a foot wide. The two holes lined up with a view of the cultural centre and a long straight street running out to the eastern outskirts of the city. When I looked through them, however, I could see that I was still slightly exposed. So I repeated the procedure, stretching the wool from the second hole to a third wall behind me, marking the spot once more and making another hole so that all three were in line. Beyond that back wall was the building's stairwell. I grabbed a table and jammed it into the bannisters, steadying it with some pillowcases that I filled with earth. I put another pillowcase of mud on the table and, after testing it with my weight, laid my Dragunov down on it and checked the view. I could see clear through all three holes to the cultural centre and the giant red-and-blue curtain the jihadis had erected. From their point of view, however, it would be almost impossible to see me, let alone for an opposing sniper to line up his shot to pass through all my holes.

I wrapped myself in a blanket and lay down behind my Dragunov. The main street down which I was looking, to the side of the cultural centre, was about thirty metres across. The range of my targets started at about one hundred and fifty metres and extended to two kilometres in the far distance. I could also see several hundred metres down three other streets stretching away to the east and the south. I spent three hours observing. There was no movement. My attention kept being drawn back to the large screen made out of red-and-blue curtains that ISIS had hung from the left side of the building to block our view of the street, which was billowing in the wind. I could see that what I had taken to be one giant piece of fabric was in fact two separate parts held together with clothes pegs. Both parts had been strung on a white wire stretching from the side of one building to a lamp-post. The wire gave me a thought. I hadn't fired a Dragunov since Jazaa. I wanted to hear its sound again. I also told myself I needed to check my new base. We were short of ammunition. But I could try just one bullet, just to see how it felt.

I told the comrades in my building that I was going to shoot. The curtain was about one hundred and fifty metres away. I dropped my crosshairs on the cable and, when I was ready, I began breathing out.

One . . .

Two . . .

Keeping my aim, I began squeezing the trigger. Punch. The curtain dropped and hung limply across the street.

'Yeah!' shouted the guys with me. 'You really did it!'

One comrade ran downstairs with excitement. I could hear him below, shouting about what had happened. There was a rush of other comrades up the stairs to my position. They looked at me, and at my holes, and the curtain. Zahra came. 'You brought the curtain down with a bullet!' she grinned.

I was a little embarrassed. It was a lucky shot. But the others kept telling me that I was being modest, and word spread. Weeks later, Nasrin told me how, all the way over on the southern front, she'd heard about how I'd shot down a curtain from three hundred metres. People would ask her to do the same. Comrades even started trying to do it themselves. A few days later I came across a fighter in another building with a BKC who was blasting away at the enemy. I took a hole next to him and waited for ISIS to appear. I could see nothing.

'Where are they?' I whispered.

'Who?' he shouted above the noise of his weapon.

'ISIS!' I hissed.

'I'm trying to bring down the curtain!' he yelled.

All through the war I'd be introduced as the sniper who shot down curtains. The truth was that I might have fired a hundred times and never hit that wire. But on that one occasion, the curtain came down and ISIS couldn't use the street any more – and that was undeniably in our favour.

After a few days, Haqi came to fetch me. He took me northeast along our line, showing me a building where there had been a lot of movement. Opposite was a new four-storey block of apartments under our control. It had been built to house several generations of one family. Most of it was empty, set aside for children and grandchildren who might one day move in. But the second floor, where the owners lived, was expensively decorated: Persian carpets, hand-carved doors and silk furnishings in the two large bedrooms, ceramic floor tiles and yellow-and-white marble surfaces in the kitchen.

Ascending to the roof, I found I could see into a street directly in front, across which ISIS had hung six curtains, and four more streets, two on either side, down which I could see more than a kilometre. It was perfect. I took a carved door off its hinges and carried it upstairs. To hold up the back end of the door, I ripped out a pole that was carrying a TV aerial and dug it into opposing walls of the top-floor room. Next, I took a pile of sandbags, filled them and built a five-foot wall on which I placed the other end of the door. To add further support to my platform, I collected silk scarves from a chest of drawers in one of the bedrooms and tied them to each corner of the door, and then to the wall. I found a ladder up which I could climb onto my platform. Then I dug sniper holes the size of a fist, one in the wall in front, two more in the walls to the side, and then, for bullet-proofing, surrounded them with heavy marble slabs that I tore out of the kitchen. Finally, I hoisted a mattress onto the door, plus a pillow for my legs and a sandbag for my rifle. The idea was to be as high up as possible – no one would expect a sniper to be lying two metres above the floor – and for every part of my body to be supported and relaxed. Only my eyes and my finger would need to move. Since I was still sniping by day, the entire base took me two nights to build.

Moving between my two positions, I developed a routine. I would wake every morning before sunrise, when the Islamists would pray and change shifts. That was always a good opportunity to spot them. The early morning sun also assisted me. Even if they were hiding behind curtains, in the morning their bodies would throw long shadows that peeked out from underneath as they ran back and forth. I almost never managed to hit the first figure I saw. I shot a number of the second or third figures, however, six from my position in Zahra's building and four or five from my second nest. After several days of this, a few of the jihadis started running across my line of sight carrying metal doors on their backs as shields.

The quiet times were the hardest. We knew the enemy was there. But if you couldn't see him, it preyed on your mind. Zahra, though, never seemed affected. She was constantly visiting the front, checking in on each of us, and giving us her broad smile. Later, I discovered she had been raised in a refugee camp in Iraq after her parents had fled Turkey. To watch her was to understand that the hardship in her life had shaped the character she had become. A lot of the comrades were like that. You rarely met one who needed lessons in resilience. More likely, even amid the devastation, was a kind of incongruous cheerfulness. If I was on duty through the night, as the sun was coming up I would say into the radio '*Rojbas*', which means 'Good morning', and from all over sentries would respond with a chorus – '*Rojbas!*', '*Rojbas!*', '*Rojbas!*' – as if we were neighbours in some quiet and orderly town greeting each other on our way to work.

By now we were regularly coordinating our advances with warplanes from the US and other countries. When I had arrived in September, the US were flying only a few bombing sorties a week against ISIS. But by October, in response to our dire situation, Secretary of State John Kerry had convinced more than sixty countries to join the US in a coalition to intervene against ISIS. Our new friends included Britain, France and, at least publicly, Russia and Turkey. It felt like our struggle was finally being noticed.

General Tolin coordinated our attacks with the pilots. She had also decided that when we advanced, our whole eastern front would move forward together so that no unit would find itself exposed. Her strategy was, first, to direct the warplanes to destroy the houses that were one or two blocks ahead of us to create a no-man's-land. In the meantime, our teams would resupply and re-equip, and Zahra and Haqi would plan which unit would take which building. Each ground advance was generally set for the middle of the night. Our fighters moved quickly and secretly, using the shadows. They taped up their ammunition belts to stop them clanking. They even put socks over the outsides of their shoes so that their steps made no noise.

At the moment of an advance, a message would come over the radio: 'Be prepared for the first step.' That meant be ready in five minutes. Then the command would come: 'Now!'

Our tactic was for our men and women to approach a building stealthily, then feel around the door and windows with their fingers for wires and booby-traps. If the door was locked or felt heavy, like it had been rigged, they were to push it open with a broom handle, crouching next to it. If nothing happened, they would enter. If jihadis were suspected to be inside, they would throw grenades through the windows, then enter while opening fire.

Inside these buildings, the dangers increased. One time, I entered one long after our fighters had passed through. After doing my own check of the rooms, I went through to the back door. I was about to step out of the house when I noticed something in the yard that made me freeze: a fishing line and a reel. I squatted down and tried to adjust my eyes to the dark. The fishing line was strung right to left across the yard. Following the lines to the walls, I could see they were hung with mines. Working quickly but carefully, I reached into my pack for some scissors, then began cutting the lines one by one. I must have cut seven of them by the time I reached the back wall. For weeks afterwards I had nightmares about fishing trips with friends going violently wrong.

NINE

Kobani,

October 2014

As the light began to dim in the afternoon of a cloudless, freezing autumn day in late October 2014, word came that we would be attempting to capture the cultural centre. I took up position under a blanket on top of the Zahra building, giving cover. Below me our forces would move forward silently in small units. The plan was for a softening air strike by the coalition to begin at dusk and last several hours. Then different teams would advance to within a few metres of ISIS-occupied buildings around the cultural centre and, once in place, all attack together. After we had captured every surrounding building, our forces would concentrate on the centre itself. It would be bloody, dangerous, room-by-room work and would likely take hours or even days. The only way we would succeed, we told ourselves, was if we observed machine-like discipline.

I watched our teams set off, one hundred and fifty men and women walking without sound, hugging the walls and shadows. After a few hundred metres, they were gone, vanishing into gaps in the walls and the darkness between the houses.

But we had one comrade, an energetic man in his late

twenties from Kirkuk called Guevara, after the famous revolutionary, who had his own plan. From the moment the advance began, Guevara could barely contain himself, sprinting towards the ISIS positions. Soon he started shooting and throwing grenades. As the others tried to calm him, then chase after him, they realised he was moving too fast, skipping past rooms without clearing them, then whole houses. He quickly made it to the walls of the cultural centre. But instead of stopping there, he ran straight past in a wild gallop, right into the Islamist line of fire. By now, everybody was yelling at him to stop. But he kept going. Within minutes he was four or five blocks ahead, out on his own and across the ISIS frontline, with the jihadis between us and him. We could hear him yelling on the radio. He'd almost lost his voice.

Zahra called him.

'Guevara?' she said.

'Yes?' he replied, his voice suddenly soft.

'Can you come back?' asked Zahra.

'Sure,' replied Guevara.

And with that Guevara turned around and started running back towards our lines, hollering and shooting once more as he passed several houses full of jihadis. Our fighters ran towards him, trying to give him cover. As they did so, seven ISIS men ran into the street, shooting at Guevara and at the teams bearing down on them. Within seconds, all seven jihadis were cut down.

And that was it. Somehow Guevara's suicidal run had coaxed all the Islamists into the open. They were all dead. A battle for which we had been preparing for weeks and which we had expected to last all night was over in minutes. The cultural centre was ours. Our fighters ran to its roof, tore down the black and white ISIS flag and hung the Kurdish yellow, red and green banner in its place, and decorated each corner of the building with small YPG and YPJ standards.

A favourite ISIS tactic was to retreat, lull us into a false sense of victory, then counter-attack. As we tried to digest Guevara's extraordinary luck, we steeled ourselves for what we knew had to come. Our guns had fallen silent at around 3.30 a.m. At about four I walked to the cultural centre with Zahra and two novice snipers whom I was training.

As Zahra went to see about erecting more curtains to cover our new positions, the three of us continued towards the centre along a muddy path and through a number of buildings. We passed through a department store strewn with clothes, some of them brand new. I made a mental note to return so that I might replace some of the torn and filthy rags I was wearing. After a few minutes, we found ourselves approaching a small copse of tall pine trees that stood next to the gates of the centre. The gates themselves had been rent off their hinges by a blast of some kind. Through a shattered window, I saw a theatre: rows of red velvet seats covered in dust and the remains of a sound and lighting rig that had crashed down from the ceiling.

We found our way into a ground-floor corridor. It was blocked by piles of broken statues, traditional Kurdish clothes, bright silks and embroidered white cotton, and even a pair of ancient millstones. It seemed the jihadis had taken offence at an exhibition of Kurdish culture and, with characteristic articulacy, smashed it to pieces. In the hall where the display had once stood I found the walls graffitied with the usual black Arabic lettering: *La ilaha illallah, Muhammadur Rasulullah,* meaning 'There is no God but God; Mohammed is the messenger of God'. To one side, next to a sniper's hole, was more interesting writing, six pin-men symbols next to a name in Russian and a number, giving the range. These were shorthand notes for all the targets available from this one hole, made so that any sniper could position himself here and fire immediately. The use of Russian seemed to indicate snipers from the North Caucasus, probably Chechens.

My plan was to ascend to the roof and prepare a sniper's base inside a small apartment that I had spotted from Zahra's building. The only access was via a central staircase, now exposed to the street after losing all its windows. As we were mounting the stairs, one of my comrades whispered, 'Azad, Azad! Who are they?'

I looked out into the street. Two ISIS fighters, instantly recognisable by their long beards and ankle-length *thawb*s, were ambling across the street below. Maybe they hadn't heard about the battle. Maybe they thought we were busy making our defences. I was close to reaching the roof and could have opened fire instantly. But my trainees below me would have likely been caught in the return of fire.

'Shhh,' I whispered back. 'We're too exposed. Stay calm and keep climbing.'

We hurried to the roof. Below us, one of the ISIS fighters was still strolling down the street, oblivious to our presence.

'Safeties off,' I whispered. 'Let these ones pass. There'll be more. We need to be in position and be sure of our shots so we can get them all.'

As we made ready, I turned to the man who had first spotted the ISIS fighters. 'Take out the next fighter who appears,' I said. Seeing him tense, I tried to reassure him. 'Stay calm. Prepare your rifle. This is the work.'

I fixed my scope at two hundred metres and breathed slowly and steadily. A third ISIS fighter entered the street below.

Suddenly I heard a shot. Peering into the street, I strained to locate the body. But I couldn't see it. I turned to the shooter next to me.

'What happened?' I asked.

He dropped his head in shame. He had pulled the trigger by accident. Almost immediately, we started receiving fire. I told the two men with me that now we needed to make ourselves more secure and, as the jihadis' rounds whined overhead, we crawled away from the parapet on our bellies.

The rooftop apartment consisted of one large room, a kitchen, a toilet, a bathroom and two offices. Small windows in the kitchen and toilet looked out over the front of the building into enemy territory. It was ideal for double-hole shooting.

One of my apprentices started hacking away at a wall separating one office from the kitchen. The other attacked the wall between the bathroom and toilet. The walls were load-bearing, made of thick concrete, and my two comrades were soon exhausted, ready to give up. But the position was too good. I took one of the hammers and started pounding on the office wall. Forty minutes later I went into the kitchen and began on the other side. After an hour, we had one hole. A further hour after that, my trainees had made two more in two different walls, giving us a sixty-degree field of vision. Finally, I dragged over a filing cabinet, positioned it beneath one of the holes and tossed a mattress on top.

We were finishing our preparations when an announcement came over the radio that the Islamists had left a car packed with explosives in front of the building, ready to detonate. Our fighters had fired two RPGs at the vehicle in an attempt to blow the charges but the car had not exploded. Now our commanders requested a coalition air strike: one on the car, and another on a house close by where ISIS had taken up new positions. The radio announcer said the planes were ten minutes out.

We gathered up our equipment and began descending to the ground floor as the countdown came over the radio.

'Five minutes . . .

'Two minutes . . .

'One minute . . .'

By now we were safely behind cover on the ground.

'Thirty seconds . . .

'Ten seconds . . .

'Five seconds . . .'

A couple of seconds later a jet screamed directly overhead. We tensed for the explosion.

None came. I later discovered that at the last second the pilot had been called away to a different target. At the time, all we knew was that we would have to detonate the car bomb ourselves.

We quickly re-entered the building and began climbing back up to the roof. On the second floor, however, one of the YPG volunteers called to me urgently.

'Azad! Azad!' he said. 'ISIS are in that house right across the street!'

'You have a gun, don't you?' I said. 'What are you waiting for? Shoot them! Kill them!'

But the man was terrified. Pushing past him, I dropped to my knees in front of a window and tried to peer into the house he was indicating. I caught a glimpse of two jihadis with Kalashnikovs bolting down the street below me, about a hundred metres away. They were heading for the booby-trapped car, most likely to detonate it. The man in front was in his late forties with long hair, a full beard and black robes. The figure behind was smaller, had no beard and was wearing a red leather jacket.

The second one is too young, I told myself. *He's just a teenager.*

96

The pair made a dash from left to right across an alley-way, making for a doorway. Twice I fired, and twice I missed. Panicked by my shots, the two fighters changed direction and sprinted away from me. I looked through my scope. The teen-ager was following the older man.

I won't kill a teenager, I told myself. *He could have a life.*

But I had to kill the older man, and quickly. In seconds, the pair would dive into a side street and this man would be gone, free to detonate the car. But it was impossible to get a clear shot. Through the scope, the teenager's head was bob-bing directly in front of the bigger man. I knew what I had to do. I could feel my mind start to collapse with the weight of it.

It has to be now, I told myself. *Any longer and they'll be gone.*

I shot the teenager cleanly in the back of the head. He hit a wall and collapsed on the pavement. The older man turned and ran back to pick him up. I waited for him to reach the boy, then fired as he knelt over him, catching him in the arm and spinning him round. The man dropped the boy and fell to one side. I felt I had him. But in a flash, he was on his feet again, hurling himself towards a nearby door. *If it doesn't open*, I thought, *I've got him*. I fired, the door gave way, and the man vanished.

The teenager's body lay out on the street. I studied him through the scope. His head was slumped between his legs. His red leather jacket was marked by dust where he had smashed into the wall. An image of the older man brushing the boy down leapt into my mind. Maybe he was the boy's father. Maybe his uncle. He would want to take away the body to be mourned and kissed one last time by those who had raised and cared for him. Or maybe the boy was a kidnapped Yazidi, forced to fight his own people. Either way, the boy had to have been the man's responsibility. He would want to come back for him. I'd wait until he did.

'How do you feel about this kill?'

I glanced to my side. Standing next to me was a journalist from our media department with a camera and a microphone. I had heard his question clearly enough. But I could make no sense of it. For close to a year I had tried to shackle my emotions. How did I feel? About killing? About shooting a boy?

'Now is not the time,' I snapped, staring down my scope. 'The enemy is still in the house in front.'

'What is wrong with you people?' the journalist retorted. 'You just shot a jihadi but you're scared of a camera?'

This was insane. 'Go away,' I spat. 'Leave. Me. Alone.'

Ignoring the journalist, I focused on my scope. Ten minutes later, the older man reappeared, sprinting back towards the booby-trapped car. I aimed at his chest but missed and he was gone once more. By now I had been kneeling on the tiled floor for twenty minutes. My weapons, ammunition and grenades were weighing me down and my knees were shaking. I felt someone shove a blanket under them to ease the pain.

Suddenly, I saw movement again. I was about to fire when I realised that I was looking at a car tyre. The older man was trying to distract me. I held my fire. I could sense my enemy waiting, too. Was he trying to get me to reveal my position? My shoulder was beginning to tremble from the weight of my straps. I tried to stay focused. Finally, I dropped the rifle and reached for the straps. The instant I did so, two ISIS fighters ran across the street. It was uncanny, almost as if they had been watching me. Furious, I filled my magazine with more bullets, rearranged the blanket under my knees and tried to calm myself.

After a while I saw something move at the corner of the street. At first I couldn't make out what it was. Then I glimpsed the head of a rocket. The older man had returned with an RPG. All at once, he shouldered the weapon, stepped out from the corner and, as he took aim, looked straight at me.

'RPG!' I yelled to my comrades. 'Everybody down! Take cover!'

I still had him in my sights. I was about to shoot when he ducked back behind a wall. I could see the tip of the rocket protruding. I aimed at that and was about to fire when abruptly the man strode out into the street a second time, the launcher on his shoulder. He was walking directly towards me. Surprised by his boldness, I struggled to follow him in my sights. The man stopped. Through my scope I could see he was looking straight at me.

I fired.

His shoulder dropped. I was sure I'd got him. I steadied my aim for a second shot. But when I looked through the scope, I glimpsed the flash of a rocket flying towards me.

I have no visual memory of the impact. But my muscles still remember being barrelled across the room as though I had been caught by a wave. When I came to, there was dust everywhere. I looked around. One of my comrades was sprawled on the floor, silent and motionless. Another was holding his right arm and screaming silently, two fingers missing from his right hand. A third was clutching his left foot. All his toes had been blown off. I realised I couldn't feel my right leg. I looked down. Blood was oozing from my thigh. I punched it to see if it would respond. Nothing.

Seeing volunteers in the stairwell, I called out to them to help the wounded. Too frightened to enter the room, they hesitated. 'Take the injured out now!' I shouted.

They ran in with blankets on which to carry away the fallen. Seeing one of my trainees among them, I shouted, 'Bring me my rifle!'

The man remained still.

'Bring me my rifle!' I screamed.

Still he did not move. I realised that he was shouting back at me. His mouth was moving but I couldn't hear him.

Someone brought me my Dragunov. I checked the scope – still intact. Dragging my wounded right leg behind me, I crawled back to the window and resumed my position. The waiting began again. Rocket or no rocket, I was going to put a bullet through that bearded bastard's head.

A second blast wave hurled me back against the wall. This time when I came round there was brick and glass everywhere. I guessed the car bomb had finally gone up: it seemed to have been a much bigger explosion. I could feel my strength ebbing. Dragging myself up, I grabbed a Kalashnikov from the floor and hobbled to the stairs. ISIS would be sure to attack in force any minute.

Once on the ground floor, I limped through the front door of the building and sat down in the road, legs splayed, not bothering with cover. As I waited for the blast cloud to subside, I lined up the Kalashnikov's sights on where the bearded man had been hiding. I was sure he would attack from out of the dust. *I'm ready for you*, I thought. *I'll destroy you. I'll eat you alive.* This jihadi had wounded my friends and me. He was not going to survive the day.

Behind me, I heard a voice calling me: 'Azad!'

I turned around to see Zahra. My hearing was returning.

'Azad, come,' she said.

I shook my head. 'I'm fine,' I said. 'I'm OK.'

Zahra called again, more of a command this time. When I refused a second time, she turned to a group of YPJ beside her and said, 'Bring him in.'

The women approached. Something about their quiet and insistent manner persuaded me to let them lift me under my arms and drag me back inside the building. Reinforcements were arriving and began shooting towards the ISIS positions. 'My name is Nuda,' puffed one of the women carrying me. 'Give me your rifle and put your arm around my shoulder. I'm taking you out the back.'

Nuda walked me out to a backyard where a pickup had arrived to take away the wounded. I radioed in to say I was returning from the frontline, then climbed into the cab.

A few houses back, I was carried into a basement where our fighters had set up a medical centre. We didn't have a qualified doctor, only a fighter who had seen wounds treated before. He cut away my trousers with a pair of scissors. Sweating and blood-spattered, he asked whether I wanted anaesthetic.

'I can't feel a thing,' I replied. 'Just do what you need to do.'

He gave me a shot anyway, then started digging around in my wound, trying to locate the shrapnel. I realised that my fellow fighters were in the basement too. The man I'd thought was dead turned out to have been only knocked unconscious. The other two, bandages wrapped around their missing fingers and toes, hobbled over to ask how I was. I told them our 'doctor' was having a hard time finding the shrapnel.

The medic regarded me. 'Why are you smiling?' he asked.

'You want me to cry?' I replied.

'I can't find it,' he complained.

I pointed to another hole on the other side of my leg.
'Maybe it came out the other side,' I said.
At that point, I think I passed out.

TEN

Mahabad,

2002

In 2002, when I was nineteen, I was accepted to attend university. But my grades were insufficient for a scholarship and, too proud to ask my father for a loan, I declined the offer of a place. In Iran, my decision had profound consequences. Two years' military service was compulsory for every man in Iran. As a graduate, I would have been able to join as an officer. But as a school-leaver, I would be conscripted as a foot soldier.

I detested the thought of joining the army of my occupiers. But the way Iran's bureaucracy worked, even if I went underground as a full-time activist, without my certificate of military service I would never legally be able to work or own a business or become a husband or a father. I considered joining the Kurdish freedom fighters. But Shina, who had visited the camps, said Komala's armed wing was inactive and uninspiring. Also, I didn't want to leave my family. In the end, I decided that I had little choice.

I walked to the police station in Sardasht and handed over my identity documents to the military registrar. A few months later, my mother received a phone call summoning me to the bus station. When I arrived, there was a minibus waiting and a small queue of young men. We were told we were going for three months' training in Mahabad, a city two hours away.

We were taken to a military barracks outside Mahabad. Once we had passed through the large metal gates and were inside the ditches and barbed wire, we were shown to a building that looked like a factory, which contained hundreds of bunk beds in three rows. We were stripped of our clothes, given a buzz cut and handed a uniform and a tiny grey blanket. Then it was lights out. At half past five the next morning, we were woken by an officer shouting that we had three minutes to be up and dressed. Thus began my short, ignominious career in the Iranian army.

The training, conducted under the slogan 'changing donkeys into men', was mostly an exercise in tedium, centred around learning by rote. We were instructed in Shia Islam, the glories of the Iranian revolution and Iran's great victories in the Iran–Iraq war. We were taught elementary soldiering and tactics. We were shown how to use and maintain weapons: mortars, rifles, Kalashnikovs and heavy machine guns.

Mainly we learned to endure injustice. The barracks ran on the principle of collective punishment. If anyone was late, or untidy, or caught smoking, or talked at night, or stood out of line, or even fell out of bed simply because he was unaccustomed to sleeping in a triple bunk, his whole unit had to do squats or stand outside in the cold, sometimes until dawn. Recruits who answered back or fought the trainers were thrown into solitary or prison. Worst of all was when the officers added days, weeks, sometimes months to your two years of service.

The oppression, bullying, insults and humiliation were relentless. To my mind, they were also pointless. This was no way to build fearless soldiers or create brotherhood. This was how to ensure disloyalty, disunity and meekness. The only part I enjoyed was hiking in the mountains. Recruits who fell behind were forced to carry stones in their packs. But I just ran and ran. If I put enough distance between me and the drill sergeants, I found it was possible, just for a moment, to imagine I was free.

When my three months' training was finished, I was posted to the city of Urmia on Iran's western border near Iraq and Turkey. There was something strange about the unit to which I was deployed. Everyone in the ranks seemed to be Kurdish and from Sardasht. The officer in charge, Colonel Abbasali, was Iranian but the word was that he had been chief of internal intelligence in Sardasht for eight years.

In Turkey, a brutalist state simply denied that Kurds or Kurdistan existed. In Iran, the authorities were subtler. They used the word 'Kurdistan' freely, even adopting it for the name of a small northwestern province. The most senior administrators would take pains to flatter us, hailing Kurds as the most ancient of peoples whose antiquity was sanctified in the Koran. 'We are brothers,' they would say. 'And you are the eldest in the family.'

But it was all lies. Iran's religious police shot dissidents. The regime had no intention of allowing their declarations of equal stature to translate to equal rights. Advantaging Persians and excluding Kurds – and Azeris, Baluchis, Ahwazis, Lurs, Mazandaranis, Gilakis and many others – was how they divided and ruled those they oppressed. Their public praising of us was a calculation. They were daring us to call their bluff, treating us as outsiders and third-class citizens and all the while telling us we were superior to them. Their way of making it difficult to hate them was telling us they loved us.

It says something about human vanity that such tactics were

often effective. But in our people's defence, the Iranian state was a very skilled deceiver. Col. Abbasali, for one, carried off the act faultlessly. He was warm and charming, with an approachable humility that belied his position. I watched him methodically make friends with everyone in our unit. Many apparently believed that he was genuinely their ally and confidant. A number openly admired him and tried to emulate him. Others cooperated not out of innocence but a cynical desire for position and money. Those, like me, who refused to be complicit in our own oppression were a minority. And an unliked one. We had to avoid loose talk. We kept to ourselves.

I did find a friend in Urmia in whom I could confide, however. Qader was older than the rest of us, a career soldier in his mid-thirties who was happy to take the state's rials but had managed to hold on to his soul. When Col. Abbasali told us that we didn't have to wear our uniforms when we went on operations along the border and that our traditional Kurdish clothes would suffice, Qader told us not to listen. Abbasali was only pretending to be giving us the freedom to dress how we liked, said Qader. What the colonel had neglected to mention was that the infiltrators for whom we would be searching were Kurds like us. 'The colonel is hoping your dress will confuse them,' said Qader. 'They're trying to manufacture a situation in which Kurds kill Kurds.'

I wanted to know more. When I questioned Qader further, he told me the 'enemy' we were expected to fight were the PKK, or the Kurdistan Workers Party. Iranian state propaganda described them as traitors. Back then, I knew nothing of the PKK's ideology. But I knew they were Kurds fighting for Kurdistan, and I wasn't about to go to war with my own people.

A few weeks after I arrived in Urmia, I discovered a village near our camp had a *hammam*, a hot spring bath, and I was granted permission to walk there and take a wash. Once in the village, I found a public phone to call home and speak to my father. When I had been conscripted, one of my main concerns was that at some point I might have to take a life. Now I had learned that I would likely be shooting at fellow Kurds. When my father answered, I told him I wanted to desert. He advised against it.

A few days later, it was Eid and I was given leave to travel back to Sardasht. When I walked through the door, I told my parents, 'I'm not going back.'

My father didn't challenge me. The decision was mine alone, he said, and whatever I decided, my family would support me. Then he gathered the entire family and all our neighbours for a huge dinner where everybody was so kind and thoughtful in the ways they entreated me to return to the army that I felt I couldn't refuse. That was something I always loved about my father. His friends beat their sons into submission. My father used persuasion. We might have lived under the yoke of the state, but inside our family my father was teaching his children how to discuss and debate as free people.

Once I was back with my unit, we began going out on patrol through villages near the Iraqi and Turkish borders. We kept it up for four months, hiking, tracking and camping out in the mountains for four or five days at a time. One day, high up above the snowline, we walked through the fog all day until, without warning, we came across a PKK camp in a wood. The guerrillas had just left. I could see piles of cigarette butts where the lookouts had stood watch. The fire was still burning and there were potatoes and onions frying in a pan. 'Careful,' warned Qader as I eyed the food. 'It might be booby-trapped.'

A few weeks later, we were out in the mountains again, way up in the snow near the border. Col. Abbasali was taking us to a peak from where we would be able to look down on a PKK position. After climbing all day, we reached the summit around 4 p.m. But as the lead man approached the top, he was immediately fired on. *Fzzz! Fzzz!* The bullets were passing close over our heads. We threw ourselves to the ground and inched forward on our elbows.

From the lip of the ridge, I could see a deep valley below us, with several mountain ranges behind. Far away below, three men as small as ants were shooting up at us and taking cover behind several big boulders. *Fzzz! Fzzz!* Their bullets were getting closer.

'Bring me the BKC,' said Col. Abbasali. 'Bring me more weapons.' He grabbed a Kalashnikov and started shooting. 'Be clear what you're firing at,' he ordered. 'Shoot to kill.'

It was an idiotic order. There was little chance of hitting a target at that range with a Kalashnikov. Seeing my expression, Qader told me not to worry. 'Just pretend by firing over their heads,' he said.

After fifteen minutes of this, Abbasali's voice came over the radio, ordering me to reposition myself on a small hill in front and fire down into the valley. I moved as instructed. But at that altitude even breathing was exhausting, and when I reached the new summit I lay down in a small ravine and, without meaning to, fell asleep. I woke up to find the radio operator nudging me with his foot and holding out a handset to me. I took it.

'You're sleeping!' shouted Col. Abbasali over the radio. 'I can see you! You've been asleep since you got there!'

He was swearing, revealing his true colours by cursing my family and my people. I was incensed. But his words also removed the last of my doubt. This was my land and my people.

Abbasali was the intruder. He was trying to make us kill each other.

I climbed back up to his position. *If he touches me*, I told myself, *I'm going to shoot him. Then I'll go down to join these Kurdish fighters.* A thick fog was coming in, hiding my expression as I walked towards Abbasali. But when I reached him, he seemed to take the measure of me. He looked in my eyes. He noted the grip I had on my weapon. He did nothing.

Up there on the ridge, being ordered to shoot and kill my countrymen, something crossed over in me. Forced to choose between my people and their persecutors, I made my decision. This was the dilemma that had haunted me since my conscription. Abbasali's pursuit of the PKK meant there was no avoiding it any longer. As long as he kept us out patrolling the mountains, the same thing was going to keep happening. Abbasali was giving me no alternative.

The fog grew thick enough that I couldn't see the end of my arm, and we had to descend. After several hours' walking down the mountain in silence, until long after it was dark, we found a village in which to camp. When it was my turn on guard duty, I relieved my predecessor, waited until he was snoring in his tent, then laid my Kalashnikov on the ground and walked out of the camp into the mist.

I walked through the night, heading down the mountain. Around dawn, I came to a village. I took a minibus leaving for Urmia, then another going to Mahabad, then walked across the city to Shina's house. He was shocked to see me but ushered me inside. I was a deserter, hiding from one of the world's most repressive regimes. But finally I was free.

Top Herdem in Kobani. The picture is part of a series by AFP photographer Bulent Kilic that have become iconic. Herdem was killed a few weeks later. (BULENT KILIC/AFP/Getty Images)

Above left Hayri in Kobani. This photograph captures Hayri as I knew him: surrounded by destruction but somehow cheerful and pleased to see you. (YPG archives)

Above right General Medya (right) with Evindar, a team commander who died in the battle to take back Sarrin. A veteran of more than a decade of fighting and a capable and intelligent warrior, Medya was the perfect soldier to face ISIS. (YPJ archives)

Above Yazidis entering our territory after fleeing ISIS's attempted genocide on Mount Shengal in Iraq. Our volunteers stalled the ISIS slaughter, allowing 500,000 to escape. (Emrah Yorulmaz/Anadolu Agency/Getty Images)

Left Zahra. Raised in a refugee camp, the hardship in Zahra's past seemed to have given her an indomitable spirit. Here she is pictured on the roof of the Zahra building. (YPJ archives)

Left My view of the cultural centre from the Zahra building. (YPJ archives)

Above The battle for Kobani. This picture was taken from the Turkish side of the border in October 2014. (Emin Menguarslan/Anadolu Agency/Getty Images)

Below Around 70 per cent of Kobani was flattened during the battle to save it from ISIS. This picture, taken in January 2015, shows the extent of the damage. (BULENT KILIC/AFP/Getty Images)

Abdullah Öcalan, our leader. For two decades he has been locked away on a one-man prison island off Istanbul. (YPG archives)

Guevara. One of most enthusiastic volunteers, his suicidal charge into and beyond the ISIS lines won us the battle for the cultural centre. (YPG archives)

Above left Nuda. When I was wounded, she and other women carried me out of the line of fire. She died a few weeks later in an ISIS suicide attack. (YPJ archives)

Above right Servan. One of our most gifted marksmen, Servan's innocent nature meant he never learned the deception and manipulation that a sniper must also deploy. (YPG archives)

An air strike on Kobani in January 2015, in the last few days before we took the city. (Associated Press)

Above Herdem with Keith Broomfield. Keith had made some bad decisions in his life, so his journey to becoming a freedom fighter was a shining example of human redemption. (**YPG** archives)

Left Tolhildan (left) with his brother. Three brothers from the same family joined the **YPG**, which was a strict violation of the rules. Tolhildan refused his mother's entreaties to leave Kobani. (**YPG** archives)

Herdem with the nine jihadis he killed single-handedly. (BULENT KILIC/AFP/ Getty Images)

Gunter Helsten had served in the German army and French foreign legion. At 55, he was a father figure to many of us. (YPG archives)

The graveyard at Kobani. (YPG archives)

A field of spectacular red fritillary flowers at the foot of the Zagros mountains. To us, the red fritillary denotes the death of an unknown warrior. (YPG archives)

ELEVEN

Kobani,

November 2014

After capturing the cultural centre, I think all of us had had the same dangerous thought: we might beat them. Alone at night, in the quiet of a turn on watch or during an unguarded daydream, the idea grew in us that the ISIS tide was ebbing. The evidence was there with every forward step we took.

Nobody spoke about it. Saying it out loud would bring it into the world and such a fragile and premature idea would never survive in such a place. We had reached this point by focusing only on enduring and surviving – and only by enduring and surviving would we continue. On our backs we carried our homeland and the friends we had lost. Lifting up our heads to survey our progress, even for a second, was how we would get them blown off. Death was everywhere. Even if we did rout ISIS and take back our land one day, hundreds more of us would die before then. Besides, we had only recaptured a few hundred metres of devastated streets and a handful of smashed buildings. Swapping one set of ruins for another hardly guaranteed the liberation of this small town, let alone Rojava, and we could lose what we had won in seconds. So we buried our hope deep in our broken land, like pirates hiding secret treasure, praying that we might return to find it some day in the future.

I put my effort into returning to the fight. My medic had confined me to a logistics and supplies base a few hundred metres behind the frontlines. When Herdem came to see me, I told him the injury to my leg wasn't crippling and that I should get back to the front.

'To reach the front, you need to be able to walk,' Herdem observed.

'I'm going whether you send me or not,' I replied. 'Besides, the doctor told me that I need to exercise my leg.'

Without taking his eyes off me, Herdem radioed the medic. The medic told him that, yes, I did need to exercise my leg, but no, he didn't consider the frontline the best place for recuperation.

'I'm not going to be running around,' I protested. 'I'm just going to be lying on a mattress behind a wall.'

Herdem smiled. The next day, he accompanied me as I hobbled through the streets to our new front. We found Zahra, who invited me on a tour of our positions. I wanted to see Nuda to thank her for dragging me back from the front. But it took me all day to limp around our new lines and it was not until the evening that I came across her on the second floor of a ruined house, the last building on our eastern front. She was wrapped in a blanket, her eyes red, her face drawn and her hair matted with dust. Recognising me, she got up slowly and we joined a group making tea. We sat there for a while in silence, looking at each other and drinking from our glasses. I felt something pass between us, a warmth between two human beings in a shattered house on the edge of a cold and bitter war.

The next morning, almost without thinking, I found myself up before sunrise, climbing inside a ruined building a block from the cultural centre. From my new position, I guessed we now held a little more than a third of the city. I tried to tell a group of comrades setting up in a building across the street where I was so they wouldn't shoot me or leave me behind. But I was in pain, they were exhausted, and neither of us had the strength for talking. When they didn't hear me, I just turned around and worked my way up to the roof.

My new building was a wreck: parts of the balcony and the walls had collapsed, and much of the floor had fallen through. I didn't have the energy to build a nest right away. Instead, I grabbed a blanket I found lying in the rubble, threw it over the debris, lay on it, then pulled a couple of empty sandbags over myself, much as Yildiz had once suggested. The blanket was very thick, with a beautiful design – scarlet and olive and sea-blue in a finely knotted pattern – and I had picked a good spot: from where I was, I could see the entire front and a large building known as the Black School, which was ISIS' new base of operations.

But lying out in the open under a cloth covering, I was exposed – to the wind, the cold and the eyes of my enemy. As the sun rose, I realised the light would reveal my position to any ISIS sniper just as clearly as I could now see their new lines. The pain in my leg was also wearing. Around 10 a.m., I decided that, whether or not anyone had me in their sights, I had to move. When I tried, however, I realised I couldn't. My leg, previously frozen in a spasm of pain, was now numb. I couldn't feel anything below my waist.

I was debating my next move when the mortars started up. I

saw the first round arc through the sky, then land a few blocks ahead of me. The second came a block closer. The gunners were sighting their weapons. Shells were rolling steadily towards me like a wave. As one round hit, another would already be flying behind it through the sky. Watching one, I caught a flash of blue. I'd heard the jihadis had worked out a way to attach a detonator to the nose of a gas canister and fit fins and a tail to its base. This had to be the result. The gas bombs were said to be capable of bringing down entire buildings. If one hit my roof, I was done for. But if I moved I was finished too. ISIS marksmen would be watching the bombardment to cut down anyone who ran. I comforted myself with the idea that a flying gas cylinder was not a precision weapon. If I was equally likely to find myself underneath a gas bomb wherever I went, then it made just as much sense to stay put as to move elsewhere.

A mortar landed a street away. Another landed in the building opposite. I hugged the floor. Out of the top of my eye I saw a dark object nosedive in front of me, disappearing into the floor below. The building bounced. I saw another mortar overhead. A building to my left leapt in the air, then collapsed. Another mortar flashed just over my head. I was in the air. I was on the ground. My eyes and nose were stuffed with dust. I scrabbled sideways, into the stairwell. The mortars kept coming.

I might have lain in the stairwell for a minute or an hour. When the barrage began to ease, I hit my legs and rubbed them to bring them back to life. I checked myself. No blood.

In front of me was a small, unfurnished room, the doors blown in but three walls still intact. As I stirred, the noise seemed to alert someone on the other side of the wall. Through a broken window I saw a pair of eyes looking back at me. I thought I recognised them.

'Who are you?' the man demanded in Kurdish. He seemed alarmed.

What was his name? Where had my voice gone?

'Who are you?' he shouted again.

I wanted to reassure him, to call him by his name and tell him it was me, Azad. He would know me if I could remember his name. But already he had his gun up. It was probably too late.

'Azad!' I managed. 'It's Azad!' I held up my hands. 'Comrade – it's me, Azad. How are you?'

Slowly, the man's eyes and face opened. He dropped his gun and walked on.

As I watched him go, his name finally came to me. 'Qandil!' I shouted after him. 'You're Qandil from South Kurdistan!'

He kept walking.

After the mortar attack, I didn't object when Zahra suggested I spend my nights back at the cultural centre, our new logistics centre, now five hundred metres back from our new front. I was there on a foggy, freezing, rainy evening a few days later when an explosion tore through the air and the radio began screaming: 'We are under attack! We are under attack!' Another voice shouted: 'We need bread, now! We need bread!' 'Bread' was our code for assistance.

Instinctively I grabbed my rifle and limped to the roof to provide cover. It was pouring with rain. Rounds were *fzzz*ing past. Up ahead it looked like New Year: sparks were flying through the air in every direction. I could hear gunfire and the jihadis' cries of '*Allahu Akbar!*' Every few minutes there was a deafening explosion which seemed to lift up the houses and walk them towards us. The sharp tang of explosive hung in the air. On the radio, I could hear a commander calling his teams but getting no response. Others were shouting. 'We're being attacked on our left flank!' 'We need more ammunition!' 'We need assistance now! ISIS is coming around the side!'

After a few minutes, I saw Yildiz run past on the street below, M16 in hand. I was no use where I was, so I hopped down to the street after her. The wounded were already starting to arrive, their blood mixing in with the mud. Some were screaming. Others, missing a leg or holding their guts in their arms, were past that. More and more kept arriving, until we had twenty men and women lying down in the street, rolling in the mire, crying out in pain. I tried to help one man, a big comrade, who was crying out and bleeding from the stomach and the leg. But as I put my hands under him, a shock of pain ran through my body from my wounds and I felt myself fainting and collapsing backwards onto the street.

'What are you doing, Azad?' a comrade yelled at me.

I was doing nothing to help. I could only watch. I pushed myself against a wall, trying to melt into it, and observed as my friends and comrades were brought in dying. Others ran around trying to save them. When I couldn't hear or see any more, I covered my ears and closed my eyes and let the rain wash away my tears.

Walking the scene the next day with Yildiz and skirting what remained of eight ISIS suicide bombers, I listened as she described the battle. ISIS had mounted an intense counter-attack using waves of kamikazes. It started when one jihadi drove a car into our lines and detonated a pile of explosives. That was the cue for a second car bomber to race in and detonate. A third then did the same.

The three explosions knocked out the two teams either side of them, breaching our line. ISIS then sent in ten suicide bombers on foot through the gap. They ran through our lines and headed for the most crowded area they could find. 'They had dressed themselves like ninjas, all in black, with only their eyes showing,' said Yildiz. 'They didn't blow themselves up straight away. Only when they failed to break through our lines or were stopped, that's when they exploded.'

Yildiz had brought two of them down herself. 'Through my thermal, I saw this guy looking around a corner of a house,' she said. 'He was trying to find a way forward. I fired. He exploded like a balloon. There were pieces of him everywhere, all over the walls, and a pile of mincemeat where he had been standing.' Of the second bomber, she told me, 'I shot him in the head through his moustache. He was wearing a vest of explosives and he had his finger through the pin of a grenade in his vest.'

I went to look. The man's forefinger was still hooked through the grenade pin, frozen in place. His face was like a stopped clock.

Thirteen of our men and women died instantly in the attack. Twenty-three more were wounded, seven of whom died later. I knew three of those killed. Qandil was beheaded and dismembered by the blast from one of the car bombs. Nuda had been defending her position in the building where we had shared tea when a suicide bomber ran into the ground floor, detonated his device and brought the building down on top of them both. Guevara also finally ran out of luck. He had become separated from his unit and, though they told him to wait, he ran to them anyway. Rounding a corner at his usual sprint, he found himself confronting two of the bombers. They shot him in the arm but he kept running, firing as he did so and yelling on the radio to his comrades: 'I'm fine. I'm doing well. I'm coming to you.'

TWELVE

Kobani,

November 2014

Every day brought another storm. We were united in trying to save our city. But so many of us were being cut down it was difficult to know whether we were fighting or dying together.

One day in early November 2014, as I crossed the street, I ran into Hayri as he emerged from the ruins of a building. He had grown a short beard but he still looked neat and tidy, with the same scarf around his neck. He had been stationed on the front next to mine for a month, a kilometre away, but in all that time I hadn't seen him. Now he was being redeployed. We looked at each other. Hayri had one hand around his Dragunov and his trigger hand in his pocket. He smiled.

'Everything good with you, Hayri?' I asked.

He nodded. 'Yes, it's good, it's good,' he said. 'We are good. And you?'

I told him I was fine.

Hayri was jiggling something metallic in his pocket. He showed me: a clutch of M16 bullets. He said he had found them in a house that he'd helped capture. 'They were on the floor in a bedroom,' he said. He wasn't sure if they had been left behind by dead comrades or by jihadis he had killed.

'Use them,' I said. 'You'll need them.'

'You sure you don't need them?' he asked me.

We chatted for a little while longer. Then he walked on.

I recall almost every word of that conversation. Every time I met someone, I tried to fix them in my mind and my heart in case I never saw them again. It might not even be a bullet that would take them. My wound, though still raw and bloody, was closing up. But by now all of us were living on the cusp of exhaustion. After two months with only scraps to eat, our flesh lay like sheets over our bones and our eyes were sinking back into their sockets. Tiredness ate at our minds and confused our bodies. One evening, curled up in the base, I woke with a start, my heart bursting. I was sure I had been shot. After checking myself all over and finding nothing, I realised what I was feeling was not a fresh injury but the muscle memory of being caught in an RPG shockwave. This went on for months.

To keep my focus, I tried to eliminate everything from my life but the craft. Planning, watching, firing; cleaning, building, hiding; deceiving, breathing, withstanding – this became my character. A rifle is a machine with an unswerving function, fast and powerful, speaking only when it must. To be right with the rifle, to be its friend and comrade, I had to be the same: just being and acting. I went for days with my mind blank and my mouth shut. It wasn't that I had nothing to say. It was that I had found a different way to say it.

But everybody has their limits. Once, after a long day watching the street, I saw a jihadi walking towards me. There was something disgusting about this man. Under his headdress he had yellow teeth and eyes, his mouth seemed to be in the middle of his face, and he was covered in filth. He was acting crazily, just strolling in front of his curtain in the middle of the road. Just at the moment when I had his head in my crosshairs, he turned to look at me. I was about to fire when suddenly I heard the word '*Rojbas*'.

I looked up to see a comrade looking down at me.

'Why did you disturb me?' I demanded. 'Why didn't you let me kill him?'

He looked around the empty room. 'Who?' he said.

I sat up. I was under a blanket in a corner of a room. My rifle was leaning up against the wall beside me.

I was far from the only one corroded by fatigue and hunger. I began to observe a new phenomenon among a few of my comrades. When we were waiting for the next battle, everyone would be vigilant, kept awake for days by the terror in our imaginations. But the moment a fight started, the instant we could see the shape of the next attack and even that there was a possibility of living through it, some would relax and fall asleep, right there in the middle of a firefight. One time I watched a group of our fighters take it in turns to spray the inside of a room in a building they had just taken over, only to discover that inside it was one of our own, asleep. The man dozed on even after his comrades shot a book-case down on top of him. We were moving forward, of that there was no more doubt. But it was an open question how many of us were even capable of reaching the finish.

In mid-November the Islamists introduced a new tactic that seemed to speak of an impatience with our resistance. I was making new holes for a sniper's nest high up on the top floor of a wrecked building one afternoon, trying to work out how to be safe behind a wall that had a giant five-metre crack in it, when suddenly the gaps in the wall on either side of me exploded with ricochets. All along the front I could hear what sounded like a huge firecracker, a rolling *crack-crack-crack* that lasted several seconds.

Almost immediately, voices began screaming for assistance on the radio. When I went to investigate, I found every base had been hit. There were pools of blood on the floor in every position we held. Comrades were pushing past me, ferrying out the wounded and the dead. What had happened?

We concluded that ISIS' commanders had instructed every one of their men to fire all their guns at once. They had unleashed a deadly volley along the entire front. Ten of our men and women perished in the fusillade. Another thirty were injured. With so many bullets fired at the same time, some found unlikely trajectories. One of our team commanders was shot and killed when a round that had already travelled several hundred metres passed through a hole in a wall and then a tiny gap between two sandbags. It hit him right in the forehead.

Most of us viewed ISIS' new strategy as another obstacle with which we had to cope. But Herdem saw it as something we could turn to our advantage. Why not use ISIS' tactic against them? he asked. Why not make it even more deadly, so that we fired into their gun holes not just along one front but across the whole city? Four days later we did just that, firing every weapon we possessed at a prearranged signal on the radio. I emptied several magazines. It was devastating. We killed scores of jihadis and wounded many more. You could hear them screaming and panicking all along the line. A few days later we did it again, then again, then again. I don't know why the jihadis never repeated the tactic against us. But we were happy to steal it from them.

*

Day by day, week by week, we inched forward. In late November, Herdem's voice came on the radio, asking me where I was. I told him I was in a tall building close to an old girls' school which at that time marked the beginning of no-man's-land. An hour later, Herdem found me. With him was a new comrade with a boyish face, blue eyes and ginger hair whom he introduced as Servan. Herdem took me aside. 'He's very polite, a very good person, very honest and quiet,' he said. 'He can also hit targets extremely well. But he has no sense of tactics and doesn't understand bases or keeping himself safe. I need you to teach him.'

I was doubtful. Servan seemed to have the calmness and patience of a good sniper. But I could see just from looking at him that he had no feel for the psychological side – the ability to calculate, analyse and manipulate. Despite my misgivings, I found myself warming to him. After more than two months of shooting and deceiving and lying in the dirt, there was something refreshing about Servan's pure nature. You felt you had no choice but to protect such innocence.

The next morning, when I woke at half past four, Servan was already up and waiting. We walked together to the front, leaning into an incline and a wild wind that was rushing through the streets. Our new target was the Black School, which stood on a hill with a wide view over the city and which had earned its name from the black mesh barricades nailed across its windows. It was another building of huge strategic value. If we captured it, we would control more than half the city.

Once we arrived at the front, I told Servan to stay put in a tall four-storey building under the control of a women's team commanded by a YPJ leader called Sama. I was going to check along the front for firing positions that would allow us to target the Black School and another nearby college in ISIS hands. I was ascending the staircase of a building next to the college when I heard several dozen ISIS fighters shout their war cry: '*Allahu Akbar! Allahu Akbar!*' The chorus came from around two hundred and fifty metres away and was followed by the noise of an arsenal of guns firing. The Islamists were making a fresh attack.

I ran to the roof and hurried towards the parapet. Abruptly, ISIS stopped firing. That was the signal for around twenty jihadis to appear in the street three or four blocks away, yelling and running towards our lines. Another ten were running across the rooftops.

I lay down and fixed my scope to two hundred and fifty metres. The jihadis filled my sights. I started shooting into them, once, then again, then a third time. Two or three collapsed while they ran, to be trampled by the others. A dozen or so reached the college and started sprinting across the playground. They were heading for one of our teams but, out in the open, had no cover. I continued to fire at them as they went. Another down. And another.

They were running over each other now.

I took down another.

And another.

I switched to the figures on the roof. I took one more. Then a second. A third to the side.

I switched back to the playground. The jihadis were scattering for cover behind a small wall and shouting at each other to fetch their fallen comrades. Then they began running back towards their lines. I hit one of the bigger ones in his side as he ran away from me. He pirouetted around and dropped to the ground. A friend grabbed him under his shoulders and tried to drag him off. I hit him too. By now several of my comrades were also firing, including one on a BKC and another on a mini

Dushka. A few more Islamists fell. Then they were gone and the attack was over.

I was ecstatic. I had shot twelve jihadis in two minutes. What an opportunity! The right place. The precise time. Even if I was wounded, I could still be part of it. I was still effective.

After a while, I remembered that Servan wasn't with me. I descended the building and went to find Sama. She told me Servan was above her on the top floor. I climbed up. On the higher floors of this building almost the entire facade had been obliterated. What remained was punctured by holes the size of basketballs. Instinctively, I threw myself to the ground and tried to find cover. Servan, I noticed, was lying directly behind one of the holes, his rifle protruding into the street.

'Servan!' I shouted. 'You can't lie there! Move away! Get out of there!'

Servan got up and ambled over to me.

'What are you doing?' I asked.

'Making a base,' he said. I saw that he had piled up four mattresses behind the hole he had chosen.

'That's not a base,' I told him. 'That's a target. You're right behind a hole. Even someone with a pistol could hit you there. If any ISIS spots you, you're done.'

Now Servan looked worried. 'How do I make a real base?' he asked.

I spent the next hour instructing Servan. I showed him how to stuff the holes with pillows so that his position was concealed. Even then, I told him, he was not to stand behind any hole. I showed him how to build a platform out of shelves and pillows. I told him to set it a few metres back from a small hole and right at the top of the wall, just below the ceiling. 'They're unlikely to shoot the holes at the top as they can't imagine how anyone could be lying down just below the ceiling,' I explained.

Servan was excited by what he was learning. 'Great!' he kept saying. 'Great!' Once I was sure he knew what to do, I went downstairs to talk to Sama. When I came back up, to my amazement Servan had nearly finished his base. 'I used to be a builder in Aleppo,' he grinned. Once he was done, Servan built me a base too, on the other side of the building.

We stayed in our building for three days. Nothing was moving. On the third afternoon I heard a noise that sent an electric shock through my stomach. Scanning the horizon, I saw a familiar outline in the distance, crossing the street from one side to the other, billowing black smoke and crushing debris beneath it. I froze. It was the first time I had seen a tank in Kobani. What could rifle rounds do against that?

I grabbed my radio and asked for Haqi. When he came on, I blurted out, 'There's a tank, between the Black School and the college! It could obliterate us all!' I requested he talk to the coalition about an immediate air strike.

From its position on the hill next to the Black School, the tank would be able to fire down on a large section of our front. I made a quick calculation. There was no doubt the tank could blast Servan and I out of our vantage point high up in our buildings. But because its barrel couldn't dip below the horizontal, it would have more difficulty hitting the fighters below us.

'Everybody down to the ground now!' I shouted.

I stayed on the top floor. Sama arrived with an RPG and a bag of rockets. 'The air strike won't make it in time,' she said. She ran to the roof.

I could hear the tank moving again. I thought I could see a plume of black smoke behind the Black School. To the side of the building was an abandoned, rusty yellow combine harvester. From behind the harvester came more noise and another jet of black smoke, then the tank's nose rumbled into view. Its barrel swung around until it seemed to be pointed directly at me.

Fire spat from the barrel. The shell flew towards us and crashed into the floor below. The building shook like the branch of a tree. When the dust cleared, I caught sight of the tank backing up and disappearing again. But after a few seconds I heard it advancing once more. As soon as it appeared, it fired again, this time directly towards Sama. The shell went wide. Through a crack in the floor above me, I saw Sama drop to her knee with the RPG over her shoulder. She fired.

Her grenade missed by inches and slammed into the harvester. Sama, shrouded in dust, immediately reloaded and fired again. Then again. Then one more time. All her shots slammed into the harvester. By this time I had run up to the roof and was racing across to her.

'Wait!' I shouted. 'You're hitting the harvester! The tank is to the left.'

We waited for the dust to clear. But the tank had gone. A fighter jet screamed overhead. Half an hour later, a predator drone began circling. We never saw the tank again. But for the rest of our time in Kobani, we all felt its presence around the corner.

Come late November, ahead of our planned advance on the Black School, coalition planes had been hitting ISIS' lines for days, raining down five-hundred-pound bombs guided by our spotters on the ground. Watching the planes from below, we could feel the world coalescing behind us. A month later, after two Islamists massacred twelve journalists and staff members at the offices of the *Charlie Hebdo* magazine in Paris, we watched as a French female pilot screamed overhead all night, bombing ISIS in run after run. She radioed our air coordinator on the ground. 'I am a member of the YPJ too,' she declared.

The air strikes were devastating. One rocket could blow a hole the size of a swimming pool in a building. The detonations would send eruptions of dust and debris hundreds of metres into the sky. Even if the jihadis survived, many would be deaf, blind and numb. Even so, this remained a street war. ISIS not only held its ground, often the jihadis counter-attacked during the strikes, trying to mingle with our forces so the strikes would stop. You had to respect their courage. Hundreds of them were vaporised but they were not giving up.

Once we reckoned the jihadis had been pummelled enough from the air, our teams would advance on foot. At this stage, the strikes would become as much a risk to us. Crossing no-man's-land on the southern front one day, five of our men and women were killed by an errant bomb. There was also no way of knowing where ISIS had set mines or hidden pockets of fighters. And now that the jihadis were in retreat, sniping was becoming one of their favoured tactics. Rather than give cover from the rear, I began to advance with commanders directing the attacks. As he or she went forward, I tried to shoot down any Islamists fleeing the bombardment or staying behind in no-man's-land. There were always a few die-hards.

The Black School attack was no different. We set off up the hill on a dark night in late November. As we were advancing, a coalition bomb wounded three of our fighters. To my left, one of our snipers cut down three jihadis holding out in the front yard of the Black School. After suffering a few more casualties and killing some more jihadis, we took the building. I'm sure I took my share of shots and kills, but now I struggle to remember how many. For weeks it had been just steady, methodical slaughter. When I try to recall that time, what I remember most is a vague feeling of rhythmic accomplishment.

THIRTEEN

Iran to Europe,
2003–2004

When I look back further, to the days after I deserted the Iranian army, when I was still just a teenager taking on God, Iran and any other injustice or untruth that offended me, I can't help but smile. Such stubbornness. So alone. In those days I had no way of knowing the turmoil my actions would unleash. But even if I had, I don't think I would have hesitated. What connects the child I was then to the man I am today is purpose and spirit. Back then, I was just a boy who liked to go swimming in a mountain stream. Today I am a freedom fighter, a veteran of fifteen years of struggle. But I am not changed. That's who I was then. It's who I am now. The path between these two figures is bounded by turbulence. But the way is straight and true.

I probably should have left Iran the day I deserted. I could have simply walked over the mountains to the PKK's camps. But it was never my wish to abandon my family and friends. Shina and I also wanted to stay and fight for our rights.

We lived together as subversives for more than a year, sleeping during the day and leafleting at night. Many other young men had deserted and were doing the same work. The numbers didn't make it any less dangerous. Dissidents like us were jailed or 'disappeared' in their hundreds.

Perhaps inevitably, one day Shina returned to the house with news that his name was on a watch-list. It couldn't be long before mine was too. A few days later we heard that the authorities had raided a garage owned by my father where I'd been secretly storing books and newspapers. A day after that, while we were out, security officers broke into the house where Shina and I were living, searched it and questioned the neighbours. Shina and I had to disappear immediately.

Shina decided that his colleagues in his movement, Komala, could hide him. That night, after so many years as friends, we said farewell. It would be an age and thousands of miles before I saw him again. Unlike Shina, I wasn't ready to put my life in the hands of others. My only choice was to leave Iran immediately. At first, I had no idea how I would do this. Given the unpopularity of the regime, however, perhaps I shouldn't have been surprised to walk into Mahabad's market and find a people smuggler sitting in an office just off the main square.

Mustafa was an older Iraqi man from the south of his country with a crippled leg and a walking stick. He specialised in trafficking what sanctions had made attractive to middle-class Iranians: colour televisions, laptops, rare teas, French crystal, candlesticks and Chinese porcelain. Mustafa had the air of a wealthy man, well groomed and at ease. His office, however, was stark and bare. Mustafa, I guessed, hid his contraband outside the city.

Mustafa spoke plainly. He could send me to Europe. Passport and identity papers were no problem: I wouldn't be going through any checkpoints. I said I needed to be sure of the route and that there was no risk of being captured either by the Iraqis or the Turks, as either one would probably send me

back to Iran. Mustafa reassured me. Though I would have to
pass through at least one of those countries, he said, I would
not be stopping.

Where did I want to end up? asked Mustafa.

Europe, I replied.

Mustafa nodded. The price was seven thousand five hundred
dollars, he said. We shook hands.

The only problem with my plan was that I didn't have a rial
to my name. But others were willing to help. In 1997, when
Saddam once again turned on Iraq's Kurds, this time massa-
cring a hundred thousand, tens of thousands had fled across
the border into Iran. We had distant relatives in Iraq – my father's aunt had married a Kurd on the other side of the border
– and when the refugees began arriving, my father went to the
frontier to see if our relatives were among them. He waited for
hours. Towards the end of the day, he noticed a man with his
wife and their three girls, standing in the rain, cold and hungry.
'They looked like the branches of a willow tree,' my father said
later. 'Slack and listless, dragging themselves along the ground.'
My father approached the man and said that since all Kurds
were family, the man was welcome to bring his wife and children to stay in our home.

The five of them were with us for a few months before they
were accepted by the UN as refugees and given a new home in
Canada. While they were living with us we discovered the man
had a heart condition that required pills, and since the medicine was cheap in Iran, my father bought him an enormous
supply. From Canada, the man wrote to say he had found a
job as a gardener, bought a house and was sending his girls to a
Canadian school. He called my father 'brother' and my mother

'sister'. Now, when he heard I was in trouble, he wrote to say he would gladly lend me the first payment of three thousand five hundred dollars. He did not know how the money would be spent. He just knew that I needed help.

This was wired to Mustafa. I told Mustafa I would borrow the rest from my extended family. We agreed a system of payment by stages. The money would be held by an intermediary, a doctor and mutual friend whom everybody trusted, and released bit by bit according to how far I had travelled. Mustafa told me he was satisfied with the arrangement. I was to make ready to leave in a few days. There was no time to say goodbye to my family.

A day later, I took a bus from Mahabad back to Urmia, close to the border with Turkey. I had nothing on me apart from some chocolate, a water bottle, five hundred dollars and my family's phone number in my head. In Urmia, a man was waiting in a pickup to take me to the border. In a clearing off the main road, a group of seven weathered-looking men were saddling twenty horses ready to depart, directed by another man in a filthy overcoat who appeared to be in charge. Most of the animals were carrying barrels of diesel and petrol. Several of us who were travelling to Europe would be going at the same time. The plan was to head out that evening, cross the border high up in the mountains during the night and be inside Turkey by the following morning. The smugglers gave us tea and yoghurt to fortify us. Then we set off.

We started climbing immediately. We passed through thick forest, followed narrow paths up precipitous ravines, crossed mountain streams, hugged cliffs and, finally, leaving the trees behind, pushed up into the snow. It was a dark and moonless night, and freezing cold, but my horse was sure-footed and I felt the exhilaration of a new journey underway. I became mesmerised by the way the horse's metal shoes would shoot out sparks when they struck crystal and flint on the path. The smugglers, too, were formidable, walking all the way, never tiring and always making sure the horses were calm and still had spirit for more. 'Why don't you ride?' I asked one. 'Can't afford to,' he puffed back. 'The horses are reserved for cargo.' At times, we could hear Turkish border guards close by and we had to hurry away. 'For the next ten minutes, you just ride as fast as you can,' the head smuggler would say, and off we would go, galloping into the night, racing ever higher into the mountains.

Some time in the night, we came to a clearing by a river. I heard voices. Then somebody shone a torch in my face. 'Stop that!' I shouted angrily. 'You are blinding me!'

The head smuggler came to talk to me. 'These people are PKK,' he said. 'They're collecting donations.'

I refused. I had been forced to leave my home partly because there was no active revolution in Iran for me to join. To my mind, the militants were a disappointment. 'I'm not going to pay,' I sniffed. 'I don't want anything to do with them.' The smuggler shrugged and handed over ten dollars on my behalf.

Finally, we neared the pass. The wind was roaring and piercing. I could feel my horse tiring. The smuggler urged me not to let him stop for anything. 'If the animals stop moving here, we'll never get them going again,' he shouted over the wind. We crested the pass and began descending the other side. A green morning light started to creep up into the sky. After an hour or two we came to a village where the smugglers called a halt and fetched water for the horses, and lentil soup for us. I ate, then fell asleep where I sat, leaning against the wall of a village house.

*

Later that morning, I awoke to the sound of an old taxi struggling up the track into the village. Now it was daylight, I could see there were five of us Kurds travelling to Europe – me, three other young men and an older man with a prosthetic leg – and we crowded into the car, which took us further down the valley to a bigger village, then onto smooth asphalt. The driver gave my travelling companions and me a Turkish identity card each. When he dropped us at a bus station on the edge of a city, these allowed us to buy tickets.

For the next few days we skipped across Turkey from city to city in small journeys of a few hours. Always there would be a smuggler waiting in a café at the next bus terminal who would buy us our new tickets and direct us to the next middleman along the route. Soon we reached Istanbul. What little I saw of the city seemed immense, a wonder of noise and light and strange food smells. But we were quickly ushered through the back streets to a house where we were shut in with dozens of others.

All were hoping to travel to Europe. Many had run out of money and were in limbo, waiting for a relative to send more cash so they could restart their journeys. We were told none of us could leave the house, so we sent somebody out to buy food for us. That evening they called our five names, then took us to a lorry park where we were told to climb into the back of a truck transporting planks of wood. We waited for an hour in the dark, silently eating biscuits and drinking water. Then we heard an engine start and we were en route again.

After seven hours, we stopped at what we took to be a checkpoint. We waited silently and without moving. After a while, we drove onto what felt like a ship. The boat sailed through the night. The next day, the lorry disembarked in what we guessed was Greece. Hours later, it pulled off the main road. The doors were opened. We were in a forest. A man took us to a small, abandoned cottage – ugly, with broken windows and dirty floors – where there were around seventy other people: Afghans, Pakistanis, Iranians, Arabs and Africans. Some had been there for months. A lot of the talk was about the scores of refugees who were said to be drowning in the Mediterranean or suffocating in the back of shipping containers. Refugee graves were now said to dot the route.

On our third day in this ruined house, a smuggler came and asked me to call the doctor to release another payment. I refused. 'I'm hungry,' I said. 'I need food first.' So these rough-looking smugglers, unshaven and covered in badly drawn tattoos, took me out to a restaurant. I ate well. I smoked a few cigarettes. Then I called my father.

'I am OK,' I told him. 'I am here.'

'Who are you?' my father replied sharply. 'Where is my son?'

'Father, it's me, Sora!' I said. 'It is your son!'

'What blanket do you use when you sleep?' demanded my father.

'Father, for God's sake, I can't remember,' I replied.

'Who is your best friend in the neighbourhood?' he insisted.

I said the man's name.

'Describe our house.'

I described it.

My father considered my answers for a moment. Finally, he relented. 'OK, OK,' he said. 'But you sound very strange, my son.'

Reluctantly, my father agreed to call the doctor and ask him to send more money to Mustafa.

*

That conversation with my father was my first experience of how misunderstanding can often be measured in kilometres. It had been more than a year since we had spoken, as it was always my mother who was home whenever I called. I later also discovered that Mustafa had told my father that he could guarantee to take me somewhere but not necessarily that I would arrive alive. My father, it seems, had convinced himself that there was a good chance I was already dead and an impostor was trying to take my place.

A few days later I was taken to another lorry with the four other Kurds. It was a refrigerated trailer, full of chocolate. That lorry just drove and drove. We huddled against the cold in the back as best we could. After what seemed like most of a day, we stopped once more in another hidden place in another forest, and again we were led to a house crammed with people. By now we were losing track of how long we had been travelling like this, in and out of windowless trucks and abandoned houses in nameless forests. But after a few more days, we five were loaded once again into a car, driven into the hills to a lorry park, pushed into a trailer full of baby milk and transported for seven or eight hours. When we stopped, the doors were opened to reveal another lorry park, and a smuggler hustled us across to another truck and trailer that contained a few cardboard boxes. This part of the journey was especially secret, the man said. The driver wouldn't know we were on board. Once we arrived at our destination, said the smuggler, 'we will wait for a few hours and then we will come for you. At that point, our job is done and you'll be on your own.'

We hid quickly behind the cardboard boxes and the smuggler closed the doors. After a while, the driver returned and started his engine. He drove for an hour. Then he slowed for what seemed like a series of checkpoints. The time taken to negotiate these barriers made us suspect that the authorities knew someone was inside. Then the doors opened. Someone called for us to show ourselves. I stayed where I was, hidden under a pile of boxes that I had pulled on top of me. Three of my travelling companions were also well hidden. But the older man had left his prosthetic leg sticking out. They found him and took him away. Then – miracle! – they closed the doors once more. After that, we felt the truck board another ship. It sailed for a few hours, then we disembarked.

We wanted to know where we were. The sides of this truck were made of canvas and one of my companions cut a tiny hole in the fabric with a little knife he had so he could try to read the road signs. But he couldn't understand them. When I looked, I saw a blue sign that read 'London'.

'We are in England,' I announced.

There was a murmur of approval from my three companions. Though I hadn't said where I wanted to go, evidently the others had been more specific. I suggested we bang on the cab so the driver stopped. I was planning to hand myself over to the police. But my companions had arranged to stay with relatives. We were still discussing what to do when the man who had cut the hole in the canvas interrupted us.

'There are two police officers driving alongside us,' he said. 'They're looking right at me.'

'There's no way they can see you through that tiny hole,' I replied. 'You're just scared.'

But after a few minutes, the lorry slowed down, pulled over on the side of the road and parked. Then two police officers opened the trailer doors.

'How many?' asked the officers.

There was no point hiding any more. We had arrived safely, and we were exhausted. I held up four fingers. Behind them, I could see the truck driver was furious. He was shouting and pointing at us. He grabbed a tyre iron and started swinging it, ready to attack. 'If he attacks us, we attack him back,' I instructed the others. They looked terrified.

In the event, a police officer pulled the driver to one side, a police van arrived and we were show... into a little cage in the back. The other men were dismayed at the disruption to their plans. But I was so happy. My only ambition had been to leave Iran. Now, when the police officers closed the doors behind us and took us away, the noise had a finality to it. There was no going back. I was twenty years old, I had made it safely to Europe, and my new life could begin.

FOURTEEN

Kobani,

November–December 2014

As we steadily took back Kobani street by street in the last weeks of 2014, we discovered the jihadis had left us some surprises. The remains of takeaway food, still in its plastic cartons. New cars and motorbikes, often with the keys still in the ignition. The morning after we took the Black School, a comrade discovered a tunnel inside a nearby house, dug straight down into the earth then angled directly towards our lines. They had been trying to dig under us so as to be able to pop out and attack us from behind. Inside was a wheel-barrow to move the earth, a generator to power a drill and a battery-powered lighting system.

The next day I was scouting the area for places where Servan and I might build new nests when a comrade ran in shouting, 'A sniper has been shot!'

I froze. 'Where?' I asked.

'That building over there,' replied the man. He pointed at a neighbouring block, next to a building where I had told Servan to wait.

'Where is Servan?' I asked. 'Has anyone seen Servan?'

There was silence.

'Take me to the sniper,' I said.

Numbly, I followed my comrade into the neighbouring building. It had been nearly levelled by air strikes and we had to climb up a two-storey field of rubble to get inside. The building was like a skeleton: the stones and bricks had been blasted off and only the steel remained. There, on a small piece of floor that was somehow still intact, I found piles of sand drenched in blood. As I squeezed onto a small ledge that had a clear view over the city, I saw Servan's dark-grey baseball cap lying on the ground, blood all over it. The way it was lying suggested it had fallen off his head as his comrades carried him out. There were two fighters crouching on the ledge. Advising me to stay low, one of them told me Servan had taken a shot to the left side of his face, just above the eye. He had probably died instantly. Even if he hadn't, there was no way he could survive losing all that blood.

I shuffled past the two fighters. In a corner with a wide view over the enemy front I found Servan's scarf, backpack and rifle. I could see he had been working on a new hole, just as I had taught him. There was a pair of pliers there, with which he had been bending back a piece of metal that was blocking part of his vision. To get the purchase he needed, he would have had to lean out of the building and expose himself fully to the enemy. I like to imagine the danger didn't even cross his mind.

We were now in control of more than half the town. But we had lost more than a dozen people capturing the Black School, and I had lost Servan, and as the battle for Kobani ground on, our worlds narrowed until it became impossible to imagine a horizon beyond those tunnels and streets or even to think back to yesterday or forward to tomorrow.

I felt angry that I had been asked to care for Servan. I was angry that he had extracted my affection so easily, then abandoned it so carelessly in the dust. I couldn't move on from his death, as I had from so many others. When someone dies in your care, maybe it is right that you are haunted for ever. But there was something else. There had been times in Kobani when I was awed by the depth of human resilience, and others when I marvelled at how conflict sharpened our senses. Now I wondered whether darker forces were at work. Servan had been a flower, so polite, so pure, and his innocence had killed him. He had been too good to live. What did that say about those of us who remained?

Servan's loss made me unsure of how to interact with other people. Was I clear when I spoke? Did I give too little or too much? Where did I get my conviction that I was right? Servan had been sent to me to train. Now he was dead. What if I'd radioed him to sit tight and wait for me to help him make his hole? What if I'd been more explicit and detailed in my instructions? From then on, everything I did took on even greater seriousness. There was no place in my life for much more than mechanical exactness. Servan's death taught me that even one wrong or omitted word might be fatal. I began to see things in purely binary terms: black or white, life or death, friend or enemy. I was far from the only one.

One night I was scanning the streets we had captured around the Black School when I caught a glimpse of a figure about four hundred metres away moving furtively and tensely from shadow to shadow, checking left and right like a thief. At one point, he entered a building and vanished. When I finished my shift the following morning, I went to the logistics centre to ask if we had anyone stationed in the house the man had entered. A group of wounded men lying on the ground shook their heads. A fighter called Janiwar jumped up and suggested five of us go to check.

We found the house and began to search it. After a while, one of them called over to me: 'Azad! Come. We've found something.' I followed him through the kitchen. 'There's someone sleeping there,' said one of my companions, gesturing through a window that looked out onto the garden. I peered through. There was the shape of a body under a blanket.

'Is he one of us?' I asked. 'Do you know him?'

They shook their heads. Janiwar spoke up: 'He has to be ISIS. Let's kill him.'

'Let's take him prisoner,' I said.

'What if he has a suicide vest?'

'Fire a burst over his head,' I said, 'then you run in and grab his arms and pin them to his sides. I'll have his head in my sights the entire time.'

They reluctantly agreed. At my nod, the first man fired and the other two ran in and threw themselves on top of the man. The sleeping figure woke with a start. 'I'm Kurdish!' he cried out. 'I'm Kurdish!'

We dragged him out. He looked shocked, as lifeless as a dead body. When I demanded an explanation, he confessed he had been fighting on a neighbouring front and had lost his nerve. 'I can't do it any more,' he said. 'So many dead. I can't fight any more. I ran. I just thought I'd hide out until the city was liberated.'

Fear is contagious. The man's face was a whirlpool of hopelessness. I didn't want to look at it. 'Nobody is forced to be here,' I said, glancing away. 'If you don't want to be here, you don't have to be.' Then I told the others to take him behind our lines, and left.

Once out in the street, however, I could hear shouting. I ran back in. The others were beating him.

'What are you doing?' I shouted. 'Nobody touch him!'

'But he is a coward!' they said.

'Nobody has to fight,' I told them. 'That is our belief. We are all volunteers.'

I understood their anger. They were all from Kobani, and had all been wounded defending their home city. Hundreds of us had sacrificed themselves and this man was saving his skin. Black or white. Friend or enemy.

To distract them, I suggested they search him. Out of his pockets came euros, dollars, Chinese money, Georgian money. He said he had taken it from the bodies of dead jihadis. To me, this sordid thieving was a second reason not to have this man in our ranks. To the others, it was something else to punish him for.

We decided to march him to Zahra and let her decide what should happen. Thankfully, she agreed with me. 'He doesn't have to fight if he doesn't want to,' she said. 'He's free to go. But he shouldn't hide here as we might kill him by accident.'

The others argued, but in the end Zahra's word prevailed. I heard later that the man observed Zahra for a few days, deliberating with himself, before asking if he could stay and become part of her team. Weeks later, Zahra told me he had become a great fighter.

The way we were deteriorating was reflected in how grim the battlefield was becoming. ISIS rarely retreated, and every street we took was filled with their bodies. As we advanced, we began to find the corpses of our own people, too, volunteers who had fallen when ISIS first overran them. One day I entered a house on the frontline where five of our fighters had been based, to find them prone on the floor, their hands tied behind them, their heads neatly balanced on their backs. We began to notice that dogs, cats and even chickens were growing fat on this harvest of cadavers. We had to shoot them, to stop the spread of disease.

The bizarre landscape that Kobani was becoming offered some surreal moments. One team, finding themselves in a sugar store, built a base out of fifty-kilo bags. Every time they were attacked, the bullets would tear into the sacks and cover them in a sweet-tasting cloud. When I visited, I found them reaching into their fortifications for fistfuls of the stuff to put in their tea. Another confusing sight was bits of shop mannequins lying next to real bodies. No clothes store in Kobani, apparently, had been complete without these unblinking pink plastic figures, and months of air strikes had scattered their slender, unbending limbs all over town. When you looked closely, it was clear that many of the mannequins had also been smashed and set on fire by ISIS. It seemed the army of the pure took no chances with temptation, not even with the sexless nakedness of a plastic doll.

Once or twice I even witnessed death take on a kind of winsome quality. Because the Black School was such a natural crow's nest with a commanding view of the city, I based myself there for more than a month. Herdem brought me an M16 with a thermal that we had captured from ISIS. One perishing night in November, around 11 p.m., I was lying on the ice on the roof when, through my thermal, I saw a hole in a wall about a hundred metres away turn white.

Haqi's latest intelligence, gleaned from listening in to a captured radio, was that ISIS would be trying to sneak through our lines and attack us from behind, just as we had done when

I first arrived in Kobani. Haqi had overheard an ISIS commander say they would be coming singly or in pairs.

I was sure this white light I was seeing was the heat signal from a jihadi. I watched it for a while. Was he the commander? Were there more Islamists coming? Did he have night vision? In the end I decided he was a scout, collecting what information he could on our positions from peeking through the hole and listening to the sounds around him. I couldn't let him go.

I fired a single shot.

The heat signal slowly began to dim. I watched the white light fade for a full ten minutes. Then it was gone.

I think we all realised that even if we survived, we would be walking out of Kobani very different people. Our standards for what was normal behaviour had begun to shift. We had one comrade who was always insisting on going forward. 'Why are we taking so long?' he would say. 'Why aren't we moving?' On one occasion some of my comrades had to pull him to the ground when he set out walking alone towards ISIS' lines in broad daylight. When they tried to explain to him that there was a strategy to a military operation, that we had to wait until all our fronts were ready to move forward together, he argued back. The waiting was taking too long, he said. It was costing too many lives. And what were we so afraid of when many of the houses we captured turned out to be empty?

He spoke well and made some good points. But that wasn't it. The man wanted death. After seeing so much suffering and so many lives lost, he wanted to be next. It wasn't that he had lost hope or that he especially wanted to die – and he certainly wasn't about to shoot himself. Rather, he wanted to achieve something, to claim a piece of land with bravery and integrity in the name of freedom, and he had convinced himself that his death was the best way to do it.

I noticed that I, too, had become unafraid of the sound of war. I no longer ducked or flinched at explosions or the slapping of bullets on a wall. I'd even begun to welcome the jihadi cry of '*Allahu Akbar!*' that used to so terrify me. Now it told me where they were. As war transformed me, I understood some changes would be permanent. The lack of sleep, the constant vigilance, the endurance – these things would mark my body and my mind for ever. And while sometimes these alterations horrified me, at other times I embraced them. I might have been surrounded by death but my senses had never been more alive. When I stalked, I was like a leopard, all my senses charged, my alertness so high it was almost deafening. One day when we were clearing a house I burst into a room in which I expected to find ISIS fighters and glimpsed a gunman by the far wall. I raised my rifle to shoot. Then I hesitated. I was looking in a mirror. That stone-faced, cold-eyed figure levelling his weapon at me – that was me. Most people would have been bewildered. I burst out laughing.

All the while as we advanced through Kobani's streets, we felt the presence of fate. When I thought of Servan, I realised that part of me had always thought of him as doomed – that one day, whatever he did or I did, the war would catch him and he would be gone. That was the nature of war: a succession of catastrophes that battered your capacity for endurance, then killed you or broke you or, if you survived, rewarded you with pain or guilt. This was the destiny of all of us the moment we had picked up a gun.

Perhaps hardest to accept was that some of us were fated to die in friendly fire. But a few made their peace with that, too. Chia had been born without a heel on his left foot, or it had been shot off – he never said, and I never asked – and when he arrived in mid-December as part of a group of reinforcements from the mountains, he was immediately given command of a unit on the south side of the Black School, based in a house where the bodies of five jihadis still lay in different rooms.

Because of the danger of infiltration, we had orders not to move around our lines at night and to shoot anyone we saw. I was on watch one night when Sama, the YPJ commander, radioed to say that someone was calling out in Chia's area, likely pretending to be wounded as part of an ISIS trap. I went to check and, as I was passing a house on my left, I heard a noise inside, like someone moving his jacket. Then I heard it a second time. It was the sound of someone getting ready to attack.

I always kept a bullet chambered in my rifle with the safety off – my safety was my finger. As a rule, I also never slung my rifle over my shoulder but carried it in my hands so that I would be ready to fire just by dropping to a knee. That night, for some reason, I had hoisted my rifle onto my shoulder. *I've got no chance to turn around*, I thought. *He already has my head in his sights.*

I walked on as casually as I could towards a deep shadow in the overhang of a tall building on the other side of the street. I passed one house, then a second. As soon as I was safely inside the shadow, I ran for position, spun around and swung my rifle to my shoulder so I had the doorway in my sights. *If I wait for him to show himself*, I thought, *I'll have a chance.*

At that moment, a voice called out in Kurdish from the doorway: 'Who's there?'

I stayed silent.

'Who's there?' came the voice again.

'Chia?' I shouted back.

'Azad?'

A figure stepped out of the doorway. Through my thermal I could see him limping.

'I nearly took your head off,' I exclaimed.

Chia walked over to me. 'Azad,' he said. 'I know that when I die, it will be one of us that pulls the trigger.'

It was a strange thing to say, almost like he was forgiving me in advance. But in the end, Chia turned out to be half-right. Months later, I was told one of his own team shot him in the arse during a village firefight. Sent for treatment over the border, the Turks caught him and threw him in prison.

As time went on and our positions became known to the jihadis, we had to make ever more elaborate attempts to deceive them. One day, I was called by a commander named Alisher to his base, a bunker he had built out of cement bags in an old builder's supply store that now formed part of our line. Alisher told me that earlier in the day he had narrowly avoided being shot by a sniper as he walked across his base. He showed me two fresh bullet holes in the wall at chest height. Looking out into the street, I calculated that the sniper must have set up in one of several houses opposite.

I made a plan to make the enemy shooter show himself. By gathering up different mannequin parts from the streets, I was able to piece together a complete figure, which I dressed in a military uniform. Then I asked a new comrade who was an apprentice with me to lie down on his stomach and 'walk' the doll back and forth past the place where Alisher had had his near miss. The doll needed to look as realistic as possible, I said, like someone inspecting the spot where the sniper's rounds had hit.

At about 4.30 a.m., I took up a position on a rooftop one street back, protected by a parapet about half a metre high. The wall was punctuated by several holes, each about the size of a basketball. I lay down behind one that gave me a clear view of the houses opposite and started scanning. The only possible location from which the bullets could have been fired, it seemed to me, was through a small hole in a chimney that was attached to the outside of a building facing me.

I lined the hole up in my sights and waited. It was raining. I tried not to move. But the rain crept into my clothes and slid down my neck like a snake. I felt my body slow. Five a.m. passed, then six. By now it was light, but the winter dawn brought no relief. I was shivering and tensing and willing my body to keep fighting the cold. Seven a.m. By now, I knew, I was losing the ability to do much beyond lie there and wait. Eight a.m. How come I could still feel the cold? I should have lost all feeling by now. Or passed out.

Nine a.m. Suddenly, I saw a small change in the light behind the chimney hole. Narrowing my eye, I relaxed my body, ready to shoot. I wanted my rival to shoot first. When he raised his head to check whether he had hit his target, I would have him.

After a few minutes, I saw another flicker of light behind the hole. Something felt off. Snipers make slow, deliberate movements. The movement of the light had been frantic, like someone waving. Had my enemy somehow spotted the trap I had laid for him? Was he waiting for me to fire so *he* could shoot *me*?

There was another strangely hurried movement of light behind the hole. Quickly, I rolled away, crawled towards the stairs and found a thick wall behind which to catch my breath. How had I been rumbled?

The answer awaited me in Alisher's base. Instead of walking

the mannequin back and forth, my apprentice, perhaps lazy, perhaps scared, had simply propped it up against a wall. The sniper had been able to see that someone was trying to fool him and had reacted accordingly, trying to spring my trap so that he could counter it. I had become the hunted instead of the hunter.

A few nights later I turned on my M16 thermal scope, pointed it towards Alisher's position in the cement store and immediately saw a figure jump over a wall next to it. All week there had been reports of ISIS movements in that location. I fired without hesitation. A gunfight broke out and I ran to the roof to find a better position. When I arrived, I could see several figures on a roof above Alisher's base shooting in. I made a radio call, directing all fire onto the attackers. Then I aimed at one fighter who was firing a BKC directly at Alisher's position and shot.

'Ah, Azad, you shot me!' Alisher cried out on the radio. 'You shot me!'

My whole body went numb. My trigger finger began to shake. I sat up, pushed my rifle away and hugged my knees, trying to breathe. My stomach was tightening into a knot. *What did you do? What did you do?*

After a while Alisher's voice came back on the radio. 'Azad?' he said. 'Azad?'

I grabbed my rifle and ran downstairs. As I stepped inside Alisher's base, I felt the ground move beneath me. I was walking on a body. I felt around my feet. The corpse was warm. It had a long beard. Then I heard a laugh. Alisher was on the other side of the room, watching me. 'I heard you describe my location over the radio,' he said. 'I tried to hide but you were

152

too quick! Don't worry, my friend, don't worry. You only grazed my leg. I don't even need to see a medic!'

Alisher later explained that while I had been running to the roof, ISIS had broken into the back of the house where he had his base. He and his team had had to abandon their position and counter-attack it from the outside. I had missed seeing the changeover and assumed the figures firing in were ISIS. The body I had felt was one of the jihadis that Alisher's team had killed.

Alisher thought my mistake hilarious. I was mortified. It was all I could do to stop my confidence from shattering into a million pieces right there on the ground.

FIFTEEN

Kobani,

December 2014

One afternoon, walking down a street close to the Black School, I caught sight of the outskirts of the city and, beyond it, fields. I was transfixed. My whole world had been reduced to these narrow streets, pushing forward metre by metre. Now I could see that Mistenur Hill was seven hundred metres to my south and, beyond it, open country. We only needed three or four more big pushes and we would have the city.

Suddenly, a firefight erupted around the base of the hill. I watched a big-bellied figure take up a position next to a wall, level a BKC in front of him and fire off almost an entire belt. The man had two other fighters with them. They seemed to be firing down on our forces but at that distance it was impossible to be sure: they might also have been our men and women.

It was unreal just to stand there in the street and watch a battle. Around me, our men and women were strolling un-hurriedly from one place to another, obliviously chatting and laughing. I took cover behind a lamp-post and began sighting my Dragunov. If those distant figures were jihadis, they would be able to see right into the street and shoot our people like chickens. Only one other fighter, Serhad, seemed to understand the danger.

'Azad!' he shouted. 'Azad! Shoot them! Shoot them!'

'I'm not sure who they are,' I replied.

Haqi, who was nearby, called around on his radio, trying to get confirmation.

'Off the streets!' I shouted at our fighters around me. 'You're in the line of fire! They can shoot you at any minute!'

It was a mess. Nobody seemed to understand that, though we now held this street, we could still be targets in it.

Haqi called back. A neighbouring commander had told him that, yes, he was being fired on by three ISIS fighters on the slopes of Mistenur Hill.

'Shoot them between the eyes,' Haqi told me.

I lay down on the street. A second sniper, Haroon, took up a position on the roof of a building. As we sighted our weapons, a crowd of fifty gathered. 'The big guy with the BKC is Number One,' I shouted to Haroon above the hubbub. 'The man in the dark green is Two. The one in grey is Three. You go for One. I'll take Two. We'll both go for Three.'

Haroon shouted his assent. The three jihadis were now firing from the corner of a house. We waited for them to reload. Two was saying something to One, who turned around to reply. I counted down to Haroon: 'Three, two, one . . .'

I aimed for Two's chest and neck. Punch. He went down. The crowd cheered. 'You got him!' Serhad exclaimed.

One ran over to Two and tried to drag him to safety. Haroon fired at One. Two was still alive and reaching for his gun. I shot him again. Then I moved to Three. He and One were now sprinting for cover inside a house. Haroon was still firing steadily at One.

'Shoot him!' I shouted.

Haroon fired again. 'He's down!' he shouted back.

Another cheer. The women began ululating. We stayed until nightfall trying to shoot the third man but he never re-appeared. Bored, the crowd drifted away. Eventually, the coalition unleashed a furious series of air strikes on the ISIS positions which were captured on film and broadcast around the world. Mistenur was ours.

The firefight on Mistenur Hill should have been a reminder to us all of an age-old Kurdish truth: even when we possessed territory, we couldn't expect to be safe in it.

That night, scores of comrades came with clothes and blankets they had scavenged and worked until morning sewing together a giant curtain, which they strung from base to base across the road. Despite that, two days later a man from Alisher's team was shot in the head as he crossed the street. When I examined where he had been hit, it seemed that the bullet had to have come from the girls' school that we had captured two weeks earlier. It didn't make sense. Then, a few days later, one of Serhad's team was hit in the leg at a nearby intersection. A day after that another man was shot in the hip as he walked down the side of the Black School. Haqi called me on the radio. I was to stop working nights and hunt down the ISIS sniper. It was clear that ISIS was learning from us and infiltrating our lines to take us down one by one.

I arrived at the scene of the last shooting to find Alisher's team hugging the walls around the spot where the shootings had occurred. 'This is the third person to be killed!' one young woman shouted. She had been with the dead man when he was hit. 'I was just chatting to him and he was shot right in front of me.'

I planted my feet on the bloodstains where he had been shot. Looking towards ISIS' lines, I could see I was protected from every angle by curtains and walls. I sat down against a wall. How was it possible to be hit here? Absently, I looked down the street back into our territory. About nine hundred metres away, I could see a two-storey building jutting out into the road. Windows on its different floors had a good view of the street. After a while, I recognised it as the girls' school. I called Haqi.

'Are we sure that the girls' school has been cleared?' I asked, looking at the building. 'Is the entire building occupied by our forces?'

Haqi said he would check. When he came back, he told me the girls' school consisted of two buildings on either side of the road. We held one part. But the part I could see was in ISIS' hands. This was a grave misunderstanding. We had all assumed we had complete control of the street. In reality, there was an island of jihadis in our midst with a clear line of fire. Right at that moment I was in all likelihood looking down the sights of an ISIS sniper rifle.

Trying not to betray my discovery to the shooter, I walked around the corner as calmly as I could and, as soon as I was clear, started running and turned into a back street that headed towards the girls' school. When I felt I was about four hundred metres away, I climbed up inside a three-storey building that would give me a view down on my target. After crawling into position on a half-collapsed roof, I could see the school playground below me. Moving some bricks out of the way and making myself comfortable, I settled in to watch.

I waited for hours. In the mid-afternoon, I saw two pigeons fly out from a window on the first floor. Someone was walking around inside. I crawled back from my position, took the stairs down a floor and lay upwards on the first few steps of the next flight, looking out through a blown-out wall. From my new position I could see a window on the second floor whose top quarter was open and shielded by blinds. I studied those blinds. After half an hour, I saw a shadow move. I fired quickly, then again, then again, then again. There was a distant return of fire but nothing from the window.

The next day, coalition planes executed several bombing runs on the building. As soon as they had finished, our men and women stormed in and engaged the survivors in a fierce fire-fight. By the evening, the building was ours. Walking through the ruins that night, we found five of our own fighters, killed months before in the ISIS advance. But behind the sniper's window I also found a large, fresh bloodstain and a wide smear running out of the room and down the corridor where his fellow jihadis had dragged the man away.

One comfort we had was that, however worn down we were, the jihadis were just as fatigued. Even their famous suicidal discipline was beginning to crack.

Down one side of the Black School was a street that ran straight and wide, west to east, all the way out of the city. We called it Forty-Eighth Street. Based there was a commander called Tolhildan, one of three brothers who had joined the YPG – something that strictly was a violation of a YPG rule about sending more than one member of a family to the front. When Tolhildan discovered his mother had complained, he called her from his base in Kobani and said, 'Do that again and I'll not call you mother any more. I'll only leave this city dead.' That was a measure of his commitment. So was the way he looked. I was amazed one day when Tolhildan told me he was only twenty-three. He looked forty.

One morning, Tolhildan's voice screamed over the radio: 'They've got a Hummer. We need an RPG.' A machine gunner ran to his position, fired at the vehicle and stopped it. Tolhildan then shot the driver.

Haqi came on the radio. The Hummer, he said, had been on its way *back* to the ISIS lines. It had already burst through our frontline and driven as far as the cultural centre, a kilometre or so behind us, where it had dropped off seven jihadis. They had tried to storm the building, killing three of ours, before scattering. Herdem had brought down two in the street. The surviving five were holed up in a house surrounded by our people. When I arrived, Herdem had already left – 'It's easy now,' he had said – and the others were bombarding them with grenades and RPGs from all sides. All five were dead inside a minute.

Something made me want to see their bodies. Climbing through the house, I found an older one, with blue eyes, perhaps fifty. The others were much younger, maybe seventeen or so, their legs all smashed, their bones sticking out and their faces chewed up by bullets and shrapnel. Later Haqi told me that as they shot at us, the jihadis had been on the radio, asking over and over for assistance. The response? 'God is great!'

One of them had answered, 'I know God is great, but we need help! We need an ambulance! We need another Hummer!'

'God is great!' came the answer again.

'I don't care!' screamed the jihadi over the noise of his gun. 'We need help!'

Three days later, the jihadis drove another Hummer at us. We killed four of the five inside instantly and dropped a grenade on the fifth after he jumped into a well. After that, we brought up a digger to make giant holes in the roads, big enough to stop either Hummers or tanks. We had no doubt we would need them. Retreat seemed to be making the jihadis even keener to throw themselves into our guns.

SIXTEEN

Leeds,
2004–2011

After a few weeks in a refugee centre in Ashford, southeast of London, I was told I had been assigned a place to live while my application for asylum was considered. A minibus picked up a few of us, skirted east London and drove north, dropping off the others at hotels and guesthouses along the way. I watched the English countryside pass by. The farmers were at work in the fields, cutting hay, harvesting wheat and setting fire to the stubble. They had bigger tractors, the grass was more lush and the gardens behind the endless rows of houses seemed too small for growing many vegetables. Otherwise, I was struck by how familiar the scene looked.

After six hours, I was left at a hostel just south of Leeds in a city called Wakefield. There were four floors in the building, with eight rooms on each, plus a shared toilet and a kitchen. My housemates included another Kurd, a few Iranians and two Africans. No one spoke much English. But we were all in the same position and my new housemates were kind, showing me where to buy food on the small allowance we were given and where to find a bus into town.

Once a week, I would call home and speak to my mother, father and sisters. They would always tell me that when they spread a rug on the floor and set it for dinner, 'your place is empty'. I missed them terribly, of course. But their words reminded me that I was on my own, and it was up to me and me alone to make the most of my new country.

The summer of 2004 was a tempestuous few months of storms, floods and blazing afternoons in England – not the fog or placid grey drizzle I had read about in children's books – and I took advantage of the warm spells to explore my new home on foot. Wakefield was an ancient market city, once a centre for wool, cloth, grain, coal and cattle trading, built around a grand yellow-stone cathedral. A cool wind blew in off the Pennines to the west, sweeping past red-brick buildings and the old mills down on the River Calder. It was grander and prettier than Sardasht – some of the main streets were quite beautiful – and everything was spotless. I was astonished by the buses, whose arrival at a stop was announced in advance on an electronic board and timed to the minute. How different from the drivers in Sardasht, who made their passengers wait for hours as they crammed their vehicles ever more tightly.

On my first wander around town, I stopped for a while on a bench near the cathedral. I was curious to see people feeding the pigeons. Back home, we would have shot and eaten them. The way people dressed and walked was also interesting. There seemed little difference between men and women. I even saw one man pushing a pram. When I was a boy, my father used to carry me on his back but he was an exception, and his friends would tease him about it. In Wakefield, men and women seemed content to be equals. Another surprise: contrary to what I'd heard about British reserve, people were friendly. On my first day, I was approached by a young couple who could see that I was lost, or at least new, and who wanted to help me. I didn't need their help but I was touched by their kindness – and so embarrassed by my inability to thank them that I resolved to learn English as a first priority.

At the hostel, I found an English dictionary and started with the 'A's. My primary-school English started to return. Soon, by applying myself for an hour or two, I was able to decipher the letters I was receiving from the Home Office detailing the progress of my asylum claim. After a couple of weeks, I was given my own apartment in a house: a bedroom, sitting room, bathroom, toilet and kitchen. It was more than generous. I wasn't allowed a television – I couldn't afford a licence – so in the evenings I listened to the radio and practised my English.

Under the conditions of my temporary stay, I was allowed to study but not work. I enrolled in English classes at a college of further education in town. I also found an illegal job at a fruit-packing factory on the city outskirts where a lot of refugees worked. I had to take the baskets in which the fruit was transported and lay them on a conveyor belt which passed through a stream of hot water. I hated it. The CCTV cameras and the punch-code entry system made the place feel like a prison. My fellow workers timed their work to the second, dropping whatever they were doing the moment it was break time or the end of their shift. I quit after three days. But I quickly found more work, as a waiter and cook in a Pakistani restaurant in Leeds, working part-time and weekends.

Slowly, Wakefield and Leeds became my life. I passed my driving test. I saved five hundred pounds, bought a car and became the restaurant's delivery driver, taking curries all over the city. One day I received a letter telling me my asylum application had been approved. I was given a council flat in Leeds. Transferring my English course to a college in the city, I studied by day and drove by night. In time, I paid back my family's friend in Canada. I developed a taste for fish and chips and full English breakfasts. I went to a nightclub. I had a girlfriend, then another. I spent my weekends travelling up and down the country, visiting Liverpool, Edinburgh, Portsmouth, Southampton and London, touring monuments and old houses, hiking in the soft rain and swimming off the beaches. What I enjoyed most was the freedom to do whatever I wanted. One day at college, I wrote an essay about winter in Sardasht, describing the snow and how people dressed. My teacher, an Australian woman in her sixties, showed it to her husband, a university professor, and he wrote me a note saying he thought I could be a writer one day. I'm sure he was just being polite. But I was delighted by the possibility the professor's words implied: that in Britain it was perfectly reasonable just to wake up one morning and decide to be a writer. This was what it was to be free.

My gratitude towards my new country didn't mean I was uncritical of it. Like many, I was sceptical of the American and British military occupations of Afghanistan and Iraq that followed 9/11, which seemed to be less about defending freedom than pushing smaller, weaker countries around. But I remained just as distrustful of religious hardliners. A handful of the mosques in Leeds were regressive, dictatorial and explicitly exclusive. Their imams would tell their congregations that they were living in a land of unbelievers. They said that Islam required them not to interact with British people. I found this attitude hypocritical and dangerous. These people would enjoy the security, rights, prosperity and welfare the unbelievers gave them, while secretly encouraging their flock to despise them. A year after I arrived, four British Islamists, three of them from Leeds or nearby, killed fifty-two people in simultaneous bomb attacks in London. What struck me was that, although the bombers had never even been to the Middle East, in their pre-attack videos they cited the Saracens and the Koran as inspiration. It reminded me of how the authorities in Iran had used the same things to sow fear there.

As the novelty of my new life began to wane, I also found myself slipping into the immigrant's paradox. To Westerners who have never emigrated, the idea that a person might pay thousands of dollars he didn't have and risk his life travelling halfway around the world only to arrive in a new place and surround himself with people from his old life can seem a contradiction. Actually, it is much the same instinct that sees Britons fly around the world on holiday, only to herd themselves into replica 'pubs' serving pints and Sunday roasts. Immigrants set off in search of freedom and happiness and travel thousands of miles to attain them, only to discover that, for human beings, freedom and happiness are collective conditions. You can't have either in isolation. Unless you have your own place in your own land with your own people where you can love, sleep, live with honour and integrity and wake safely in the morning, whatever liberty and joy you think you have eventually reveals itself as empty. To be happy, you must have a home. Some immigrants manage to make a new one. Many don't. The only mystery is not in why immigrants bundle together in their new lands but why so few of us were aware of this yawning flaw in our plans before we set out.

I found myself meeting up regularly with other Kurds. Since many of us had been dissidents, politics was often high on the agenda. At first, I was suspicious of these oppositions in exile, which seemed to be all talk and little action. But a friend was continually telling me about PJAK, the grandly named Kurdish

Free Life Party in Iran, and the PKK, the Kurdistan Workers Party in Turkey, and its founder Abdullah Öcalan, or Apo.

One day, out of politeness, I asked him to give me the best of Öcalan's many books. He gave me several, a couple of political tracts and a biography. For want of anything better to do, I began reading. The more I read, the more I felt like Apo was making sense of my own life. In Sardasht, my mother had refused to bow to my father and the idea of a male hierarchy. This was how she had forged her freedom. Her rebellion had bred in me an antipathy towards religion, or any state or economy based on ethnic exclusion. This was how I had become a dissident.

But somehow since my arrival in England, I had abandoned my purpose. Maybe I had thought I could be happy with supermarkets and a flat and weekend hiking trips across the moors. And maybe, for a while, I was. But now I saw those things for what they were: distractions. It was like a veil was being lifted. By untangling my past, Apo's words made me see my present for what it was, and set a course for my future. Though I had yet to articulate it, Apo made me realise that there had been an emptiness and uncertainty creeping into my life. With all the stress of escaping from Iran and travelling across Europe, then all the bureaucracy and procedure of asylum and my everyday worries about work and rent and fitting in and making a new life, I had forgotten why I had first set out on this path. Apo was drawing me back to my original purpose. I could feel it filling me like a flood.

In the summer of 2010, a cousin and I took a car and drove south from Leeds. We drove onto the train to France, then on through Belgium, Germany, Austria, Hungary, Serbia and

Bulgaria down to Istanbul, from where we headed east for a thousand miles before dropping into northern Iraq and finally Irbil. For a total of five days and a few hundred pounds in petrol I was retracing the route that six years earlier, in reverse, had taken weeks, risked my life and cost my family thousands of dollars. Such were the privileges of a rich-world passport.

To anyone who asked, my cousin and I were visiting family in and around South Kurdistan. My cousin, in fact, had no other motive. But my intention was to visit the Kurdish revolutionary army in the southern Turkish mountains that, by now, I had been reading about for years. Finding it proved surprisingly easy. I took a bus towards the peaks and climbed ever higher until I came to a checkpoint. Presenting myself to the Kurdish guards, I explained that I had come to see free Kurdistan for myself. By their reaction, they were used to visitors.

'What's your name?' one of them asked.

'Sora,' I said.

The guard laughed. 'Not your real name,' he said, 'your movement name. You need to keep your true identity secret.'

Behind the guards, one of their comrades was wheeling a barrow of tomatoes, potatoes, lemons, garlic and spinach. 'What's your name?' I asked the man.

'Azad,' he replied with a smile.

'Perfect,' I said to the guards. 'My movement name is Azad.'

I travelled on for another few hours until I arrived at a camp. There I was shown to the team with whom I would be staying. The camp was in a stunning position in a valley ringed by towering snowy mountains, carpeted with summer flowers and watered by a river of fast, cold, grey melt-water. I wasn't there for the scenery, however. I wanted to see for myself if Apo's ideas were as inspiring in practice as they were on the page.

I was allowed to wander freely around the camp. Though the

volunteers moved every few months, they were well organised. They stuck pipes into the river to channel water to kitchens and shower blocks around the camp. The threat of an attack obliged everyone to carry a gun. The more immediate threat of bombing by Turkish warplanes also meant living quarters were generally built in caves or underground. As well as places to sleep, there were libraries, lecture halls and eating tents furnished with large wooden tables that the comrades had made themselves. Before I arrived, I had wondered about food supplies for so many thousands of people in such a remote place. Now I saw that the camp grew its own vegetables, raised its own animals and managed its environment. Litter was kept to a minimum. Plastics were collected, shovelled into a hole well away from the river and burned. Paper, wood and anything else that could be recycled was kept. Even cigarette butts were collected in old cans.

For a month and a half, the volunteers let me watch, observe and take part in meetings and debates. When they discussed politics, I saw how independent men and women were of each other. There was little cheap, meaningless interaction. Even in the smallest of things, they were honest and friendly. There was something in the way they treated each other, how they talked to one another with respect – the way everyone looked each other in the eye. They were confident and clear in their minds about the values and principles with which they wanted to live. Another thing that impressed me: no one tried to recruit me. They fed me and gave me a bed but otherwise let me witness them and their work and make up my own mind. They even listened to my criticisms.

The hub of camp life was the academies, dedicated to education and discussion. Comrades could propose themselves or others for a course in political theory and they would be accepted if they were judged ready and thirsty for knowledge. The length of the courses was calibrated according to experience and aptitude. After two years in the movement you could apply for a beginners' course, which lasted three months. Every four years after that you could apply for a more advanced level of education, courses that lasted four and a half months, then six months, then nine months, the last of which was reserved for potential generals and commanders. For many, this was their first real education. A few struggled. Many more found the experience thrilling and spiritual.

Perhaps the most important feature of the camps was the equality between men and women. In the West, such equality is often understood in terms of absorbing women into positions or structures previously fashioned by men. The camps were attempting a more fundamental change. While the volunteers ultimately wanted men and women to live together as equals, in order to undo millennia of sexism they separated the two genders into different areas and allowed each complete autonomy to build their own institutions and procedures. Once these were established, men and women could come together as equals to discuss how they might collaborate with each other.

I studied the different camp territories, those areas run by women and those run by men. Mostly women and men organised themselves in similar ways, with command structures, administrations, logistics offices and academies. The point was, they had the freedom to do whatever they wanted. It wasn't about men giving power to women. It was about erasing any role for power in a relationship between men and women and, instead, living alongside each other in mutual respect and dialogue. Walking into a women's area and seeing nothing but women going about every task and duty was to understand how different a world we were trying to create. It was quietly magnificent.

After a while, I realised that one reason I enjoyed the freedom to wander where I liked was that our people had bigger concerns than baby-sitting me. The prospect of war was ever-present. The PKK was fighting in Turkey. PJAK was fighting in Iran. The movement's libraries were decorated with pictures of some of the thousands of Kurds who had died in three decades of struggle. No one doubted there would be more war to come. And there came a moment a few weeks into my stay when I realised that I would be happy to stand beside them. In search of freedom, I had travelled thousands of miles only to circle back almost to where I had started. But now I knew. This was where I belonged. These were my people. Whatever troubles were to come, this was my home.

I returned to Leeds. When Syria erupted in civil war in the spring of 2011, I quit my job as a delivery driver and moved to Sweden to work as a journalist for a Kurdish channel. One day in the summer of 2013, for a report I was preparing, I emailed the Kurdish administration in Qamishli, Rojava, asking for details of the resources they lacked.

Volunteers, they replied.

SEVENTEEN

Kobani,

December 2014 to January 2015

By the end of December we had been fighting in Kobani for four months. The days passed unnoticed in a fog of frozen numbness and fatigue. I had been shooting from the roof of the Black School for more than five weeks and it was becoming hard to remember an existence prior to trudging up and down those stairs, staring out at the same buildings in the same streets. Fighting exhaustion had become so routine that it had bled into an inability to sleep. Every time I curled up on the ground, I prepared myself for hours of wrestling my pinched, nervy body, trying to convince it to rest.

Much of the fighting could be seen from the hills in Turkey across the border. On New Year's Eve, some of the Kurds who had fled the city and who had watched the battles progress street by street began letting off fireworks. Was it a gesture of support? A celebration? With all the journalists also stationed on those hills, training their cameras on us, sometimes it felt like we were gladiators in a circus.

Still, the more surreal and disorientating Kobani became, there were always some comrades you could count on to keep their heads. Travelling to Kobani from Jazaa four months earlier, I'd gone with a small group that included Serhad. To reach Kobani, we had had to hike for several hours over frozen ground, crawl under a border fence, run past a couple of Turkish border patrols, then travel west for hours in an old bus. Serhad had done the entire journey, twenty-four hours without a break, with a fresh gunshot wound in his stomach.

By mid-December, Serhad was fully healed and in command of a group of six young enthusiastic volunteers, whom I nicknamed the Young Wolves. The Wolves were never far from the action. After our latest advance, they were basing themselves in a house to the south of the Black School that looked directly at ISIS' positions. The Wolves, I knew, were energetic and smart, surrounding their positions with broken tiles and glass and sheets of corrugated iron so that they would hear anyone approaching. But they valued their independence and often didn't respond to radio checks. Around 1 a.m. one night, with the temperature around minus five or so, I saw a figure run towards their building. As I shifted my aim to their position, I saw a second figure dart across the street. I was about to fire when I thought better of it and decided to radio Serhad first. When I described what I was seeing, he replied, 'Don't shoot! That's us!' It was a lesson in how I needed to understand our own people as well as I understood the enemy.

A day or so later, around noon and in broad daylight, the jihadis attacked the Wolves' position in full force. Hearing the firefight, I ran over to their base. By the time I arrived, the Wolves had already cut down six Islamists, three right at the doorstep of their base, where their bodies now lay slumped.

The Wolves' base was little more than rubble. There were RPG holes in the walls, and bullets and shrapnel had turned what remained into something approaching a giant sieve. But my comrades were unharmed. I made my way upstairs to find Serhad, who had fashioned a position out of a collapsed staircase. He was sitting stock-still with his neck stretched out and his rifle pointed out through a small hole at the houses across the street. 'Good that you came, Azad,' he said, without lifting his eyes. 'About twenty to twenty-five of them attacked. We killed three in the street and three up against our own wall. There's about fifteen of them left.'

I sat next to him and readied my rifle. Once both of us were still, I realised the jihadis were so close that I could hear them talking.

'There's a guy hiding in the front yard opposite,' Serhad whispered.

I moved my scope to where Serhad was indicating. There was a small copse. Dangling from the branches of the trees were hundreds of strips of cloth, apparently a kind of camouflage meant to simulate leaves.

'The guy has a mask on,' Serhad continued. 'He's moving around, trying to see what's happening. I think he's coordinating the attack, trying to get his men inside our building. He looked right at me two times. But he doesn't fire, as he's trying to hide.'

I told Serhad I couldn't see the man.

'Watch this,' said Serhad.

He fired a single shot.

Something moved. Next to the end of a wall, I could just make out a pair of eyes looking back at us. As I brought my crosshairs down to his head, however, they disappeared.

We lay there, waiting for the man to reappear. After a while, Serhad said, 'I can hear them talking inside that house two blocks over to the left.'

I swung my Dragunov in the building's direction. In a

driveway I saw a man in a YPG uniform peering inside an abandoned jeep as though trying to work out if there was anything in it worth taking. 'YPG or ISIS?' I whispered to Serhad.

Serhad glanced at the man. 'ISIS,' he replied. 'All the comrades are inside.'

I fixed my sights on the man. He was three hundred metres away. It was a clean shot.

One . . .

Two . . .

My bullet hit him in the right lung. He screamed and jumped in the air. His rifle, which he was carrying in his hands, spun backwards and landed on the ground. Somehow, the man landed on his feet.

One . . .

Two . . .

My second shot hit his left lung. He fell backwards onto a pile of rubble.

All around, the Young Wolves were cheering. '*Biji biji Y-P-G! Biji biji Y-P-J!* [Long live YPG! Long live YPJ!]' they shouted.

There was no way for the jihadi to escape. He was in pain, probably dying. We could hear him crying out. Then, as Serhad and I watched, his left arm moved. He seemed to be trying to push himself up. He scrabbled around with his hands until he found two pieces of concrete, then pushed down on them to raise himself up, before finally sitting back on his knees.

Now I could see that my target was a tall, broad-shouldered man in his late thirties. He was tanned, athletic and healthy, with a full head of long black hair and a short beard that he kept neatly trimmed around his thick lips. I had hit him once in either lung, one shot just above his heart, one slightly below it. A small trickle of blood ran from each wound. Beneath his strong arching eyebrows he had calm brown eyes. He was looking directly at me and his expression was composed and unafraid. He knew who he was and what path he had chosen and that he had reached its end. He did not beg. He did not surrender. He accepted his fate. And as I watched this man, proud in death, without fear or regret, I realised that with all that we stood for, all our fine words about conduct and progression and morality, and everything we said about the Islamists' savagery and regression, in that moment I was being taught a lesson in dignity by a jihadi.

I fixed my sights on the point between his two eyebrows. His right arm started to lift his rifle. I moved my finger to my trigger. He raised his weapon until it was almost level. I held his eyes until the last moment.

After it was done, Serhad let me lie there behind my gun for a while.

Then he said, 'The other guy is back,' and fired off a burst. The man went down and we heard a choking sound.

We waited half an hour. A coalition jet flew overhead and fired several rockets into the ISIS positions. We waited some more, then went over to check the bodies. I had hit mine between the eyes. Serhad had shot his through the Adam's apple.

Three weeks later, on the morning of 27 January 2015, we liberated Kobani.

The day before had been an uncertain one. Thick black smoke had hung over the entire front like a dark blanket in the sky. Haqi had radioed around to tell everyone to be prepared. 'They're setting fire to the entire city,' he said. 'It's a full-frontal attack.' I positioned myself in a minaret to protect the teams who were advancing. But my suspicion was that the fires were to cover the jihadis' retreat. The smoke lasted all day. No one

177

fired at us. Finally, Haqi radioed again. The last surviving jihadis were pulling out of Kobani.

The next morning, one by one, our men and women began
to emerge from their bases and walk through the streets. They
walked to the edge of the city. Covering the teams that I could
see, I watched one walk right through to the outskirts of the city
and into the fields beyond. Then another made it, then another. The city was ours. After watching a fourth team walk clean
out of the city, I radioed Haqi and said I wanted to join them.
'I need to be part of this,' I said. 'I've been dreaming of this
moment. I want to feel how it is to put my feet on the ground.'

'Be my guest,' replied Haqi.

I descended the minaret, slung my rifle on my shoulder and
walked down the middle of a street that I had been watching
and observing for all these months. I felt like I had wings. Some
of our men and women were still checking the last houses for
any remaining ISIS. But most of us just looked at each other.
Around me, comrades were crying. Others were dancing and
singing. There was a lot of shooting in the air. Everywhere I saw
dusty, exhausted faces, long, straggly beards, and red eyes, smiling, laughing and crying at the same time. It was an explosion
of freedom. A documentary crew found Herdem in the street,
his gun slung across his back, reeling with happiness. 'Kobani is
not sad any more,' he proclaimed. 'Kobani's heart is no longer
burning. Kobani can be proud once more and hold her head
high. Let the world witness this day! People of Kobani! We
have claimed our city back!'

A comrade who knew me approached. '*Heval*, you are smiling!' he exclaimed. He was right. I hadn't smiled for months.
I thought about that for days afterwards. In many ways, it was
hard to digest the enormity of what we had achieved. With our
old guns and a few hundred men and women we had stopped

the most ruthless, richest and best-equipped militia in the world. ISIS had terrorised the region, abused the name of God, and murdered, tortured, raped and destroyed for years. Their medieval malevolence had seemed unstoppable. They had called a bluff on all the good in the world. But we had stopped them. Then, step by step, building by building, we had pushed them back. We had broken the spell of ISIS' invincibility and the world could breathe again. It was a new beginning for the Kurds and for the world.

But what price had we paid? We had lost thousands. The jihadis had also left their mark on those of us who survived. They had made us killers. They had forced us to live as animals. They had made us love our friends more fiercely than most human beings can ever know, then forced us to watch them die. I had taken so many lives that I now did it without thinking, sometimes without even remembering. Even if we managed to rebuild Rojava and restore some normality, how could we, the fighters who had saved it, ever be a part of it?

I came across Zahra with a group of volunteers, raising our flag on a hill overlooking the city. As ever, she greeted me with a smile. But for the first time since I had known her, she allowed sadness into her voice. 'I just wish all our friends could have been here to see this day,' she said. 'Only a few days ago I was talking to some of them about what we would do to celebrate. None of them made it to this day. They should be here too.'

I climbed up the tallest building I could find, one of the southernmost in the city. There I put my rifle down, took my jacket off, then my shoes and socks, until I was stripped to the waist, just to feel the openness and the freedom. Our commanders were shouting on the radio: 'Take up positions! Build bases! This is a very important moment! We could be attacked at any time!' But nobody was listening. Everyone was just wandering around and feeling the thrill of liberation. The city echoed with their release.

When I climbed down, I realised I was feeling uneasy. I think part of me was afraid of the celebrations, of letting go of the will and determination that had got us through the past four months. During our training, they had taught us to be wary of the time after a victory. 'You lose more people after a success,' our instructor had said. 'You forget yourselves, you lower your guard and you become vulnerable. Happiness exposes you.' When I ran into a young YPJ fighter from Kobani handing out chocolate and what she called 'the sweets of liberation', I snapped at her. 'We haven't even cleared the city yet,' I reminded her. 'After that there's the villages, the farms, the rest of West Kurdistan, then North and East Kurdistan.'

The woman's face dropped. I immediately regretted my words. 'Come, come,' I said. 'Don't stop. Let's celebrate.'

But she replied, 'No, you are right. We need to liberate more. We need to go on.' And she put away the sweets and walked away.

All afternoon I wandered around the city in a daze. As evening approached, I turned a corner and was stunned to see a family – a mother and her two children who seemed to have chosen the first possible moment to return. They appeared dumbfounded by the devastation around them. So much of what they knew was gone. I could see them struggling to imagine the diabolical forces that had transformed the city into the ruin it now was.

I couldn't help staring back at them. For months I had been crawling through the grey, funereal, frozen dust of the dead. It lay across the city like a shroud. Now here were the colours of life: a mother in a bright-blue traditional Kurdish dress, her children in pink, red and blue silks. I felt like I was looking at a distant memory.

I sat down in a doorway, my rifle across my lap, and watched that family until night fell. My mind had held my heart at bay for so long. Watching this family and others like them, I told myself, was how my heart would begin to repair the space between them.

The day after Kobani's liberation, I had my first shower in months. I warmed the water using an old oil heater in a house we were using, then stood there for what seemed like hours, soaping and washing, soaping and washing. I hadn't felt so clean since swimming in the river outside Sardasht as a boy.

Around noon, a call came over the radio for the snipers to assemble at our base in the city. It was a strange reunion. Herdem, Yildiz, Hayri, Nasrin and I each could have talked for months. Inside my head, it felt so loud. But it was not the time, and if we began with our stories, none of us knew when we would stop. So we just sat silently together, touching each other on the shoulder, peaceful and calm and happy to be in our group of five again.

After a while, Herdem and Yildiz stood and faced us. Of our original seventeen snipers, they said, four were badly wounded, four had lost their minds and one, Servan, was dead. Eight of us had survived, and for us, Herdem said, there would be no let-up. We all needed to return to the war immediately as our forces pushed south from the city into the countryside. 'We have freed the city,' he said. 'But Kobani is in a very weak position. ISIS is waiting outside and they want it back. We need to move to the villages as soon as we can to deny ISIS the space to counter-attack.'

Yildiz added that outside Kobani lay three hundred and seventy-four villages that needed to be recaptured. The terrain would be largely flat. Our new targets would be a series of gently sloping hills that held height advantage over the surrounding area and on which ISIS had built fortified bases. We should expect to encounter these redoubts all the way to the Euphrates to the west and the border of Iraq to the east.

I spoke up. From Jazaa, I had experience of sniping in villages. 'It's mobile, and lots of walking,' I said. 'Not sitting and watching life and death through a hole like we've been doing for the last four months. Now we're going to be able to see the sky. Now we'll have room to roam.'

Everyone laughed at that. I suppose it was funny. But it was also true that we had been living our whole lives through these tiny holes, and our minds had narrowed as a result. It had affected my vision, too. For weeks after Kobani I would find myself spooking people by talking to them with one eye closed, as though I were lining up a shot. Even today I'll walk down a street in London or Leeds and catch myself scanning windows for sniper nests and sizing up passers-by.

I asked to rejoin Haqi and Serhad on the western front, pushing towards the Euphrates, which marked the traditional border of Kurdistan, in whose waters I had begun to dream of washing my face. The others said they were happy to take the eastern and southern fronts. Once our deployments were agreed, we cooked some rice and beans, and ate. It was the last time Herdem, Yildiz, Hayri, Nasrin and I would be together.

EIGHTEEN

Outside Kobani,

January–February 2015

Herdem left as soon as he had finished eating, picking up a pistol and a black Dragunov. A few hours later he returned in a truck, parked, opened the back, hauled out the bodies of nine ISIS fighters, dragged them to the side of the road and lined them up in sequence.

I learned later that Herdem had walked straight from our meeting to a village three kilometres beyond our frontline where he knew ISIS were repositioning. There he'd crept up to a house inside which he could see the enemy and started firing through the windows – shooting, ducking down, popping up at another window, then shooting again. As the jihadis panicked inside, thinking they were surrounded, Herdem took his time. In ten minutes, he cut all nine of them down. Then he heaved their bodies onto their truck and drove it back to the city.

Part of me understood. On one of the last nights before we retook Kobani, he and I had teamed up for an assault on one of the remaining sets of buildings still in ISIS' hands. We were watching a street in which several teams had positioned themselves. The opposite side was controlled by ISIS. I took first watch. When Herdem relieved me, I was in the middle of showing him our positions when I was interrupted by another commander, who took over my briefing.

At around 2 a.m., Herdem saw the top of a man's head pop up behind a wall of sandbags on the balcony of a house on the ISIS side of the street, around two hundred metres away. Not wanting to miss the shot, he fired immediately. After just seconds, the radio exploded with the news that one of our most popular commanders, Hamza, was down. I went to check. There was so much blood it looked like ten men had been hit. The trajectory of the single bullet that had passed through Hamza's neck suggested it came from our lines. When I found the hole where the round had burrowed into the wall, I dug into the brick and pulled out an M16 slug. There was no doubt that this was Herdem's shot.

Herdem was devastated. His distress was exacerbated by the men in Hamza's units, who loved their commander and immediately ostracised Herdem, declaring they would never fight with him again and asking him to stay away from their positions.

Herdem blamed himself, of course. But over the next few days I watched as his agony turned to rage at everything ISIS had done to him. Hamza's death, the death of Herdem's friends, the destruction of the city and all the years of killing – none of it would have happened were it not for ISIS. Herdem had been fighting for his people and for a cause. Look what they made him do! Look what they made him into! From then on, I think he decided he would be fighting to show ISIS what they had created.

Herdem was also displaying the same wholly unnatural absence of caution that many of us were exhibiting. We had begun to feel untouchable. Fear, in the end, is about what you don't know, and Herdem, I and the others had made such a study of the colours and forms of death that it was impossible to be scared of it any more. Over the next few weeks I would hear story after story about how Herdem was attacking villages and hills single-handedly, killing every ISIS fighter he found. I was even told that one day he shot two ISIS fighters then, to keep warm that night, bedded down between them.

Because I spoke English, Herdem asked me to chaperone a volunteer from Hungary called Zuli. At forty-seven, Zuli's burning ambition to kill a few ISIS fighters had persuaded him to leave his job as a nurse in Budapest, say goodbye to his wife, three daughters and two sons, and travel to the war. 'It was when I heard the news that ISIS were raping women and killing children and beheading people,' he told me. 'I had to do something about it.' Zuli was good company. But his anger troubled us. 'Try to keep him back from the front,' Tolin told me. 'If you find a way to let him kill a few of them safely, let him do it and then maybe he'll go back to his family.'

Herdem drove Zuli and me outside the city to a village called Selim, west of Kobani, where Haqi was stationed. 'ISIS has mined everything,' said Herdem. 'Don't ever walk in the fields. Don't even think of visiting the graveyards. Stay on the roads. Our de-miners have cleared the roads.'

We arrived in Selim to find Haqi in an old radio station building, making a fire and planning an attack that night. The village was in a valley. ISIS were about two kilometres away on a hill to the west. They were harassing our positions, advancing to a group of fifteen houses between our two fronts, firing their Kalashnikovs and RPGs, then retreating again. Haqi and I agreed we should take these houses first. To assist the advance,

185

I would crawl to within a few hundred metres to scout the target and provide cover.

I spent the evening creating a camouflage suit by pulling the threads out of empty farmers' sacks and sewing the tassels onto my clothes. I set off at 3 a.m., crouching and elbowing my way forward until I was a hundred metres from the target houses. I couldn't move or shoot as I would be discovered. My job was to stay hidden and count how many jihadis there were and which of the houses they were using. I stayed in the frozen mud all night and all the next day, stock-still, observing, pissing in my clothes, even watching a jihadi drop his trousers and take a crap. After sixteen hours, I was sure there were nine of them. When ISIS returned to their main base for the night, I radioed Haqi and he sent up a group of volunteers who took over the vacant houses without a fight.

It was just as well that they didn't need me. I was more tired than ever. Inside one of the houses the next day I was eating a piece of warmed cheese and drinking a glass of tea when a bullet came through the window and slapped into the wall behind me. Chilled to the bone and stiff as a board, I wasn't sure I could have moved even if I'd wanted to. The team commander apparently felt the same and, like me, remained at the table, eating and sipping his tea. A second bullet hit the wall behind us. Then a third. Eventually, I picked up my rifle, walked out through the back door, sighted up the ISIS position a kilometre away and, noticing an anomalous black shadow inside a hay manger, fired. The black spot disappeared and the shooting stopped.

As we advanced west, we came across two villages in ISIS' hands, Big and Little Boban, and, to the south, a smooth and gradual rise called Sûsan Hill, where commander Cudi had been run over by a tank five months earlier. Our plan was to take Little Boban and Sûsan Hill, then fire down on Big Boban from both positions and force ISIS to retreat. We always tried to leave the jihadis a way out. This meant we might have to fight them again, but our priority was always taking back our land, not killing.

With the help of a few coalition air strikes, we took Sûsan Hill without a fight. Around 4 a.m. the next day, I left Zuli and advanced alone to a small clump of trees to observe Little Boban. If there were only three or four jihadis, my idea was to take them out myself. Around 8.30 that morning I saw two figures set out on foot from one of the houses. Ten minutes later, another five followed them. An eighth man on a motorbike came and left, presumably delivering orders. The jihadis on foot were striding purposefully with long, firm steps, not stopping or looking back, and carrying several spare bags of ammunition. I was sure I was watching the start of a counterattack on Sûsan Hill.

I snuck back the way I had come, called Haqi, relayed my observations, then set out across the fields for Sûsan Hill. It was heavy going, soft and muddy. At one point I was challenged by a woman's angry voice on the radio: 'Who is walking in the fields alone?'

'Azad,' I replied. 'I'm a sniper. I'm always alone.'

The woman was a commander called Golan. She told me she had been listening in to ISIS' radio and heard them say that our fighters were fleeing Sûsan Hill.

'I'm not running away,' I shouted. 'I'm coming towards you!'

Before we had time for more disagreement, ISIS began shooting at me from their positions around two kilometres away. A round hit the earth near my feet, then another. From the sound,

I could tell the jihadis were using a BKC, a large-calibre Dushka and a Kalashnikov or two. A BKC or a Kalashnikov could kill with a single round and a Dushka would cut me in two. But none of them were accurate over distance. I kept walking. I had little choice: the mud was too sticky for running. After a few more steps, without really thinking what I was doing, I stopped, turned to face my attackers, opened my arms wide, closed my eyes, and just stood there. *I won't be hit*, I told myself. *I can't be hit.* Several bullets slapped the earth around me. After a while, I lowered my arms, opened my eyes, turned back in the direction I had been headed and trudged on. The jihadis seemed to give up and the bullets stopped. It felt like I had proved something, though what, and to whom, I wasn't sure.

I made it to a cluster of houses at the foot of Sûsan Hill in the thick of the midday heat, took a seat on a doorstep and caught my breath. To the east were my comrades. To the west was ISIS. The summit of Sûsan Hill was our frontline dividing the two. There were four comrades in two shallow foxholes on the top of the hill, trying to hold out against the ISIS counter-attack. I walked around the back of the hill and made it to a group of our fighters who were providing cover fire for the foxholes. 'Most of the guys out on the hill are just new arrivals,' warned one. 'Never been in battle before.'

Fzzz! Fzzz!

We pressed our faces into the dirt as bullets flew over our heads. In the distance, I could hear a Dushka starting up. I drained a bottle of water which the others had passed to me and, when I felt a pause in the fire, set off up the hill for the first foxhole. As I was running up, I saw one of our men, a teenager, running down towards me. As we passed each other, I grabbed him by his collar, flipped him onto his back, dragged him back into the hole and stuck my knee on his chest.

'What are you doing?' I shouted. 'Nobody is leaving! This is where Cudi fought and died. So will we if we have to! Nobody leaves here as long as I'm alive!'

In the foxhole was a second man, bleeding from the head. I looked at the teenager under my knee. He looked scared half to death, though now perhaps more of me than ISIS. The enemy fire was intensifying, thumping into the ground around us. I rolled off the boy, pressed my body into the foxhole, all of half a metre deep, and waited for the next pause in the fusillade.

After a minute or so, with no sign of a break in incoming fire, I jumped up and ran the twenty metres to the second, higher foxhole, skidding in next to two comrades and an old, broken BKC covered in dirt and blood. One of the two, another young man, was screaming into his radio: 'We're surrounded! They're everywhere! We need to leave!'

I reached over and turned off his radio. 'You can't talk like that,' I told him. 'You'll scare people.'

The second comrade, in his late twenties, was calmer. Registering my Dragunov, he anticipated my purpose. 'There are five on that hill six hundred metres away to the right,' he told me. 'Two are creeping up towards us behind that low wall over there four hundred metres to the front. Three more are in the houses down the hill five hundred metres to the far left. And there are three Dushkas, on the right, on the left and straight ahead on the far side of the valley, all out of our range. In the foxhole you came from, one comrade was hit in the head by shrapnel kicked up by a Dushka round.'

'Got it,' I said.

I zeroed my scope to six hundred and fifty metres. To the right, I could see the five jihadis. They were standing together out in the open, as casual as cowboys, with their forward feet resting on rocks as they shot at us. I fired at them, once, then again. It was like a grenade had gone off. All five threw themselves to the ground and took cover behind a small rise.

'Watch them with your binoculars,' I said to my spotter. 'I'll scan the other side.'

I switched to the wall running up the hill. As my comrade had said, there were two ISIS men crouching behind it, edging towards us. One was carrying a BKC. I went for him. He went down, though I couldn't tell if I'd hit him or whether he was taking cover.

Next were the houses at the base of the hill. On the roof of one was a guy firing a BKC from the hip. I hit him in the chest. He flipped over backwards, somersaulting off the roof as though he was doing a backwards dive.

It was suddenly much quieter. There was still the occasional *fzzz* of an incoming round but the barrage had stopped for now. I took the chance to adjust my position in the foxhole, pull my camo over myself and reload my magazine.

'Nobody is leaving,' I insisted.

The jihadis soon recovered and restarted their attack. Just when the incoming fire seemed to reach a new pitch, I felt it veer off to my right. I looked around to see the two youngsters from the other foxhole lying outside it on the ground, their faces in the dirt. They'd tried to make another run for it, then come under fire and thought better of it. Bullets were kicking up dust all around them. They weren't dead yet, but death was one well-aimed shot away.

'Stand up!' I shouted at them. 'Stand up!'

I grabbed a large stone and threw it at the nearer man, hitting him in the back. Startled, he looked round at me.

Enunciating as clearly as I could above the noise of the bullets, I said, 'Pick up the wounded man and take him to the back. I will give you cover.'

The young man nodded and got to his feet. I began firing in rapid succession, two quick shots to the left, two more at the wall, two more at the houses. I was through my mag in seconds. I reloaded a second, then a third. Behind me, my two comrades were shuffling away slowly towards cover. I shouted at the teenager in my foxhole to take the ammunition belt off the BKC, clean the dirt and blood off the bullets, then load them into my spare mags. I kept firing. In my left hand, I could feel my barrel overheating. I was down to my last thirty rounds.

'I need gun oil and more Dragunov rounds,' I shouted into my radio.

As I reloaded once more, I lifted my rifle to my eye to begin firing again when it flew out of my hands. My scope hit me in the eye, knocking me back and into the dirt. It felt like my eye had been ripped from my skull. I put my fingers to my face. My eyelid was closed but my eyeball was still there.

I prised my eyelid open with my thumb and forefinger, trying to blink back the rising bruise. My rifle was behind me. Next to it was a large white stone, shattered into pieces. I could read what had happened: a heavy-calibre bullet had hit the stone, knocked it into my barrel, and the force of the collision had ripped the weapon from my hands and smashed it into my face.

I checked the Dragunov. The scope was fine. Aside from a scrape on the barrel and some peeling paint due to the overheating, the gun was also functional. So was I.

*

By now, I had been shooting at a steady pace for more than an hour. During a lull, a comrade skidded past and dropped off more gun oil and a big box of ammunition, including some armour-piercing rounds. The two men in the foxhole with me kept me supplied. I tried to slow my shots, firing only when I saw movement. Another hour passed. I noticed the enemy's Dushka had gone quiet, either broken or out of bullets.

I was so focused on the battle in front of me that the first I knew of Janiwar's presence was when I heard a clanking metal sound behind me. I looked back to see him working on the old Dushka. 'If we can get this thing working,' he said, 'we'll hold them off easily.'

Suddenly he screamed and fell on me. 'I've been hit in the leg!' he cried. 'They shot my leg.'

I looked at his wound. He was bleeding but it didn't seem life-threatening. 'It's just your leg, comrade,' I said. I grabbed his scarf and threw it at him so he could make a tourniquet.

Janiwar went quiet, tying his scarf tightly around his leg to stop the bleeding. Once he was satisfied, he looked up. 'Azad,' he said, 'you fire at the enemy and I'll run back.'

'That's it?' I asked. 'You come, you get wounded and you leave?'

I was only teasing. But Janiwar grimaced.

'Three, two, one, GO!' I shouted.

But as Janiwar got to his feet, I realised I'd made a mistake: my rifle was empty. 'STOP!' I shouted. 'Duck back down – I'm out!'

Janiwar scrambled back into the foxhole. I could see he wanted to hit me in the face. But he controlled himself and watched me reload. When I was done, he said, 'Test it first. And this time, I'll count it off.'

I fired a shot.

Janiwar nodded. 'Three, two, one, GO!'

I fired two shots left, two centre, two more right, then repeated until I finished the mag. For a moment, the battlefield was deadly quiet. I looked over at my spotter. He caught my eye and nodded at the younger comrade squatting next to me.

The teenager was huddled in a ball, his arms around his knees, his face in his hands. Sticky dark blood was pouring through his fingers. It had already made a deep, dark pool in his lap and was spilling onto the ground around him.

'Tie his wound!' I shouted.

'I can't!' the other man shouted back. 'He's been hit in the mouth. He would choke.'

'Press some cloth on it and take him back,' I said.

I waited until they were ready, then counted them off.

'Three, two, one . . .'

I knelt up and started firing once more. Beside me, my spotter pulled the boy's arm over his shoulder, lifted him to his feet and began walking him across the hill. They went slowly, the older man heaving the younger one along, leaving a trail of dragged feet and blood in the dust. Eventually, they disappeared down the hill. Later, Janiwar told me that the bullet that had hit his leg was the same one that had passed through the boy's mouth then out of his neck.

It was 4 p.m. by now. My comrades had left me. I realised ISIS was departing too. Down the hill to the right I could see one jihadi helping a wounded man off the battlefield. The two behind the wall were either dead or had left. The group on the cluster of houses to the left had moved back a few hundred metres into the valley. It was the first time I had seen ISIS retreat with my own eyes. But I was in no mood for mercy.

My comrade had been hit in the mouth. Another had been hit in the leg, and another in the head. I'd nearly lost an eye. Whenever I spotted the jihadis, I fired. I dropped one more at a thousand metres. Then I jumped up out of the foxhole and began running down the hill towards them, firing as I went.

'Wait! Wait!' came a voice on my radio. 'Where are you going?'

The voice steadied me. I walked back up the hill, rejoined my comrades, and together we descended the hill to make sure the jihadis were gone. I found the bodies of at least two that I had hit. The guy I had shot on the roof was a mess: my bullet had knocked a wad of white fat out through his back and onto his vest, as though squeezed from a tube of toothpaste. Over to the right was another dead jihadi who was wearing new leather zip-up boots. I was pleased to see that one of my rounds had hit him in the foot and the blood had ruined the silk lining.

Of all the engagements I fought, Sûsan Hill remains the one of which I am most proud. Cudi had died for that hill. Outnumbered ten to one, with only a rifle against BKCs and Dushkas, I'd used my Dragunov like a machine gun to hold it. When I left the foxhole, it was filled with more than a thousand bullet casings. The camouflage paint on the barrel was all burned off. For days afterwards, my shoulder was purple and yellow with the bruising from the recoil. But they hadn't taken Sûsan Hill. With Cudi beside me, they hadn't come close.

NINETEEN

Southwest of Kobani,
March 2015

As we moved south and east, our lines widened and thinned, and we found ourselves working in ever smaller groups. After the confines of Kobani, this new spread-out war threw up some surprises. Haqi, who came from the area, began asking families he knew to return from Turkey to the north, saying they were needed to fill the gaps in our forces in case the jihadis tried to slip over the border and attack us from behind. One day I came across a man with a long beard in black clothes with a gun in his hands and raised my rifle at him, only for him to address me in Kurdish. He had responded to Haqi's request and returned from Turkey but hadn't stopped to consider how his appearance might describe him.

As we advanced, we managed to solve some of the mysteries of what had happened to our men and women who disappeared in the first days of the ISIS attack. One morning we found seven of their bodies lying next to each other in a room in an abandoned house. All had been executed with a single bullet to the head. Their bodies were lying where they had fallen. The exposed parts of their flesh were turning to parchment. The skin on their faces was drawn back over their bones as tight as stretched leather. When we tried to lift them to take them back to Kobani to be buried, they fell apart in our arms. The smell of putrefaction was unbearable. Several of us vomited. Eventually, we gathered their body parts into some old grain sacks, tied them up and carried them out.

The new distances between us and the enemy also gave the jihadis a chance to try fresh forms of deception. A few weeks after the battle at Sûsan Hill, we came across another gently sloping incline called Qeregoyê. On it was a farmhouse and several outbuildings in which our commanders said a large group of Islamists were making a stand, holding up our entire advance. I volunteered to scout the farmhouse and crawled forward behind a small stone wall until I was three hundred metres away. Through my scope, I saw one of the Islamists throw a bottle of water down to a small shed that was the ji-hadis' most forward position. A few minutes later, another figure ran across the top of the hill behind the main house. Then a third sprinted down to a small barn to the side, ferrying a pillow to be used as a sandbag. A fourth appeared carrying a blanket. Then a fifth came into view ferrying a mattress. There had to be at least ten of them, I thought.

I radioed Haqi and Golan. 'We need an air strike,' I said. 'There's a lot of them and they're digging in.'

As I was talking, however, another figure made a dash across some open ground and I realised I had seen this man before, or at least part of him: he was wearing the same jacket as one I had seen further up the hill. Now that I knew what to look for, each time a jihadi made another run, I focused on the jacket. It was the same jacket every time. I realised I had been looking at the same man all along.

'You know what?' I called Haqi and Golan again. 'It's only

one guy. He's faking the whole thing. He's pretending to be resupplying a force of ten people or so. But he's the only one moving.'

'We're bringing up the tank,' Haqi replied.

Our 'tank' was actually an old Toyota fitted with heavy metal plates to cover its sides and tyres. It took fifteen minutes to reach me. As it clanked past, the men and women inside opened fire, then advanced to the farmhouse firing continuously, at which point five of our fighters jumped out of the back and stormed inside. I joined them and we repeated the manoeuvre for each of the outbuildings. We met no resistance in any of them.

The jihadi in the jacket was lying on the ground in front of the farmhouse, his head split open by a Dushka round. There was a second ISIS fighter nearby who had been hit seven or eight times in his stomach and legs and who might have been dead for some time. A third body was inside one of the out-buildings. And that was it. Three jihadis against one hundred of us – and they had held us off all day. War is often imagined like a great battle scene in a movie where dozens of extras are wiped out at once. In real life, there are no extras in war. Every-one gets to play a central character.

Out of habit, I inspected the third body. The corpse was lying on the floor, and from the size of the torso, it was the body of a boy, perhaps thirteen or fourteen. He was wearing blue jeans but was otherwise stripped to the waist, revealing his pale-pink skin. There was a terrible smell in the room. When I walked around the body, I realised the boy's face was lying in a smouldering fire. Most of his features had been burned off. On and around him were magazines of bullets. Some of the rounds were still exploding.

I grabbed him and started to drag him out of the fire. A com-rade shouted at me to stop: the boy was dead and it might be a booby-trap. I felt in the boy's pockets. There were no papers. There was a mobile phone next to him but it had nothing on it – no music, no pictures – except three local numbers and a detailed military map of the area. We never found out any more about this boy. Who was he? A Russian? A Chechen? A European? Why had his fellow jihadis taken such trouble to obscure his features? Perhaps he was important. Perhaps he wasn't. What struck me was the gruesomeness with which the jihadis had erased any hint of his earthly identity. *There is nothing we won't do in this world*, they seemed to be saying. *None of what happens here matters.*

War had levelled Kobani, turning it into a hot, dry Dresden. Out in the villages, however, we were met not so much by the ruins of war as the absence of life. Our people had abandoned their homes. Then the jihadis had looted everything they'd left behind. There wasn't a sheep or chicken that had escaped ISIS' kitchens. They stole cooking oil, grain, rice, flour, cheese, tea and even the kettles and glasses that went with them. They pilfered dried grapes, urns of honey and sacks of salted pistachios. They took cars, tractors, petrol, diesel and generators. They forced farmers they captured to pick the olives off their ancient trees. They even stole donkeys to carry away their loot, and guard-dogs to protect it. It was remarkable, really, how even as we began to understand that the war for Rojava was in its final few months, ISIS' band of rapists, murderers, thieves and thugs would offer us new outrages to renew our fury.

One of our last objectives was the village of Misko, a place of several hundred houses surrounded by rolling hills and a scattering of smaller settlements a day's walk east from the Euphrates. From some of these hills you could see the greenness of the marsh banks running either side of the great river, perhaps ten or fifteen kilometres away. Misko was too big and well defended for our hundred or so men and women to capture immediately, so our plan was to whittle our way in by taking all the villages that surrounded it one by one, then close in on Misko from all sides.

It was in one of these villages that, to settle a dispute between returning farmers by appealing for unity in the face of a common enemy, I told the story of Sûsan Hill. In an aside, I said I assumed the young fighter who was hit in the mouth had died of his injuries. After the farmers dispersed, a man came over to me and introduced himself as Mohandis, an engineer.

'This wounded guy is not dead,' he said.

'I want to believe you, brother,' I replied. 'But he lost so much blood.'

'No,' said Mohandis. 'I *know* he's not dead. I know his sister. We're from the same village. I spoke to her just now.'

'Can you call her?' I asked.

He could. A few seconds later, a woman was telling me on Mohandis' phone that she had just returned from Turkey where she had visited her injured brother in hospital. Her father was still with him, she said, and she gave me the number. When we phoned her father, the man told me his son was unconscious in intensive care and, looking through the glass, he described his boy to me. 'Big thick brown eyebrows, brown skin, not too tall. Shot in the mouth on Sûsan Hill. He can't talk but the doctor says he may be able to in the future. But he is alive.'

'You don't know what you are giving me,' I said. During the battle for Sûsan Hill, I had had no thought for anything but fighting. From the moment the adrenalin subsided, however, I had been haunted by how I had forced this boy to remain in the battle. The image of his blood pouring out of his mouth and welling in his hands had become my new nightmare. He hadn't even been able to call out. He might have died right next to me and I wouldn't have noticed.

'When he wakes up, tell him Azad called,' I said to the father. 'The sniper in the foxhole. Tell him that I am overjoyed that he is alive.'

The man promised to do so. Then he said he had a request for me. 'My house in the village,' he said. 'Can you check that the Islamists are not stealing everything from me?'

It was early spring in South Kurdistan but that February brought the heaviest rain anyone could remember. The downpour lasted a month. The villagers explained it by saying Nature was reminding us that nothing man-made, not even war, could match its power. Our men and women found the weather sapped as much of their strength as the fighting. On the fourth consecutive night of rain I went to visit a team who had been out in the open since it started. Shortly after I left, the commanders decided to move forward. As this team entered a house, the first shelter they had experienced in four days, five of them were killed by a landmine. A few days later another three were badly wounded by an RPG.

I felt that I might help prevent some of these deaths if I had a night scope: my previous one had been requisitioned by another unit weeks earlier. I radioed Herdem to request a new one. But Herdem wasn't available and my call was answered by a junior comrade.

'He is wherever the front is moving forward,' the comrade said. 'He goes and takes over villages and hills, then leaves and goes to another attack.' The man on the other end sounded worried. He described Herdem as exhausted but relentless. 'He kills any jihadi he finds. In one attack, he shot forty-five ISIS single-handedly.'

The man's words made me so sad. It was too much, even for Herdem. He had lost so many friends. He was consumed by a killing rage.

A day or so later, I managed to speak to him on the radio.

'I need a thermal,' I said.

'We only have one and you will need to find an M16 on which to mount it,' he told me. 'But I will send it.'

'Are you OK?' I asked.

'Am I OK?'

'I heard about what you've been doing.'

Herdem was quiet.

'Even if you kill a thousand ISIS, it will not equal one drop of Hamza's blood,' I said. 'I understand how you feel. When I wounded Alisher, I nearly collapsed. But it can happen to anyone.'

I could hear Herdem breathing heavily.

'Maybe take a break,' I said. 'Maybe get some rest back at the sniper base for a few days.'

'How can I rest?' he replied. 'How can I send you to the front and rest back at headquarters?'

I had no answer for him. Herdem repeated that he would send the thermal.

There was a silence.

'If you have anything else you need to say, I am listening,' I said.

'Likewise,' he said. 'If you have anything you need to say, I am listening too.'

'Success, Herdem,' I said, finally.

'Success, Azad.'

*

After a few weeks in the rain and cold, General Golan gave us a new target: Haroon Hill. This tall mass of bare rock, one of the last pieces of high ground before the Euphrates, was named after one of our social workers who had lived and worked there, and who had picked up a gun when ISIS invaded and died there. The hill was more of a mountain, a giant plinth of rock several hundred metres tall. With two ISIS positions on the summit, Golan said Haroon Hill was all but untakeable by ground troops alone. The coalition had agreed to continual air strikes, day and night. We would stand back and watch and, when we were sure the jihadis had all either died or fled, we would take the hill unopposed.

It was a strange sensation to sit back and watch your war being fought in front of you. For ten days, the warplanes bombarded the hill. They were using their most powerful missiles, which would send clouds of dust hundreds of metres into the air. Again and again the bombers came. Underneath the explosions, we would see the Islamists scurrying around like ants under boiling water. Most were enveloped in the dust. More than one seemed to just disappear – a tiny black figure fleeing the bombs one second, nothing there the next. But somehow the survivors managed to keep their black-and-white flag flying.

During a break in the bombardment, I saw nine ISIS fighters emerge from their base and walk down the hill. At first, I couldn't understand it. After enduring the bombing for a week, they were just leaving? I watched them as they strolled over a rise until, one by one, they all disappeared. No more came and there was no movement, not in their base and not in the rocks to the side. When I looked again, however, I realised their base flag was still up.

'They're pretending,' I radioed to Haqi. 'They never forget their flag. It's a very spiritual thing for them. They're trying to make it look like they're retreating but they're preparing to fight. It's a trap.'

Haqi agreed I should go forward and check. Sure enough, I spotted a group of Islamists hiding out in a small cluster of houses down the back of the hill, spread out so as to avoid the air strikes. I radioed to Haqi what I had seen. That night the bombers came again, this time targeting the houses and hillside where I had seen the jihadis. After that, a drone kept circling the area, looking for survivors to pick off. Finally, Serhad went forward with his team. Within an hour he called back to say he had taken the hill without firing a shot.

I joined Serhad on the summit just as dawn broke on the horizon. Behind the ISIS base were four small graveyards. In the first, there were four fully completed graves. The next contained another three graves which were half-dug: the bodies were mostly buried though only a thin scattering of earth had been thrown over the top. Here and there arms and legs protruded. One of the jihadis' faces was showing. To me, he looked as though he was still alive, pretending to be dead. I watched him for a full minute, my rifle to his head and my hand over his mouth to check if he was breathing.

In the third set of graves, two bodies were lying in shallow scoops on the ground. What covering they had seemed to have been thrown over them by the force of an explosion. A toe was sticking out of one small mound of earth. I felt it. Cold. Finally, I came across a pile of corpses and body parts lying out in the open, the remains of perhaps seven or eight people. At least three of them had white skin and ginger hair.

More fighters from the Caucasus, I assumed.

From what I was seeing, an air strike had hit the initial group of jihadis. Another team had come up to bury them and take their places, then another strike had hit them. So a third team had arrived, and a third strike had killed them. Finally, a fourth team had taken over and they had been killed too. It was terrible tactics. It also made no sense to travel all the way from Chechnya or Georgia and fight for so many months and years only to hurl yourself into death. The only possible answer was that they always knew they were going to die, and they welcomed it.

Even then, looking at their bodies, maimed and burned and ripped apart, you had to wonder whether they had thought it through. This didn't look heroic. It looked agonising, stupid and pointless, like some horrific misunderstanding. Maybe they had made a mistake. Maybe they had been misled. Maybe they were just fools. After all, there were easier, more commendable ways to commit suicide than trying to enslave a land and its people. Their sacrifice didn't justify their crimes. It just made them even more blinkered and narcissistic. I wondered whether, in the moment of their death, they had experienced enlightenment at last. But when I studied them, nothing in their blank, frozen expressions suggested illumination – quite the opposite. I have to think that they died dumb.

TWENTY

Close to the Euphrates,
March–April 2015

As the war continued, we inevitably made more mistakes of our own. One evening Serhad and his unit advanced on a village that had not been cleared and, to fool ISIS into thinking they were camping somewhere else, lit a fire, then bedded down a few hundred metres away. When a second group of comrades arrived, they saw the fire and assumed Serhad had checked the area for jihadis before warming himself. So they lit their own blaze and settled in around it. Several more units did the same. In the morning, a comrade called Jamal was stoking the embers to warm himself in the dawn cold when he looked up and, speechless, watched one, two, then three jihadis run out of a house not ten metres away and disappear.

Another time, we took over a small village on a road leading directly towards ISIS' lines to the west. Our Hungarian volunteer Zuli still hadn't fired a shot in anger, the village was easy to defend and I had other places to go, so I placed him on the roof of the last house in the village and told him to shoot anything that came towards him. A small group of new volunteers also took up position on either side of the road.

I returned in the evening to find Zuli in a state of high distress, pushing the other volunteers around, looking like he was going to hit someone.

'This guy wouldn't let me kill him!' he shouted when he saw me. 'I had him right in my sights and they wouldn't let me shoot!'

Between outbursts, Zuli told me that a lone motorbiker with a long beard, dressed in black and wearing a *thawb*, had approached from the west. Zuli was convinced the man was ISIS and was about to shoot when the volunteers called to him that the man might be one of ours. The motorbiker came to a stop. The volunteers shouted across to him, asking for his name and unit. At which point the motorbiker turned around and sped off back in the direction he had come. They showed me the tyre marks. The jihadi had been ten metres away from Zuli.

'You're lucky he didn't steal your tea!' I exclaimed. 'Zuli – why didn't you get him?'

'I did!' cried Zuli. 'I fired again and again but I couldn't hit him.'

I examined Zuli's rifle. His scope was zeroed to a thousand metres. The bullets would have passed clean over the jihadi's head.

I thought the incident was hilarious. For days afterwards I made fun of Zuli, making the sound of a revving motorbike. Zuli didn't think it was funny.

It was during the same advance to the west that Serhad, Jamal, a commander called Dado and I walked into Chargle, a place of forty to fifty mud-walled, tin-roofed houses which turned out to be Haqi's ancestral village. We were half-expecting to run into ISIS. Instead, in a room in a deserted house we found an Aladdin's Cave of supplies. Boxes of ammunition and RPGs, sleeping bags and rain ponchos, American-made backpacks, socks, cots and blankets. In the corridor outside we found a small mountain of fresh food in takeaway containers: meat, onions, orange juice, cakes, pistachios, biscuits, rice, plus gas cookers and piles of spare cylinders.

It could have been poisoned, of course. The thought of taking from ISIS was also unpalatable. Nor had we finished checking the houses for stray jihadis. But we were famished. We lit a stove, found a large pot and threw in some boiled rice, onions, tomatoes, steak and chicken to warm it, then flipped it all out onto a large tray. We must have eaten a kilo each. The feeling in my stomach was one of shock and surprise – it gurgled for days afterwards – and it took all the willpower we had not to stretch out afterwards in the middle of a warzone and take a nap.

ISIS left other gifts. Not far away, I forced the door into the backyard of another house to find a brand-new Honda motorbike with the keys in the ignition. *It has to be booby-trapped*, I thought. I checked the stand, the engine, the seat and the tyres but found nothing. I threw my leg over the seat, turned the key and kick-started it. It was fine. Jamal, who had more experience with bikes, suggested he steer on the muddy roads and I hop on the back. I gathered up a box of RPGs and another of ponchos to take back to our forces and we rode out of the village back up Haroon Hill.

'Can you believe we ate ISIS' food?' shouted Jamal over his shoulder. 'I thought your principles wouldn't have allowed you to swallow!'

I was about to answer when, in front of us, I saw a fishing line running across the road. I quickly traced it to the right-hand side, where there was nothing, then followed it to the left, where was a large gas cylinder sitting on the verge. Jamal was changing into a higher gear. I grabbed him, trying to pull him down onto the road. But as I gripped him, I saw the bike's front wheel hit the wire.

I released Jamal and threw my arms in the air. Finally, my moment had come. I felt the wild grip of death. An image of my mother flashed into my mind, and another of my home-town, Sardasht, and the waterfall and the green beauty of the countryside. I saw Jazaa. I saw Kobani. I was at peace.

After a while, I realised I could hear somebody's voice. It sounded quiet and distant. I opened my eyes. I was on the back of the bike. It was Jamal talking.

'It didn't explode!' I screamed at him. 'It didn't explode!'

'What?' replied Jamal, braking hard and dropping the bike into the dirt.

I grabbed him by the hand and we ran back the way we had come.

'Where?' demanded Jamal.

One hundred and fifty metres behind us, the large gas cylinder attached to the fishing line was now lying in the road. As we approached, I saw that the other end of the line was tied to a stick that was also lying flat on the ground. We had burst through the trip-wire but instead of tightening it and triggering the detona-tor, the stick holding it taut had popped clean out of the muddy ground. We had cursed the rain for weeks. Now it had saved us.

After a month, we finally took the last village surrounding Misko. We were now able to attack it from the north, south and east, squeezing the jihadis out through a gap running to the west. We wanted to give them an alternative to fighting to the last man, but we wouldn't let them run unmolested. Serhad and his men would cut them down as they went.

I took up a position about a thousand metres out to the southeast, driving the jihadis to the west. I quickly shot dead three of them. It seemed to energise the others. I could hear them shouting and screaming '*Allahu Akbar! Allahu Akbar!*' as they ran into the middle of Misko.

After a few minutes, Serhad called me: 'Azad! Come here! There's a lot of ISIS here.'

I made my way towards him. Serhad was on the roof of a house on the eastern outskirts, ready to attack.

'They're just behind that wall over there,' said Serhad. 'One of them is close.'

I surveyed the wall through my sights. As I did so, a jihadi stood up in full view five hundred metres away. I shot him as he was walking.

Serhad told me he wanted to take over the houses that stood between us and ISIS. When he called Haqi and Golan, however, they requested him to wait for reinforcements. Serhad just switched off his radio.

'Let's do it ourselves, Azad,' he said. 'You cover me. The generals can wait for us this time.'

I reasoned Serhad was going to attack with or without me. 'OK,' I said.

I watched Serhad creep towards the jihadis. As he reached a house, two men stood up and ran behind him. I shot one immediately. He went down screaming, dragging himself behind a rock, his free hand trying to stop the blood pumping from his neck. I moved to his friend and shot him as well. I couldn't help but enjoy it – the skill, the success. I'd become so used to killing that I felt no hesitation, just the feeling of a debate long since settled and a necessary job done.

I spotted two more ISIS nearby and another further away, moving fast. 'Don't move!' I radioed to Serhad. 'Don't go any further! They look like they're about to make a run for it.'

The three men ran to a chicken shed on the edge of the village. Just as they reached it, a missile released by a coalition warplane overhead slammed into it. Dust shot into the sky and the wooden boards of the shed tumbled through the air.

Serhad had kept up a constant rate of fire and was down to his last fifteen rounds. Two novice YPJ comrades next to me volunteered to resupply him. Serhad refused their help, saying there were jihadis all around him. 'I'll do it,' came a voice on the radio that I recognised as Jamal's. Before anyone could stop him, I saw Jamal darting through a grove of olives in front, taking a second comrade with him. The earth started exploding around him. I realised one of our Dushka gunners was blasting away at Jamal, thinking he was a jihadi.

'You're firing at Jamal!' I screamed into the radio.

Jamal came on the radio. 'That's not me, Azad!' he shouted. 'I'm shooting too!'

At that, everyone opened up on the two figures in the olive grove. I think even ISIS was firing at them. When I went to check on them later, I couldn't find a single part of their bodies which hadn't been hit. There were more holes than flesh.

We kept up the pressure for another hour or so. Finally the moment came for which we had waited. A large crowd of ji-hadis suddenly made a break to the west. As they ran into an open field, I did a quick count: thirty-seven. They were within easy range. I waited until they were close, then began firing. One. Two. Three. Four. Five. Six . . .

I had at least fifteen kills that day. Seven Islamists escaped, though most of them were quickly picked off from the air. The field through which they ran was carpeted with bodies. We had waited so long to capture Misko, and we made them pay a price for that.

*

The last few weeks before Tolin relieved me went by in a waking dream of exhaustion. New memories still come back to me every now and then, but mostly only fragments. After Zuli suffered a near miss in an RPG strike, I finally convinced him to go home to Hungary. I have a memory of it snowing a few days later. Then I was nearly hit in the face by a Dushka round: the splinters from the wall next to me shot into my cheek. I also recall coming across a mine in the road over which we had all walked a hundred times.

One night a house where a group of five of our fighters were based was blown to smithereens. In the usual manner, they had lit a fire to distract ISIS from where they planned to spend the night – but the site they had chosen for their blaze was on top of a mine connected to a series of other explosives that the enemy had rigged up all around the house. I spent an hour gathering up fingers, eyeballs and lumps of flesh and placing them on five separate blankets, trying to put them back together.

I also have a memory of following the roar and howl of an animal through a village at night. Eventually, the noise led me to an empty swimming pool behind a grand stone house. In it was a wild-looking dog, fat, dirty, growling and showing me his teeth. Next to him was a pile of human bones and two YPG uniforms. I lowered a bucket of water into the pool to give the animal something to drink. Then I found a plank and lowered it in so that it made a gangway for the dog to leave. Two days later when I returned, the dog was gone and we were able to collect the remains of our comrades.

The trauma would hit me much later, but at the time I functioned like an animal, just instinct and purpose. One day I noticed I had even developed the habit of pissing every time we took over a new position, as though I was marking my territory. It was also around then that we received new battle orders. We were to stop allowing ISIS to escape. What the instruction didn't say, but what we understood, was that we needed to end the war. We were to kill or capture them all.

One day I ran into Herdem and Yildiz at our new sniper base behind the front. Yildiz only managed a brief greeting: she was stopping by to pick up more ammunition. Herdem wanted me to meet some foreign volunteers who had recently arrived, an Algerian-Italian called Karim, a Spanish revolutionary from Madrid and an American called Keith Broomfield from Massachusetts. Keith told me he had once been to prison but was now making a conscious choice to side with right against wrong. He had found his cause in the Kurds' fight against ISIS, he said. I liked Keith, and he was a great shot. There was something about his enthusiasm that reminded me of who I once was.

Such interludes, however, were only brief distractions from what had now become an obsession: washing in the Euphrates. I stank, and was dressed in filthy rags. For weeks I had tried to have a shower, only to be interrupted by a new firefight just as I prepared to step under the bucket. I felt encased in dirt and gore. I had to break out. I had to get clean.

One night we were advancing on the last village before the Euphrates when I found myself almost feverish with thirst. As we checked one house, then another, I asked for spare water but there was none. My knees began shaking. I slowed to a crawl, managing only one or two hundred metres at a time before I had to rest. When the sun started to rise around 5 a.m., my comrades spotted two litre-bottles of water and passed them to me. I drank one, then the other, then grabbed a child's blanket and, barely able to walk, hauled myself up onto a roof with a clear view of the Euphrates on which two YPJ were keeping watch. I sat up against a wall, wrapped my arms around my rifle, and tugged the blanket around me. 'If they attack,' I said to the two women, 'just leave me here. I can't move.' One of the women began to object but at that point I fainted.

I awoke sweating, with the sun on my face. There was a mattress underneath me, a large blanket on top of me, a lit wooden stove in the corner and a large red apple placed carefully on the ground nearby. When I checked the time, it was 2 p.m. I rose, descended from the roof and walked out into an open field. I followed a path through some sugar-cane fields towards the river. After a while, I could hear the sound of the water. I could smell the damp earth and taste its coolness.

I turned a corner and there it was, wide and quiet and deep green-blue. I ripped off my jacket, then my scarf, then my boots and my socks and my T-shirt. I stood my Dragunov and my M16 against a bank of reeds. Spring was at its height and the sun was shining brightly. I walked leadenly towards the water, my feet sinking into the sand. The water was sharp and cold and clean. That freshness! That liberation! My people had found shelter in these curved riverbanks for millennia. The river's restless currents had been their source of life, its ever-flowing strength the renewal of their hope and the sustenance of their purpose. I cupped its waters in my palms and splashed my face. I drank and drank.

Finally, I opened my eyes. About five hundred metres downstream, two jihadis were sitting on a motorbike, watching me. I ran for my Dragunov. But before I could fire, they gunned the bike and disappeared into the sugar cane.

TWENTY-ONE

Kobani,

April–May 2015

Maybe I should have stopped at the Euphrates. Ever since Sardasht, immersing myself in cold river waters had felt to me like the promise of a new beginning. But the war wasn't done with me. I fought on for a few more weeks, dispatched to the eastern front to help hold the line against a deadly ISIS counter-attack against Hamza's old team, then sent back to the southwest to lead the operation to take the hills around Sarrin.

The way I was being called across ever larger distances reflected our success. We had stopped ISIS, turned them back and were on the point of throwing them out of Rojava. The momentum was with us. Within two more years, our forces and those of the Kurds in northern Iraq and the warplanes of the coalition would kill thousands more jihadis, destroy ISIS as a military force and reduce its territory to a handful of tiny, scattered holdouts. Our front had grown from a few houses and a few streets in Kobani to a line that was hundreds of kilometres long. I should have been enjoying our new freedom. Instead, I felt like something had to give and that it was going to be me.

After observing how my composure was deteriorating, General Tolin made my decision for me and sent me back to Kobani to await further instructions. I returned to the new sniper base, a farmhouse that sat alone on a hill to the southwest of the city. The first days of summer would soon be upon us, the sky was a clear blue, the hills had turned from brown to green and the wind was heavy with the fragrance of fresh jasmine. All around the farm were fields of yellow daisies and red poppies and dark-blue lupins, like the patterns on the dresses my mother made when I was a boy. From the window of the car that took me there, I watched a pair of sparrows noisily building a nest in a tree beside the road, fighting speckled wheatears and crows for pieces of straw and grass. Surrounded as we were by the meat and metal of battle, you could imagine that the war had defiled all existence. Yet here was Nature, oblivious and eternal.

The base was manned by the same fighters who had been with us through Kobani: an anxious young YPG apprentice who always wanted to head for the front, and an elder man who seemed completely broken. By chance, Herdem, Yildiz and Nasrin were at the farmhouse when I arrived. I greeted them, then excused myself. I was finally leaving the front, and I needed to digest the moment alone. I cleaned my Dragunov one last time, then climbed with it up onto the roof. I laid the weapon in my lap and ran my hands over it. How many men had it killed, even before me? Where had it been? What had it seen? I respected this machine. It had been a good companion and a lifesaver. I took my saviour bullets out of my pocket, cleaned them, and put them back. Then I descended and leant my rifle carefully against the wall. Tolin had radioed ahead and I was glad I didn't have to explain myself to the others.

Coming back from the front, I had prepared myself for bad news. It had been three months since we took Kobani and I was bound to have missed the deaths of comrades that I knew. But I also felt it was impossible to ask who was alive and who was not. Who knew where the question might lead? There was also something ugly about enquiring about tragedy. I couldn't find the words. Instead, I resolved to wait until my friends decided on their own to tell me what they knew.

I might have expected Yildiz to be the one to talk. She was always so chatty; Herdem and Nasrin were far quieter. But in the event Yildiz was too distracted. She had been given a note asking her to return to the mountains in North Kurdistan for more training and she was busy packing. So it fell to Herdem and Nasrin to tell me about Zahra.

Zahra had been killed with another YPJ fighter on 29 January, two days after we liberated Kobani. She had been opening the shutters on a shop in a village outside the city when an ISIS mine rigged as a booby-trap exploded and cut them both in two. I received the news in silence. Zahra was such a pure and clean spirit, always smiling or labouring on a new base or putting up a new curtain or taking over a new place. She hardly slept. It took years of struggle and will for Zahra to become who she was. It seemed impossible that she could be gone in a second.

But I knew it was true. In peacetime, news of a disaster is often telegraphed in advance and you have time to steel yourself. But in Rojava, normal rules did not apply. I had seen the colour of death and I knew it could happen to anyone. We had learned to brace ourselves around the clock for bad news. Friends with whom we had the most intense and truthful relationships could be shot or crushed or ripped to pieces a kilometre away from us, and we wouldn't know for months. That was the way of this war. We mourned our friends late and alone, brought to a sudden halt by a single word during a chance conversation, or by happening across a list of the dead, or by catching sight of a photograph on a wall of martyrs. You could set your mind to endure hardship, starvation, killing and even dying. To volunteer for that kind of sacrifice had a nobility to it. But to survive the war, I was discovering, was to be rewarded with a lifetime to ponder the ways in which it had soiled us. That was our penance for living.

Zahra, my brave and cheerful friend. I didn't forget you. I didn't mean to miss our last goodbye. The scars your death carved on my heart are like marks on a stone tablet. Zahra, they didn't tell me you were gone.

Herdem said he had other news. Gentle, resolute, undaunted Hayri had died about a month after Zahra. He had been helping to take over a village when a sniper's bullet found him.

Coming on top of my grief for Zahra, the news was almost too much to swallow. It didn't make sense. Hayri was so unlikely a candidate for death. He was so careful, so calm. He had committed to pull the trigger whenever it was required and there was nothing that would keep him from his task. But it often seemed to me like he had saved a part of himself from the war to keep clean and pure. I knew the war was uncaring and thoughtless and that it took without plan or justice or remorse. I had also known that Hayri would survive. It seemed impossible that he had miscalculated. And if he was gone, if the war had managed to hunt down and kill one of its masters, then even what little I thought I knew about it was untrue. I couldn't digest it. Under my feet, I felt the universe slew. I was sure that Hayri might walk around the corner any minute and, in his knowing way, tease me about my scarf.

Then Nasrin spoke up. 'Hayri was like my brother,' she said. 'We came to Kobani together from our positions in Shengal, joking that we were sister and brother. But on the way, through everything that happened here, it became true. By the end, he really was my brother. I really feel that.'

It was the first time I had heard Nasrin really speak. Her words explained the silence that she and Hayri shared. It was something that they had arrived at together. It seemed they had agreed early on to an unspoken pact of calm, reserve and empathy to get them through what lay ahead. It had made them family. It had sustained them through all those months lying alone behind their guns in the rubble. I felt I understood it. If neither of them articulated the horror out loud, if only innocence and light passed between them, then it would have felt like there was a chance that they would pass through this hell unbroken. There was even the chance that they might reclaim the lives they'd once had. But now Hayri was gone, and Nasrin was alone, and the promise they had made one another was dead.

Herdem and I watched Nasrin. She grew restless, as if she regretted talking. Oh, Hayri, I think she felt she had betrayed you by talking. Did you know how she loved you, Hayri? What spite in this war, to bring us together only to tear us apart.

Nasrin began packing her gear. That afternoon she left to go back to the front. I sat with Herdem as he checked his kit and handed out instructions. After a while, I asked, 'Who is going to replace me at the front?'

Herdem didn't reply. He just sat there. The losses were

weighing ever heavier on him and here was I presenting him with another one. My departure from the front would also mean no more radio talks between us. But Herdem didn't say a word. He never showed me the trouble my leaving might make for him nor tried to make me stay. He was wise and he understood exhaustion and the impact war could have on people. He knew from one look at me that I couldn't continue, and he accepted it.

Herdem let me stay at the snipers' headquarters for a few days. Eventually, Tolin came to say that she had a new assignment for me. Word about how we had stopped ISIS had travelled and the numbers of foreigners now showing up to volunteer or find out about the YPG and the YPJ meant the defence minister in Kobani needed someone to run an office of foreign affairs. 'You speak their language and know their culture,' said Tolin. I told her I would do what was needed.

As I gathered my things, I remember watching Yildiz finish her packing for the mountains. As ever, she was sunny, efficient and organised. There was no question that she would always serve the movement, wherever they needed her, whenever they asked. She left that night for the border and crossed over into North Kurdistan. Later, I would wish I had watched her go so I had the memory to hold on to. Dear Yildiz, my commander and protector, our sweet companion in the ruins, I don't remember if we said goodbye.

TWENTY-TWO

Kobani,

May–June 2015

After dialling the number for my parents' house, I listened to the ring. A woman's voice answered.

'Hello?'

I said nothing. I had not spoken to my family for two years. I wasn't sure I recognised the voice.

'Hello?' the voice asked again. It was my mother.

I didn't know where to begin.

'Is that you, Sora?' she asked. 'Sora?'

'Yes,' I said.

I could hear my mother breathing heavily. She started crying. It was a minute before she spoke again.

'How are you?' she asked. 'Are you OK? Are you wounded?'

'I was wounded a few times but not badly,' I said. 'I am alive. I am not bad.'

'I knew you were wounded!' she shouted. 'I had a dream.'

'Tell me about your dream,' I said.

'I was holding you as a baby in this room,' she said. 'There was a noise. I went out into the corridor and there were two demons there. They were walking past. I thought to myself: "I

221

don't want my baby to see these distorted, wicked faces. And I don't want them to find my baby." So I stood there, blocking the doorway.

'The first demon looked at me right in the eyes and passed on. As the second one was passing, he looked over my shoulder into the room and saw my baby. I tried to stop him but he pushed past me. He went for you. I went for you. We were both holding you, the devil trying to take you away and me trying to save you. Then the other demon came and stabbed me in the back with a knife. I screamed and woke up, shaking and panicked. I knew something had happened to you.'

It was unnerving to hear my mother's dream, so fantastical and strange. But she was also a mother talking to her son about the nightmares he was giving her, and in a way the dream made some sense. Something about two devils in a corridor, the way the second one turned and attacked, reminded me of the two jihadis outside the cultural centre, the boy and the man, running down the street. 'Don't worry, mother,' I told her, 'I'm all right. I met your devils. One of them wounded me. I killed one and wounded the other. I got away. I'm doing fine. I am walking.'

To prove it, I took a picture of myself and sent it to her.

Herdem had a new truck that he had taken from a group of jihadis he had killed. He dropped me the next morning at the yellow-and-grey Syrian government building we had commandeered for our defence ministry.

The minister was Xhalo, an old man from Kobani, who was kind, respectful, meticulously organised and neatly dressed. My clothes were filthy from months of fighting and my trousers still had holes in their legs where I had been caught by small shards of shrapnel. But Xhalo pretended not to notice and even allowed me to take a mattress and a blanket up to the roof at night so that I could stay there, out in the open.

Aside from the few times when I had collapsed from exhaustion, I hadn't slept for more than a few minutes at a time for months. Now, when I tried to sleep indoors, I found it impossible. My mind had been in the war for too long. Walls blocked my view of the battlefield. Floors were unsafe. But roofs were good for seeing what might be coming. And so for months, like a bird, I returned each night to my nest on top of the ministry.

I had lost so much weight, my teeth were destroyed by lack of brushing and too much coffee, I had developed a near-permanent sniper's squint, and I couldn't eat more than a morsel. But that didn't account for the ache in my stomach. My belly seemed to be able to hear the suffering and pain of the war. When people spoke, I heard them with my ears but with my guts, too. The biggest injury was to my heart. It was howling, day and night. I tried to be kind to it. I told my mind to respect my heart, to listen to it, because I had locked it away for so long and now that I had released it, it needed to scream and shout.

In a strange way, I found myself missing the front. My comrades. The narrow focus. The lack of choice. Now that I was no longer there, I felt the absence of war, the lack of a force pushing me through its narrow channels of exigency. I had the freedom to do what I wanted – the freedom, after all, for which I had fought. But I was unused to it. I was like a pilot sitting on the runway with the chance to fly anywhere but finding he had lost all feel for the controls. I had been at peace in war, I realised. Now I was at war in peace.

As I hesitated, I felt the weight of my experience begin to crush me. This war was not something we had planned. It had been imposed on us. It was a reality far bigger than our own. And now that I was able to look back at it, I was starting to sense the size of it and how its immensity might overwhelm everything that I was. Nor had I left the fighting entirely behind. Part of me, I knew, wanted to hold on to it. I wanted to feel that kinship with my comrades. I wanted my injuries to last to keep me sharp. And in Kobani, of course, I was still in the middle of a battlefield of which I knew every brick and every hole. All my instincts told me that the dark and quiet were merely a lull in the fighting. At any moment, a word or a gesture or a sound could transport me back to the front and I would be stuck there for hours at a time. I tried to convince myself that it was over. Then I tried not to try. But my body knew better. I was still at war. It raged inside me.

When I could, I took walks around Kobani. Looking around the streets, viewing all the destruction, I felt the old fury. Why would anyone choose to destroy my land as their way to heaven? How could anyone imagine vandalism as a path to paradise? They had wrecked our city. They had killed over a thousand of us, wounded another two thousand and sent hundreds of thousands more fleeing as refugees. I was angry that even one of these imbeciles might have died with the illusion that my bullets were sending them to a glorious afterlife. I didn't want them to think I was giving them anything but the pain they inflicted on us.

If I wasn't sleeping, which was often, I would walk at night. I had discovered so many new things in this war, things which I would not have absorbed in two hundred years of living, and like a curious child I found myself returning to the places of my learning. The war had been a cruel explosion of under-standing: what friendship means, what comrades are, what an enemy is, what it means to say 'our land' and 'our people' and 'life and death'. I went back to the cultural centre. I went to the girls' school. I went to the Black School. I went to Forty-Eighth Street and Mistenur Hill. I walked the rooftops and lay down in my old bases. I spoke to bricks, to houses, to streets, to broken doors and empty chairs. Sometimes I would see a person in the far distance and my finger would reach for a trigger and I would stay there for a while, remembering how I had lain in that place for three or four days, just watching and waiting for my shot.

But the city was mostly empty. My comrades were no longer there, nor ISIS, and I could walk freely in the streets. I developed the habit of lying down in the open and looking up at the night sky, trying to accustom myself to the calm and peace. And over the weeks and months of my wanderings, as I watched families start to return to their homes, I began to see that death had lost interest in Kobani and that maybe there was the possibility of something new. This was how it was when a place came back to life. This was how it felt to have the opportunity to live again. This is what it was to be reborn. One thing of which I was certain was that, from now on, I would live with deeper meaning. My understanding of life, people and family had changed. Fear, death, freedom and love would remain my closest confidants. And that knowledge, I was beginning to realise, could light my new path forward.

Many times I found myself returning to the city graveyard. The long lines of bodies buried next to each other seemed to insist on regular visits. I would read the names: who they were, how they had died, places and dates. There were so many I hadn't met. Young ones, old ones, men, women, children, all filling the earth. I would stay for hours, lying down between the graves, conversing with my comrades.

I had heard about survivor's guilt. I wasn't sure I had it, not exactly. Why I'd lived and why others had died – and what that said about me, that I could walk out of a war, that I was good at war – remained a mystery to me. My idea was that war was not really living. It was surviving by instinct, a sharpness that was more animal than human. Now that I was becoming human again, I could talk to my comrades as people too. I would tell them that I was still willing to die a hundred times for honour and respect, liberation and history, to live a life free from back-wardness and blind ideology. But I was also preparing myself for a different existence. It wasn't easy. I could feel that the souls of my comrades were at peace. I knew I was not.

I was out among the graves one day when I received a call telling me that Herdem had been shot. He had been leading an advance on a village where ISIS were still holding out. At one point, a breach opened up in their defences and Herdem jumped into it. He survived, as ever. But hours later, after that battle was won, Herdem walked into a house that he imagined to be empty and was confronted by two terrified ISIS fight-ers. They had hidden away during the fighting. I imagine it wouldn't have occurred to Herdem that anyone could be so cowardly. He took a single bullet in his upper right arm which passed through his lungs and heart before exiting through his other side.

Herdem's body was taken to a makeshift hospital in the city. I radioed Nasrin, who was on the southern front, and she came back immediately so that we could go together to see him. When we arrived, we found our fellow sniper Haroon already there. He had been close to Herdem. As they moved his body into the back of the truck, Haroon taped Herdem's black Dra-gunov to the bonnet.

By now a number of comrades had arrived and we set off in a procession from the hospital to the graveyard. Some of us fired guns in the air. After twenty minutes we arrived and I helped carry Herdem's body to a spare patch of ground at the end of a line of graves. We dug a trench for him in the yellow soil, then lowered him in. Once he was inside the grave, I helped the grave-diggers stack breezeblocks over his body to make a stone coffin.

It was my job to cover Herdem's head. As I was placing some bricks over the last few gaps, watching his face disappear, our last conversation came back to me. 'How can I send you to the front and rest back at headquarters?' Herdem had asked. Herdem had always done what he said, right up until his death. He met that commitment with his life. And it was Herdem who taught us that a bullet doesn't know addresses or colours or ages, or care whether you are a poor man or a president. He had accepted the fate that he knew awaited him. But as I heard his voice one more time, I broke down, splitting open right inside his grave. I cried and cried. They had to pull me out.

I sat there with Nasrin next to the hole as they filled it with earth and then, one by one, started to drift away. Eventually, the two of us stood up and walked back together into the city which, more than anyone, Herdem had helped to liberate.

TWENTY-THREE

Kobani,

July 2015 to April 2016

By now, thousands of Kobani's townspeople were pouring back into the city. There were shortages of everything: food, milk, petrol, blankets, doors, windows. There were also still thousands of mines, booby-traps and unexploded mortars lying around the city. Every day, someone would be killed by the presents ISIS had left behind, many of them children. Within a few weeks of my returning, the total number of civilians who had died this way stood at thirty-three. We were also steadily losing our mine-clearers: from an original squad of twenty-three we were down to four or five.

Many of the new arrivals were looking for loved ones who had fought in the war. Mothers looking for daughters, wives looking for husbands, brothers asking after brothers. People would see the devastation around them and understand that to search through such chaos might be fruitless. That just made them more desperate. Day after day, more came. Every hour we were in the office, Xhalo and I would find ourselves wading through another family tragedy. Xhalo would just look out at his town and cry. I found that the blood and the horror of conflict had prepared me for my new work. I would listen, then try to find out information on the missing from our martyrs' committee, or from the front, or from friends and comrades I knew. If we had luck, I would take these people out to the graveyard and show them where their lost ones lay. Often I couldn't help. Sometimes volunteers had died even before they had picked up a rifle, before anyone knew their name. Sometimes there was nothing left of them, or no one left alive who might have known what had happened to them. And we had no archive that had made it whole through the war. I would lead these families of the vanished to the section of the graveyard where the headstones were just marked with numbers and dates. There were hundreds of them. It was all I could do.

One time I accompanied a YPG committee to Qamishli and the old neighbourhood where I used to be an administrator. We were there to tell the mother of a comrade that her son had died. All the way there we struggled with the weight of the news we had to deliver.

When we arrived, at first the mother misunderstood our reason for coming, dropping everything she was doing to welcome us inside her home, so happy and excited to be visited by so many friends and comrades of her son. We sat there in silence while she busied herself making tea. Some of us looked at the ground. Some stared at this strong, bustling woman whose life we were about to ruin. None of us knew how to start. Then she sensed something. Her face fell and became white. She started shaking. The glasses of tea rattled and spilled in her hands. Finally, one of the comrades broke the silence.

'Your son has been martyred,' he said.

I was the youngest-looking among the group. After a while, the woman gathered herself, looked me in the eyes, took my hands and said, 'I wish the years my son never had to you. You live your life for him.'

*

Arriving with the returnees were hundreds of foreigners: activists from Spain, politicians from Germany, film-makers from Chile, journalists from America, France, the UK and China. It felt like another kind of assault, and at the office of foreign affairs I was on the frontline of it. The journalists were writing articles and essays, interviewing people, filming the city, asking us how it was, how we felt, if we had lost anyone, what age we were, how our friends had died and how to spell our names. Sometimes I would watch the international news on CNN and the BBC. They all seemed to be talking about Kobani.

I tried to be as efficient and courteous as possible, finding out who these people were and what they wanted, offering them a glass of tea, telling them brief details of a battle or two, then trying to send them on their way. Many of them would realise that I had spent time at the front. 'You are the one we need,' they would say.

I always refused to be interviewed, as did many of my comrades. From the beginning, I found it hard to respect the journalists. They professed to be fascinated by our bravery. Actually they just wanted to steal our stories. I found it disrespectful that they would appropriate our lives in this way and sell us as if we were commodities. They called us 'victims' or 'rebels' or even 'packages'. Everything we had done was, for them, the way they made a living. They would listen eagerly and write down every word but it was all just a brief assignment before they moved on to other people and other wars. When I saw their excitement as they listened to us, it wasn't because of what we had done or what we stood for. They were just happy to have copy. They found bloodshed thrilling or heroic, or even beautiful. They said our women snipers were 'cool' and 'hot'.

One journalist proposed sticking a tiny camera on my rifle and filming as I shot jihadis. It was obscene. What we had been through was terrible and ugly. It was not a movie. To me, most of these people seemed little more than thieves.

It all made me extremely nervous around journalists. I told them I did not have the time to talk, which was true, or that I didn't want to talk, which was also accurate. For most of two years I had done nothing but look for the enemy and try to figure out how to attack and how to defend. I found it difficult to talk to anyone who had not been directly affected by the war. It was impossible for me to be interested in problems such as live feeds and deadlines.

I also believed that the right to tell your own story, to get it right, to tell the truth as only you knew it and only you could know it, was a fundamental human freedom. In the end, I came to like some of these foreigners, those who approached me with the genuine intent of learning and sharing, and some of them even became friends. But telling my story was how I defined myself in the world. None of these people knew where we had been. They didn't know how we had fought street by street, house by house. They barely knew who we were. No one was going to tell that story for us. For them even to imagine they could only showed how little they knew.

One day a journalist who was trying to interview me asked me if I realised that the whole world had been looking at Kobani as we fought. His words confused me. In battle, we had had no sense of anything beyond the street where we were fighting. The war had filled everything. We had fought out of simple necessity, because this was our land for which we would die. And because I was there, that was what I did. 'This is what we were assigned to do,' I responded blankly. 'We did what we had to.'

But the journalist's words stayed with me. Over the months I stayed in Kobani, I began to see what we had done as historic. In one way or another, more than a hundred countries had lent us their support in our fight against ISIS. The coalition had been almost unprecedented, bringing together nations such as the US and Russia who were enemies elsewhere, and even Turkey and Iran, who were killing their own Kurds at the time. I began to understand that the entire planet had realised ISIS was a threat. ISIS was backward and repressive and against civilisation – and, until we had stopped them, they had posed a threat to every corner of the world. When they attacked Mosul, a city of two million, five hundred of them took it in twenty-four hours. No one felt able to withstand their rage. You had to be suicidal to face suicidal. Only the YPG and YPJ proved up to the task.

There was something else. ISIS had been born from the American prisons in Iraq. And when you looked at who later joined their ranks, many coalition countries shared the blame. By some counts, ISIS had forty thousand volunteers from one hundred and ten countries around the world, including America, Canada, Germany, Australia, Britain and, especially, France. Often the jihadis were misfits in their home countries, disregarded and marginalised, petty criminals and dropouts. They had felt shunned in these other countries, but ISIS had given them a community and a brotherhood. It had drugged them with religion. It had even fed them actual narcotics: we found bags of ecstasy, heroin, cocaine and other drugs in the positions we captured from them. These countries had washed their hands of these feral, unwanted children. It had fallen to us to deal with their failure. No wonder the whole world appreciated what we had done. They owed us.

That didn't detract from the nobility of our fight. We had stood firm for enlightenment and principle, honesty and freedom. It had cost us dearly. But it had been the making of so many, too. I had seen this myself: how a weak character could become a strong commander. Our people had found themselves in this cause. And it was fascinating to me, how something born of catastrophe and from a small group of young Kurds committing themselves to a set of principles could be such an example to the world. Maybe, I thought, the war in Kobani had lit the beacon for Rojava.

Besides the journalists, there were thousands of other foreigners who came to see us: activists, actors, anarchists, artists, ecologists, economists, feminists, musicians, philosophers, political scientists, sociologists and writers. They saw us as revolutionaries of hope. They wanted to find out more about the ideas that inspired us. They wanted to stand next to us and against what was wrong.

That, too, was good. Ideas don't have a nationality. You don't have to be Russian to be a socialist, Greek to be a democrat or Tibetan to be a Buddhist. Ideas spread. People discover themselves in them. I had. When I first read Apo's books, I had been living in Britain long enough that I was not really Kurdish any more. I had come to recognise people, not race. I judged character. I valued ideas. When all these people arrived in Kobani, I felt I already knew why. Our philosophy is different from any other – how we view history, our ideas about democracy, feminism and anarchism, our attempt to be as close as is practically possible to real freedom. This is why others travelled so far to stand with us. Our principles had given me a sense of who I was, and they were doing the same for them. The appeal of Apo's ideas was not limited by border or race.

Many of the new arrivals became involved in our social, political, economic and media work, helping us to build our new society. Some of them fought with us, too. In the end, we received around four hundred military volunteers, from revolutionaries to former soldiers. Many had fought jihadis in Iraq or Afghanistan and Pakistan. They would say, 'Our governments should be doing more.' They had lost people, close friends, and they had come back to fight the same enemy again. Once we received a full team of five Americans: a BKC operator, an RPG man, a rifleman, a sniper and a medic. They had fought together in Iraq and now they had come to fight in Rojava. Another time, seventeen foreign volunteers arrived at once, including one man from Ukraine and another from China.

Of course, a few of them were adventurers, lost, loud people with big muscles looking for some new way for the world to see them. Some of them had been influenced by propaganda in their own countries: they told us proudly that they were there to kill Muslims. I would make these people wait a few weeks before I let them go to the front. Over that time I would see them change from wannabe killers to fellow comrades in a movement that wasn't so much against a group of jihadis as it was for a new way of living. I think the revelation, for them, was that we were not some mighty army of warriors but a group of volunteers standing up for our beliefs. Most of them also turned out to be decent people who had left their homes, friends and families, and comfortable, safe lives, to cross mountains, oceans and deserts to fight against injustice, cruelty and brutality. I gave them a phone and a laptop to share among themselves and insisted they call home every fortnight. When they wanted to leave, I gave them money for a ticket. Even if they hadn't achieved much, just by being there they were serving a purpose. Millions of Kurds had run away from their oppressors and their homeland. They were amazed to see foreigners fighting for them. It shamed them that they were trying to leave for Europe. It made many of them think again.

A number of these brave men and women died alongside us. One was Keith Broomfield, the American to whom Herdem had introduced me. In the few months he was with us, Keith built a reputation as a great sniper and a hard worker. He was shot by an ISIS sniper in early June 2015. My respect for his sacrifice is beyond words, not least because Keith never lived to see the change for which he fought. We named the foreign volunteers' headquarters in Kobani after him.

There was another, older volunteer called Gunter Helsten. Gunter was fifty-five and had served in the German army and the French Foreign Legion, for whom he had commanded troops in Africa and Asia. 'For all those years, I was fighting for governments and for business people – for money,' he said. 'Eventually I came to understand that as a soldier, my duty was to protect women and children. So I stopped.'

When he read about us, Gunter put his house in Luxembourg in his sixteen-year-old son's name and travelled to Kurdistan to help us. He said he wasn't there to fight against ISIS but to stand shoulder to shoulder with the Kurds. He was a disciplined and principled man who would wake up every morning at half past four to take a cold shower. He told me that when his son's class had been asked to write about their hero, his boy had written about him – who he was, what he was doing and how his son had taken a long time to understand why he was doing it – and had won a prize for his essay. You never saw a father so proud.

Because of Gunter's experience, Tolin asked him to set up a military training academy. Gunter agreed but eventually went to the front when the supplies he needed were delayed. In early 2016 he was killed while taking part in an operation to take the last village held by ISIS on the border between Syria and Iraq, a successful advance which split ISIS' forces into two tiny strongholds. When I heard the news, I felt like I had lost an older brother.

*

Through the end of 2015 and into 2016, Kobani was coming back to life. We had workers cleaning the city, clearing away the bodies and moving debris off the streets. A group of British de-miners from the Mines Advisory Group arrived. They collected an enormous pile of explosives and ordnance, dumped it all in an area they dug outside the city the size of a small football pitch, and detonated it.

The more normal life became, the more I found that I was troubled by it. Instinctively, I wanted Kobani to stay as it was, as a museum and a tribute to my fallen friends and comrades. I hadn't known the town before the war. I only knew it as a battleground, a place of dust and blood, and people in green and black. For thousands of us, this place had been our whole lives. For the dead, these ruins would be everything they would ever know. It was a shock to realise that the debris would all soon be cleared away and that any memory of what had happened here would begin to fade.

I wasn't the only one who felt like that. One afternoon I went to see the site of an old battle, a building where I had lain for days, and I found a young couple with a baby busy cleaning what remained. 'Are you here to see the house?' the man asked, unprompted. It seemed he had already been visited by several other comrades returning to the scene of the fight.

I looked inside their home. There were no windows, no doors, no locks, no fridge, no oven, and out in the garden the flowers and trees were dead. Everything they knew had been destroyed. The young man and his wife had tried to live in the camps but said they found it too hard. They had come back to their home and, although nothing was what it had been, they said they preferred it. 'In the camps, we never knew what was happening,' the woman said. 'We could hear the explosions. We couldn't sleep. At least now we can see what has happened.'

The couple, I realised, had come back to rebuild their memories. They couldn't bear to see what the place had become. And, of course, they were right to do so. We needed people to come home and reconstruct so that normal life could resume. But there was no escaping the fact that in order to restore their world they would have to destroy mine. In the end it was decided that the cultural centre and a few nearby blocks should be preserved as they were when I knew them. They stand there to this day, wrecks in the middle of the city, a piece of battlefield into which people can step and walk around and smell the dust into which so many of us bled.

One day I received the news that Yildiz had been killed in the mountains. Turkey considers any mountain Kurd they find actually living in those mountains to be a terrorist. A Turkish warplane was said to have spotted the truck in which she and a group of nine other YPJ fighters were travelling to a training camp and attacked it. None of them, we were told, survived.

Of our original group of five snipers, only Nasrin and I remained alive. Nasrin was still at the front. In my grief at Yildiz's loss, I suggested to Tolin that I return to fight alongside her.

'You're looking for an easy job?' she replied.

I must have looked stunned.

'You'd be running away from this important new duty,' said Tolin. 'This is your new battleground, dealing with these people, helping them, fixing things. Is it that you think this war cannot go on without you? Do you think you are the only one who can save us?'

Tolin, I recognise now, was trying to save me from the habit of war. At first, the fighting had been terrifying. When I first shot someone and saw them die, I had nightmares for weeks. But the second time I killed someone, I had maybe one or two dreams; the third time I had one; by the fifth, there were none. Like anything, you adapt to killing. It can even become an addiction. Tolin could see the front was calling to me. She knew that if I answered the call, I might finally lose my humanity. 'If you just fight at the front without understanding, it doesn't matter what you achieve there,' she told me. 'You will end up as nothing more than a killer, a criminal. Yes, you will be fighting ISIS. But you will be just as trapped as they are.'

Our movement was only too aware of the dangers of comrades becoming addicted to fighting and had a programme to deal with it. Even the most senior commanders would be sent back from the front and asked to take charge of a small village. The idea was to remember normal life and everyday things. I began to practise my own version of this process, visiting the villages outside Kobani. The people would talk about goats and vegetables. I expected it to be dull. But when I was there, I found it so pleasurable. All these emotions wrapped up in something so small – there was something simple, beautiful and profound about it. I discovered I could keep my fierce principles – beliefs I was ready to die for – without having to ignore life. These people were who I had been as a boy growing up with my family in Sardasht. I loved to hear the mothers talking about how they made yoghurt and tomato puree. They were perfectionists, and there was wisdom, calculation and planning in everything they did.

Later, when I returned to Europe and to Leeds, I would remember these villages. Watching my friends becoming excited about what clothes they wore and what TV channel or film to watch and slapping each other on the back as they enjoyed a meal, I would tell myself that their happiness was beautiful, and the common ground on which all people can come together. This was life. War was something else. The only good reason to fight, really, was to allow people in Kurdish villages or northern British cities or anywhere else to live as they wanted, as they always had, as they chose to.

I spent a year in Kobani. At the end of my time there, I began to think of writing my story. When I talked to journalists, they would encourage me. I also remembered the words of the husband of my teacher in Leeds and how he said I could become a writer one day.

When it came to why we fought, our thoughts had always been as clear as a mountain stream. For me, it was the result of a simple quest for freedom that started when I was a boy. I had wanted what any human being wants: to live with honour and dignity. The search led me to some dark places. I had to confront the most malevolent and misguided men. I had to watch so many friends die. But maybe telling the story of Kobani was a way to make the sacrifice serve a wider purpose. For decades, Turkish and Iranian propaganda had made it so hard for us to be heard. But Kobani earned us worldwide respect. In forty years we had not achieved the kind of recognition that we did from those five months. The reason Kobani connected with people was, I think, because such a pure story of free will offered them powerful and universal inspiration. Because being right didn't always mean winning. The good and progressive does not inevitably triumph over the bad and backward. We had to make sure it did. And perhaps there is no more meaningful and moving story than a never-say-die struggle for human freedom.

TWENTY-FOUR

Silemani, Frankfurt, Brussels and Leeds,
2016–2018

I left Kobani one morning in April 2016. I took off my green
trousers and jacket and pulled on some jeans and a T-shirt. It
made my head spin. I was removing the uniform that had given
us such pride and honour and stepping into the uniform of
civilians the world over.

It was in something of a daze that I retraced the journey
I had made two and a half years before, crossing back into
Iraq, following the Tigris past Mosul and Kirkuk, until eventually I arrived at Silemani. My plan was to spend some time
in the city to recover. I still hadn't gained much weight, my
teeth were bad and I wasn't sleeping more than an hour a
night. After a few months in Silemani, I planned to travel on to
Europe.

In Silemani, I began to wonder whether I could ever settle
back into life in Britain. South Kurdistan already felt like another planet. Kurdish friends tried to give me bodyguards and
a pistol – ISIS assassins might have been operating in the area
– but I refused. I had an idea about passing my days in coffee
shops or sitting on a park bench, smelling the kebabs at the

roadside stalls and listening to the voices from the fruit market and the sound of birds in the trees.

But I overestimated my ability to blend in. I looked too old and too serious for my thirty-two years. When I walked down a street, I had a very stiff and deliberate way of stepping and I was always scanning for sniper holes and nests and vantage points. In a city of yellow stone houses and cafés on leafy squares, surrounded by towering green mountains, I found myself instinctively drawn to the best places from which to defend it.

My interactions with people were also a disaster. Walking into the city market, I would become overwhelmed by all the information I was picking up with my eyes and ears. When I tried to talk to people, I found I had no answer when they asked me how I was. When I lied and said I was looking for work, I could see them wondering what kind of work I did, exactly. I saw the same look when I walked into a restaurant or came to pay the bill. It was fear. I resolved to say as little as possible. I watched the way they drank grape juice from a glass and how they played with their coffee spoons and tried to copy them. I tried to talk the way they talked. But the way I stared at them just worried people even more, and when I shook their hand, it was like they could feel my true nature through my skin. I wondered if I would always be like this: the man who carried so much death with him that people shivered when he passed by.

In December, I flew to Frankfurt, Germany. Rojava's representatives in Europe had organised for a family to pick me up from the airport. They took me home, then the next day to one of the floating cafés on the river in the city. That was when the mother, Hekmat, told me her son had died in the war. She said she had two more sons in the YPG. She showed me a picture. It was Tolhildan.

Hekmat was the mother who had tried to save her son from the war and whom Tolhildan had forsworn, vowing the only way he would leave Kobani was in a box. In fact, Tolhildan had survived the city only to be shot dead weeks later in the villages. He had always been one of the fighters I most admired and his death had floored me. Now that I was in his mother's presence, the memories came flooding back so strongly – his face, his voice – that I had to leave.

I walked up the riverbank and sat on the grass next to the water. Everybody was going about their ordinary day. I sat in the middle of them, my mind filled with bodies and gunfire and battle. I was back in Kobani. Everything was returning to me so thickly that I didn't notice Hekmat's approach. She sat next to me and hugged me.

After a while, I told her a few things about her son. About when the Hummer came and how her son had stopped it. How disciplined he was. How old he looked.

Hekmat looked up at me and smiled. 'I am happy because I can still smell him on you,' she said.

Tolhildan's mother dropped me at the station and I took the train to Brussels, where there was another family to meet me. I felt even less at home in this city. It was a freezing-cold, grey European winter. I couldn't bear to be outside for more than a few minutes. I also found I couldn't taste the food. The cucumbers and tomatoes, all grown in greenhouses and packaged in plastic, had no substance to them. I began to lose my appetite again.

But finally, with the help of a few European friends I had met in Kobani, I began writing. That work continued when I moved back to Leeds in the autumn of 2017 and for the next year after that. It wasn't easy. Just as it would take time to stitch so many pieces of myself back together, so I realised it would take a couple of years to write down all my thoughts in a way that made sense.

It wasn't that my thoughts were disordered. My story, and the story of so many of us, was a straight line that ran directly from the moment when we first stood up against injustice. In my case, my journey had taken me from my childhood across the Middle East and Europe only for me to reverse course and travel back to my land to fight with my people in Kobani. And now I had seen free Kurdistan. No longer was our freedom a place in our imagination or on a few ancient maps. Now I knew it as a land across which I had walked.

The story of my people was just as linear. After resisting injustice and oppression for centuries, we had wrested our freedom from the hands of others. Kobani unified the Kurds from Turkey, Syria, Iraq and Iran. It also briefly unified the world behind us. And there was no reversing that moment. Finally, the Kurds were establishing themselves as a people. After Kobani, the idea of Kurdish freedom was alive again. Our destiny was once more our own.

I regretted more than anyone that it took calamity to bring us all together. But that we had triumphed over such suffering, that so few had stood with forty-year-old guns against so many with so much money and the best military equipment, and won – that made anything possible. While the battle for Kobani raged, in Turkey tens of thousands of Kurds began an uprising that continues to this day. In East Kurdistan, there were protests and uprisings, including days of clashes in Sardasht. In Iraq,

Kurdish authorities briefly created a stable society in the north. There were setbacks, of course, such as in late 2017 when the Kurds in northern Iraq lost much of their territory again in an Iraqi–Iranian advance, and in early 2018 when Turkey linked up with the jihadis in Afrin in southwest Kurdistan and bombed our forces from the air as the Islamists advanced on the ground. But for the first time, these counter-attacks felt desperate and, ultimately, in vain. In Rojava, the Kurds had established their sovereignty for the first time in thousands of years. Even if the place was one day overrun and swallowed up, there was no erasing it from people's minds. It couldn't be undone. It would endure for ever. I, and thousands of others, would make sure of it.

Crucially, this was no mere triumph of one nation or race over another, as so often happened in the Middle East. This was the emergence of a new stable and peaceful social order, a stateless, autonomous democracy blind to race, religion or gender, based on self-determination, a communal economy and harmony with the environment. Rojava was unique. It was democracy with a vengeance, and it quickly became an example to the Middle East and beyond.

This new world was symbolised, above all, by the idea of a free woman. Women were the vanguard of the revolution and the mothers guiding the birth of our new world. They had fought ISIS. They would defend Rojava against its enemies in Turkey, Syria, Iraq and Iran in the struggles to come. And if women were our warriors, Kobani was our proof that liberation was vital and enduring. Our people had tasted freedom, nothing could take that away, and word of our achievement was echoing out around the world. Over there, they do not live like us. Our dictators' days are numbered. In that place they call Rojava, the people are finally free.

*

I speak to my family from time to time these days. They seem well. My father always gave me his opinion and I know he would never have let me leave if he'd known where I would go and what I would become. But he also always let me have my independence and I think he has made his peace with my life as a revolutionary.

He and my mother know I will continue to fight for our cause. Since they are watched and their phones are listened to, neither of them can tell me what they think of my choices. But I do know that when they were visited by the Iranian authorities one day, my mother shouted gleefully at them, 'He is not a child, he is a free man. Catch him if you can!'

I know my parents would like me to start a family. It is not an ambition I can allow myself. One of the reasons we fought and died was to build a new world in which patriarchy, marriage and tradition are replaced by a commitment between soul-mates to share their lives. But unless you possess that one place where you can love and sleep and wake safely in the morning, unless you have a home, everything else must wait. Most of us are still foreigners where we live. We don't have that safe place where we can exist freely and raise our children with honour and integrity. I hope that won't always be the case. But for now, like forty-five million other Kurds, I am still waiting for a home.

From time to time I receive news from Kurdistan. Tolin still commands our forces in Rojava. Serhad fights on. We used to joke that to walk unwounded out of Kobani would be shameful, but Haqi has taken that to new heights with his fourth set of injuries. He, too, remains a commander on the frontline. Janiwar, who had never thought to pick up a gun before war came to Kobani, lives still in his home town with his wife and son. Nasrin has stepped back from the fighting for now to study politics and ideology in the YPJ academy. One day, after years of living with Yildiz's death, I was stunned to be told by some old friends that she had survived the air attack in which I heard she had died. She was badly injured, but after a few weeks of recuperation she, too, had resumed her duties.

I have taken up ice-skating again, something I first learned on the frozen ponds around Sardasht. I have also started visiting my old friend Shina, who, after years living underground in Iran, was eventually granted asylum in Britain and moved to Scotland. We go walking and camping and fishing in the mountains around Ben Nevis. It reminds us of the old days in Kurdistan. Somehow those paths feel more familiar than the streets of Leeds whose layout, to my surprise, I am having to learn a second time. It is almost as though my brain has jettisoned anything from the years when I drifted away from the movement. I find myself wondering how I could have really lived like that. A car, a flat, a shopping centre, a supermarket. It does not seem like me at all.

I always walked for the feeling of liberation it gave me, but these days I find it also stills my mind. It will take a lifetime to come to terms with the cost of Kobani. How that city was ruined. How many of us died. How many we killed. The lives I took myself. I have never strayed from the conviction that it was worth it, but that doesn't stop me from measuring the price.

Lately, I've found my mind goes back to a day, soon after Tolin sent me back from the front, when I was walking around the ruins, retracing my steps as I remembered the battles we'd fought. On that day, I went to the house where I had destroyed that beautiful Italian marble kitchen to make a platform to lie on. When I arrived, there was an old man there. He looked at me.

'You know my house?' he asked me.

'Yes,' I said. 'I fought here. For two weeks. I built this huge platform on your top floor.'

Now that I saw the man, I remembered the extent to which I had destroyed his home to build my nest. I had ripped down an antenna from the roof. I made holes in the walls. I stuck pipes in the floor. I ripped a door off its hinges. I brought blankets and mattresses out of the bedroom and put those on top of the door and tied the whole platform together with scarves. I used everything. I wrecked it all.

The old man took me upstairs, to the fourth floor, where I saw that everything was the same as I had left it.

'I keep it as a memory of what happened in my house,' he said.

'I built it,' I told him.

'Why did you need it?' he asked. 'What are the holes in the walls for?'

I explained to the old man about corridors and line of sight and my system of holes. 'I shot somebody here,' I said, pointing through one opening in the wall. 'And I shot somebody over there.'

The old man nodded. We descended the stairs to the kitchen. There were the broken marble counters and the sink that I had destroyed. The old man's wife was there. I could tell the kitchen had been important to her.

'You know, it was me who broke your beautiful kitchen,' I said.

'You must stay and have a coffee in this kitchen,' she replied.

Immediately I was consumed by guilt at the knowledge that I had taken her best coffee cups upstairs to use for drinking and dampening my shooting holes.

The old woman saw the look on my face. 'You didn't break everything,' she reassured me.

She found three cups, we drank our coffee, and I tried to tell her and her husband something about the war. But it was hard, and the old lady could see that I was embarrassed about what I had done to her home.

After a while she leaned over to me and patted me on the knee.

'You didn't break my house,' she said. 'You saved it.'

ACKNOWLEDGEMENTS

This book is the product of several years of writing, rewriting, reporting and re-reporting, and that it exists at all is due to the shared efforts of a wide cast of volunteers. First among them is Heval Tolin and Heval Haqi, my commanders in Rojava, and my friends. They not only saved me from myself innumerable times on the battlefield but also understood why I wanted to tell this story and excused me from duty for three months so that I could return to the scenes of the fighting and talk to others who were there with me. Today, Tolin and Haqi remain on the frontline fighting for Rojava and Kurdistan. It is their commitment and the determination of thousands like them that will ensure that one day we will have our freedom.

Also in Rojava, I need to thank my comrades Kazm, Roni, Baran and Koma for their assistance, and Santiago, Fouad Yassin and Salaam Amin, who first encouraged me to start writing. As a first-time writer, I leant on the expertise and support of many. Francesca Couchi helped me write my first chapter in Silemani and was always there to listen and offer insightful advice. Alba Sottorra Clua from Catalonia, who listened to my

251

stories, coached me in structure and offered a critical review of the text. Jan Fermon in Belgium provided crucial legal advice. Anina Jendreyko in Switzerland and Narinder Khroud were generous with their views. Very special thanks is due to Renée In der Maur from the Netherlands, who I first met in Kobani in the first months after the war and who has always been there to help, teaching me basic computer literacy, setting aside weeks to help me with a proposal and reviewing all my drafts. For their generous welcomes, food, sympathetic ears, and spare rooms and sofas, I owe a great debt to Chia, Kamaran and Jyan, Himn and Azadeh, Rebwar, Nawzad and Farzaneh, and Delil in Brussels.

In New York, Servan Emiriki and Sue Hodson offered early support and corrective advice on my first poor attempt at a proposal. Virginia Marx offered early, insightful advice and made the connection to Patrick Walsh at Pew Literary, who became my agent. To Patrick and John Ash, I owe an unfathomable debt for seeing the potential in this book, championing it to the literary world and speedily assembling the large cast who have seen it through to publication around the world with integrity and great skill. In particular, Alex Perry, to whom Patrick introduced me, invested himself deeply and intensely in the formidable task of writing this book, putting himself entirely aside to melt into my story and find the voice and language to tell it. I am proud to say we now call each other 'brother', and he has my deepest respect and thanks.

I should also thank Morgan Entrekin, Brenna McDuffie and Alison Malecha at Grove Atlantic in New York for engaged and pinpoint editing. Paul Murphy at Orion in London offered generous encouragement and eagle-eyed reviews of the text, and Daniel Balado's copy-edit was extraordinary: precise, and brilliantly improving. I took great heart, too, from the early support of Margit Ketterle and Iris Forster at Droemer Knaur in Munich, Cristina Foschini at Mauri Spagnol and Giuseppe Strazzeri at Longanesi in Milan, Tom Harmsen at Uitgever in Amsterdam and my publishers at Kobunsha in Japan.

There are many more who are due my deepest and sincerest thanks but who, because of the way they might be treated by our enemies, must remain anonymous. My gratitude is only delayed, until we meet again and I can express it in person.

WEDDING IN
DARLING DOWNS

BY
LEAH MARTYN

KT-163-749

MILLS & BOON®

First published in Great Britain 2010
Harlequin Mills & Boon Limited,
Eton House, 18-24 Paradise Road, Richmond, Surrey TW9 1SR

© Leah Martyn 2010

ISBN: 978 0 263 87905 6

Harlequin Mills & Boon policy is to use papers that are natural, renewable and recyclable products and made from wood grown in sustainable forests. The logging and manufacturing process conform to the legal environmental regulations of the country of origin.

Printed and bound in Spain
by Litografia Rosés, S.A., Barcelona

'I th

Emma swallowed. Her heart tripped. He was bending towards her, his blue eyes capturing hers with an almost magnetic pull. 'I…'

ght about me too?' he murmured hopefully.

ad. She couldn't deny it. But would it help either of if she told him that? Did she need the complication mission would undoubtedly bring?

cian leaned closer to her, slowly.

nma…' he said, his voice low in this last second before kiss.

r mouth trembled. She lifted her gaze and stared at n, mesmerised by the yearning she saw in his eyes. The re to be kissed by him was irresistible, and before she ld second-guess the wisdom of it all she was leaning him.

clan took her face in his hands, his need materialising he softest sigh before his mouth found hers. The kiss d through his blood, and raw need slammed into him nothing he had ever known before.

ma clung to him and the kiss deepened, turned nching and wild. She felt a need inside her, an whelming need to be touched and held by him.

it wasn't going to go that far. At least not today. felt Declan pulling back, breaking the kiss slowly, y, his lips leaving a shivering sweetness like trails of stantial gossamer.

g beat of silence while they collected themselves.

we broken every rule in the official partnership ha ook?' Declan asked, wrapping her closer.

She licked her lips. 'Possibly…probably.'

Leah Martyn loves to create warm, believable characters for the Mills & Boon® Medical™ Romance series. She is grounded firmly in rural Australia, and the special qualities of the bush are reflected in her stories. For plots and possibilities she bounces ideas off her husband on their early-morning walks. Browsing in bookshops and buying an armful of new releases is high on her list of enjoyable things to do.

Recent titles by the same author:

OUTBACK DOCTOR, ENGLISH BRIDE
THE DOCTOR'S PREGNANCY SECRET
A MOTHER FOR HIS BABY

WEDDING IN DARLING DOWNS

CHAPTER ONE

IT WAS winter. Early morning. And cold.

Emma burrowed her chin more deeply into the roll-collar of her fleece as she jogged the last of the way home across the park.

The cawing of a crow disturbed the peace. Emma slowed her step and looked about her. She loved this time before sun-up. The moist atmosphere never failed to lift her spirits. And heaven knew she could do with a bit of that. Mist was every-where, as translucent and filmy as a bridal veil. It seemed to have a life of its own, breathing up from the earth, softening the stark winter outlines of the trees.

Emma clicked back into the present, regaining her momentum. She hadn't time to be indulging in fanciful thoughts. Another long day at the surgery loomed. But time for Kingsholme to keep functioning as a viable medical practice was running out. Her father's sudden death almost three months ago had left Emma in disarray. Both personally and professionally. If she didn't line up another partner quickly, the medical practice that had been founded by her grandfather would have to close. One lone doctor, namely *her*, couldn't hope to generate enough income to keep the place functioning.

The end result would be for the practice and the beautiful old home that encompassed it to go under the auctioneer's hammer.

The new owner, perhaps someone with an eye to the tourist potential of the district, would probably turn it into a bed and breakfast. And their little town would be left without a resident medical officer.

Emma's spirits plummeted to a new low. The nerves in her stomach began knotting up again.

I *should* be able to get a doctor interested enough to work here, she berated herself. Even a decent locum who could fill the gap until a suitable partner came along. Perhaps her interviewing technique was all wrong. The few people who had actually showed, had taken one look at the set-up and promptly, if a bit awkwardly, fled.

Lifting the latch on the back gate, she made her way along the path and ran quickly up the steps to the verandah. She had time for a shower and marginally less time for breakfast. And then she'd better open the surgery and start seeing patients.

In her consulting room later, Emma threw her pen aside and lifted her arms in a long stretch. It had been another crazy morning. She couldn't go on like this. She just couldn't…

A soft tap sounded on her door before it opened. 'Moira—' Emma managed a passable smile for the practice manager '—come to tell me it's lunch time already?'

Moira Connelly, who'd been with the practice for at least twenty years, came into the room and closed the door. She looked pointedly at Emma's untouched cup of tea and the half-eaten muffin and clucked a motherly concern. 'You don't eat enough, Emma.'

Emma lifted a shoulder in a resigned shrug. 'I'll be out in a tick. Perhaps we could open a can of soup for lunch.'

'I'll manage something.' Moira flapped a hand in dismissal. 'Actually, I came to tell you there's a Dr Declan O'Malley here to see you.'

A sudden light leapt into Emma's green eyes. 'Has he come about the job?'

Moira shook her head. 'Apparently, he knew your dad.'

'Oh—' Emma bit her lips together, the grief she felt still raw and unchannelled.

Moira paused, pulling the edges of her cardigan more closely together, as if warding off a sudden chill. 'I expect he wants to offer his condolences.'

'I guess so…' Emma's short ray of hope faded into a heavy sigh. 'Give me a minute, please, Moira and then ask Dr O'Malley to come through.'

Emma watched the door close behind Moira and then swung off her chair and went to stand at the picture window, looking out. She imagined this Dr O'Malley was a contemporary of her father's from Melbourne. In earlier times Andrew Armitage had forged a rather distinguished medical career before the call of *home* had brought him back here to the town of Bendemere on the picturesque Darling Downs in Queensland.

Emma had spent holidays here, been happy here. So it had seemed only natural to come flying home when her world had fallen apart. Her return had coincided with the resignation of her father's practice partner. Emma had stepped in, proud to work alongside her father. In the past year she'd begun to pull the shattered bits of her life together until it was almost making a whole picture again.

Then her father had suffered a massive heart attack, leaving her to cope alone.

Declan O'Malley prowled the reception area. In a few seconds he'd know whether Emma Armitage would welcome his visit or tell him to go to hell. God, he hoped she'd be reasonable. The situation demanded she be reasonable.

'Oh, Dr O'Malley—' Moira fluttered back into reception. 'Sorry to keep you waiting. Emma was just finishing up.' She waved towards an inner corridor. 'Second door on your left.'

'Thanks.' Declan acknowledged the information with a slight lifting of his hand. He paused outside what was obviously Emma's consulting room, took a deep breath, gave a courtesy knock to warn of his imminent entry, and then moved in with every intention of being at his diplomatic best.

Emma turned from the window. Her throat dried. Every molecule in her body felt as though it had been swiftly rearranged. She'd been expecting a man in her father's age group, a man in his sixties. But Declan O'Malley in no way fitted that description. He looked in the prime of his life, all six feet of him. Mentally roping off the very mixed emotions she felt, she went forward and offered her hand. 'Dr O'Malley.'

'Emma.' Declan ditched formality, enfolding her hand easily within his own. 'Your father told me such a lot about you.'

Well, it's more than he told me about *you*, Emma thought, blinking several times in quick succession, long lashes swooping against her pale cheeks.

'I can imagine what a difficult time this must be for you.' Declan's words filled an uncomfortable gap. 'I would have been in touch before this but I've been out of the country. I've just caught up with things in general.'

She nodded. His voice was deep and resonant. Smooth like red wine. Emma could feel its impact like a thump to her chest, momentarily disarming her. 'Please... have a seat.' She indicated a conversation area in front of the big bay window.

As they settled, Emma took several quick, all-encompassing peeks at him, recording short finger-combed dark hair, a lean face, strong features, olive complexion. And blue eyes reflecting a vivid intensity that could see things she didn't want seen...

Declan looked at the woman he had to deal with here. Emma Armitage was strikingly lovely. She had amazing facial bones and her hair looked cornsilk-soft, blonde and straight, just brushing her shoulders. But it was her eyes that drew him. They were green like the deepest part of the forest, framed within thick tawny lashes. And they were accessing him warily. He had to step carefully here. He didn't want to embarrass her, hurt her. But he'd come on a mission and, somehow, he had to accomplish it.

But how to begin?

'So, how come you knew my father?' In a lightning strike, Emma took the initiative.

Declan refused to be put on the back foot; instead he cut to the chase. 'When I was an intern at St John Bosco's in Melbourne, your father was my boss. I'm where I am today in medicine because of Andrew. In the early days of my training, I was ready to chuck it. Oh, boy was I ready! But your dad talked me out of it. He was an amazing man.'

A new loneliness stabbed through Emma's heart. 'Yes, he was...'

A pause. Awkward. Until Declan resumed gently, 'Over the years I kept in touch with your dad. Any career-change I considered, I ran it past him first. He was my mentor and I considered him my *friend*. And I don't use the word lightly.'

Emma nodded, swallowing past the lump in her throat. 'I appreciate your taking the time to come here.' Her mouth compressed as if shutting off the flow of emotion. 'You must be very busy in your own practice.'

'I'm between jobs, actually. That's another reason why I'm here.'

Emma straightened in her chair, the oddest feeling of unease slithering up her backbone. 'I don't understand.'

Declan's perceptions whipped into high awareness. Something in her eyes and the defensive little tilt of her chin held him back from explaining further. The last thing he needed was for her to start resenting him before they could speak properly. So, softly-softly. 'Uh...this could take a while.' He glanced briefly at his watch. 'Could we perhaps have a spot of lunch somewhere and talk?'

Emma held back a harsh laugh. He just had no idea. 'I don't have time to go out to lunch, Dr O'Malley. Patients will be arriving soon for the afternoon surgery.'

'You're the sole practitioner?'

'Yes,' she said, thinking that was another story in itself.

He'd assumed she'd have engaged a locum, but obviously not. Declan thought quickly. Emma Armitage had a brittle-

ness about her—she was obviously worked to death. He
cursed his lack of foresight and sought to remedy it swiftly.
'Understood.' He gave a brief shrug. 'I'm here and available.
Put *me* to work.'

So, what was he saying? That he'd share her patient list?
Emma's eyes widened. She didn't want to be blunt but she had
only this man's word he was a competent doctor. First and
foremost, she had a duty of care to her patients... She turned
her head slightly, raising a hand to sweep her loose fair hair
away from her neck. 'Is that a good idea, do you think?'

Declan sat riveted. Her little restive movement had briefly
exposed her nape, with skin as tender and sweet as a baby's.
He tried without success to dismiss the unexpected zip of
awareness through his gut. What was the question again?
Idiot. Got it. 'Sorry.' He gave an apologetic twist of his hand.
'You'll need some ID.' Reaching back, he took out his wallet
and spun it open in front of her. 'Driver's licence.'

Emma nodded, registering that the photo on the licence
matched the face of the man sitting opposite her. So he was
who he claimed he was.

'My card as well.' He held out the buff-coloured business
card towards her.

Frowning a bit, Emma took it, almost dazzled by the impressive array of letters after his name. 'You completed your
orthopaedic speciality in Edinburgh, Scotland?'

His hesitation was palpable. Then he said, 'Yes. It was
always the discipline I felt drawn to.'

She handed the licence back with the ghost of a smile but
retained his card. 'Should I be addressing you as Professor
O'Malley, then?'

'I wouldn't think so.' In a second his eyes were filled with
unfathomable depth and shadows. 'Declan will do just fine.
So—' he slid his wallet back into his pocket '—going to let
me loose on your patients, then?'

'Why wouldn't I?' Emma felt a curious lightening of her
spirits. To be able to share her workload, even for a few hours,

would be wonderful. 'I'll give you the ones who like a good chat.'

'I guess I asked for that.' Declan's look was rueful and he uncurled to his feet. 'I'll grab a burger somewhere and my bag and be back in—' he checked his watch '—twenty minutes?'

Swept along by his enthusiasm, Emma stood hastily. 'Take whatever time you need.' She began to usher him out. 'You can use Dad's consulting room.'

Declan stopped, looked down at her, his expression closed. 'If you're sure?'

Emma nodded, leading him down the corridor to the room next to her own. She opened the door and went in.

Declan followed hesitantly. Soft early afternoon light streamed in through the windows, leaving a dappled pattern across the large desk and the big leather chair behind it. A big chair for a big man, Declan thought. A man with a big heart that had in the end let him down far earlier than it should have.

'It's been cleaned but basically everything is as Dad left it.' Emma moved across to touch the tips of her fingers to the rosewood patina of the desktop.

Declan felt emotion drench him. Yet he knew what he felt at the man's loss was only a fraction of what his daughter must be feeling. He spun to face her, questioning softly, 'Are you sure about this, Emma?'

'Quite sure. It will be good to see the place being used again.' The words were husky, as though she was pushing them through a very tight throat.

Declan wanted to reach out to her. Hold her close. Feel the press of her body against his. Take her grief into himself... Oh, for crying out loud! He cleared his throat. 'I'll see you back here, then, in a half-hour or so.'

'Feel free to come straight through and get yourself set up,' Emma said as they left the consulting room and she pulled the door closed. 'I'll just need to make a call and verify your registration before you take surgery.'

Declan inclined his head, acknowledging her eyes were clearly weighing the effect of her statement on him. He gave a mental shrug. As far as his accreditation went, he had nothing to hide. 'Good,' he agreed. 'You should do that.'

'And I'll brief Moira,' Emma added. 'She'll make sure the patients find you.'

'Moira.' Declan lifted a dark brow. 'The lady I spoke to in reception, right?'

Emma nodded. 'She's been with us for years. I sometimes think she could treat most of the patients herself.' Her eyes lit impishly, her full mouth hooking into a half smile.

The impact of that curve of her lips hit him like a sandbag to the solar-plexus. He flicked back the edges of his jacket, jamming his hands low on his hips. 'Let's try to push through early, then.' He paused, his blue gaze roaming over her in an almost physical caress. 'We do need to talk, Emma.'

For a second Emma felt as though she could hardly breathe, his proximity sending a warm rush of want to every part of her body. Feminine places she'd almost forgotten existed. She pulled back, regaining her space. 'We'll arrange something...'

Even though the circumstances weren't ideal, it was good to be back in a consulting room with his feet under a desk again, Declan thought. At least he was doing something useful and if it lasted no more than the rest of the day, he'd give it his best shot.

He was amazed how the time flew. He saw a steady stream of patients, each without exception with a comment about his presence in the practice. He'd answered as honestly as he could, 'I'm helping out Dr Armitage for the moment.' And whether that situation became permanent still depended on so many things. So many.

He called in his final patient for the day, Carolyn Jones. She looked anxiously at Declan. 'I was expecting to see Emma— Dr Armitage.'

'Emma's passed some of her patients over to me today, Mrs

Jones,' Declan offloaded with a cheerful smile. 'I'll do my best to help.'

Carolyn gripped her handbag more tightly. 'I...really just wanted a chat...'

'That's fine,' Declan encouraged, leaning back in his chair, his look expectant. 'I'm here to listen.'

'I want to go back on my sleeping pills. I've tried to do without them for a couple of months now but I just can't manage—' Carolyn stopped and swallowed heavily.

For a second Declan considered a quick consult with Emma. But she had enough on her plate. He could handle this. He leaned forward, speed-reading the patient notes.

The lady was sixty-one but there was nothing leaping out at him to warrant extra caution. He raised his gaze, asking, 'Is there a reason why you can't sleep, Carolyn?'

'I've a difficult family life. Emma knows about it—'

'I see. Suppose you tell me about it as well and see how we go?'

Carolyn lifted her shoulders in a long sigh. 'My husband, Nev, and I are bringing up our three grandchildren. Their ages range from seven to ten.'

'Hard going, then,' Declan surmised gently. 'What circumstances caused this to come about?'

Carolyn gave a weary shrug. 'The whole town knows about it. Our son was a soldier serving overseas. He was killed by a roadside mine. Our daughter-in-law, Tracey, took off and then got in with the wrong crowd. Started seeing someone else. She was always a bit *flighty*.'

Declan raised his eyebrows at the old-fashioned word.

'She's with this new boyfriend now. We've heard they're into drugs. I don't understand how she could just dump her children...'

Declan's caring instincts went out to his patient. But, on the other hand, there were strategies she could try that might induce natural sleep—

'The children are still unsettled, especially at night,' Carolyn said, interrupting his train of thought. 'I just can't get off to sleep and then I'm useless the next day.' She paused and blinked. 'I've really had enough….'

So, crisis time then. Declan thought quickly. As a general rule, sleeping pills were prescribed in small doses and only for a limited time-span. But his patient sounded desperate—desperate enough to… He got to his feet. 'Carolyn, excuse me a moment. I've been out of the country for a while. I'll just need to recheck on dosage and so on.'

Declan came out of his office the same time as Emma emerged from hers. Her brows flicked in question. 'Finished for the day?'

'Not quite.' He accompanied her along to reception. 'Actually, I wanted a word about a patient, Carolyn Jones.'

'The family have ongoing problems,' Emma said quietly.

'I gathered that.' Declan backed himself against the counter and folded his arms. 'Carolyn wants to go back on her sleeping pills. I wondered about her stability.'

'You're asking me whether she's liable to overdose on them?'

'Just double-checking.'

'She cares too much about those children to do anything silly,' Emma said.

'Quite. But still—'

'The sleepers Carolyn takes are quite mild,' Emma cut in. 'They don't produce a hangover effect next day.'

A beat of silence until Declan broke it. 'You realize more than two weeks on those things and she's hooked?'

Oh, for heaven's sake! Emma almost ground her teeth. Declan O'Malley needed to stand outside the rarefied air of his theatre suite and realize family practice was about people not protocol. 'If you're so concerned, make it a stopgap solution. In the meantime, I'll try to figure out some other way to help her. But if Carolyn can't get sleep, she'll go dotty. Then where will the family be?' she pointed out.

'OK…' Declan raised a two-fingered salute in a peace sign. This obviously wasn't the time to start a heated discussion with the lady doctor. 'I'll go ahead and write her script.'

He took a couple of steps forward and then wheeled back. 'Are you around for a while?'

Emma felt the nerves in her stomach tighten. What was on his mind now? 'My last patient just left so I'll be here.'

'Good.' Declan's eyes glinted briefly. 'I'm sorry to push it, but we do need to talk.'

Emma twitched her shoulders into a barely perceptible shrug and watched him go back to his consulting room. Then she went into the work space behind reception and began slotting files back into place.

Moira joined her. With the information Emma had discreetly passed on to her about the new doctor, Moira's eyes were rife with speculation. 'Do you think he'll stay?'

At the thought, Emma managed a dry smile. 'I haven't offered him a job yet. And, even if I did, I expect Dr O'Malley has far more exciting challenges than working in a run-down practice in a country town.'

'You never know.' Moira's voice held a bracing optimism.

No, you never did. Thinking of her father's untimely death, Emma could only silently agree. 'Moira, it's way past your home time. I'll lock up.'

'If you're sure?' Moira looked uncertain.

'I'll be fine. Go.' Emma flapped a hand. 'And have a nice evening.'

There was still no sign of Declan some ten minutes later. Carolyn was obviously still with him. Perhaps it would help her to talk to a different practitioner, Emma thought philosophically. Heaven knew, she herself had no extra time to allot to her needy patients. Well, even if Declan helped only *one* of her patients in the short time he was here, it was a plus. Deciding there was no use hanging round in reception, she went through to the staffroom.

Declan found her there. He gave a rat-a-tat on the door with the back of his hand to alert her.

Emma's head came up, her eyes blinking against his sudden appearance. 'Hi…'

'Hi, yourself.' One side of his mouth inched upward and a crease formed in his cheek as he smiled. 'I smelled coffee.'

Emma averted her gaze to blot out the all-male physical imprint.

In a couple of long strides, he'd crossed the room to her.

Emma lifted the percolator, her fingers as unsteady as her heartbeat. 'Milk and sugar's there on the tray.'

'Thanks.' He took the coffee, added a dollop of milk and lifted the cup to his mouth. 'Could we sit for a minute?'

Emma indicated the old kitchen table that been in the staff room for as long as she could remember. 'You were a long time with Carolyn. Everything OK?' she asked as they took their places on opposite sides of the table.

'I hope so.' Declan's long fingers spanned his coffee mug and he said thoughtfully, 'We talked a bit and I suggested a few things. Some tai chi, a good solid walk in the early evening could help her relax enough to induce a natural sleep. Even a leisurely swim would be beneficial.'

'The school has a pool but it's not open to the public.'

'Pity. She's obviously quite tense.'

'And it's a situation that's happening more and more,' Emma agreed. 'Grandparents taking on the caring role for their grandchildren. Even here in this small community, there are families in similar circumstances as the Joneses.'

Declan took a long mouthful of his coffee. 'Does Bendemere have anything like a support group for them? Somewhere they can air their fears and worries in a safe environment?'

Emma resisted the urge to shriek. 'This isn't the city, Dr O'Malley. We're a bit short of facilitators and psychologists who could lead a group.'

'But a doctor could.'

Was he serious? 'Don't you think I would if I could?' she flashed. 'I'm so stretched now, I—'

'No, Emma, you're misunderstanding me.' His look was guarded and cool. 'I meant *me*—I could help.'

'You?' Emma huffed her disbelief. She wasn't understanding any of this. 'Are you saying you want to stay on here?'

'You need a practice partner, don't you?'

'But you know nothing about the place!' Emma's thoughts were spinning. 'Nothing about the viability of the practice. Nothing about *me*.'

He stared at her for a long moment. 'I know you're Andrew's daughter.'

'And you'd make a life-changing decision on the basis of that?' Emma's voice had a husky edge of disquiet.

Oh, hell. He was doing this all wrong. No wonder she was confused. He'd meant to lead up to things gently and objectively, explain himself, choose his words carefully. But just getting his head around Emma's crippling workload, the plight of Carolyn Jones and others like her had spurred him on to get matters sorted and quickly.

'Emma—' He paused significantly. 'I didn't just come here to offer my condolences. There's another reason why I'm here in Bendemere.'

Emma tried to grasp the significance of his words. 'Perhaps you'd better explain.'

Declan watched as she drew herself up stiffly, almost as if she were gathering invisible armour around her. He knew what he was about to tell her would come as a shock, maybe even wound her deeply. But he had to do it. 'Your father contacted me shortly before his death. He offered to sell me his share of the practice. I'm here to arrange payment and finalise the details of our partnership.'

Emma's mouth fell open and then snapped shut. She clutched the edge of the table for support, becoming aware of her heart thrashing to a sickening rhythm inside her chest. 'I don't believe Dad would have done something like that.'

'I have a letter of confirmation from your father and the legal documents.'

'Dad wouldn't have just *thrust* someone on me. Someone I didn't even know!' She felt the pitch of her anger and emotion rising and didn't care. 'And I don't have to accept your money, Dr O'Malley, nor do I *have* to take you on as my practice partner.'

Declan's gaze narrowed on her flushed face, the angry tilt of her small chin. Damn! He hadn't reckoned on any of this. 'It was what your father wanted, Emma.'

Emma gave a hard little laugh. 'Emotional blackmail will get you absolutely nowhere, Dr O'Malley.'

'Please!' With a reflex action Declan's head shot up, his vivid blue gaze striking an arc across the space between them. 'Give me a little credit. I realize this has come as a shock to you. And I'm sorry. I'd hoped Andrew might have given you some idea of what he wanted, paved the way a bit, but obviously time ran out on him. But we can't leave things here, Emma. We really can't.' His mouth compressed briefly. 'I suggest we take a break and let things settle a bit. I'm staying at the Heritage Hotel. We could link up there later this evening and talk further. Dinner around seven. Does that suit you?'

'Fine,' Emma responded bluntly. It seemed she had no choice in the matter.

'Let's meet at the bar, then.' Declan grabbed at the grudging acceptance.

CHAPTER TWO

EMMA hitched up her little shoulder bag and determinedly pushed open the heavy plate glass door of the restaurant. She loved this place. As it was winter, the lovely old fireplace was lit, sending out warmth and flickering patterns to the wood-panelled walls. The atmosphere was charming and tonight was the first time she'd come here since... Her teeth caught on her lower lip. She and Dad had come here often. The Sunday lunch at the Heritage was legendary.

But this evening her dinner companion was someone far different than her father.

Heart thrumming, Emma made her way along the parquet flooring towards the bar. Declan was there already. She saw him at once, his distinctive dark head turning automatically, almost as if he'd sensed her approach. A shower of tingles began at the base of her backbone, spiralling upwards and engulfing her. She swallowed. He was wearing dark jeans and an oatmeal-coloured sweater that looked soft and cuddly. Oh, get real, Emma! Cuddles and Declan O'Malley were about as compatible as oil and water.

'Hello again.' Declan nodded almost formally. And blinked. Wow! Gone was the harassed-looking medico. Emma Armitage could have sauntered in from the catwalk. She was wearing black leggings and a long-sleeved, long-line silver-grey T-shirt, a huge silky scarf in a swirl of multicolour around her throat. And knee-high boots. 'You look amazing.'

'Thanks.' Her shrug was so slight he hardly saw it. 'I love your outfit too.'

So, the lady did have a sense of humour after all. A quirky one at that. Declan's grin unfolded lazily, his eyes crinkling at the corners. 'We seem to have that sorted, so let's try to enjoy our evening, shall we? Would you like something to drink?'

In a leggy, graceful movement, Emma hitched herself up on to one of the high bar stools. 'A glass of the house red would be nice, thanks.'

For a while they talked generalities and then Declan glanced at his watch. 'I reserved us a table. Shall we go through?'

'It's rather crowded for a week night,' Emma said stiltedly as they took their places in the restaurant adjoining the bar.

'I've been quite taken with the town,' Declan rejoined. 'Tell me a bit about its history.'

Emma did her best to comply and it wasn't until they'd come to the end of their meal and were sitting over coffee she said pointedly, 'It's been a long day, could we wind things up so we can both get on about our business?'

'OK, then.' Declan's moody blue eyes were fixed unflinchingly on hers. 'I'll get straight to the point. About six months ago I received a letter from your father telling me about his deterioration in health.'

For a few seconds Emma stared at him in numb disbelief. 'Dad told *you* and he didn't tell me? Why? I was his daughter, for heaven's sake.'

Declan could hardly bear to watch her grief. 'I know it sounds an old chestnut, Emma,' he said gently, 'but perhaps he didn't want to upset you any further than you had been. You had other things going on in your life, didn't you?'

Emma's face was tightly controlled. 'What did Dad tell you about that?'

'Almost nothing—just that you'd had a few personal problems.'

Like mopping up the emotional fallout after her rat of a fiancé had dumped her for her best friend…

'And that you'd come back to work in the practice,' Declan finished diplomatically.

Emma curled her hands into a tight knot on her lap. 'What did he tell you about his health? That he had only a short time to live?'

Declan's frown deepened. 'Nothing like that. But, from what he told me, I drew my own conclusions. If it hadn't been for the fact that I, myself, was in somewhat of a personal crisis at the time, I'd have come back to Australia to see Andrew immediately. Instead, I called him. He was concerned for you, for the future of the practice if the worst happened. We talked at length. It was then he offered to sell me his half of the practice.'

'I see.' Emma swallowed through a suddenly dry throat. But she understood now why her father hadn't told her anything about his plans. He would have had to reveal the uncertain state of his health. So instead he'd trusted Declan O'Malley to set things right. But did that mean she had to accept him as her partner? She didn't think so. 'I'm sure Dad wouldn't have wanted you interfering in my life.'

'That's not what Andrew had in mind, Emma.'

'So, you're here as some kind of…white knight?' she grated bitterly.

'I'm here because I want to be here,' Declan said simply. 'Because it seems like a worthwhile thing to do. You need a partner. I need a job. Isn't that the truth of it?'

She looked at him warily. 'Why do you need a job? You obviously have medical qualifications beyond the norm. Career-wise, the world should be your playground. Why aren't you working in your chosen discipline somewhere?'

'It's a long story.'

'There's plenty of coffee in the pot,' Emma countered. 'And we're quite private here.'

Declan felt the familiar grind in his guts at the thought of rehashing everything.

At his continued silence, something like resentment stirred in Emma and she couldn't let go of it. 'Dr O'Malley, if you've ideas of entering into partnership with me, then I need to know what I'm getting. That's only fair, isn't it?'

He took a long breath and let it go. 'My surgical career is, to all intents and purposes, finished. I can't operate any longer.'

Faint shock widened Emma's eyes. How awful. She knew only too well what it was like to have your world collapse with no redress possible. 'I'm sorry.'

'Thank you.' The words escaped mechanically from his lips.

And that was it? Emma took in the sudden tight set of his neck and shoulders. He had to know she needed more information. Much more than the bald statement he'd offered. She felt about for the right words to help him. But in the end it was a simple, softly spoken, 'What happened?'

Declan rubbed a hand across his forehead. 'After I'd completed my general surgery training, I decided to go ahead and specialize in orthopaedics.' His blue eyes shone for a moment. 'On a good day when everything in the OR goes right and you know it's your skill that's enabling a patient to regain their mobility, their normal life, and in some instances their whole livelihood…it's empowering and humbling all rolled into one.'

'Yes, I imagine it is,' Emma said, but she had the feeling he had hardly heard.

'I was fortunate enough to be accepted at St Mary's in Edinburgh.'

Emma's eyes widened. 'Their training programme is legendary. I believe they take only the brightest and best.'

'I was lucky,' he said modestly.

Hardly. Obviously, he was seriously gifted. Which fact made Declan O'Malley's reasons for opting to come in as her partner in a country practice odd indeed, she thought, noticing he'd hadn't touched his coffee. Instead, he'd spanned his fingers around the cup, holding on to it like some kind of lifeline.

'After a long stint in Scotland, I'd decided to head back home. I was still finalizing dates when I had a call from an Aussie mate. He was coming over for a holiday in the UK, beginning in Scotland. I postponed my plans and Jack and I bought a couple of motorbikes.'

'Fuel-wise cheaper than cars, I guess,' was Emma's only comment.

'Jack and I found a couple of high-powered beauties for sale locally. Those bikes took us everywhere. Life was sweet—until we had the accident.'

Emma winced and she automatically put her hand to her heart. 'How?'

He gave a grim smile. 'A foggy afternoon, an unfamiliar road. A bit too much speed. And a truck that came out of nowhere. Jack received a broken leg. I was somewhat more compromised. I ended up with lumbar injuries.' He expanded on the statement with technical language, ending with, 'The outcome was partial paralysis in my left leg.' He grimaced as if the memory was still fresh.

Emma gripped her hands tightly. He must have been sick with worry and conjecture. And fear. Her antagonism faded and her heart went out to him. 'What was the result? I mean, you don't appear to have any deficit in your movement.'

His eyes took on a dull bleakness. 'I've regained most of it but my muscles are unpredictable, my toes still get numb from time to time. Added to that, I can't stand for excessively long periods. And that's what orthopaedic surgeons have to do. You need to have muscle strength, be in control. I can't risk a patient's life by breaking down in the middle of a long operation. So, career-wise, I'm stuffed.'

'But you could do other kinds of surgery,' Emma said hopefully.

'I don't even want to think about that. I want to do what I was trained to do—what I do—*did* best.'

But sometimes you had to compromise. Emma knew that better than most. 'You could lecture, Declan.'

He made a disgusted sound. 'Take up a *chair* in a hallowed hall somewhere? That's not me. I'm a doer. I'd rather change direction entirely.'

'In other words, come in as my partner—' She broke off. 'You might hate it.'

'I don't think so.' Blue eyes challenged her although his mouth moved in the ghost of a wry smile. When she remained silent, he went on, 'Emma, don't you think it's just possible Andrew considered he was acting in the best interests of *both* of us? He knew the extent of my injuries, the uncertain state of my career in medicine and he knew, without him, you were going to need a partner—someone you could trust. And you *can* trust me, Emma,' he assured her sincerely.

Emma felt almost sick with vulnerability. Heaven knew there was no one else beating the door down to come and work with her. But this man? On the other hand, what choice did she have? He had all the power on his side and, she suspected, the determination that her father's wishes would be carried out. There was really no get-out clause here. None at all. 'How do we go about setting things in motion, then?' Her voice was small and formal.

Declan breathed the greatest sigh of relief. They'd got to the trickiest hurdle and jumped it. 'You're overworked and under-capitalised. If we tackle the problems together, Kingsholme could be brought up to its potential again. Why don't we give it six months? If we find we can't work together, I'll get out.'

'And where will that leave me?'

'Hopefully, with a fully functioning practice. You'd have no difficulty attracting a new partner and I'd recoup my investment. It would be a win-win situation for both of us.'

Emma knew the decision had already been made for her. She wanted to—*needed* to—keep Kingsholme. Declan O'Malley had been Dad's choice of a suitable practice partner for her. She had to trust his judgement and go along with that.

Otherwise, she was back to the mind-numbing uncertainty of the past weeks. 'Have you come prepared to stay, then?'

'I've brought enough gear to keep me going for a while.' Declan kept his tone deliberately brisk. 'If it suits you, I'll continue at the surgery until Friday and then, on the weekend, we can go over what practical changes need to be made. I'd imagine you'd have a few ideas of your own about that?'

'It depends on how much money you want to spend,' Emma shot back with the faintest hint of cynicism.

He answered levelly, 'There'll be enough.'

On Friday afternoon, they held a quick consult after surgery. 'What time do you want to begin tomorrow?' Emma asked.

Declan lifted his medical case up on the counter. 'I'm flexible. What suits you?'

'I need to do an early hospital round. We could meet after that.'

'Why can't I come to the hospital with you?'

Emma looked uncertain. 'It's all pretty basic medicine we do here.'

'And nothing I'd be interested in?' Declan's gaze clouded. 'Emma, if we're partners, we share duties. Right?'

She coloured slightly. 'I was just pointing out there'll be none of the drama associated with Theatres.'

'So, it'll be a change of pace. I can handle that.'

Could he, though? Emma wished she felt more certain. On the other hand, why not think positively? She'd already ca-pitulated over him becoming her partner. It was time to just get on with things. 'Hospital at eight o'clock, then? I'll give you the tour.'

'That's what I want to hear,' he drawled with his slow smile.

For a split second Emma registered a zinging awareness between them. Raw and immediate. Like the white-heat of an electric current. She repressed a gasp. Declan O'Malley exuded sex appeal in spades. He was about to step in as her practice partner. And they were going to be working very closely together for at least the next six months...

Emma had enjoyed her Saturday morning run. Leaning forward, hands on the verandah railings, she breathed deeply and began to warm down.

'Great morning for it,' a male voice rumbled behind her and she jumped and spun round, her heart skittering.

Emma straightened, one hand clenched on the railings, her senses on high alert, as Declan O'Malley came up the steps. His sudden appearance had made her flustered and unsure. 'I run most mornings.' She felt his eyes track over her and, before she could move or comprehend, he'd lifted a hand and knuckled her cheek ever so gently. Emma felt her breath jam.

'It's good to see those shadows gone,' he said, his voice throaty and low and further tugging on her senses. His eyes beckoned hers until she lifted her gaze. 'I gather you slept well?'

She nodded, breath rushing into the vacuum of her lungs. She'd slept well for the first time in weeks. She wasn't about to analyse the reason. But she had a fair idea it was all to do with the fact that at least for the next little while, her future was settled. Her teeth caught on her lower lip. 'I thought we were to meet at the hospital.'

Hands rammed in his back pockets, Declan shifted his stance slightly as if to relieve tense muscles. 'I was awake early. Thought I might come over and persuade you to have breakfast with me.'

'Or you could stay here and have breakfast with *me*,' Emma rushed out. 'I'm sure I could cobble something together.'

'I didn't mean to gatecrash—'

'You're not.' She took a thin breath. 'Give me a minute to have a shower and change.'

He followed her inside to the kitchen. 'I could knock us up some breakfast—that's if you don't mind someone else rattling around in your kitchen?'

'Not remotely.' In a reflex action, Emma jerked the zipper

closed on her track top right up to her chin. 'Uh...I did a shop last night. There's plenty of stuff in the fridge.' She almost ran from the room.

Sheesh! Declan spun away, thumping the heel of his hand to his forehead. Why on earth had he done that? *Touched* her. He hadn't meant it to happen but at that moment his hand had seemed to have a life of its own. Oh, good grief. Surely, the idea had been to reassure her he was trustworthy. Well, that premise was shot. Instead, he'd gone to the other extreme and created a damn great elephant in the room. He hissed out a breath of frustration and tried to take stock of the kitchen. He'd promised her breakfast. He'd better start delivering.

Emma showered in record time, towelled dry and dressed quickly in comfortable cargos and a ruby-red sweater. She wasn't about to drive herself crazy thinking about earlier. It was hardly a professional thing for Declan to have done. What she couldn't work out was her instinctive response to his touch... Oh, Lord. Suddenly, her body was stiff with tension. Almost jerkily, she lifted her hands, bunching her hair from her shoulders and letting it spiral away. At least he'd got on with the breakfast. There was a gorgeous smell of grilling bacon coming from the kitchen.

'How's it going?' Emma asked, buzzing back into the kitchen, determined not to start walking on eggshells around him. They were about to become partners in practice. Nothing else. 'Find everything?'

Declan looked up from the stove. 'No worries. It's a great kitchen.'

'Tottering with age but very user-friendly,' Emma agreed. Opening the door of the fridge, she peered in and located the orange juice. She poured two glasses and handed one across to Declan.

'Thanks. I'm doing bacon and scrambled eggs.'

'Lovely.'

Declan lifted his glass and drained it slowly as he watched the eggs begin to thicken and fluff. He could get used to this.

The warmth and the clutter of the old-fashioned kitchen. The comforting aroma of food cooking. The feeling of solidness, of family. The place just breathed it. He could get some idea now of how desperate Emma had been to hang on to her home. 'Your idea?' He pointed to the sun-catcher crystal that dangled from the window in front of the sink.

Her tiny smile blossomed to a grin. 'My *alternative* period. You about done here?'

'I hope it's up to scratch,' he said, catching the drift of her flowery shampoo as her head topped his shoulder.

'Mmm, smells good.' Emma gave him a quick nod of approval. 'I'll get the plates.'

'I used to run a bit,' Declan said as they settled over breakfast.

'You can't now?'

His mouth pulled down. 'I seem to be stuck with a set of prescribed exercises these days.'

Emma looked up sharply with a frown. Did that mean he didn't trust his legs on a simple run? 'I understood you to say it was standing for long periods you had trouble with. Short bursts of running would seem OK, surely? And drawing all that fresh air into your bloodstream works magic.'

Well, he knew that. 'Maybe it'll happen. In time.'

So, end of discussion. Emma pursed her mouth into a thoughtful moue, realizing suddenly that her own emotional baggage didn't seem nearly as weighty as her soon-to-be-partner's. Determinedly, she pulled out her social skills and managed to create enough general conversation to get them through the rest of the meal. She glanced at her watch, surprised to see the time had gone so quickly. She swung up from the table. 'If you'll start clearing away, I'll just feed the cat.'

Declan gave a rusty chuckle, looking sideways to where the big tabby sprawled indolently on the old-fashioned cane settee. 'Looks like he wants room service.'

Emma snorted. 'Lazy creature. I think the mice run rings around him. He belonged to Mum.'

Declan hesitated with a response, a query in his eyes.

'She moved back to Melbourne about a year ago,' Emma enlightened him thinly. 'Dad bought her an art gallery in St Kilda. It had an apartment attached so the whole set-up suited her perfectly and Dad went there as often as he could before he died. She never really felt at home here in rural Queensland. Missed the buzz of the city, her friends.'

Declan was thoughtful as he stood to his feet, processing the information. At least now he knew where the bulk of Andrew's estate had gone and why the practice was all but running on goodwill. And why Emma's stress levels must have been immense as a result.

Between them, they put the kitchen to rights in a few minutes. Hanging the tea towel up to dry, Emma felt an odd lightness in her spirits.

'Emma, I wonder if you could spare a few minutes now? There are a couple of business decisions I'd like to run past you.'

His voice had a firm edge to it and Emma came back to earth with a thud. 'Let's go through to Dad's–*your* surgery,' she substituted shortly. 'I'll give the hospital a call and let them know we'll be along a bit later than planned.'

They took their places at the big rosewood desk. 'Fire away,' Emma invited, locking her arms around her middle as if to protect herself.

Declan moved his position, sitting sideways in his chair, his legs outstretched and crossed at the ankles. 'First up, I'll need to see some figures from your accountant. Could you arrange that, please?'

'I do have some current figures,' she replied. 'I organized that when I needed to see what state the practice was in after Dad—' She stopped. 'I'll get them for you directly. Perhaps you'd like to study them over the weekend.'

'Thanks.' He nodded almost formally. 'That will help a lot. Now, your office system—'

'Yes?'

'It seems a bit outdated. You obviously have computers installed but no one seems to be using them.'

She'd wondered when they'd get to that. 'I encouraged Dad to get them soon after I moved back and we had the appropriate software installed. Moira did an evening course at the local high school, but at the end of it she said it was all beyond her. Dad said he felt more comfortable with his own way of doing things.'

'I see.'

'I tried to get things operational myself, but then, with Dad gone, it all came to a screeching halt. Any time I had to spare has had to go on face-to-face consults.'

'The system must be got up and running,' he insisted. 'If it's too onerous for Moira, then she'd be better—'

'I won't let you sack her, Declan,' Emma swiftly interjected.

He raised his head and looked at her coolly. 'Emma, don't go second-guessing me, please. I was about to add, Moira would be better staying with what she does best. She's obviously invaluable to the practice. She knows the patients well and that helps facilitate appointments. But what we do need is someone with expertise who can come in on a permanent basis and get our patient lists up to date and their medical history on to the computers. Can you think of anyone suitable?'

'Not offhand,' she said stiffly. It all made sense though and, belatedly, she realized the shortcomings he'd pointed out had probably been one of the reasons the doctors she'd interviewed had vetoed working here. 'I'll have a chat to Moira. Better still, I'll call her now.' She felt almost goaded into action, reaching for the phone on his desk. She hit Moira's logged-in home number and, after a brief conversation, replaced the receiver in its cradle. Raising her gaze, she looked directly at Declan. 'Moira's coming in now. She says she may have a few ideas. I hope that's in order?'

Declan spread his hands in compliance. He wished Emma didn't see him as the bad guy here. But he'd promised Andrew he'd do what he could to save the practice and if along the way he had to tread on a few toes—gently, of course–then he'd do it. He hauled his legs up and swivelled them under the desk. 'I noticed we don't seem to have the services of a practice nurse. What's the situation there?'

'We used to have one, Libby Macklin. She took maternity leave, intending to come back, but found it was just too much with the demands of the baby. We didn't get round to replacing her.'

Declan placed his hands palms down on the desk. 'Would she like to come back, do you think?'

Emma nodded. 'I see her quite often. The baby's older now, of course, and Libby's managing much better. I know she'd appreciate some work but I just haven't been in a position to offer her any…'

'Sound her out then,' Declan said, refusing to acknowledge Emma's wistful expression.

'I'll go and see her after we've been to the hospital. Now, about patient lists.'

'I'm listening.'

'I'm not sure how you'd like to work it, but perhaps we could do a clean swap? You'd take over Dad's patients,' she suggested.

'That sounds fair. And I'm thinking we could schedule a weekly practice meeting, air anything problematic then. Suit you?'

Heck, did she even have a choice in the matter? A resigned kind of smile dusted Emma's lips. 'Fine.'

Declan frowned and glanced at his watch. 'How long will Moira be?'

'Not long. She lives only a few minutes away.'

'Yoo-hoo, it's me!' As if on cue, Moira's quick tap along the corridor accompanied her greeting.

Declan uncurled to his feet and dragged up another chair. 'Thanks for doing this, Moira.'

'No worries.' She flapped a hand and leant forward confidentially. 'I'll get straight to the point. My granddaughter is looking for work.'

'Jodi?' Emma's gaze widened in query. 'I thought she was full-time at McGinty's stables.'

Moira's mouth turned down. 'James, the youngest son, has returned home so he's taken over much of the track work. Jodi's there only one day a week now.'

Declan exchanged a quick guarded look with Emma. Moira was obviously a doting grandmother but they couldn't afford to be giving jobs away on her say-so. 'Moira, we'd need to have a chat to Jodi about what the job here entails,' he stressed diplomatically.

'Of course you would.' Moira smiled. 'That's why I've brought her in with me. She's outside in reception.'

'Ask her to come in then,' Declan said briefly, turning to Emma as Moira left the room. 'What do you think?' he asked quietly. 'You obviously know this young woman. Are we doing the right thing here?'

'Jodi is very bright. Providing her technical skills are up to speed, then I think she'll do a good job. Oh—here she is now.'

Declan got to his feet again as Jodi bounded in, all youthful spirits and sparkling eyes. 'Hi.' She linked the two doctors with a wide white smile.

'Jodi.' Declan stuck out his hand in greeting. 'Declan O'Malley. Emma you know, of course.'

'Hello, Jodi.' Emma beckoned the teenager to a seat. 'Moira says you're looking for some work.'

'Yes, I am.' Jodi slid her huge leather satchel from her shoulder and on to the floor beside her chair. 'Nan's told me a bit about what you need here. I could easily manage to give you three days a week, if that suits. I work track at McGinty's on Fridays and I've just got a day's work at the supermarket on Thursdays. So I could give you from Monday to Wednesday.'

Declan leaned back in his chair and folded his arms. 'How old are you, Jodi?'

'Eighteen. At present I'm taking a gap year before I start Uni.'

'What are you studying?' Declan asked.

'Applied science. Eventually, I want to be associated with the equine industry, combine research and field work. Horses and their welfare are my great passion. I'll need to do my doctorate, of course.'

'That's really worthwhile, Jodi,' Emma said warmly. 'Best of luck with your studies.'

Declan made a restive movement in his chair, his dark brows flexed in query. 'How are your computer skills, Jodi? We'd need you to be able to collate information, get the patients' histories logged in and kept up to date.'

'I'm thoroughly computer literate.' Jodi twitched a long hank of dark hair over her shoulder. 'I work quickly and thoroughly and I'm quite aware of the confidential nature of the job here. I'll sign a clause to that effect if you need me to.'

Emma bit hard on the inside of her cheek to stop the grin that threatened. This kid was something else. 'We'll probably get round to that, Jodi. But, if Dr O'Malley agrees, I think we can offer you the job. Declan?'

'Uh—' Declan's eyes looked slightly glazed. He rocked forward in his chair. 'Let's agree on a trial period, Jodi, if that suits—say a month? And we'll see how things are going then?'

'Absolutely.' Jodi shrugged slender shoulders. Bending down, she flipped open her satchel. 'I'll leave you my CV. And there are several character references as well.' She placed the file on the desk. 'If there's anything else you need to know, I'll be available on my mobile.' She smiled confidently and whirled to her feet. 'So, I'll see you both on Monday, then.'

'Good grief,' Declan said faintly after Jodi had swished out of the door. 'Do you get the feeling *we're* the ones who have just been interviewed?'

Emma chuckled. 'It's the Gen Y thing. They're inclined to set out terms and conditions to prospective employers. But isn't she marvellous?'

'Made me feel about a hundred and six,' Declan growled. 'Hell, was I ever that young and enthusiastic about life?'

Emma stood and pushed her chair back in. 'Probably we both were.'

'Mmm.' Declan's tone was non-committal. 'Well, we seem to have made a dint in what needs to be done here so, if you're ready, I'd like to see over your hospital.'

CHAPTER THREE

BENDEMERE'S hospital was old but beautifully kept. Declan looked around with growing interest. 'This place has a long history, obviously,' he remarked.

'My grandfather actually funded the building of it,' Emma said proudly. 'These days, much of the accommodation is given over to nursing home beds for our seniors. Anything acute is sent straight on to Toowoomba by road ambulance. Or, in the case of serious trauma, we stabilise as best we can and chopper the patient out to Brisbane.'

'Do you have a theatre?' Declan began striding ahead, his interest clearly raised.

'A small one—just here.' She turned into an annexe and indicated the big oval window that looked into the pristine operating space. 'Dad did basic surgical procedures. And Rachel Wallace, our nurse manager, has extensive theatre experience. She insists the maintenance is kept up. Shame it's not used any more...'

'It's all here though, isn't it?' Declan's gaze roamed almost hungrily, left and right and back again, as if to better acquaint himself with the layout. 'Who did the gas when your dad operated?'

'Oliver Shackelton. He's retired in the district. And, even though he won't see seventy again, I know Dad trusted his skills to the nth degree.'

'Interesting.' Declan pressed his lips together and took a

deep breath. This was his natural environment. But he didn't belong here any longer. Suddenly, it all came at him in a rush, a heartbeat, the past coming forward to link with the present. He felt the sudden tightening of his throat muscles. It was over. He was finished as a surgeon. He couldn't operate any more. At least not in any way that was meaningful—from his standpoint, at least...

'Declan...are you OK?'

Declan's head came up, looking at her without seeing. 'Sorry?'

'We should get on,' she cajoled gently.

'Yes, we should.' He turned abruptly, as if to shut out the scene he'd walked into so unguardedly. He felt weird, in no way prepared for the hollow feeling in his gut as he snapped off the light and closed the double doors on the annexe.

Emma's gaze moved over him. 'Sure you're OK?'

He saw the compassion in her eyes, the softening, felt her empathy. But he wasn't a kid who needed to cry on her shoulder. 'I'm fine,' he said, his tone gruff as if brushing her concern aside. 'Fill me in about hospital staff.'

Emma gave a mental shrug. He hadn't fooled her for a minute. Well, if that was how he wanted to handle it, that was his business, his life. 'I've sent out an email to the nurses to advise them you were joining the practice.' She didn't add they'd probably done their own research on the Internet in the meantime. 'Rachel is our nurse manager,' she reiterated as they made their way along to the station. 'We have three other permanent RNs who alternate shifts and Dot Chalmers is permanent nights. Ancillary staff are rostered as necessary.'

'Leave and sick days?' Declan fell into step beside her.

'Covered by a small pool of nurses who mainly live in the district.'

'That seems like a reasonable set-up,' Declan said. 'I imagine the staff value their jobs quite highly.'

'And the folk hereabouts value *them*,' Emma said, leaving him in no doubt that any changes there would be unacceptable. Just in case he was thinking along those lines.

'Hospital maintenance is covered by a local firm, as is security. And Betty Miller is our indispensable hospital cook.'

Declan nodded, taking everything on board. He began to quicken his pace.

'Patients now?'

Emma rolled her eyes. He'd have to learn to slow down if he was going to relate to the locals. 'Is there a fire some-where?' she enquired innocently.

'Forgot.' He sent her a twisted grin. 'I'm keen to get cracking, that's all.'

'Hello, people.' Rachel, tall and slender, came towards them, her nimbus of auburn hair stark against the white walls of the hospital corridor. 'And you are Dr O'Malley, I presume?' Beaming, the nurse manager stuck her hand out towards Declan.

'I am.' Declan shook her hand warmly. 'And it's Declan. I've just been getting the lay of the land from Emma. It looks like a great little hospital.'

'We're proud of it.' Rachel spun her gaze between the two medical officers. 'Um—I was just on my way for a cuppa.'

'Don't let us hold you up,' Emma insisted. Despite it being a small hospital, she knew the nurses worked hard and deserved their breaks.

'OK, then. I won't be long.' Rachel began to move away and then turned back. 'I knew you'd be along so I've pulled the charts on our current patients.'

'Take your time.' Emma smiled. 'And thanks, Rach. We'll be fine.'

'I guess you know this place like the back of your hand,' Declan surmised as they made their way along to the nurses' station.

Emma sent him a quick look. It still seemed surreal that this once highly ambitious, powerful man was now to all intents and purposes her practice partner. Her hand closed around the small medallion at her throat. No doubt, for the moment, the newness of what he'd taken on was enough to keep him motivated. But what would happen when the grind of family practice began to wear thin? Where would his motivation be then?

In a dry little twist of quirky humour, Emma transposed the scenario into equine terms. Surely what Declan was proposing was like expecting a thoroughbred racer to feel fulfilled pulling a plough…

'Something amusing you, Emma?' Declan lifted a dark brow.

'Not really,' she said, going behind the counter and collecting the charts Rachel had left out.

'OK, who's the first cab off the rank?' Declan asked, settling on one of the high stools next to her.

'Russell Kernow, age seventy-five, lives alone,' Emma said. 'I saw him at the surgery a week ago. He was presenting with an incessant cough, raised temperature. I prescribed roxithromycin. His condition didn't improve and I admitted him two days ago. He was seriously dehydrated, complained his chest felt tight. I've placed him on an inhaler twice daily and the cough seems to have diminished slightly. I've sent bloods off as well.'

'So, you're testing for what—serology, pertussis, mycoplasma?'

'Plus legionella,' Emma said.

Declan raised a dark brow. 'Is that a possibility?'

'A remote one, but Russell's house is fully air-conditioned. He spends much of his time indoors. And we've since found out the filters on his air-con unit haven't been changed for two years.'

'Still…legionella is drawing a fairly long bow,' Declan considered.

Emma bristled. If he was going to start telling her her job, they were going to fall out before the ink was dry on their partnership papers.

Their eyes met. He could see the spark of hostility in her gaze. Hell, he didn't want to blow things with her before they even got off the ground. 'Just thinking aloud,' he said hastily. 'It's your call. When do you expect the results?'

'Soonish,' Emma said, faintly mollified. 'I've requested the path lab to fax them to us here.' She turned, stroking a stray lock of hair behind her ear. 'Next patient is Sylvia Gartrell, age sixty-five. Recently had surgery—hysterectomy and bladder repair. Post-op seven days. The air ambulance delivered her to us yesterday.'

Declan ran his index finger between his brows. 'What's the problem?'

'Her bladder function hasn't yet returned to normal. She's having to self-catheterise and she's finding the procedure difficult to manage. Currently, the nurses are giving her some guidance. It seemed the safest option to have her here until she feels competent to go it alone. At the moment she's convinced she'll be stuck with this problem for ever so she needs emotional support as well.'

'Why was she released from hospital in the first place?'

Emma sighed. 'Same old story. They needed the bed.'

'Oh, for crying out loud! We'll need to keep a close eye on her, be mindful of the possibility of infection.'

'We're all aware of that, Declan.'

He sighed. 'OK, then, who's next on our patient list?'

'Only one more. Ashleigh Maine, aged eleven. Poor little kid had a bad asthma attack yesterday. Scared the life out of her.'

'So what's her prognosis?'

'She's getting some relief from a nebuliser and of course she's on a drip. Her home situation is not as good as it could be, though. Dad still smokes.'

Declan swore under his breath. 'I realize tobacco is the drug some folk cling to when they're under stress but surely, if his child is suffering, the man has to take stock of his actions?'

'Normally, Ashleigh's condition is fairly well managed but it only needs a change in routine and she's struggling again.'

'Are you aware of the study on asthmatics that's been

carried by the Jarvis Institute in Sydney?' Declan asked pointedly.

Emma's gaze was suddenly uncertain. 'It's a breathing technique, isn't it? I think there's a new physio in Toowoomba who's a graduate from the Institute. We got some leaflets. I was going to investigate it further just before Dad…died. Do you want to take the child on to your list?'

'Fine with me,' he replied calmly. 'I'll chase up the physio and get the parents in for a round-table chat. I've a few ideas that might help as well.'

Emma defended her corner quietly. 'I did try to put the parents in touch with the Asthma Foundation. They run camps and things that Ashleigh could attend with other youngsters with the same health problem. They declined.'

Declan's response was swift. 'Leave it with me, Emma. I'm new to the place. They'll take notice, believe me.'

Emma opened her mouth and closed it. She hoped he wouldn't jump all over the family. It wasn't the way things worked in rural medicine. If the Maines took offence, that would be the end of the doctors getting access to Ashleigh. Oh, help. Which way should she jump? Forward, if she had any sense. 'You will tread gently, won't you, Declan?'

His jaw hardened. 'I'll do what I need to do, Emma.'

'Not with my patients, you won't,' she flared. 'Bendemere is a close-knit community. You can't go around upsetting people.'

Hell, this was a minefield. She was guarding her territory, whereas he was used to giving orders and having them carried out immediately. OK, then. Back off, he told himself. 'If we want this partnership to work, Emma, we have to trust each other's medical skills. You haven't had any complaints about my patient contact, have you?'

'No…' She lifted her hands in appeasement. 'It's just— we're not used to working with each other yet.'

His mouth pulled tight. Was this what he was about to sign on for—bickering over someone who couldn't grasp that his inability to quit smoking was stuffing up his child's health?

He lifted his gaze to glance meaningfully at her. 'Just let's try to keep it professional, then.'

Emma gritted her teeth. That was a low blow. She'd done everything she could under very difficult circumstances to keep their relationship professional. He'd been the one to overstep this morning when he'd touched her cheek! She tried to steady her thoughts. She'd have to swallow her angst with him if she didn't want everything turned into ashes. New jobs had been promised and already there was an air of expectation about the town. She breathed a sigh of relief when she saw Rachel heading towards them, a tea tray in her hands. 'I thought you might need this,' she said. 'And Betty's made us some of her special ginger biscuits,' she added brightly, sensing an air of tension between the two.

'Lovely,' Emma said faintly.

'I'll take a rain check, thanks, Rachel.' Declan spun off his stool. 'I'll get on and make myself known to our patients.'

'Then I'll accompany you,' Rachel said.

'There's no need.' He gave an impatient twitch of his shoulder. 'I'm sure I can manage.'

Rachel's raised brows spoke volumes, before she swept up the patient charts. 'My hospital, my call, Dr O'Malley. Besides, I need to strut my stuff occasionally,' she said cheekily. 'It's ages since I walked the wards with a posh doc.'

Emma watched them walk away together, saw Declan turn his head, heard his rumble of laughter as he interacted with Rachel. She made a little sniff of disapproval. Shaking off a disquiet she didn't understand, she took up one of Betty's ginger biscuits and dunked it in her tea.

By Sunday afternoon Emma was going stir-crazy. It wasn't that she didn't have a million things she could be doing. She just couldn't settle to anything. Declan had offered to be on call for the weekend so that had left her with more free time than she'd had in months. She'd done a tour of the garden and picked a bunch of winter roses to bring some warmth and friendliness to reception. At least Moira would appreciate her gesture. She doubted Declan would even notice.

She was back to *him* again. She still had the feeling of things being not quite right between them. He'd erupted into the practice and into her life and she'd hardly had time to take stock. He hadn't exactly steamrollered over her but he hadn't wasted any time in putting his plans into action. But then she'd given him tacit permission, hadn't she? Because the alternative had been too bleak to contemplate.

Oh, help. Emma turned her restless gaze towards the kitchen window. It would be dark soon. Suddenly she was beset with a strange unease. She couldn't begin the first week of their new partnership with so many of her questions unresolved.

They needed to talk.

Now she'd decided, she wouldn't hold back, although her heart was slamming at the thought of what she was about to take on. They'd already exchanged mobile phone numbers. She'd find him about the place somewhere.

He answered on the fourth ring. 'O'Malley.'

'Hi—it's me—Emma.'

'Problem?'

She took a shallow breath. He wasn't making this easy. 'Are you busy?'

'Er—no. I've just been for a jog.'

Emma blinked uncertainly. 'How did it go?'

'Pretty good,' he said, sounding pleased with himself. 'What's up?'

'Nothing, really. I wondered whether we could get together this evening—just sort out a few things before work tomorrow…'

'OK…' He seemed to be thinking. 'Want to grab a bite to eat somewhere, then? Or, better still, come to me. I've moved into the log cabin at Foley's farm. Know where it is?'

'Yes.' Emma's fingers tightened on the phone. The Foleys lived about a kilometre out of town. 'I thought it was only a holiday let.'

'I struck a deal with the Foleys. It's mine for as long as I need it.'

'I see…well, that's good. About dinner—I've made soup. I could bring some over.'

He curled a low laugh. 'You're obviously intent on feeding me. But soup sounds good. I did a shop this morning. I'm sure we'll find something to go with it.'

Declan felt a new spring in his step as he threw himself under the shower. How odd that Emma must have been thinking about him just at the same moment he'd been thinking about her…

Emma was glad he'd found somewhere to live, and the log cabin was a comfortable option for the time being, she thought, guiding the car carefully over the cattle grid that marked the entrance to the farm. The cabin was barely five minutes drive further on and in seconds she saw the lighted windows come into view. As she pulled to a stop in front of the cabin, her heart began its pattering again, the nerves in her stomach lurching and flailing like a drunken butterfly.

Out of the car, she took a moment to look up at the sky. It was the same night sky she'd been seeing since she was a child, the same stars. But tonight she noticed them in a way she never had before. The Milky Way was its usual wash of grey-white light, peppered with twinkling stars. But tonight, as she watched, one lone star shot across the heavens, leaving a glittering trail of light before it disappeared.

'Stargazing?' Declan's deep voice was husky behind her.

'Oh—' Emma spun round, giving a jagged half-laugh. He was standing on the sheltered front porch. 'I didn't know you were there.'

'Saw your headlights. Coming in?'

'Mmm.' Suddenly, for no reason at all, anticipation was a sweet ache in her chest, a flutter in her breathing. She held her vacuum jug of soup tightly and followed him inside.

The cabin was open-plan and modern with the lounge area and kitchen melded into one living space. 'Oh, good,' Emma said lightly. 'You've got the fire going.'

'Glass of wine?' Declan offered as they moved across the timber floor to the kitchen. 'I have a nice local red.'

'OK, thanks.' Emma placed her soup on the counter top. 'You should be comfortable here.'

Declan didn't comment. Instead, he took up the wine he'd left breathing and poured two glasses. He handed one to Emma, unable to stop himself gazing at her with an intensity that made his heart stall for a second and then pick up speed. She was wearing jeans that clung to her legs and outlined a pert little backside. Her top was a frilly button-up shirt, the neckline open just enough to expose a hint of cleavage. Her hair had a just-washed, just-brushed shine about it and when their gazes met and she smiled at him he felt a jolt to every one of his senses. Hell. How was he going to get through the evening without wanting to…?

'What?' Emma raised a quick brow.

He shrugged, breaking eye contact quickly. 'I guess we should drink to the future of our *partnership*.'

Emma's mind went blank. They seemed to have travelled half a lifetime in a few days. Even this morning, she'd woken with a start, wondering whether she'd dreamed it all—that she actually had a partner for the practice, someone to rely on, to confer with—to trust. 'I guess we should.' She gave a tinny laugh to disguise the sudden attack of nerves. Lifting her glass to his, she echoed, 'To our partnership.'

'What kind of soup did you bring?' Declan cringed at the banality of his conversation. But his brain felt like shredded cheese.

'Minestrone.'

'A meal in itself.' He sent her a crooked grin. 'I put some herb bread in the oven to warm when I knew you were bringing soup.'

Emma savoured another mouthful of the full-bodied wine. 'You know about food, then?'

He lifted a shoulder modestly. 'I went along to the farmers' market this morning. I thought I might have seen you there.'

Emma blinked rapidly. 'I used to go when I had time to cook.'

'The produce is amazing,' Declan said, indicating they should take their wine through to the lounge area. 'I couldn't stop buying stuff.'

Emma chuckled. 'And I'll bet the stall-holders couldn't wait to sell you *stuff*. The whole town will know who you are by now.'

'They will?' He looked startled.

'And that you're living here and fending for yourself.'

He groaned. 'It won't be daily casseroles at the surgery, will it?'

'Not just casseroles.' Emma sent him an innocent wide-eyed look and curled herself into the big squishy armchair. 'There'll possibly be apple pies as well. Bendemere will want you to feel at home here.'

'I think I'm beginning to already.' He'd taken his place on the sofa opposite her. 'By the way, I released young Ashleigh this afternoon.'

'Any problems?'

He was about to ask if she'd expected any. Except he'd seen the flash of worry in her eyes. 'None at all,' he elaborated. 'And I have Aaron and Renee coming in for a chat tomorrow.'

Emma felt a flood of relief. If he'd already got on first name terms with the Maines, then he must have at least listened to her concerns and trod softly. 'They're not bad parents. They're just—'

'Young?' Declan gave a rueful smile. 'I'll be gentle with them, Emma, but I promise I'll get through to them, whatever it takes.'

Well, she guessed she couldn't ask for more than that. She took another mouthful of wine and then leaned forward to place her glass on the coffee table between them. In a second her thoughts began racing like an out of control juggernaut. She'd come to ask Declan something. She tried to think of the best way to say what she'd come to say but, in the end, there was really no lead-in for the questions she needed answers to.

'Declan—' she paused and wet her lips, tasting the sweetness of the wine '—I need to run something past you.'

'About the practice?'

'No.' Emma swallowed hard. 'I want to know the extent of your involvement with my father.'

'I thought I'd told you.'

Not nearly enough. 'You mentioned Dad was your boss when you were at John Bosco's and that he took a special interest in you. Was there a reason for that? I mean, there must have been a large group of interns. Why did he single you out?'

So here it was, sooner than he would have liked. Deep down, he'd known someone as astute as Emma would not have been content with the glib kind of scenario he'd painted about knowing her father. Very deliberately, he took a mouthful of his wine and placed his glass next to hers on the coffee table. His jaw tightened. 'I was about ten, I suppose, when your dad started visiting our home.'

Emma stared at him uncertainly. 'Was someone ill?'

He shook his head. 'My mother was a nurse. She and Andrew worked together in Casualty at the Prince Alfred in Melbourne.'

Oh. She hadn't expected that. She quickly put dates and ages together in her head. Dad would have been married to Mum by then… 'What were the circumstances? How did— why did Dad become involved with your family?'

He looked at her steadily. 'Are you sure you want to hear this, Emma?'

Emma had no idea where their conversation was leading and her stomach was churning. But she knew she needed answers. 'Yes.'

He rocked his hand as if say, *so be it.* 'My parents, me and my two younger sisters were just a regular little family living in the suburbs of Melbourne when my dad was killed in an industrial accident. Suddenly our lives were turned upside down. Overnight, Mum was a sole supporting parent with three kids to feed and educate. She had no choice than to switch from part-time to full-time work.'

Emma shook her head. She'd been indulged as a child and had wanted for nothing in a material sense. 'It must have been very hard on you all.'

'No, not hard, exactly.' His mouth lifted in a token smile. 'Just different. I know I had to grow up pretty fast. Erinn and Katie were only little girls.'

'You had to be the man of the house.'

He shrugged. 'Mum worked an early shift. We went to a neighbour's until it was time for school and Mum was always home for us in the afternoon. We missed Dad, of course, were bewildered for a time. But, after a while, kids being kids, we accepted our lives as they were, changes and all. But I guess Mum had worries she never told us about. Well, how could she?' The muscle in his jaw kicked for a second. 'It was about that time Andrew began calling round. Mum merely said he was a friend from the hospital. Sometimes he brought groceries, had a kick of the football with me. He seemed to enjoy being around us kids. Told us he had a little girl called Emma.'

Emma licked lips that seemed bone-dry. 'H-how long did he keep coming to see you? Weeks, months…?'

'Couple of months, I guess. I was a kid, Emma. Time didn't mean much. I just remember when he stopped coming. I asked Mum about it. She said he'd left the PA and gone to another hospital. He wouldn't be able to see us any more.'

Emma lifted eyes that were wide and anguished. 'Do you think they were…*involved*?'

'I don't know,' he said evenly.

She swallowed hard, as if unable to voice the questions crowding her head. Had Dad fallen in love with—? 'What was your mother's name?' she asked.

'Anne,' Declan said quietly. 'She was called Anne. She died a couple of years ago.'

Anne O'Malley. The name sat frozen inside Emma, along with a block of emotions. She'd never heard her father refer to anyone by that name. Never. But obviously Dad's involvement with Declan hadn't ended there. 'Was it pure chance you and Dad met up again when you were an intern?'

'It seemed like chance. Perhaps he'd simply seen my name on the intake list. I do know he was extremely interested in my welfare. But he was discreet. I never felt I was treated differently than the others. But I knew I could go to him with any problems.'

Emma smiled sadly. 'That sounds like Dad. But you mentioned wanting to chuck in medicine. Why was that?'

'My mother had a stroke…' Declan's words were drawn out softly, seeming to echo in the close confines of the cabin. 'She was only forty-eight. Both Erinn and Katie were at Uni. Money was tight. I figured I could get a *real* job, start bringing in the big bucks.' He rubbed at his jaw. 'God only knows what I thought I was capable of doing. When I told Andrew, he was shocked. He told me I had the potential to make a fine doctor.' Declan gave a rough laugh. 'At the time I remember wondering how *potential* was going to pay the bills. Mum's rehab was dragging on and I knew it would be a long time before she could work again—if ever. Then, suddenly out of the blue, she was whisked off to a private clinic with the latest methods. I gathered Andrew had arranged it. I have the feeling he paid for it as well.'

Emma just nodded. If she'd had any doubts before, then she had none now. Dad had fallen in love with Anne but he'd stayed with his wife. *For my sake?* she wondered now. Or maybe Anne had sent him away so as not to break up his family. They'd never know. Emma was not about to ask her own mother. Ever. Sometimes, it was better not to revisit old wounds, old memories.

Somehow, they got through the rest of the evening. They ate their soup and the warmed herb bread and made desultory conversation.

'What made you decide to go for a jog?' Emma asked later, washing the platter they'd used for the local cheeses and crisp slices of apple they'd eaten instead of dessert.

'I went out on to the porch, took one look at the paddock and all that space and thought, why not?'

'And it was good?'

'It was fine,' he hedged. He didn't tell her he'd begun to ache all over. He felt almost relieved when Emma glanced surreptitiously at her watch. The evening had strained them both. 'Cup of tea before you go?'

'No, I won't, thanks,' she said almost hurriedly. 'I'll just grab my Thermos jug.'

Declan managed a quick smile. 'I'll walk you out.'

'Thanks.' Emma's return smile was edged with vulnerability.

On the lighted porch, Declan paused and looked down at her. 'Are you OK?'

'You've given me a bit to think about.'

His mouth drew in. She'd sounded shaky and the eyes that lifted briefly to his were guarded and shadowed. Almost in slow motion, he took the Thermos from her unprotesting hands and set it on the outdoor table. 'Come here…'

Emma fought a losing battle as he gathered her close. Every caressing detail of his hands was conveyed to her through the thin stuff of her shirt, lapping at the edge of her resistance. Confusion and need struggled for supremacy.

'Half-truths wouldn't have done,' he said quietly.

'I know,' she said huskily, not trusting her voice too far.

Declan frowned down at her. A tiny chill wind had come in a flurry behind her, separating tendrils of her hair from around her face and fluffing them out. For an instant, she'd looked so young. And so alone.

'It's just—I don't quite know where I fit any more,' she said quietly, an admission that was heightened by her evident uncertainty about *what* to think.

'You were the sunshine of your father's life, Emma. Hell, you must know he'd have moved mountains for you?'

Her mouth trembled. 'Perhaps he was just overcompensating. Perhaps he felt guilty that he'd rather have been with Anne and all of you.'

Declan swore under his breath. 'That's rubbish. Did you ever feel second-best?'

She shook her head. 'It's been a bit of a revelation all the same. About Dad.'

'With hindsight, would you have rather stayed in ignorance?'

Letting her breath go on a heavy sigh, she stepped away from the weight of his hands. 'I honestly don't know.'

CHAPTER FOUR

DECLAN immersed himself in his Monday morning surgery. It was better he did, he thought, grabbing a quick coffee between patients. Anything to keep his mind from flipping back to last night and Emma's reaction to what he'd told her. Now he wondered whether he'd done the right thing in telling her anything.

He could have pleaded ignorance. But secrets had a way of surfacing when you least expected. And, in reality, did any of it matter now? Emma seemed to think so. He sighed and reached for his phone when it rang softly. 'Yes, Moira?'

'Your eleven o'clock's cancelled, Declan, and the Maines are here already.'

'OK, I'll come out. And don't forget I'm going to need extra time for this consult, Moira.'

'All taken care of.'

'Thanks.' He replaced the handpiece and got to his feet. Moments later, he was ushering Aaron and Renee Maine through to his office. When they were settled, he said, 'Just for the record, you're not on trial here. But obviously I need your input if we're to sort something out for Ashleigh. Do you have any idea what may have triggered her asthma this time?'

'She had a cold.' Renee kept her gaze averted. 'Sometimes, no matter what we do, she can't seem to throw it off.'

'I know my smoking doesn't help…' Aaron came in. He paused and chewed his bottom lip. 'Renee and me have talked a bit—' He stretched out his hands, his knuckles white as he clasped them across his jeans-clad thighs. 'I reckon I have to quit. And no mucking about this time.'

'Well, that's very good news.' Declan leaned forward earnestly. 'There's a great deal of help I can give you for that.'

Aaron shook his head. 'I'm gonna chuck out my cigarettes—go cold turkey.'

'That's pretty drastic, Aaron.' Declan was cautious. 'And I'd like to give you a physical before you start, if that's OK?'

'Yeah, whatever. I just want the poison outta me system.'

'Dr O'Malley—' Renee paused, nervously winding a strand of dark hair around her finger '—could you explain just what happens when Ashleigh gets an attack? This time, it scared us spitless. We had to call the ambulance.'

'Sure.' Declan swung round to the bank of filing cabinets behind him. 'I actually put together some reading matter for you.' He pulled out a file and opened it. 'There's a chart here that will give you an idea of the body's reaction during an asthma attack.' So saying, he flipped out the chart and placed it in front of the young parents. 'As you know, asthma affects the lungs,' he explained. 'When someone experiences an attack the tubes begin narrowing, making breathing difficult.'

'Oh—that's the wheezing sound Ashleigh makes?' Renee looked at Declan fearfully, fisting her hands and crossing them over her chest.

Almost an hour later, during which Declan had drawn diagrams for the parents and explained in depth the crippling effects of an asthma attack on their daughter, Renee said, 'I feel like we're really getting somewhere at last. And we'll need to go to the physio's appointment with Ashleigh, then?'

'It's essential.' Declan was unequivocal. 'One of you should be there and learn the breathing technique with your daughter.'

'We can do that.' Renee's mouth trembled into a shaky smile. 'We're ever so grateful to you for explaining everything. Thank you, Dr O'Malley.'

'Yeah. Thanks, Doc,' Aaron said awkwardly. 'Thanks a lot.'

'Ashleigh's a great kid,' Declan complimented them. 'Take care of her.'

'Oh, we will.' Renee linked hands with her husband and they stood together.

'Er—when do you want me for this medical, Doc?' Aaron's chin came up and his shoulders straightened as if he'd at last taken charge of his life and his family.

'The sooner, the better.' Declan opened the door of his consulting room for them. 'Sort out something with Moira as you leave.'

Emma was in some kind of shock. She knew the signs and she also knew it would pass. But finding out about Dad... Clicking off her computer, she got to her feet. Possibly, it had had the same impact as finding out as an adult that you were adopted.

But she and Declan had got through the first week as practice partners without any major dramas. She should be glad about that. Not that they'd seen much of one another. Well, not for long enough to have talked about anything other than the patients. Now it was Friday and they were about to begin their first staff meeting. Moira had been invited to attend.

'Let's keep this as brief and to the point as we can,' Declan suggested as they sat at the table in the staffroom.

'I don't have any complaints,' Moira said in her forthright style.

'How's Jodi shaping up?' Declan flipped his pen back and forth between his fingers.

'Very well,' Emma came in. 'She's caught on exactly to what we need.'

'Good.' Declan turned to face Emma. 'Libby still OK to start with us on Monday?'

'She can do a four-day week,' Emma said. 'If we're happy to work around that?'

'Fine with me,' Declan said economically.

'Libby's coming in for some orientation tomorrow,' Emma

relayed. 'She and I will go over things so she's up to speed and then she'll start officially on Monday—if that's all right with you, Declan?'

'Sounds very proactive. And make sure we pay Libby for the Saturday hours, please, Moira.' He lifted his head and raised an eyebrow between the two women. 'If that's all the staff business, then?'

'I've nothing else,' Moira said.

'Nor me.' Emma shook her head.

'Right.' Declan scooted his chair back from the table and stretched out his legs. 'Moira, feel free to take off, then. And thanks for making my first week such a smooth ride.'

'Oh—how nice of you to say so, Declan,' Moira responded coyly. 'I think we're going to make a great team.' She stood to her feet, sending the two doctors a broad smile. 'See you both on Monday.'

'Have a nice weekend,' they chorused.

Moira was barely out of the door when Declan rounded on Emma. 'Any patients you want to consult about?'

'A couple.' She gave an inward shrug. Did he always conduct his meetings at this pace? 'The lab confirmed Russell Kernow has whooping cough.'

'Poor old boy! Probably jabs for that weren't around when he was a kid. Not much we can do, though. It will just have to run its course. And the good thing is he's not infectious any longer. So, you'll release him then?'

Emma nodded. 'From a funding point of view, we can't justify keeping him indefinitely. Someone from the Rotary has been round to his home and replaced the filters in his air-con units and the meals on wheels will start calling again.'

Declan ran a finger across his chin thoughtfully. 'We should probably keep up a regular home visit, though.'

'I'll tee up with Libby to pop in on him each day. Anything untoward, she can report to us,' Emma said.

'Great.' Declan smiled and raised his arms and locked them at the back of his neck. 'How about your gynae patient, Sylvia?'

Emma was surprised he'd remembered such a small detail as a patient's first name. 'She's gone home. Her bladder function is still incomplete but she's managing much better. Her husband is at home for support and I aim to see her regularly until everything is back to normal. How was your consult with the Maines?' Emma pressed back a strand of hair behind her ear, shifting the angle of her gaze to look fully at him.

'Er—productive, I think.' Declan caught the concentration of her gaze, noting how the forest-green of her eyes was unusually dark, her expression almost wistful. His heart thumped, the memory of her feminine softness under his hands making his body tighten uncomfortably. Hell…he was almost tempted to cancel his plans for the weekend. And do what? the practical part of his brain demanded.

'And?' Her mouth was smiling. Just. More a tiny upward flick at the corners. 'Wakey, wakey, Doctor.'

'Huh!' Declan gave a crack of laughter. 'Slipped out of focus there for a minute. What were we talking about?'

'The Maine family.'

'Right.' He spun a finger up in comprehension. 'Aaron is chucking the smokes and Ashleigh is booked to see the physio next week. All on the file.' He cranked a dark eyebrow at her. 'You all set to cover for the weekend?'

She nodded.

'Good. Looks like we can wrap it up, then.' He clicked his pen closed and pushed it back in his shirt pocket. 'I'll just grab my bag and be off.' In one fluid movement, he'd stood to his feet and pushed his chair in.

Somewhat more slowly, Emma followed suit. She caught up with him again as he came out of his office, pulling the door closed and locking it. 'You seem in an almighty hurry to get out of the place.' Emma tried to dismiss the odd stab of disappointment she felt, almost running to keep up with him as he strode back out to reception.

'I'm driving to Brisbane.' Declan hoisted his medical case on to the counter top and wheeled to face her. 'Erinn is flying in for a conference. It's been ages since we've been able to catch up.'

'No wonder you're excited, then.' Emma managed a quick smile. 'So, what kind of conference is it?'

'Erinn is an OT,' he said, as if that would explain everything.

Emma blinked. An occupational therapist. 'And Katie? What does she do?' Emma knew she was holding him up but suddenly, for reasons she didn't want to analyse, she needed to put him together with his family. See them as a unit. Something *she* didn't have any longer.

'Katie teaches high school. Year eights. The *littlies,* as she calls them. Loves it.'

He laughed and then drawled sing-song, 'And they're both married to good guys and both have two kids each.'

Emma wrinkled her nose at him. 'So why aren't *you* married?' she asked lightly.

'Dunno. Never happened.' Raising an arm, he flipped his case off the counter top. 'Er...if there's a crisis of any kind—call me,' he instructed. 'I'll come galloping back.'

Her laugh cracked in the middle. 'On your white charger?'

'You bet. Isn't that what knights do?'

'Very cute.' Head thrown back, Emma caught his gaze. Her smile widened. Declan smiled back and, for just a moment, a blink of time, there was a connection of shared awareness. Sharp. Intense. Then, suddenly, their smiles retracted as quickly as turning off a light switch.

They both looked awkwardly away at precisely the same moment. And Declan was gone in the time it took for him to stride down the ramp to the parking area at the front of the surgery and cross to his car.

Against her better judgement, Emma watched from the window. In seconds he'd taken off, the bonnet of his silver-grey Audi a flash in the setting sun as he passed the border of flowering plumbago and was lost to sight. Emma stifled a sigh and drew back. He was on his way.

Suddenly all the places in her heart felt empty.

A peculiar kind of separateness engulfed her. She had nowhere to go.

And she realized she'd wanted to go with Declan. Be close with him. Meet his sister. Gather the warmth of family about her. *Oh, dear God.* Lifting a hand, she pressed it against her mouth. Where did she think she was going with any of this?

She needed to get a serious grip.

Keep busy. That was the best option. The only option. She locked up and set the alarm and then looked at her watch. It was still relatively early. She had time to pop in on Sylvia.

'How is everything going?' Emma asked as they sat side by side in the Gartrells' comfortable lounge room.

The older woman smiled. 'Tom's treating me like a queen. Doing the washing and everything. And we do the cooking together.'

'You know not to lift heavy pots and things,' Emma warned.

Sylvia flicked her hand dismissively. 'I just give the orders and Tom takes direction. We're quite a team.'

Emma chuckled. 'I'm sure you are. Now, how about the rest of you?'

Sylvia leaned forward confidentially. 'I think I may have had a breakthrough with the water. It's coming much better.'

'That's brilliant, Sylvia. You're still measuring the output?'

'Like you told me.'

'And how much are you still retaining?'

Sylvia thought for a second. 'About fifty mils. And I used the catheter to get that away. But I must say it's getting a bit tiresome.'

'Well, I think you can stop, now.'

'I can? Really?'

'Yes. Most of us retain that amount of urine naturally. I'd say nature's taken over and your body is well on the way to a complete recovery.'

'Oh, my!' Sylvia's hand went to her chest. 'You know I thought it would never happen. Even turning on the water at the basin like the nurses said didn't help. I was beginning to think I was some kind of oddity.'

'Oh, Sylvia, of course you're not! It's been a struggle but you'll reap the rewards of having the surgery done now.'

'Yes. And now I can power on again, get into my garden and help with the grandkids much more.'

'But not for a while yet,' Emma cautioned. 'You've had major surgery, Sylvia. Now, barring emergencies, could you come and see me in two weeks and we'll check everything is where it should be?'

'I can do that, dear.'

'About medication…' Emma flipped open the file she'd brought with her. 'I'd like you to stay on the hormone cream the specialist prescribed. Do you have enough for the next two weeks? If not, I'll write you a new script.'

'I have one repeat left,' Sylvia said. 'That nice new partner you have wrote me a script when he popped in on me at the hospital.'

'Oh—' Emma frowned. That would have been on that Saturday morning when they'd only just firmed up their partnership. But there was nothing on file… She lowered her gaze and rechecked the information. Oh, yes—there it was, in Declan's precise handwriting. So, why hadn't she seen it? She bit her lip thoughtfully. Probably because she hadn't been looking for it. Hadn't expected Declan to have become involved so quickly in a hands-on kind of way with their patients. She blinked a bit, not quite able to admit that she was missing the solidarity of his presence already.

Emma got to her feet. 'I'll see myself out, Sylvia. Don't get up.'

'Tom should be back any minute,' Sylvia said. 'He's just gone to get our usual Friday fish and chips for tea. Why don't you stay, dear? He always buys extra.' A grin tweaked a dimple in her cheek. 'Still can't get used to the fact there's only the two of us now. Stay,' she invited again.

Emma was tempted. Lord, how she was tempted. The need to be with family, surrogate as it was, was almost unbearable.

But, in reality, it would solve nothing. 'It's a lovely thought, Sylvia. And thanks. But...er...I've another patient I need to catch up with,' she invented hurriedly.

Sylvia nodded. 'Another time, then. And Emma?' Reaching up from her sitting position, the older woman squeezed the tips of Emma's fingers. 'Be kind to yourself, dear. Your dad would have wanted that for you.'

CHAPTER FIVE

HE WAS back.

Declan blew out a calming breath and switched off the ignition. He'd made good time from Brisbane and driven straight to Kingsholme, telling himself if Emma was out it was no big deal.

He stretched, felt a crack or two in his spine and shoulder joints, shrugged inwardly and swung out of the car. He'd go round to the back of the house. If the kitchen door was open, he'd know Emma was home.

Oh, hell. He worked his legs as he walked along the path at the side of the house. His joints felt as stiff and rusty as the Tin Man from *The Wizard of Oz.* Mounting the shallow steps to the verandah, he stood, quietly absorbing his surroundings.

It was a typical back verandah found in countless rural settings in Australia. A mish-mash of everyday items, from the outdoor shoes left to dry to the weathered wooden ladder that was being used as a plant stand. Two lovely old wicker chairs painted a silvery-blue were parked against the wall and in between sat a matching round wicker table covered with a patchwork cloth. On the table sat a little tea tray, a cup and saucer and a glass jar of…what? Shortbread? Something like that…

Declan took a hard breath and tunnelled a hand back through his hair. There was an odd feeling about the setting. A loneliness. Emma? His heart twisted. He hated that conclusion.

Moving purposefully across the verandah, he called a greeting from the open kitchen doorway. And waited, his heart banging like a drumbeat in his chest. There was no reply. Yet he knew she was here. He could *feel* it.

Warily, he took a couple of steps into the kitchen and looked around, his eyes widening, his face working at the sweetness of what he saw.

Emma was lying curled on the cane settee. It was obvious she was asleep, her pose unconsciously sexy yet vulnerable. Desire and need slammed into him with the intensity of a punch to the solar plexus, dizzying, like sudden gravity after weightlessness.

He felt a hard wedge in the region of his stomach and his jaw clenched. Oh, sweet heaven. This felt almost like voyeurism. Swallowing the dryness in his throat, he moved closer. 'Emma…'

His voice seemed to fall on Emma's skin like a caress, easing her out of sleep into wakefulness. 'Declan?' Her eyes shot open, her voice foggy with confusion. She jack-knifed to a sitting position. 'How long have you been there?'

'Just arrived. I didn't mean to intrude. Your kitchen door was open—'

'It's OK.' She lifted her hands, sweeping her hair back behind her ears. She gave a husky laugh. 'I started reading— must have fallen asleep.'

He frowned. 'Do you do that often—leave your door open? I could have been a burglar.'

She sent him a weighted look. 'What were you intending to steal—the kitchen chairs? The cat? This is a country town, Declan. No one locks their back doors.'

His mouth grew taut. 'I was concerned for you, that's all.'

Soft colour licked along Emma's cheekbones and she protested gruffly, 'Well, as you can see, I'm fine.' She stood to her feet. 'I thought you'd be back much later than this.'

Declan gave a twitch of his shoulder. 'Erinn's conference broke up at lunchtime. We both took off soon after. How was *your* weekend?'

Lonely without you, she was tempted to reply. But quickly thought better of it. 'Couple of call-outs,' she said. 'Nothing serious. So you had a good time with your sister?'

'Yes,' he said economically. 'Erinn and I had a few laughs, caught up on the family news.'

'As you do. Something to drink?' she asked, moving to the fridge, opening the door and peering into the contents, trying in vain to stem the smile that just wouldn't go away. He was back and somehow, in some odd way, her world felt right again. Which was crazy, she decided, leaning in to extract pear juice, a ginger cordial and soda water. She spun round and moved back to the bench. 'You'll like this,' she said, expertly mixing the three ingredients and then pouring the finished product into two tall glasses. She topped each glass with a sprig of mint and passed one across to Declan. 'It's delicious,' she promised when he hesitated over a taste test.

He held the glass to his lips and tasted once and then again, licking the residue from his lips. 'It's good,' he agreed and drank thirstily.

'Let's catch the last of the rays,' Emma invited, putting her own half-finished drink aside and leading the way out on to the verandah.

Ignoring the outdoor chairs, Declan moved to stand with his back against the railings. 'I'm a bit stiff after the drive,' he explained.

'So, was the trip back all right, then?' she asked, her hip almost touching his as she stood beside him.

'Mmm.' Why on earth were they talking such generalities? Stuff it. He couldn't hold back any longer. He turned to face her. 'I thought about you a lot over the weekend…'

Emma swallowed. Her heart tripped. He was bending towards her, his blue eyes capturing hers with an almost magnetic pull. 'I…'

'Thought about me too?' he murmured hopefully.

She had. She couldn't deny it. But would it help either of them if she told him that? Did she need the complication an admission would undoubtedly bring? She felt her heart bang out of rhythm, her gaze moving restlessly, almost fearfully, as though to find a way out of the dilemma.

The late afternoon sun felt intoxicatingly warm against her back. There was no urgency in the air. Just a languid kind of sweetness.

Declan leaned closer to her, slowly.

In a second, Emma felt her body trembling from the inside out. Was this what it felt like before a first kiss? Her mind went blank. After Marcus had defected, she'd thought she'd never again trust a man enough to experience another *first kiss*.

But she wanted it. How she wanted it.

Declan was so close to her now she could see the faint shadow across his jaw line, the slight smudges under his eyes. His face reflected a toughness, a strength.

'Emma…' he said, his voice low, this last second before his kiss.

Her mouth trembled. She could feel his breath on her face. It smelled minty, a faint residue from his drink. She lifted her gaze and stared at him, mesmerized by the yearning she saw in his eyes. The desire to be kissed by him was irresistible and, before she could second-guess the wisdom of it all, she was leaning into him.

Declan took her face in his hands, his need materialising in the softest sigh, before his mouth found hers. The kiss rolled through his blood and raw need slammed into him like nothing he had ever known before. Her lips parted and her own longing seemed to match his, overwhelming him like the heady aroma of some dark heated wine.

Applying a barely-there pressure through his hands, he whispered the tips of his fingers down the sides of her throat, then in a sweep across her breastbone to her shoulders, gathering her in.

Emma clung to him. And the kiss deepened, turned wrenching and wild. She felt a need inside her, an overwhelming need to be touched like this, held like this.

And *stroked* to the point of ecstasy by this man.

But it wasn't going to go that far. At least not today. She felt Declan pulling back, breaking the kiss, slowly, gently, his lips leaving a shivering sweetness like trails of insubstantial gossamer.

A long beat of silence while they collected themselves.

'Have we broken every rule in the official partnership handbook?' Declan asked in a deep voice, wrapping her closer.

She licked her lips. 'Possibly…probably.'

He bent to her, pressing his forehead to hers. 'It's all been a bit…'

'Unexpected?' Emma was dizzy with the newness of it all.

'Huge understatement,' he declared. 'Bone-rattling would be more apt. Ah, Emma…' His fingers lifted her chin, his mouth only a breath away as he said her name and then his lips were on hers. Again. And it felt so right the second time around. To taste slowly and blissfully instead of devouring as if there were no tomorrow.

Emma felt intoxicated, as though she were swimming through warm treacle toffee, loving the vital male taste of him, the warmth of his arms around her, the long, slow getting-to-know-you kind of kiss that she guessed neither of them wanted to end. Because then there would be questions, post-mortems.

And no answers.

But of course the kiss had to end. Good things, unexpected pleasurable things, always did. This time at Emma's instigation. Slowly, she pulled back, untwining his arms from where he'd looped them around her shoulders and took a decisive step away from him.

Declan's shoulders lifted in a huge sigh. 'I guess I should go,' he murmured and hesitated. Then, as if still compelled to touch her, he reached for her, running his hands down her arms, lacing his fingers with hers. 'Before we get into any more trouble,' he added wryly, placing the softest kiss at the side of her mouth. 'See you tomorrow.' He let her go abruptly, turning away and making a swift exit across the verandah and down the steps to the path.

He didn't look back.

At work on Monday morning, Emma was still dazed by what had happened, her whole body still sensitized by Declan's kisses, her thoughts far from clear. She'd been woefully un-prepared for the avalanche of emotions she'd felt—and never experienced before. Not even with Marcus, whom she'd almost married.

She went along to her consulting room, lifting a hand to touch the corner of her mouth where Declan had imprinted that last lingering kiss. He'd be arriving at the surgery very soon. Suddenly she felt fluttery, the expectation of seeing him intense, sizzling and her former safe world was spinning out of control.

Declan left the log cabin hardly noticing the chilly winter morning, still trying to untangle the strands of emotions inside him. He'd *kissed* Emma. God, how had he let that happen? He should have been concentrating on cementing their pro-fessional partnership, not reacting to his hormones like a randy adolescent.

But they'd only kissed, for crying out loud. People did that all the time. It didn't mean they were about to move in together! Emma would see it for what it was. Opportunity, time and place, the uniqueness of their circumstances and no doubt capped off by a build-up of emotional overload. He heaved in a controlling breath and concentrated on the road.

But, by the time he reached the surgery, the rationalisation he'd concocted was rapidly being drowned out by the clang of warning bells. He was kidding himself. It was nothing to do with hormones. It was about feelings. It was about Emma Armitage.

OK, play it by ear, Declan self-counselled as he made his way along the corridor to his consulting room. He stowed his medical case and straightened his shoulders. Moira had informed him Emma was already in. Closing the door to his surgery, he moved along to her room. Her door was slightly open. Nevertheless, he rapped before he went in. 'Morning.'

'Good morning.' Emma lifted her gaze from her computer, snapping a smile into place. 'You're in early.'

Declan held out the cake tin he'd brought in. 'Thought we could share this for morning tea for the next hundred years or so,' he said deadpan.

Emma frowned a bit. 'What is it?'

'Fruit cake—old family recipe. Katie sent it via Erinn.'

'That was nice of her.' Emma looked at the rather battered cake tin with its old-fashioned English hunting scene on the lid. 'My Nanna had one of these,' she said with a laugh and got to her feet. 'May I look?'

'Help yourself.'

'Mmm…I love that smell,' Emma inhaled the classic lusciousness of rich dried fruit laced with brandy. 'Pity, though.'

He raised a dark brow.

'I think it'll be long gone before a hundred years are up. I'll leave it in Moira's safekeeping,' she added, replacing the lid carefully. 'Thank Katie when next you speak to her, won't you?'

He nodded absently. There was a beat of silence. Then, softly, as if the words were being pushed up through his diaphragm, 'Are you OK about yesterday, Emma?'

Emma didn't try to misunderstand him. Looking up, she saw the uncertainty clouding his gaze. Lord, she didn't want to have this conversation. She gave a little twist of her shoulder and asked a question of her own, 'How *OK* are you about it?'

Declan felt his heart walk a few flights of stairs. His mouth worked a bit before he answered, 'I'm not.'

'Did you enjoy kissing me, Declan?'

He looked startled at her frankness. Then, throatily, 'I'd have to be dead from the feet up not to have enjoyed kissing you, Emma. You're lovely…'

'Oh!' Suddenly, there was an ache in her stomach that was

half pleasure, half pain. And a new awareness was beating its wings all around them.

'We shouldn't let it happen again, though.' Declan sounded as though he was trying to convince himself. His hand reached out towards her cheek, then drew back sharply before it could connect with her skin. 'We're supposed to be operating a professional partnership here, aren't we?'

Her mouth dried. Was he saying they couldn't have both? Yet she ached for him. For the physical closeness they'd found yesterday. For more and more of his long, slow kisses. She was still searching for an acceptable reply when the harsh jangle of the phone in reception split the air.

'Monday morning,' Emma said resignedly.

Within seconds Moira's head popped around the door. 'We have an emergency at the primary school, folks. Neal Drummond needs a doctor there.'

Declan looked a question at Emma. 'Neal's the head teacher,' she said. 'What's happened, Moira?'

'Adam Jones has fallen out of a tree and impaled himself on the fence. It's his upper arm. The child is Carolyn Jones's grandson,' she added for Declan's benefit. 'He's only seven.'

'Then I think we should both go,' Declan said firmly. 'It all sounds a bit iffy.'

'Tsk...' Moira shook her head at the unfairness of it all. 'As if that family needs more trouble.'

'Let's not get bogged down in sentiment, Moira,' Declan growled. 'We can sort all that out later. Let's move it!' He flung the words at Emma from the doorway. 'I'll gather up some gear. Meet you in reception.'

'That's a bit unfeeling.' Moira's feathers were clearly ruffled. 'This could well be the last straw for Carolyn.'

'Declan's still finding his way in rural medicine to some extent,' Emma said diplomatically. 'I imagine the school will have contacted Carolyn but the last thing we need is for her to go into orbit at the accident scene. Whatever else, Adam will have to be kept calm.'

'I'll get her on her mobile then.' Moira as always was one

step ahead. 'I'll tell her to go to the school office and wait there. She'll listen to me.'

'Thanks, Moira.' Emma nodded gratefully. 'And prepare her for the fact that Adam will probably have to be sent on to Toowoomba Base. Carolyn will want to go with him.'

'So she'd better pack a bag then.'

'Yes.' Emma picked up her medical case and hurried through to reception.

Declan was already there, taking delivery of the emergency supplies Libby had hastily assembled.

'Paeds drug box, IV kit and emergency oxygen—is that all you need?'

'That's brilliant, Libby, thanks.' Declan slung the emergency pack over his shoulder. He sent a quick grin at the nurse. 'In at the deep end on your first day.'

Libby returned a pert look. 'That's what I'm here for.'

'Not sure how long we'll be,' Emma warned.

'Go!' The RN shooed them towards the outer door. 'Moira and I will juggle the lists around somehow.'

'We'll take my wheels,' Declan said as they sped across the car park. In seconds they were seated and belted up. 'What kind of fence are we talking about here?' He ignited the motor and shot the car towards the street.

'Probably the ten-foot wrought iron fence at the rear of the school grounds,' Emma said. 'There are several huge Moreton Bay figs close to the fence line. I'd guess Adam's scrambled up one of those and fallen.'

'For crying out loud!' Declan muttered, anger and dread in equal portions catching him by surprise. 'Those old spiked fences have no place anywhere near a school!'

'It's precisely because they are *old*,' Emma pointed out patiently. 'They're heritage-listed.'

It was barely half a kilometre to the school but time enough for Emma's uncertainty to intensify at the thought of the possible scenario they were facing.

Neal Drummond was waiting for them. 'Thanks, both of you, for coming,' he said after Emma had made swift introductions.

'What action have you taken so far?' Declan asked quickly.

'Our year one teacher has gone up to Adam. She's physically supporting him as best she can. We've also positioned a couple of ladders so that you'll have access of sorts to the injured child.' Neal escorted them swiftly along to the accident scene.

'So, do you have any idea why Adam went climbing?' Emma asked carefully.

'Don't know yet.' Neal's mouth tightened. 'His grandmother's on her way in. We'll perhaps get a clearer picture then.'

Emma explained what initiative she'd taken to keep Carolyn at arm's length from the accident scene.

'Thanks for that, Emma.' Neal nodded his relief.

'Ambulance, fire and rescue services been alerted?' Declan queried.

'Both ambulances are out on other calls. The base will get one to us asap. Fire and rescue will be here when they can muster a team.' The head teacher ran a hand distractedly over his crew cut. 'We do have a staff member who does regular climbing. He could be of some help in the interim. He's just nipped off home to get his ropes. Right, here we are.'

'Hell's bells!' Declan's face was grim. One look at the accident scene told both doctors it going to need a painstaking and skilled team effort to achieve a successful outcome for Adam.

Just then, the boy's plaintive little cry, high-pitched and heart-rending, brought the doctors into swift consultation.

'He'll be bordering on shock with the pain.' Emma shaded her eyes, frowning up to where the dense foliage of the tree overhung the fence where the child was impaled. 'That setup with the ladders isn't going to be effective, Declan. There's no way we can work on Adam like that.'

'Well, not for long,' Declan agreed. 'But if you could manage to get up there and begin the drugs regime…'

'What will you do?' Emma looked worried.

'Wait until the abseiling ropes arrive. Hopefully, I'll be able to secure myself to one of those big branches.' Declan raised his gaze to where the giant fig spread upwards towards the heavens. 'From there I can lower myself almost to the exact spot where Adam is impaled and support him on my lap. That'll allow me the freedom to use both hands to work on him.'

They'd need to intubate. Emma asked hesitantly, 'Sure you're OK with that?' She'd noticed the sudden tautness in Declan's stance. The thinly veiled tension. He was wound tight. Oh, sweet heaven. The uncertainties of his physical fitness must be eating him up. She dived in feet first. 'Do you want to swap roles here?' she asked in a swift aside. 'It's no big deal, if you'd rather…'

'I'm not a cripple, Emma,' Declan shot back with dark impatience. 'Yet!'

'I know—I didn't mean—' Emma swallowed the constriction in her throat, steeling herself as Adam's agonized sobbing almost jettisoned her composure entirely. 'Do what you have to do, then. Just, for heaven's sake, let's get this child some pain relief. Oh—' She turned, catching sight of the male figure sprinting across the quadrangle. 'Here's the bearer of the promised ropes, by the look of it.'

'Mike Foreman,' the young teacher introduced himself. 'What do you want me to do, Doc?'

'We'll need to set up a pulley system.' Declan's response was clipped. The two men went into a huddle.

Emma left them to get on with it. Quashing her fears, she slung the emergency pack over her shoulder and began moving purposefully up the ladder. Her stomach swirled. She breathed deeply and then collected herself. 'Hi.' She looked up shakily to where the young teacher was perched. 'I'm Emma.'

'Chrissy. Are you the doctor?'

'Yes. And you're doing wonderfully, Chrissy.'

'It's been awful, just trying to hold him like this. Poor little boy…'

'I know. Just keep on doing what you're doing. That'll be a great help.' Emma was aware of curtailing her movements, doing everything in slow motion. Adam's broken little sobs spurred her on.

'Hush now, baby,' Emma soothed gently, popping the oxygen mask over the little boy's face. She began assessing her small patient. His skin was cold and clammy, indicating shock. But his pulse and BP were better than she'd feared, raised but stable. Good. She could safely administer the pain-killer and anti-nausea drugs. She'd follow up with midazolam. Its light anaesthetic properties would help to combat post-traumatic shock and ease the youngster through the ordeal ahead.

She selected the wide-bore cannula. She was taking no chances with this little one. If Adam began bleeding or, heaven forbid, going into sudden shock, they'd need to run through high-volume fluids to resuscitate him.

But, as long as the foreign object stayed where it was in Adam's arm, until it could be surgically removed, then the child was reasonably safe from haemorrhaging.

Although they still had a way to go.

With the drugs safely administered, Emma leaned more of her weight into the ladder, using both hands to secure a light absorbent pad around the child's injured arm, and then carefully and gently tucking the youngster into a space blanket. She sent the ghost of a smile to her counterpart.

Chrissy looked on in awe. 'I wouldn't have your job for anything. But, whatever you've given Adam, it's starting to work. I can feel him relaxing.'

'The drugs are doing their job, then. And that sounds like our backup arriving.'

Leaves swirled above them and then Declan's command rang out, 'One more hitch should do it, Mike. Right, I'm here—thanks.' Sitting suspended in his harness, he eased the weight of the child across on to his lap. 'Well done, team.'

Emma felt her heart lift. 'And you,' she rejoined quietly.

'Hmm.' He looked at her narrowly for a moment. 'How's our patient doing?'

'Drifting off.'

'Enough for me to get an airway in?'

'I should think so.'

Declan nodded. 'OK, I'll have a go.'

'I think this is where I leave you, guys.' Chrissy began backing down the ladder.

'The fire and rescue crew are ten minutes away,' Neal Drummond relayed from the foot of the tree.

'Have you got the airway in?' Emma's concern was more immediate.

'Almost there… Right, it's done. With a bit of luck—and heaven knows we've earned it—Adam will be in la-la land by the time the rescue guys get here.'

At last Adam was cut free. At the fireman's signal that the mission had been successful, a subdued cheer went up and, from his anchor in the tree, Mike paid out the guide rope, lowering Declan and his precious cargo to the ground.

'Nice work, folks.' The paramedics had arrived to witness the rescue. 'We'll take over now.' Gently, Adam was stretchered to the waiting vehicle, one officer supporting the little injured arm with the foreign object still *in situ*. 'Heading to Toowoomba Base, right, Emma?'

'Yes, please.' Emma bent over Adam for a final check of the IV line that was running in fluids.

'Just hang on a tick, guys.' Quickly, Declan scribbled some notes to go with their young patient.

'Declan?' Emma said in an urgent undertone. 'I can manage the patient lists if you'd like to go with Adam to the hospital.'

'And what possible use would I be there?' he growled, adding his signature and handing the notes across to the waiting ambulance officer. 'Thanks, mate. We'll be in touch with the surgeon later.'

'No worries, Doc.'

'Adam's grandmother is going with you,' a subdued Emma reminded them.

Jim Yardley, the chief paramedic, raised a hand in acknowledgement. 'All covered, Emma. Thanks.'

There was a strange lull for a few moments after the ambulance had pulled away. A kind of eerie hiatus. Emma heard the soft rustle of leaves above them and looked up. 'I hate this feeling,' she said.

Declan eyed her sharply. 'Adam will be all right, Emma. His arm will be a bit iffy for a while but kids spring back remarkably quickly.'

A furrow etched between her eyes. He just didn't get it. 'I know all that. I just meant the feeling of uncertainty. Wondering why this child did what he did this morning. Was there an upset at home? Should we be taking better care of Carolyn and her needs—the whole family?'

'For crying out loud!' Declan began gathering up their paraphernalia, impatience in every beat of his movements.

Emma felt her spine stiffen. What kind of response was that? Declan O'Malley had a lot to learn about family medicine, that was for sure. Her teeth bit into the full softness of her lower lip. She didn't need this aggravation. And she didn't need a practice partner who was on a completely different wavelength. After checking they'd left nothing behind, she followed him across to his car.

'Look—' Declan stood awkwardly beside the open lid of the car boot after loading everything inside '—just give me a bit of space here, all right?'

Emma felt a needle of guilt prick her conscience. He sounded on edge and the eyes that lifted to hers were guarded and shadowed. She swallowed. 'Are you OK?'

The corners of his mouth tightened. 'I'm fine.'

Of course he wasn't fine. Her heart bounced sickeningly. She should have realized. He'd spent most of the morning on an emotional roller coaster, no doubt agonizing whether he was going to be able to cut it in a rural practice where physical stamina counted just as much as his medical skills. But he'd done so well. So well. Her gaze faltered. 'Declan—I realize this morning has been difficult so if you feel we need a debrief, you only have to say.'

His blue eyes bored into hers. 'I'll bear it in mind.'

In other words, butt out. *Great.* Emma felt completely put in her place. At this rate they'd be lucky if the contract they'd signed lasted as long as six weeks—let alone six months!

By the time they'd got back to the surgery, Emma knew what she had to do and, by the end of the day, she'd accomplished most of it. She hesitated about telling Declan what she'd done. Would he even care…? Her train of thought was interrupted by the rap on her door and the man himself poked his head in.

'Moira said you'd finished for the day,' he said by way of explanation.

Emma beckoned him in, drawing back in her chair as if to reclaim her space. She took a deep breath, ultra-conscious of him as he walked forward and planted his hands on the desk in front of her. 'What's up?'

'I've an update on Adam. They've operated. Bit of a mess but the foreign object came out cleanly. They'll hit him with antibiotics for the next little while. Should be a straightforward recovery.'

Emma nodded, feeling the awkwardness between them cloy and magnify. She made a quick decision and swung off her chair. 'Let's go through and get a cup of tea. I'm parched—unless you need to be somewhere else?'

Several expressions chased through his eyes before he said with a rough sigh, 'No… A cuppa sounds good.' He tacked on a forced smile. 'Perhaps we can make some inroads into that fruit cake as well.'

'We'll give it a good shot,' Emma said, relieved that he'd at least agreed to have some down time, if only for a little while.

Switching on the electric jug, she got mugs down from the cupboard, all the time conscious of Declan's restive movements about her kitchen. She cut slabs of the fruit cake and set them on a plate and then, when the water boiled, she made a pot of tea. She didn't care how many cups it took, she was going to make Declan O'Malley talk to her about this morning.

'Delicious cake,' she said a bit later, swiping a crumb from the corner of her mouth. 'Family recipe, you said?'

'Mmm.' Declan was on his second cup of tea. Taking up his mug, he looked at her narrowly over its rim. 'Spit it out, Emma.'

Her eyes widened innocently. 'The cake?'

'No, not the cake.' His voice rumbled with dry humour. 'You want me to spill my guts about my reactions this morning, don't you?'

Her shoulders twitched. 'I wouldn't have put it quite so bluntly. But if it would help you to talk…'

His blue eyes traced her features one by one, then flicked back to lock with hers, their expression uncertain. 'I—realize I lost it a bit. I jumped all over you. It's the last thing I wanted to do.'

Emma drew in her breath sharply, and suddenly it was there in the air between them. The raw, overwhelming need, the awareness. The fear if it all went wrong. But, for now, they had to stay on track, keep it all professional. She moistened her lips. 'It's OK.'

'It's not OK,' he contradicted. 'I'd like to think it was a one-off but, realistically, I guess I'm going to have to face more of those knife-edge moments in the future—'

'But you'll also learn to cope, Declan,' she responded earnestly.

He snorted. 'Well, let's hope so. Otherwise, I'm not going to be much use to you as a rural doctor, am I?'

'Was it just the fact you doubted your physical capability in the situation?'

'That and the frustration I felt.' He sat back, linking his hands around his mug and staring broodingly into its contents. 'The fact is I *should* have been able to whip Adam into surgery here. Think how much easier it would have been for the family. How much more comfortable for Adam not to have had the road trip to Toowoomba.'

'But it would have been quite the wrong decision for *you*!' Emma's voice was ripe with emotion.

'I know that too,' he agreed, a small rueful twist to his mouth. 'It doesn't make the frustration any less, though.'

'Frustration you can live with,' Emma declared quietly. 'It would be a far worse outcome if you were to rush in when you're not ready.'

'Just to prove a point,' he tacked on dryly.

'Exactly.'

She was wise as well as beautiful. Declan ached to hold her again, feel the silkiness of her hair glide through his fingers. He closed his eyes briefly. He'd better face the fact. Emma Armitage had got to him as no other woman had. Ever. He wanted—*needed* her to think well of him. It mattered. A hell of a lot. He certainly didn't want her to think of him as some kind of lame dog she had to carry in the practice. He blinked and focused as Emma began speaking again.

'Don't keep beating up on yourself over this, Declan. In an ideal situation, the firemen would have been on hand to do the tree climbing today. We should have had only to carry out our role as doctors. But, like it or not, that's run-of-the-mill rural medicine,' she ended, spreading her hands in a philosophical shrug.

Declan frowned and changed the subject. 'I had a long conversation with Neal Drummond this afternoon.'

'About what?'

'Opening the swimming pool for use by our senior citizens.'

Emma's widened gaze registered her surprise at his proactiveness. 'What was his response?'

'He's willing but he'll have to confer with the school's P&C committee before he can give us an answer. I figured if we could get some water aerobics going for the seniors, it would be of immense benefit health-wise, lessen their stress levels, be a social outlet as well.'

'It would certainly benefit patients like Carolyn Jones. Well done, you.'

Declan's mouth kicked up in a crooked smile. 'Well…I'm slowly getting the hang of this kind of community medicine. Perhaps, by the end of our six months' trial, I'll be taking it in my stride.'

Emma's heart skipped a beat. But if he wasn't—what then? 'Um—I've done a bit of organizing of my own. While Carolyn's away in Toowoomba, I'm having Adam's two older siblings to stay with me.'

He huffed dryly, 'Why am I not surprised?'

'I'm a hands-on kind of girl,' she defended.

'I'd have to agree with that.' The look he sent her was blue-metal hot.

Emma's insides heaved crazily. She felt heat rising, warming her throat, flowering over her cheeks. Suddenly, her train of thought was gone, her thoughts all over the place. 'It just seemed the logical thing to do.' The words pumped up jerkily from her chest. 'Lauren and Joel know me. Before their lives went pear-shaped, Carolyn did some housekeeping for Dad and me. The kids used to come with her sometimes. They had the run of the house. Moira's round there now, helping them pack a few clothes. The school bus can pick them up from here in the mornings and drop them back. It'll be good.'

Declan's gaze softened. 'You're so like your father, Emma. He believed in actions speaking louder than words too.'

Emma dipped her head, sudden tears blurring her eyes. He couldn't have given her a nicer compliment.

CHAPTER SIX

CHILDREN made the house a home, Emma thought indulgently, watching as Lauren and Joel scooped up their breakfast cereal with obvious enjoyment. 'Now, I'll get on and make your school lunches,' she said, placing some buttered toast on the table between them. 'What would you like on your sandwiches, guys?'

'Anything will do,' ten-year-old Lauren said shyly.

Blue-eyed Joel sent an innocent look at Emma. 'It's tuck shop today.'

'We're not allowed tuck shop.' Lauren gave her younger brother an old-fashioned look.

Probably because their grandparents couldn't afford to hand out money they didn't have. Emma's soft heart was touched. Poor babes. 'Why don't we have a treat today, then? Let's do tuck shop.'

The children stopped eating and looked at Emma. 'Could we?' Lauren fisted a small hand across her chest.

'You bet,' Emma said.

'Yay!' Joel yelped with delight. 'Can I have a burger?'

'Please,' Emma directed, hiding a smile.

'Please…' Joel parroted with a grin.

'What about you, Lauren?' Emma sent the little girl a warm smile. 'Like a burger as well?'

Lauren nodded her wheat-blonde head. 'Yes, please, Emma.'

'Good. Now, what do we have to do—write out an order or something?' Emma racked her brains thinking back to her own primary school days.

'We write what we want on a piece of paper and put it in our lunch box with the money.' Joel was only too happy to provide the answers.

'And the tuck shop ladies make up the lunch orders,' Lauren filled in quietly.

'Right.' Emma looked from one to the other. 'That sounds easy-peasy.'

Lauren giggled.

'And you can get other stuff too,' Joel said around a mouthful of toast.

Emma reached for her scribble pad and a pen. 'Let's get started, then.' While the two pairs of young eyes watched intently, she wrote the orders for the burgers and then asked, 'Now, what else would you like, Lauren?'

The little girl thought for a minute. 'Could I have a straw-berry yoghurt, please?'

'Of course, you may.' Emma wrote diligently. 'Joel, honey?'

'Packet of chips—please?'

Emma raised a brow. It wasn't the most nutritious of choices, but hey, today's lunches were meant to be a treat. 'OK, done.' Emma stuffed the notes into the waiting lunch boxes and enclosed the appropriate money. 'Now, if you've finished breakfast, hop off and brush your teeth.'

Joel took off along the hallway, making *vroom* noises as he flapped his arms like an aeroplane coming in to land, almost colliding with Declan, who was making his way in. 'What's that all about?' Declan cranked a dark brow in query.

Emma chuckled. 'Joel's on a high because I said they could have tuck shop today.'

'He's not the only one on a high.' Declan's eyes and voice teased.

'It's lovely having them here.' Emma's blood sang. 'This house was made for children.'

And perhaps she'd fill it with her own one day. The wild idea of him being the father of those imaginary children stopped Declan in his tracks, sending rivers of want and doubt and sheer amazement cascading through his bloodstream. The thought was crazy… 'Er…I came in early. Thought you might want a bit of a hand. But I see I needn't have worried.'

'No—' She saw his gaze settle on her mouth and linger. And suddenly she could feel his presence, his masculinity like the ticking of a time bomb… 'They're great kids. Ah—here they are again. All set?' She snuggled them into their anoraks, gave Lauren a hug and laughed as Joel squirmed away. Handing them their backpacks, she ushered them outside to wait for the school bus.

'It's cold out there—' Emma was rubbing her arms as she came back into the warmth of the kitchen. 'Would you like a cup of tea?'

'I've put the kettle on for a fresh pot.'

'Oh—good. That's good.' Emma's voice trailed away and she glanced at her watch. 'You *are* in early.

'I couldn't stay away. It's more fun here.'

There was a moment of awkward silence while they smiled at each other in a goofy kind of way. Then the water boiled and Declan turned away to make the tea. Tea made, he turned back with the pot cradled in his hands. 'Am I making myself too much at home here? Just yell if I am.'

'No—it's nice…' The words spilled out on their own and she squirmed at her transparent honesty. 'I'll get the mugs.'

'So—did you happen to find out the reasons for Adam's misadventure?' Declan asked her.

'Mmm, I did, actually. I had a little chat to Lauren last night when she was getting ready for bed. I didn't press her,' she added, seeing Declan's sharp look of concern. 'Lauren volunteered the information. She said her gran lost her temper and smacked Adam on the legs.'

Declan's mouth drew in. 'Hard?'

'With a rolled-up newspaper.'

So, not too hard, then. They didn't need a case of child

abuse to add to the already difficult situation. 'What was the problem?'

'Adam wet the bed—again.'

'He's obviously disturbed. Poor little kid.' Declan shook his head. 'So, as doctors, what do we do—start looking for definitive solutions for this family?'

'If there are any.' Emma sighed. 'Carolyn will be beside herself.'

'Wallowing in guilt is not going to solve anything.'

'That's a bit hard.'

'So is what's happening to these kids. Be realistic, Emma. Do we know where the mother is?'

'Tracey?' Emma pulled her thoughts together. 'Toowoomba somewhere, I think. Carolyn has an address.'

'So, will she let Tracey know what's happened?'

'I don't think they speak much.'

Declan blew out a frustrated breath through his teeth. 'So, Tracey is living in a twilight zone with her junkie boyfriend while the grandparents slave their guts out to raise *her* kids. That's not good enough. Those kids need their mother.'

'They need a functioning mother,' Emma countered. 'And stability—which they have now with their grandparents.'

'They could still have that but Tracey should be there as well, sharing the load. Carolyn and Nev are nearing an age when they should be thinking of enjoying their retirement. They shouldn't have this extra burden of having to rear their grandchildren because their daughter-in-law chooses to opt out of her responsibilities.'

Emma rolled her eyes. 'So, what are you going to do—drag Tracey back by the hair and make her be a proper mother to her kids?'

'No, Dr Armitage.' Surprisingly, Declan grinned. 'I'll go and see her, talk to her and try to get her into some decent rehab programme.'

'You're quite serious about this, aren't you?'

'Yes, I am.' Declan's look turned pensive. 'I'm remembering my own childhood, when our lives suddenly turned upside-down.'

'I don't see the connection,' Emma said. '*Your* mother appears to have made a wonderful job of raising you and your sisters.'

He shrugged. 'Given a different set of genes, who knows how she might have coped? It's both as simple and as complicated as that. Anyway, I'd like to try to see Tracey. Ascertain what I can do to help.'

Emma was about to offer to accompany him but she held back. She guessed this was something he needed to do off his own bat. He was on a steep learning curve but he seemed to be getting the hang of family medicine with all its uncertainties and pitfalls. She should be grateful. 'When will you go?' she asked instead.

'This afternoon, if I can get away reasonably early. I'll make a few phone calls first, see what's out there in the way of help for Tracey. When I get to Toowoomba, I'll swing by the hospital and see Adam, have a word with Carolyn and hope she can give me Tracey's address.'

'Just—don't expect too much, Declan, from yourself or—' Emma's flow of words was interrupted by a loud banging on the front door of the surgery. She jumped to her feet.

'Wait!' Declan cautioned. 'Let me get the door.'

Emma stopped mid-stride. 'But surely it's an emergency!'

'We don't know that for sure. And people are aware you live alone, Emma.'

'Oh—' Beating back a shadowy unease, Emma fell in behind Declan as he went to the front door. Switching off the alarm, he unlocked the door and slid it open. 'Yes?'

A man dressed in workman's clothes rocked agitatedly from one foot to the other. At Declan's appearance, he pulled back uncertainly. 'You a doctor, mate?'

'Yes, I am.' Declan's response was clipped. 'What's happened?'

The man jerked a thumb over his shoulder. 'I'm the foreman from the building site across the road, there. One of the guys slipped off the scaffolding—tore his hand on a bloody wall spike. Bleeding's pretty bad.'

'You go!' Emma practically pushed Declan out of the door. 'I'll follow with my bag.'

As quickly as she could, Emma followed the men across the road to the site. 'Who and what do we have here?' She hunkered down beside Declan.

'Brett Cartrell, de-gloved hand.' Declan's dark head was bent over his patient. 'Did you bring morphine?'

Emma delved into her case and handed him the drug plus an anti-nausea medication. Ah…not good. She clamped her teeth on her bottom lip, seeing where the skin had been forcibly pulled back from the workman's hand. The injury would surely need microsurgery.

'Crikey, Doc…' Brett was pale and sweating. 'This is killin' me—'

'I know, mate.' Declan slipped the oxygen mask into place. 'Breathe away, now. That's good. IV now, please, Emma.' He shot the painkiller home. 'Normal saline.'

Emma knew it was their best option to stave off shock. Prompting a vein to the surface, she slid the cannula into place.

'What's the ETA on the ambulance?' Declan brought his gaze up, addressing the shocked faces of the men around him.

'They'll be a while, the base reckoned,' Cam Creedy, the foreman, said.

'God, I love that euphemistic term,' Declan growled, running a stethoscope over Brett's chest. 'Breathing's OK,' he relayed in an aside to Emma. 'Could you get a pressure bandage over the injury, please?'

Quickly and gently, Emma secured the bandage. 'Sling now?'

Declan nodded. 'I'll hold his hand steady while you do that.' He addressed the site foreman. 'I take it you'll be doing a report for the Workplace Health and Safety people?'

'Goes without saying.' Cam Creedy pushed back his hard hat and scratched his head. 'I don't know how it could have happened. I always get the guys to check and double-check before they climb anywhere.'

'Accidents happen,' Declan said darkly. 'I can vouch for that.'

Emma sent him a sharp look. He seemed in control and there was none of the edginess of yesterday. She daren't ask him if he was OK. He'd probably shoot her down in flames and she didn't want that. Not when they seemed to be forging a more positive kind of relationship.

'Here's the ambulance,' someone said.

After the handover, they walked back across the road to the surgery. 'So, when can we expect the third?' Declan asked.

'Sorry?'

'Accidents usually happen in threes, don't they?'

'Who said that?' Emma looked at him with scepticism.

'No one of note, but haven't you noticed when, for instance, your car packs up, then something else breaks down and then you wait with trepidation for the third thing to go wrong?'

'That's rubbish!'

'That's what the guy said when he accidentally threw out an antique vase worth thousands.'

'You're making it up.'

'We'll see,' he grinned, standing aside for her to precede him through the front door of the surgery. 'Morning all.'

Jodi avidly sought details of what had occurred. And then shrieked, 'Yeuch! Declan—look at your shirt! It's all bloody.'

'That's the third one,' Declan deadpanned, holding the offending garment away from his chest. He turned to Emma. 'My shirt's ruined. See, told you so.'

'You fool.' Emma's chuckle was rich and warm. 'Come through and I'll find you a spare one.'

Later that afternoon, Declan made his way to the address Carolyn had given him—reluctantly. 'Tracey won't come back,' the grandmother had said as they'd sat over a cup of coffee in the annexe off the children's ward.

'Have you told her about Adam's accident?' Declan had asked gently.

'She wouldn't be interested. Nev and I will have to rear these children as best we can.' Her shoulders lifted in a weary sigh and the corners of her mouth wilted unhappily. 'Ryan wouldn't have wanted this for us.'

'I don't imagine he'd have wanted this for Tracey either,' Declan pointed out with quiet diplomacy. 'Was he your only son?'

'Our only child. We couldn't have any more.' She paused. 'And I suppose I could have tried harder with Tracey…' Carolyn's mouth trembled. 'She's only a little thing. The babies took it out of her…her own mother was useless, no help there.'

Now, Declan hesitated before gingerly ascending the shallow steps. What a falling-down dump. The verandah was crumbling and sagging on rotten footings and saplings and long-stemmed weeds were shoving up through the cracks in the floorboards. He stood on the edge of the verandah and looked out, feeling a surge of anger swell in his chest. This just wasn't on…

'Whaddya want?'

Declan turned, his jaw tightening.

A young man was standing at the front door. He looked malnourished and unkempt, his hair dreadlocked and grubby, his skin pasty. 'You a cop?'

'No,' Declan said clearly. 'I'm a doctor.'

'We didn't send for no doctor. You're narc squad, ain't yer? Leave us alone…'

'Sorry, can't manage that.' Declan took a step forward. 'I need to see Tracey.'

'You can't—just—just leave us alone…' the young man whined, trying to block Declan's entry, but his slight build was no match for Declan's powerful bulk. 'Hey—you hurt me!' he yelped accusingly, trying to regain his balance. 'I'll get ya for this—'

'Whatever works,' Declan said through clenched teeth. A few strides took him to the end of the short hallway leading to an enclosed back verandah-cum-kitchen. There was a sight that had his worst fears realized. Tracey Jones looked a washed-out, defeated figure.

She was standing against a set of louvred windows, the light from the solitary naked bulb elongating her shadow. She was barefoot and wearing a threadbare dressing gown. Her stance spoke of defiance mixed with a fear so tangible Declan felt he could almost reach out and touch it. 'Hello, Tracey,' he said gently. 'I'm Declan O'Malley, your children's doctor from the Kingsholme practice. I've come to tell you Adam's had an accident. He's in hospital.'

Tracey gave an audible gasp and her hand flew to her mouth. 'It's not my fault—' She shrank back as if she'd been threatened with violence.

'No one is saying it is, Tracey. But you're Adam's mother and we need to talk about that.'

There was a long silence. Then Tracey slowly moved forward as if sleep-walking and sank down on one of the old wooden chairs set against the rickety kitchen table. She bowed her head and clasped her hands between her knees. 'My kids must hate me…'

Declan let the statement go unanswered. Instead, he cast a quick all-encompassing look around him. It was a scene of abject poverty. He'd expected no less but he'd also expected chaos and there he'd been wrong. Every surface was scrubbed clean; even the mismatched crockery was washed and stacked neatly on the shabby dresser. Declan's jaw worked for a second. It was a pathetic sight, yet he sensed hope that something could be salvaged here.

He pulled out a chair and sat down with Tracey at the table, his hands placed squarely in front of him. 'Would you like to see your children again, Tracey?'

'They wouldn't want to see me,' the young woman whispered brokenly. 'I—left them.'

'Mind telling me why you did that?' Declan's voice carried a gentle reassurance.

There was a long silence while Tracey rubbed at a spot on the edge of the table.

'I guess you were gutted when Ryan was killed,' Declan surmised. 'Maybe you flipped out, lost the plot for a while. Am I right?'

Tracey's gaze sprang to his. 'Yes…' she said on a ragged breath. 'H-how did you know?'

'I've been there.' Declan's voice flattened. 'Life gets complicated. Sometimes it's hard to ask for help, even when we know we should. I can give you that help now, Tracey, if you want it badly enough.'

Tracey made a sound somewhere between a sob and a moan. She looked at Declan, the pain of loss and uncertainty in her eyes.

'Your kids miss you…' Declan's smile warmed the bleak little kitchen. 'They need you. And I think you need them. If I didn't think that, I wouldn't be here.'

'Where are they now?' Tracey's gaze widened in query, her question a whispered plea. 'And what happened to my baby?'

Quietly and non-judgementally, Declan filled her in.

'I don't suppose Carolyn will ever forgive me,' Tracey said bitterly. 'She never wanted Ryan to marry me but I was pregnant with Lauren and we loved each other, despite what she said. But I had the kids so quickly and Ryan was away a lot. It was hard…'

'I know. Carolyn knows that too now. I think she and Nev would be over the moon if you came back.'

Tracey pressed a lock of hair to her cheek, her eyes wide with fear and doubt. 'I couldn't just rock back as if—as if nothing has happened. I'd need someone to help me.' She sent Declan a beseeching look. 'Could you… Dr O'Malley?'

Declan nodded, as if her response was what he'd hoped for. 'I can do that, Tracey.' He paused and then, 'When was your last fix?'

Tracey drew back sharply, her expression shocked. 'I never injected! I only took a few pills and that—not enough to get hooked on anything. It was just something to…make the pain go away. And Robbie kept getting them for me.' Her teeth came down on her bottom lip. 'He's garbage. I never want to see him again.'

'I don't think you need worry about *him*. I'd say he's done a runner. Now—' Declan pushed his chair back and stood to his feet '—let's get you sorted, Tracey Jones. What do you say?'

Tracey scrambled awkwardly to her feet. 'I'd like a shower but there's no hot water.'

'Do you have clothes?'

'Some—the ones I brought with me. And they're clean,' she added with an edge of defiance.

'Go and get dressed, then,' Declan said kindly. 'And pack up what you want to take with you.'

'Everything?' It was a frightened whisper.

Declan's look was implacable. 'You won't be coming back, Tracey.'

Her throat jerked as she swallowed. 'Then what?'

'You'll come with me to the women's shelter. You can have a shower and a hot meal and they'll give you a bed. I'll leave you a mild sleeper so you'll get some decent rest.'

'How...long can I stay there?'

'As long as you need. No one is about to judge you, Tracey, please believe that. The people at the shelter will arrange a medical check-up for you and, later on, some counselling, if that's what you'd like.'

'OK…' Tracey nodded. 'I s'pose I could talk to someone.'

'Good.' Declan smiled again. 'I'll check in with the shelter each day and, as soon as you're feeling up to it, I'll take you to see Adam.'

About a kilometre out of Bendemere, Declan pressed Emma's logged-in number on his hands-free phone. She answered on the third ring. 'Where are you?'

'Nearly home.'

'How did it go with Tracey?'

'OK, I think. Long story. Could I swing by?'

'Of course. Have you eaten?'

'No. Have you?'

'Not yet.'

'I'll pick up some takeaway, then.'

'No need.' There was a hint of laughter in her voice as she added, 'I've made a curry.'

'It must be your destiny to feed me,' he responded, matching her jokey tone.

'Mmm. Must be.'

'Are the kids OK?'

'They're fine. I've just tucked them in. Lauren's reading *The Wind in the Willows*.'

'Ah—I loved those guys—especially old Badger. Who's Lauren's favourite?'

'Moley, I think. She says he's cuddly.'

'Nice.' Declan laughed lightly. Oh, boy. He began to feel almost punch-drunk. The tone of the conversation was doing strange things to his insides. It could have been *their* kids they were talking about. An unfulfilled yearning as sudden as a lightning strike filled his veins.

Emma.

Who else in the whole of his adult life had ever made him feel this way? As though his feet were hardly touching the ground, his head in the stars.

But at the same time scared him to blazes…

What was happening here? Emma began to set the table, a mixture of a kind of thrilling uncertainty and just plain happiness flooding her. *Declan.* Her practice partner. Her friend. Yes, he was both of those. But he had become more than that. Unless she was reading it all wrong.

But she didn't think so. Lately, he'd been watching her in that way he had. Kind of thoughtful and expectant all mixed up together. And a little bemused, as though he didn't quite know what universe he'd stumbled into. Let alone why he had.

And there was more. Emma pressed her fingers to her mouth, reliving his kisses all over again. Parting her lips, she imagined tasting him again, just the action flooding her body with sensation and desire...

'Emma?'

'Ooh!' she squealed and spun round from her X-rated reverie to see him hovering at the kitchen door. Her hand flew to her throat. 'I didn't hear you arrive,' she said, all flustered.

'I was quiet,' he said, moving inside. 'Didn't want to wake the kids.'

'I've just checked on them. They're well away.' She went towards him and they met in the middle of the kitchen. 'What do you have there?' Emma indicated the carrier bag he was toting.

'Some wine and a chocolate dessert.'

'Lovely. But you didn't need to—' Emma felt she could hardly breathe.

'I can't keep letting you feed me.'

Oh, you can, you can.

Emma savoured the last of her dessert as it rolled off her tongue. 'Oh, that was gorgeous,' she said with a sigh.

'Not bad,' Declan said. 'I think the packaging might have been a bit deceptive all the same.' In fact the dessert had turned out to be nothing more exotic than a rich vanilla ice cream with a swirl of chocolate and a sprinkling of hazelnuts. 'No doubt the kids will finish it off.'

'Mmm, they'll love it. Coffee?'

'No, thanks.' Declan rolled his shoulders and stretched. 'Do you have a green tea, by any chance?'

'I have a whole selection of organic teas,' Emma said grandly, getting lightly to her feet. 'I'll have a peppermint, I think.' She made the tea quickly, passed a mug to Declan and then resumed her chair. 'Are you going to fill me in about your visit to Tracey now?'

Declan did, quickly and concisely.

Emma looked thoughtful. 'You don't think she'll do a runner from the shelter, do you?'

Declan took a mouthful of his tea. 'No…' he said eventually. 'Her self-esteem has taken a battering. But, unless I'm a very poor judge of character, I think she'll be back with her kids quite soon. She's had a huge wake-up call. And Carolyn's anxious to mend fences as well. I'm tipping they'll forge a workable relationship when things settle down.'

'Should we say anything to Lauren and Joel yet?'

'Not yet. I have faith in Tracey but I'd hate to raise the kids' hopes and see them dashed. Let's tread carefully for the next little while.'

'You're right.' She gave a short nod. And then the emotions from a very crowded couple of days kicked in and she said without thinking, 'You've no idea how wonderful it is to have someone to talk to about this stuff. And not even on a professional level—just to talk to.'

'Oh, but I do, Emma,' he said softly. 'I couldn't wait to get back and talk to *you*.'

She blinked. He was watching her in *that* way again. 'I guess it's good, then—that we can communicate so well. For the success of the practice,' she concluded, the words so far from where her thoughts had travelled, they made no sense at all.

'Why are you spinning this, Emma?' Declan kept his voice low. 'What's happening here is about us—you and me. We could have met anywhere in the world but we just happened to meet here. The practice has nothing to do with it.'

'I'm afraid…' she heard herself say.

'Of me?' His voice rose. 'Or of what we could mean to each other?'

'You were all for cooling things between us very recently,' she accused bluntly.

'Yeah—well, I was nuts to think emotions could be put in little boxes and only opened when it seemed the right time. There's no *right time*. Is there?'

Emma's green eyes flew wide with indecision.

'Don't you trust me?' His tone was still patient.

She licked her lips. 'I once trusted a man with my whole life…'

'I know about that.' Declan's gaze didn't waver.

'Dad told you?' Emma fisted a hand against her breast. 'He *told* you?'

'Normally, he wouldn't have broken your confidence. You must know that. But he was worn down, worried about the future—your future. And, whoever he was, the man who let you go was an idiot.'

'So you're implying I fell in love with an idiot?'

'He might have been a charming idiot,' Declan compromised. 'They exist.'

'He was sleeping with my best friend.' With the benefit of time blurring the pain, Emma found she could talk about it objectively. 'It was going on right under my nose and I didn't twig. And when Marcus finally had the decency to tell me he wanted to break our engagement, *she* had the gall to suggest there was no reason why we couldn't still be friends!'

'I hope you got mad.'

'Mad enough.' Emma smiled unwillingly. 'When I finally steeled myself to go round to our apartment to collect the rest of my things, Marcus was there.'

'And?' Declan's mouth twitched.

'He was embarrassed as hell. Said he was just nipping out to the shops. In other words, he hoped I'd be gone by the time he got back.'

'Bad move.' Declan's eyes glinted wickedly. 'And you *were* gone, of course.'

'Of course.' Emma sliced him a grin. 'But not before I'd interrupted the wash cycle he'd left going and chucked in a pair of my red knickers with all his obscenely expensive white business shirts.'

'Wow!' Declan looked impressed. 'I see I'll have to watch my back around you, Dr Armitage.'

She made a face at him and then, 'I was in a well of self-pity for a long time. That's probably why I didn't notice Dad's deteriorating health.'

'But you're over this guy, Marcus, now?'

'The man was indeed an idiot,' she said with asperity.

'So, we agree on something at last. Come on.' Declan reached for her hand across the table. 'Walk me out. It's time I went home.' There was regret in his voice and his eyes had gone dark.

'You could stay here tonight.'

There was a beat of silence.

A thousand questions wanted to leap off Declan's tongue. But he held back. Obviously, she hadn't meant stay as in *stay*. And, even if she had, it was too soon.

For both of them.

'There are a zillion bedrooms in this place,' Emma explained jerkily—just in case he'd imagined...

'There would be. It's a big house.'

'Um—thank you for today and everything. I have a feeling it will all turn out—'

'Stop.' He pressed his finger against her lips. 'This is about us, Emma.'

'Is it?' Her hands went to his waist. 'Shame we don't seem to have come up with any solutions *about us*.'

'On the contrary.' His voice dropped to a husky undertone. 'I think we've lit a bit of a lamp tonight, don't you?'

A lamp to find their way? Could it be as simple as that? Emma closed her eyes, giving herself up to the pure sensation of his hands running over her back, whispering against the soft cotton of her shirt.

'Come on the journey with me...' Declan bent to kiss her, tenderly at first, as if to soothe away her doubts and fears, then with an eagerness and urgency, as if to imprint his faith on what they had together.

Was this the time to let her feelings run free and just *trust* him? Emma agonized as she opened her mouth under his and kissed him back.

CHAPTER SEVEN

IT WAS two days later and Lauren was icing cup cakes with Emma at the kitchen table after school. 'Is Mum ever coming home?'

Oh, please heaven, *yes*, Emma thought, her eyes clouding, but what to tell this sweet child? 'Lauren,' she said carefully, leaning over and gently curving her hand around Lauren's slender little wrist. 'Your Mum's been sick.'

'Like vomiting and stuff?' Lauren asked.

'Well, not quite like that. But a lot of worries have made her sad and just not able to be with you all.'

Lauren set two huge dark eyes on Emma. 'How do you mean?'

Emma's mind scrabbled for a truth that might be acceptable. And then in a flash she remembered the explanation one of her trainers in paeds had given to a child whose circumstances had not been dissimilar to Lauren's.

'You've seen a balloon burst, haven't you, Lauren?'

The little girl's eyes widened and then she nodded.

'Well, your mum's problems just kept piling up and up and each problem was like another puff into the balloon. And then it was just one problem too many and the balloon exploded.'

'And she ran away…'

'Yes.' Emma met the child's gaze steadily.

Lauren looked suddenly lost. 'Was she mad at us?'

'Oh, honey, no…' Emma scooped the little girl close to her. 'Your mum was just mixed up.' Emma smoothed a hand over Lauren's fair hair. 'But she's been staying with some people who are helping her and she's feeling so much better, we think she'll be home with you again before too long.' Emma mentally crossed her fingers about that. But, from what Declan had said only that morning, it seemed Tracey had made a remarkable turn-around and had begun a tentative re-connection with Carolyn. Tomorrow, Declan was taking her to see Adam at the hospital.

'She might be back in time for our sports day,' Lauren said, her little hand still trustingly in Emma's.

'Yes, she just might.' Oh, Tracey, please don't screw up, Emma pleaded silently to the absent mum. Please come home where you belong.

The next morning, Emma welcomed a new patient, Rina Kennedy, into her consulting room. 'You're new to our community?'

'We've just bought the garden centre,' Rina answered in her soft Irish brogue.

'That's interesting,' Emma said. 'It looked like closing there for a while.'

Rina made a face. 'I don't think the former owners had a clue what they were doing. But we aim to fix all that. It'll be grand when we've done a makeover.'

'Very good luck with it, then.' Emma smiled. 'Now, Mrs Kennedy, what can I do for you today?'

'Call me Rina for starters. And I hope you don't think I've gone soft in the head for coming to see you, Doctor, but I wanted to ask you about the best way to avoid getting sun damage to our skin. We've been hearing such terrible things about skin cancer since we've moved to Australia and our two little girls have the fairest complexions.'

'You're right to be concerned,' Emma said. 'Our summers here are hotter and the sun's rays far more intense than you'd be used to in the Northern hemisphere.'

'That's what I thought…'

'But mostly,' Emma went on, 'folk who suffer sun damage to their skin can only blame themselves, because they don't take a blind bit of notice of what health professionals have been telling them for years. And that is to stay out of the sun in the hottest part of the day, to cover up with light protective clothing and, most importantly, to use sunscreen with the highest protection factor. A thirty-plus rating is the best.'

'Could you write all that down for me, please, Doctor?'

Emma smiled. 'I'll give you some fact sheets and you can read up on it. But if you're sensible and keep a healthy respect for what excessive exposure to the sun can do, you shouldn't have any problems.'

Rina jerked a hand at the window. 'It's a lovely garden you have out there,' she said with an impish grin. 'But there's always room for another shrub or two,' she added, unashamedly drumming up business. 'You must come along to our official opening when we've done our revamp. We'll have some grand bargains.'

Emma's head went back as she laughed. 'Let's know the date and I'll make sure all our folk from the practice are there with bells on and nice fat wallets,' she promised. What a nice cheery person, she thought. Spirits lighter, Emma began to make her way through the day's patient list and, at the end of it, she popped in on Declan.

'Hi.' He looked up from his computer, his eyes crinkling into a smile.

'Is our Friday staff meeting still on?'

'Hell, yeah. This is where we function properly as a practice. Thrash out all the hairy bits.'

Watching his strong mouth, so sexy in repose, curve upwards in a smile, Emma felt her heart pick up speed. 'See you shortly, then.'

'I can't believe how the time seems to be flying these days.' Moira looked around the team with a happy smile. 'Mind you, they say it does when you're having fun.'

'It's certainly been interesting,' Declan said. 'OK, folks, any problems?'

'Cedric Dutton,' Libby said with feeling. 'One of our patients on the list for a home visit.'

Declan reclined in his chair and stretched out his legs. 'What's up with Mr Dutton?'

'For starters, he lives alone. He had a stroke some while ago. He was treated in Toowoomba Base. But he's not re-claiming his independence at all.'

'Do we know why not?' Declan cut to the chase.

Libby shook her head. 'The Rotary arranged the necessary safety modifications to his house, and the meals on wheels folk call but he appears to be just sitting in front of the tele-vision. It's not like he doesn't know better—he's an educated man. He used to work as a surveyor with the council.'

Declan's eyes lit with sympathy. 'The stroke will have come as a great shock to him.'

'If Mr Dutton's not moving about, we have to be con-cerned about pressure sores.' Emma looked keenly at Libby.

'We do,' Libby agreed. 'And he's so very thin. But he wouldn't let me touch him, let alone explain anything. There are a dozen things he could be doing to gain a much better quality of life.'

Declan's mouth drew in. 'Possibly there's a residue of post-trauma. Sounds like he's scared to try himself out. Does he have family?'

'He's a bachelor,' Libby said. 'Extended family in Brisbane.'

'Has anyone talked to him about the stroke itself?' Declan queried. 'The repercussions to his body?'

'I imagine the nurses tried but he's such an old chauvin-ist,' Libby emphasized with a roll of her eyes. 'He called me *girlie*!'

Declan cracked a laugh. 'Want me to have a word, then, Libs?'

'Please, Declan, if you have time. He lives in one of the

cottages along by the old railway line, number fourteen. Seems very much a loner, from what I could gather.'

'Possibly another candidate for our water walking if we can get it up and running,' Declan considered. 'Which reminds me, I've been invited to a meeting of the school's P&C committee on Monday night. It's on the agenda to be discussed.'

'Hey, that's great,' Libby enthused. 'I've a list a mile long of folk who'd benefit. We'd possibly need to arrange transport, though.'

'The council could be pressed into doing that,' Moira contributed.

'Hang on, people.' Declan lifted a staying hand. 'We've only got to first base yet.'

'But it's a positive first step and all down to you,' Emma said, enthusiastic and proud on his behalf.

Declan acknowledged Emma's praise with a twist of his hand. Rocking forward, he doodled something on his pad and thought life played weird tricks sometimes. *Very weird.* A year ago, he'd never in his wildest dreams have imagined he'd be here in rural Queensland practicing family medicine. Rather, he'd expected to be planning a quick rise to the top in his chosen field in one of Australia's big teaching hospitals…

Emma was now so tuned in to his body language she could read Declan like a book. He was doing his best to settle in, even enjoying the challenge to some extent. But was he also acknowledging that community medicine could never match the heart-pumping discipline of being a top-flight surgeon? And, if he was, could he let his dreams go so easily? Suddenly, the six months he'd promised for their trial period seemed so little time to work out whether they had a future together.

Or apart.

'Oh, Emma, while I think of it—' Moira cast a quick enquiring look across the table '—Jodi wondered whether Lauren and Joel would like to spend some time out at the stables tomorrow. Apparently, there are a couple of quiet ponies they could ride and Jodi would be there to supervise them. She thought—well, we both thought—it might be a nice treat for them and, being Saturday, it could help fill in the time a little?'

Emma was touched by Moira and Jodi's kindness. In truth, she'd been wondering how she could keep the kids occupied over a whole weekend. There wasn't a lot to do in Bendemere. She jumped at the offer. 'I'm sure they'd love it, Moira. But is Jodi sure it's OK with the McGintys?'

Moira shrugged. 'My granddaughter could sweet-talk a crow into singing like a canary if she had a mind to. I'll tell her it's all right then, shall I?'

Emma nodded. 'Did she mention a time?'

'Morning's good. And, speaking of the children—' Moira looked at her watch. 'Do you need to see to them?'

'No, they're spending the night back home with their grandfather.' Emma smiled. 'He was picking them up from school. Promised them pizza for tea, I believe.'

'Good old Nev,' Moira nodded in approval. 'How's Tracey doing?' she asked gently. The whole practice in one way or another was now involved in the Jones's ongoing saga and were all rooting for the family to be healed and reunited.

Declan rubbed a hand across his chin. 'I'm visiting Tracey tomorrow. She thinks she's ready to see Adam. I'm picking up Nev and taking him along with me. He, at least, seems very optimistic things will work out.'

'He's the calming influence on Carolyn,' Moira said wisely. 'And he's always had a soft spot for Tracey.'

'There's still a fair bit of sorting out to do yet.' Declan was cautious. 'Now, anything else on the agenda, guys?'

There wasn't a lot, so the meeting wrapped up quickly and Libby and Moira left.

'How optimistic are you, really, about Tracey getting things together?' Emma looked earnestly at Declan, her chin resting in her upturned hand.

'Reasonably.' He flexed a hand. 'I've spoken to her on the phone each night and she's surprised me with her turnaround. But then, the folk at the shelter have been working with her and her self-esteem has received a huge boost. Apparently, she's been absorbing the counselling sessions like a sponge.'

'Lauren has been quietly eating her little heart out about things, worrying whether her mum left because she was mad at them. I tried to reassure her and I hope I haven't jumped the gun but I indicated Tracey might be back home soon.'

'It's best to keep positive around the kids,' Declan said slowly. 'I mean, what's the alternative?'

Emma bit her lip. 'Awful,' she agreed.

'Hey, don't let's drop the ball.' In an abrupt gesture of re-assurance, Declan pressed her hand and then got to his feet. 'Are you busy tonight?'

'Er...no.'

'Like to go out somewhere to eat later?'

'Um...' Emma flannelled. He'd taken her by surprise. 'Where would we go?'

'You choose. Better phone and book, though. It's Friday night.'

'OK... Are you heading home now?' she asked as they walked slowly along the hallway and through to the main part of the house and eventually to the kitchen.

'I thought I'd call in on Libby's old chap first. See what I can sort out for him. I'll pick you up about seven?'

'Or we could meet at the restaurant.'

'Let's be old-fashioned.' His mouth tipped at the corner. 'I'll call for you.'

Emma pulled back, her nerve ends pinching alarmingly. So, were they going on a date? The thought thrilled her and panicked her in equal measure. 'Fine. Seven's good.'

As Declan opened the back door, a gale-force wind nearly knocked him back inside. 'Hell's bells, when did the weather turn foul like this?'

'Ages ago, probably without our knowing. We've been cloistered indoors. And it's freezing, Declan.'

'Rats!' Declan turned up the collar on his windcheater. 'After Scotland, this is nothing.'

Emma began to rub her upper arms vigorously. 'You won't say that when the power lines come down.'

'Is that likely?'

'It's happened a few times since I've been here.'

'Snap decision then.' His eyes narrowed on her face and suddenly the intensity of his regard hardened, as though he'd made up his mind about something. 'Change of plan. I'll drop by Cedric's, then head home for a shower and, on my way back to you, I'll grab some stuff for dinner. Not a takeaway,' he promised. 'I'll cook.'

How could she refuse? It would be such a relief not to have to venture out on such a wild night. 'If you're sure? But I've stuff in the freezer—'

'Please. Let it be my treat, Emma.'

Emma gave an uneasy huff of laughter. 'And you *can* cook?'

'I promise it'll be edible. Just trust me on this, all right?'

Well, she had to, didn't she? Emma thought as she closed the door after him and turned back inside. About dinner and about a lot of other things too.

Declan felt the wind tear at his clothes as he made a dash to his car. But, far from being intimidated by its force, he felt exhilarated, wild, powerful. As if he could do anything he really set his mind to.

If only that were an option.

Following Emma's directions, he soon found his way to the row of neatly kept cottages and drove slowly along until he found Cedric Dutton's. Hefting his case off the passenger seat, he swung out of his car. Making his way to the front door, Declan lifted his hand and banged loudly. When there was no response, he called, 'Mr Dutton? I'm a doctor from the Kingsholme surgery. I'd like a word. Could you let me in, please?'

Declan waited and listened and, finally, there was a shuffling inside and the door was opened just a crack. Two faded blue eyes under bushy brows looked suspiciously out. 'Who're you?'

'I'm a doctor from the Kingsholme surgery,' Declan repeated. 'May I come in?'

A beat of silence while the elderly man digested the information. 'No law against it, I suppose,' he said, unlocking the chain and holding the door open.

Once inside, Declan extended his hand. 'Declan O'Malley, Mr Dutton.'

'New around here, are you?' Cedric looked over the imposing male figure while he held Declan's hand in a fragile grip.

'Yes. I'm in partnership with Dr Armitage.' Unobtrusively, Declan watched his patient's general mobility as Cedric led the way back inside to the lounge room.

It took a little time for the elderly man to settle himself into his armchair. 'So—why did you want to see me?' he asked, seeming to sense the importance of Declan's visit. 'That girl's being talking to you, I'll bet?'

'Libby Macklin is a Registered Nurse, Mr Dutton. It's part of her job to check on our senior patients. We depend on her to tell us how your health is. She was concerned for you and she's a skilled professional, otherwise, she wouldn't be employed at our practice. You should have let her check you over.'

'Maybe.' Cedric shrugged a skinny shoulder.

'How's your general health, Cedric?' Declan's voice was gentle. He didn't want to antagonize his new patient from the outset.

'Days get a bit long. I'm not as fit as I used to be.'

'I understand that. What about your exercises?' Declan asked. 'Are you doing them? You know they're essential to help your muscles recover from the stroke.'

The elderly man hesitated. 'Sometimes I do them. But it's hard when everything's crook…'

'I know.'

Cedric looked sceptical. 'What would you know about it—young fella like you?'

Declan snorted a hard laugh. 'Oh, believe me, Cedric, I know.' Briefly, Declan explained something of his own circumstances.

'I get a bit *down*,' Cedric admitted. 'Like you said—'

'Depression is all part of the syndrome.' Declan leaned forward, his hands linked between his knees. 'When your body won't do what you want it to, you feel robbed of self-respect. And it's hard when you lose everything you could once be sure of.'

'My word, that's it!' Cedric looked impressed. 'For a while there I couldn't even get my pants on.' His mouth compressed in a reluctant grin. 'Or do up any buttons. And shoelaces were a lost cause.'

Declan nodded sympathetically. 'Was it explained to you just what a stroke is?'

'Something about a blood clot, isn't it?'

'Exactly. A stroke happens when a clot blocks a blood vessel or artery in the brain. It interrupts the blood flow and suddenly the body is out of whack.'

'Like damming a river,' Cedric acknowledged thought-fully. 'I never cottoned on. But I do now you've explained it.'

'So you can see why those exercises are so important, can't you?'

'Reckon I can.' Cedric thought long and hard. 'So, this Libby, the nurse, she could help me with that, could she?'

'Yes.' Declan nodded. 'But I want you to come into the hospital one day a week for the next while and see our regular physiotherapist, Michelle Crother. I'll arrange transport for you.'

Cedric sighed resignedly. 'I suppose that'd be the thing to do.'

While he had Cedric's tacit acceptance of the changes he wanted to implement, Declan thought he'd push gently ahead with another suggestion. 'What about getting back into a bit of social life? Do you play cards?'

'I don't mind a game or two.'

'Then you might enjoy coming along to the seniors' club.' Since his involvement with Carolyn Jones, Declan had done his homework and clued himself in on what was available to the older residents of the town. 'They meet regularly on a

Wednesday at the farmers' hall and the CWA provide lunch. From what I hear, it's a friendly group. They'd make you welcome.' Declan grinned disarmingly. 'You'd possibly know most of them anyway, an old-timer like you.'

'Probably would.' Cedric looked down at his hands. 'I lost touch a bit when I had the stroke…'

'So, how's your appetite?' Declan infused enthusiasm into his voice, sensing Cedric was apt to drift off into introspection. 'Are you managing with the meals on wheels?'

'Food's OK.' Cedric shrugged. 'Sometimes I don't feel like eating much.'

'Once we can get you out and about a bit more, all that will improve. Get yourself out into the sun as well. That will keep up your vitamin D requirement. Very important, whatever our age.'

Cedric nodded, taking it all on board. Then he lifted his eyebrows in a query. 'What did you say your name was, Doctor?'

'O'Malley. Call me Declan. I'll be your medical officer from now on, if you're agreeable?'

'You seem all right,' Cedric said grudgingly. 'Not bossy like some.'

Like the women, Declan interpreted wryly. But at least he'd made headway with this old man. Stirred him up enough to take an interest in his own welfare. And that felt surprisingly good. 'Now—' Declan flipped open his medical case '—how would you feel about me checking you over while I'm here?'

'Fair enough, I suppose.' Cedric looked around him with agitation. 'Where do you want me?'

'Just there's fine.' Declan slung his stethoscope around his neck and grinned. 'And I promise I'll keep the prodding to a minimum.'

Emma's heartbeat was thrumming. Surely he'd be here soon. It seemed ages since he'd left to visit his patient. An age in which she'd had a leisurely bath and dressed in comfortable trousers and a fine woollen black top. She'd brushed her hair and left it loose and kept her make-up to a minimum.

Why was she fussing so? They were simply sharing a meal. He'd probably prefer to eat in the kitchen. But then, perhaps she should make the evening special and set the small table in the dining room. Would that look a bit contrived? He'd hate that. Although, just in case, she'd go ahead and light the fire in the dining room...

Finally, a knock sounded at her front door.

'Hi.' Hands occupied with his shopping bags, Declan leaned forward and planted a lingering kiss on her mouth when Emma opened the door. 'Sorry, I'm a bit late. It's a wild night out there. I nearly got blown to bits.'

'Hello...' Emma said when she could breathe again. The touch of his mouth had sent up sparks. She wanted to stop him right there, wrap her arms around his body and just *hold* him. She wanted him. So much. But he was already at the worktop unloading his shopping. 'What are we having?' she asked, peering over his shoulder.

He tipped his head on one side and grinned down at her. 'Char-grilled spiced lamb cutlets with ratatouille.'

Emma gurgled a soft laugh. In other words, grilled chops and vegetables. 'I'm impressed.'

'You're not.' He sent her an indulgent half-amused look. 'But give me my moment of fame here.'

'What can I do to help?'

'Ah—' he indicated the array of vegetables he'd bought—red and yellow peppers, zucchini and vine tomatoes. 'These have to be cut into bite-sized pieces.'

'Even though we're starving hungry?'

'Even though.' Declan gently elbowed her out of the way to select a knife from the kitchen block. 'Just do what the main man tells you, please? It'll be worth the wait.'

Emma was still chuckling to herself as she set about her task. Since he was going to so much trouble to feed her, she definitely *would* set the table in the dining room.

* * *

They took a long time over dinner, as though neither of them wanted it to end. 'How did I do, then?' Declan asked finally.

Emma smiled. He'd given her a look so warm, she'd felt its impact skidding and sliding across her nerves and along her backbone before settling in a swirling mass in her belly. 'You did so well, I just might have to keep you. This was such a good idea,' she rushed on. 'To have dinner at home.'

'Yes, it was.' Declan's gaze shimmered over her face and then roamed to register the gleam of lamplight that threw her tawny lashes into sharp relief against her flushed cheeks. He moved a bit uncomfortably as his body zinged to a new awareness. He took a careful mouthful of his wine, his eyes caressing her over the rim of his glass. He ached to touch her intimately, to breathe in the sweet scent of her silky hair, stroke the softness of her naked body as she lay next to him...

'Coffee?' Emma felt a quicksilver flip in her stomach. She'd been aware of his overt scrutiny.

'Not for me, thanks.'

She swung to her feet. 'I'll clear the table and stack the dishwasher, then.' She sent him a quick smile. 'Go through to the lounge. We'll be more comfortable in there.'

Declan extinguished the candles they'd used on the dinner table and then crossed the hallway to the lounge room. He went to stand at the window, drawing back the curtains slightly in order to check the state of the weather himself. In the glow from the street lights he could see the trees bending, their foliage swirling into a mad dance in the wake of the wind's rushing passage.

He turned when Emma came in. 'How long do you think the storm will take to get here?' He opened his arms in invitation and she slid into his embrace.

'I'm no expert.' Emma rested her head against his shoulder. 'But I'd rather be here than out driving somewhere—wouldn't you?'

'That's a no-brainer,' he said. 'Of course I'd rather be here.' He looked down at her. 'That's if it's all right if I hang about?'

'I'd have turfed you out ages ago if it wasn't.'

Declan gave one of his lazy smiles. 'Would I have gone, though?'

'Of course you would.' Emma stroked the tips of her fingers across the small of his back, her hands already addicted to the sensation. 'You're an old-fashioned kind of guy.'

Declan looked pained. 'Are you saying my clothes need an update?'

Emma's mouth widened in a grin. They were shadow dancing again—fooling around, as if it was obvious to both of them that if their conversation became too serious, too personal, then anything could happen…'Stop fishing for compliments,' she said. 'You know you dress very well.'

'I undress very well, too,' he rejoined daringly.

Emma's heart twanged out of rhythm. 'Do you?'

'Mmm.' Declan registered the tiny swallow in her throat. 'So,' he said softly, moving so that his hands rested on the tops of her arms and feeling the tremble that went through her, 'what do you want to do with the rest of the evening?'

Emma opened her mouth and closed it again, knowing deep in her heart that this was a moment of no return. Was she ready? Were *they* ready? They'd never know unless they put their trust in one another, reached out and gathered life in. 'You could stay—if you like…?'

His eyes locked with hers, dark in shadow, tender in their caress. 'My whole body aches with wanting you, Emma. As long as you're sure?'

'Yes.' He should have come into her life sooner, but he was here now. And that was all that mattered. 'Yes.' She looked at him and smiled, feeling the weight of indecision drop from her like an unwanted heavy garment. 'I've never been more sure of anything.'

Declan made a deep sound in his throat that could have been a sigh. Then he drew her close, lowering his mouth to claim her lips.

That was all it took. Like a spark on straw, the fire of their passion took hold and in a breath it was raging.

Declan whispered harshly against her mouth. 'I meant to take it slow…'

She arched back with a little cry. 'No—not slow.' Her hands threaded through his hair and she trapped his face, holding him. 'I need you, Declan—'

He turned his head and gently nipped the soft flesh below her thumb, his eyes pinpoints of desire when she gasped an indrawn breath. 'Which bedroom?'

'Mine.'

Clothes flew off in a flurry, Declan swearing over a leg of his jeans that refused to leave his foot. Finally, he stepped back and stared at her. At the tendrils of corn-silk hair draping gently on to her creamy naked shoulders. At the swanlike gracefulness of her neck. At the small line of muscle delineating the length of her upper arm. The sweet roundness of her breasts. The shallow dip of her tummy…'Emma—' He felt his voice catch on a painful swallow. 'You're—' He shook his head. 'You're beautiful.'

'And you…' She hardly realized what she was doing, reaching out to slide her fingers down over his diaphragm, over his belly and dip into the shallow nook of his navel.

Suddenly, Declan made a gravelly sound of protest, jamming his hand over hers to stop its movement. 'Wait…' He looked around blankly and then hooked up his jeans, slipping a tiny packet from the back pocket. 'I never know whether there's a right time to do this,' he growled.

Emma felt herself blushing, crossing her arms tightly across her ribcage. He'd turned his back and she could see the shallow hollow just above the base of his spine. A tiny jagged laugh left her mouth. 'No need for diagrams, Declan—just do it…'

Oh, God…it was like stumbling into paradise. He touched her teasingly, his hands light and seductive in their rhythm. Instinctively, he knew what would please her, excite her, bring her to the brink but not quite tip over.

Emma was wild for him, a wildness she'd never known,

drawing him closer, feeling him hover at the core of her femininity before plunging in. She gasped, dragging him in more deeply, her head arching back as she called his name, feeling the sweet ripeness of her release gathering and then splintering her into a thousand pieces. Her name exploded on Declan's tongue as his climax followed hers a millisecond later, their hearts thumping a wild tattoo as they fell back to earth.

After a long time, they pulled back from each other, two sets of bruised lips, two pairs of eyes hazed with a new kind of wonderment.

'So…' he said.

'So,' she echoed huskily.

Lifting a hand, he knuckled her cheek gently. 'Why did we wait so long?'

CHAPTER EIGHT

EMMA had no time to answer.

'I don't believe this!' Declan's expletive hit the air as his mobile rang. 'Can't we get two minutes to call our own?'

'Where's your phone?' Emma was out of bed and reaching for her gown.

'Pocket of my jeans.'

'Here.' She hooked them off the floor and tossed them to him. It had to be an emergency somewhere. She knew that instinctively.

They had trouble, the police sergeant, Gary Bryson, informed Declan. Part of the roof at the farmers' hall had blown off. The hall had been packed with the usual Friday bingo players. There was confusion, to say the least. No one was sure about injuries but could the doctors come? Declan closed off his phone and in clipped terms relayed the message to Emma.

'Right.' She snatched up her own mobile off the bedside table. 'I'll get on to the hospital and alert them we might be sending patients in. They'll automatically recall any staff who are available.'

'Let's just be grateful the power lines haven't gone down,' Declan said as they dressed hurriedly.

'Don't count your chickens quite yet,' Emma warned. 'But at least the hospital has a backup power supply. It'll kick in if the worst happens.'

Declan grunted a non-reply, looking broodingly at Emma as she twisted her hair quickly into a ponytail. A frown touched his eyes. He felt as though he'd been catapulted from a delicious dream with no time to wallow in its aftermath. But he could still smell Emma's perfume, still feel the softness of her skin beneath his hands.

His mouth tightened. He wanted more and he couldn't have it. They'd taken a huge step into the unknown tonight. They'd needed time and closeness to talk about it, wind down, make love again, this time slowly, softly, sexily—

'Your top's inside out,' Emma said, breaking his thought pattern.

Impatiently, Declan dragged the T-shirt over his head and rectified it. 'The timing's all wrong for this, Emma.'

Well, she knew that. Emma's head was bent as she pulled on a pair of sturdy boots. But they were rural doctors. They had to attend. Emergencies didn't choose their time to happen. Heaven knew what they'd find when they got to the hall. And she didn't want to be doing this any more than Declan. The timing *was* all wrong. She'd wanted a blissful few hours with him. Their newness as lovers surely demanded that. She'd wanted to hold him and have him hold her and just *talk*. About nothing. About everything. But it seemed as though an unkind fate had stepped in and now her emotions were all over the place. Declan's too, if she was a betting woman. She popped upright from the edge of the bed. 'Ready?'

They went in Declan's car. Halfway to the hall the street lights flickered and faded and the night around them was plunged into darkness.

'I've a couple of lantern torches in the boot' was Declan's only comment.

The rain had started in earnest by the time they got to the hall. 'Let's proceed with caution,' Declan warned, handing Emma one of the torches and taking the other himself.

'We should go through the front entrance,' she said. 'It seems the least affected.' To her relief, the State Emergency Services people were already on the scene, their bright orange overalls lending a sense of security. Emergency lighting was rapidly being put in place. 'That's John Cabot, the team leader for the SES,' she told Declan. 'We'll speak to him first.'

Introductions were made swiftly and Declan asked the question on both their minds, 'What's the damage, John? Do we know yet?'

'Less than we feared, Doc. Most of the folk had already left. Just a few stragglers having a last cuppa, from what we know. The roof over the rear of the hall has pretty much gone but the rest seems intact. I've a couple of guys up there presently checking and getting tarpaulins into place to keep out the rain. Let us know if you need more lighting.'

'Thanks, John.' Declan nodded, taking it all in. 'We'll let you get on with it, then.'

'Oh, look—' Emma made a dash forward. 'There's Moira! What on earth is she doing here?'

'I'm on the driving roster for our seniors' group at the church,' Moira explained agitatedly. 'And I'd just come to collect them when the roof went. This is Agnes—' She indicated the elderly lady slumped in a chair beside them. 'I think she's hurt quite badly,' Moira added in a frightened whisper.

Declan had already sized up the situation. His seeking gaze went quickly around the hall. 'Moira, is there a first aid room or somewhere we could make Agnes more comfortable?'

'Er—yes—yes…' Moira visibly pulled herself together, pointing to a room at the side of the hall. 'And, mercifully, it's still intact.'

'Over here!' Declan hailed the two ambulances officers who had just arrived and explained what he needed.

'Take it easy,' he instructed as they settled the elderly woman on the narrow bunk bed. Agnes looked glassily pale against the deep purple of her cardigan. 'Can you tell us what happened, Agnes?' he asked gently as he began his examination.

'Sitting at the table…' Agnes moistened her lips slowly. 'Something hit me—fell forward—hard, terrible hard…'

'That must have hurt, Agnes.' Emma held her hand to the injured woman's wrist. 'Thready,' she reported softly.

Declan replaced his stethoscope. 'Let's step outside for a minute.'

'What's the matter with me?' Agnes asked fretfully.

'It'll be all right, dear.' Moira took the older woman's hand and held it. 'The doctors will look after you.'

Emma followed Declan out of the room. 'What do you think?' she asked quietly.

'Hard to tell, but she could have a splenic haematoma. She'll need a CT scan asap.'

'We'll send her on, then?'

'Obviously.' Declan gave a dismissive grunt. 'We don't have the equipment to do it here, Emma.'

It was hardly her fault if their little hospital didn't have the advanced facilities of a city radiology department! 'I'll escort Agnes across to the hospital, then,' she said shortly. 'Stabilize her before the road trip to Toowoomba.'

'Do that.' Declan's voice was clipped. 'And call through to Toowoomba, please. Tell them we want a CT scan immediately on arrival. And to make sure they have a supply of O-neg blood ready in case she needs to go to surgery.'

For heaven's sake! Emma's fine chin darted a centimetre upwards. She knew what protocol to follow. Did he ever stop to consider how they'd managed before he'd come? Well, amazingly enough, they had! Then she softened. Giving orders came as naturally to him as breathing. 'Are you worried about a bleed?'

'Without a scanner we can only second-guess.' And it was frustrating him like hell. 'If you'll do the necessary for Agnes, I'll see if there are any more casualties here. So far it looks pretty quiet.'

They went back to the first aid room and Emma explained what they needed to do.

'I'll follow across to the hospital directly, Agnes.' Moira squeezed the older woman's hand. 'Don't worry about a thing.'

'Right, let's get you on board, sweetheart.' The paramedics moved in to make the transfer.

With Moira disappearing out into the night, Declan took a quick look around. Thankfully, the damage was only in one part of the hall. He was still considering the injury to Agnes when he heard his name called. He turned sharply. John Cabot was heading towards him.

'One of my lads has hurt himself, Doc. Breaking all the rules and trying to lift debris on his own.'

'I'll take a look at him.' Declan hitched up his bag and followed the SES leader. 'Who do we have, John?'

'Jason Toohey. One of our local football stars.'

Declan found the young man sitting hunched over, hands crossed, supporting his elbows. 'Where are you hurt, Jason?' Declan hunkered down beside his patient.

'Shoulder.' Jason pulled in a harsh breath. 'Put it out again, I reckon.'

'What do you mean *again*? Does this happen often?'

'I play league, Doc. It's contact sport.'

'I'm well aware of what rugby league is,' Declan muttered. 'I want you over at the hospital so I can look at you properly.'

John Cabot looked on worriedly. 'What do you think, Doc?'

'Shoulder dislocation,' Declan said briefly. He looked about him. 'Is the other ambulance here?'

Gary Bryson joined in the conversation. 'Just heard they've gone to collect a pregnant woman. Roads to Toowoomba are flooded. Looks like she'll have to have the baby here.'

Bendemere didn't take midwifery patients. At least not on a regular basis. But Declan guessed there would be protocol in place for just such an eventuality. And he guessed too that Emma, as usual, would have things well in hand. 'We need to get Jason over to the hospital.'

Rachel Wallace arrived just as Jason was being settled into the treatment room. 'Sorry, guys.' She looked from Declan to the young nursing assistant, Talitha, and made a grimace. 'I'd have been here earlier but when I went to reverse out of the garage, I found a damn great tree had fallen across the driveway. Took me a while to move it.'

Declan's eyes widened ever so slightly. 'You moved a fallen tree on your own?'

'With the help of a chainsaw.' Rachel coughed out a self-deprecating laugh. 'And it was more of a sapling really. But there was no way I could have reversed the car over it. Hi, JT.' She made a sympathetic face at the young man on the treatment couch. 'Is it the shoulder again?'

'Yep.' Jason managed a weak smile, raising his hand in acknowledgment, then wincing as he lowered it quickly.

'Let's get Jason on some oxygen, please,' Declan directed.

'We've all become accustomed to popping Jason's shoulder back in,' Rachel said, adjusting the oxygen. 'Relax now and breathe away, JT. Big tug coming up.'

Not if he could help it, Declan thought. 'I'll just try a manoeuvre here, Rachel,' he informed the nurse manager quietly.

She went to the head of the bed and waited. She watched intently as Declan gently and smoothly reduced Jason's dislocation until his shoulder was safely back in its socket. 'Wow…' Rachel puffed a little breath of admiration. 'You're good.'

Declan's mouth compressed for moment. It was what he'd trained for, for heaven's sake. But nevertheless Rachel's compliment had warmed him like a favourite woolly jumper on a winter's morning. 'Let's get a sling on that arm now, please.'

'Thanks, Doc,' Jason said, perking up. 'Looks like I'll be back in time for the semi-finals weekend after next.'

'No, you won't, old son.' Declan flipped out the patient chart from its rack and took the pen Rachel handed to him. 'You're out for the rest of the season. That shoulder needs resting.'

'Stuff that!' Jason struggled upright, dangling his legs over the side of the treatment couch. 'The team needs me. I play second-row forward.'

'And correct me if I'm wrong.' Declan's tone was profes-

sionally detached and even. 'But isn't that the position where
you regularly shoulder-charge your opposite number?'

'So?' Jason looked sulky.

'So,' Declan elaborated, 'if you continue playing, you'll be
lucky if your shoulder's not hanging by a thread by the end
of the season. And you'll be very unlikely to have a future in
league at all. How old are you, Jason?'

'Nineteen.'

'So, you've plenty of time to get your footy career up and
running again.'

Jason gave a howl of dissention.

'Hey, JT, listen to Dr O'Malley, hmm?' Rachel came in
with an overbright smile. 'This is his special field of medicine.
He knows what he's talking about.'

Jason's lip curled briefly. 'So—what do I have to do, then?'
he asked ungraciously.

'I'd like you to have a CAT scan on that shoulder,' Declan
said. 'We need to know why it keeps dislocating. In the
meantime, chum, it's rest. Want me to have a word with your
coach?'

Jason shook his head. 'I'll tell him at training.'

Declan replaced the chart, backing against the treatment
couch and folding his arms. 'It won't be the end of the world,
Jason.' His tone was gentle. 'We'll make a plan of action
when we see the results of your scan. Maybe the problem can
be resolved with some appropriate physio. In all probability,
you'll be back on the field next season. Call the imaging
centre first thing on Monday. They'll give you an appointment. And I'd rather you didn't try to drive, so can you get a
lift across to Toowoomba?'

Jason nodded and stood gingerly to his feet. 'Uh—thanks,'
he added grudgingly.

'You're welcome, Jason.' Declan's mouth tightened frac-
tionally. 'If you could hang around for a bit, I'll organise a
request form for your X-ray.'

'We can fix you up at the nurses' station for that,' Rachel
said helpfully. 'And JT, I'm sure you could do with a cup of

tea. Or an energy drink, if you'd prefer. Talitha will show you where to go.'

'Follow me.' The young nursing assistant grinned impishly. 'Unless you'd like a wheelchair?'

'No way!' Jason looked horrified. He paused for a second and then, as if he could see he had no other choice, shuffled out after Talitha.

Declan worked his shoulder muscles and lifted his arms in a half-mast stretch.

'Long day?' Rachel commiserated. 'Got time for a hot drink?'

'Perhaps later.' Declan smiled. 'I'll look in on Emma first. See if she needs any backup.'

'Oh—OK, then. I'll be around for a while, if you change your mind.' She sent him a quick grin. 'We'll raid the kitchen.'

'Oh— Hi.' Emma had stepped out of the room that had been quickly rearranged as a delivery suite, to find Declan hovering. She blinked a bit. 'Is something wrong?'

'I came to see if you needed any backup.'

She shook her head. 'We're fine. Dot's a midwife and the baby's well on its way. Shouldn't be any problems.' She looked closely at him and put her hand on his arm. 'You look tired. Why don't you take off? You've a big day tomorrow with Tracey.'

Declan's gaze narrowed. Was she patronizing him? It sure felt like it. His eyes swept over her pale blue hospital gown. 'I'll wait.'

'You don't have to, Declan. I can get a lift home with someone.'

By the time Declan had formulated a reply, she'd turned away and re-entered the delivery room. He had a frown in his eyes as he made his way back to the nurses' station. Damn it! he raged silently. What an awful way for their evening to have turned out.

With the baby boy safely delivered and his mum tidied up, Emma felt a surge of relief. In the little annexe, she stripped off her gown and tossed it into the linen tidy. It had been a very long day. Day and a bit, she realized after a glance at the wall clock. Oh, Lord, she needed her bed. She stretched, feeling the protest of internal muscles, and felt heat rising from her toes upwards until she flushed almost guiltily. She couldn't believe she'd been so wild with Declan, almost frenzied. She stifled a groan. She hoped he'd gone home. She needed time to gather herself. They'd taken a giant step into the unknown. It had seemed the right one at the time but now, in the fuzzy light of the early hours… The smell of coffee, fragrant and rich, drew her towards the hospital kitchen.

And that was where she found her new lover and the nurse manager. All her insecurities from her past relationship, coupled with the most awful kind of disappointment, washed through her like a power-shower of pain. She pulled back, freezing at what she saw—Declan and Rachel were sitting very closely together, their foreheads almost touching, utterly engrossed in quiet conversation. At least Rachel was the one doing the talking, while Declan seemed enthralled, drawn towards her, listening. Emma felt the drum-heavy beat in her chest, the sudden recoil in her stomach. Surely she hadn't misplaced her trust again? Surely…

It was the longest minute of Emma's life. She stood undecided, wanting to run, yet with all her heart wanting to stay. The decision was taken out of her hands when Rachel looked up. 'Emma…hey… Everything OK?'

'Fine.' Emma took a deep breath. 'I smelled coffee.'

'Help yourself.' The nurse manager pressed a strand of auburn hair behind her ear and got to her feet. 'I'm off to crash for a while. I'm on an early.'

Two sets of eyes followed Rachel as she left and then Declan pushed up out of his chair. 'I'll get you a coffee.'

'Don't bother. I've changed my mind.' The words were said tonelessly, like a recorded message.

'Let's get you home, then.' Declan moving with speed, was already ushering her out of the door.

* * *

'You seemed very cosy with Rachel back there,' Emma said as they drove. Suddenly she felt she was fighting for her very existence, her emotions unravelling like a ball of string.

'Just killing time,' Declan answered evenly. 'Waiting for you.'

A beat of silence and then, 'I—guess you'd have a lot in common with Rachel. She's worked all over the world in the OR. She's smart and savvy. *And available.*'

'Don't do this, Emma.'

Emma felt her throat thicken. 'She was practically in your lap.'

Declan pulled air into his lungs and let it go. 'Emma, if you're waiting for a reaction, I'm not biting. We just have to accept the evening turned out light years from what we'd hoped for.' He paused. 'What about coming home with me?'

'To the cabin?' He must be out of his mind.

'That's where I call home at the moment.'

'Declan—' Emma made a weary little gesture with her hand '—I'd rather be on my own, if you don't mind.'

'So you can do what?' Declan felt nettled. 'Talk yourself into believing that making love with me was a huge mistake? Or, better still,' he revised with heavy sarcasm, 'that you can't trust me now?'

Emma felt her stomach churn. He was too near the truth for comfort.

Declan gave a fractured sigh and then he spoke quietly. 'I realize you feel vulnerable—hell, don't you think I do as well? But don't blow this up into something it's not, Emma. Come home with me. I'll sleep on the couch. There's hardly anything left of the night, anyway. But at least we'll be together. I hate the thought of you rattling around in that great house on your own.'

'I was doing it long before you came on the scene, Declan. I'm used to it,' she dismissed. 'Besides, the power's back on. I'll be fine.'

With a weary shake of his head, Declan aimed the car towards Kingsholme.

When they turned into the driveway at the surgery, he cut the engine.

Emma's head spun round in query.

'I'll come in with you,' he said. 'Make sure it's all safe—that no water's come in, or worse.'

'Thanks—but there's never been any problem before.'

In other words, I can get along without you very well; you don't need to come in at all. Declan's hands tightened on the steering wheel. 'It won't take a minute.'

Once inside, Emma stood stiffly in the kitchen, listening as Declan went from room to room, checking things were in order. It seemed only seconds until he was back and poking his head in the door.

'Seems fine, very snug. I'll say goodnight, then.'

'Yes— OK—thanks.' Emma voice sounded thick and vaguely husky.

'I'll be here about eight in the morning,' Declan said. 'To drop the kids off as arranged.'

She nodded. Words, all of them mixed up, tried to force their way from her lips. Words like, *Perhaps I was wrong. Perhaps we need to talk. Can things ever be right between us again?* Instead, she stood there awkwardly. 'Take care on the road back to the cabin.'

Declan's lips twisted in self-mockery. Obviously, she couldn't wait to be shot of his company. He lifted a hand in a stiff kind of farewell but no words came readily to mind. He turned and left quietly.

The next morning, Emma made a concerted effort to corral her private thoughts and concentrate on the children's chatter as they drove to the stables. But it was difficult. Declan had had very little to say when he'd dropped them off—well, nothing personal anyway. But she'd hoped, unrealistically perhaps—? 'There's Jodi waiting for us!' Lauren was beside herself with excitement.

'Now, I want both of you to do exactly what Jodi tells you,' Emma instructed. 'Horses can be a bit tricky.'

Jodi spent some time showing them the basic skills in looking after the horses. 'Now, I'll have to take each of you separately for a ride,' Jodi explained to the children. 'Lauren, you can go first. Joel, you'll have to wait a bit, OK?'

'I don't wanna ride.' Joel tugged his cap further down on his forehead. 'I'd rather help feed the horses.'

'Right, you're easily pleased.' Jodi grinned. 'Come with me, then, dude.'

Jodi was back in a few minutes and began saddling a chestnut pony. 'This is Lady Marmalade,' she told an entranced Lauren. She showed the little girl how to mount and then positioned her feet in the stirrups. 'Lady has a soft mouth,' Jodi explained as Lauren took up the reins. 'That means she'll go exactly where you want her to with just a touch on the bridle.'

Watching on, Emma said, 'Thanks for doing all this, Jodi.'

'No worries.' Jodi gave a dimple-bright grin. 'It's good for kids to learn to be safe around animals and have fun while they're doing it. All set?' She looked up at her young charge. 'I'll lead Lady for a while until you get used to sitting on her back and then I might let you have a ride by yourself.'

Lauren's little face was alight with happiness.

Jodi pointed to the paddock adjoining the track. 'Now, for starters, we'll be taking Lady over there.'

Lauren small hands clutched the reins, her thin little shoulders almost stiff with anticipation of her first riding lesson.

Jodi looked a question at Emma. 'Coming along?'

'I thought perhaps I should keep an eye on Joel.'

'He'll be fine.' Jodi flapped a hand. 'He's with the guys. And there's a new puppy over at the barn. He'll have fun with him. Isn't it a gorgeous morning after the storm?' Jodi chatted light-heartedly as they made their way towards the big paddock.

Emma began to feel her spirits lighten. It was indeed a lovely morning. The sun had risen, dispersing the mist, and a brilliant burst of gold-tipped fingers spanned the horizon.

* * *

Lauren was going beautifully, Emma decided and, even though she didn't know terribly much about riding in general, she could see the little girl was a natural. Already her seat was easy, her little back straight, her body moving in tune with the pony's rhythmic gait. She watched as Jodi gave a thumbs-up sign and then stepped away, leaving Lauren in charge of her mount. With a tap of her heels, Lauren urged Lady forward and the pony responded, picking up her pace into a bouncy brisk walk.

Emma thought the smile on the child's face would have dimmed even the Christmas lights. Oh, sweetheart, Emma's heart swelled. I wish your mum could see you now. She'd be back home in a flash.

And then it happened.

A black streak in the form of a wilful, naughty puppy tore across the paddock in front of Lady. Without warning, the pony took fright, breaking into a jerky canter and racing through the grass. Lauren cried out…and so did Emma.

Jodi began sprinting to try to contain the pony but Lady was having none of it.

'Oh, no!' Emma's hand went to her heart as Lauren lost her seat and tumbled to the ground. Emma ran as if she was possessed. Lauren was in a little heap on the ground, hunched over and looking into the distance at the pony that had careened away to the far side of the paddock. 'Is she hurt?' Emma skidded to a stop and dropped to the ground beside the child.

'She landed like a pro.' Jodi had her arm around Lauren. 'She's one smart little girl.'

'Ooh…' Emma felt a sob of relief in her chest.

'I fell off,' Lauren said as though the fact amazed her.

'Yes, you did.' Jodi squeezed her shoulders. 'I did too when I first began to ride.'

'Did you?' Lauren looked a wide-eyed question at her mentor.

'Broke my wrist.' Jodi held up a strong, straight arm. 'But you'd never know now, would you?'

Lauren shook her head. 'I don't think I broke anything.'

'Just let me take a little look at you, Lauren.' Emma bent to the child. She did a quick neuro check and asked Lauren to turn her head and lift her arms. 'Now, can you squeeze my fingers really hard? Good girl. Now, stand up for me, Lauren. And walk a straight line, please, sweetheart. Good. That's lovely.' Emma's heart fell back into its rightful place.

'I'll go and catch Lady.' Jodi scrambled upright. 'And we'll get her back to the stables.'

'Can I ride her back?' a now recovered Lauren asked eagerly.

Emma looked doubtful but Jodi said, 'If you feel up to it, Lauren—of course you can. But I'll lead her, just to make sure she doesn't get up to any more tricks.'

The ride ended with no more mishaps. 'I'll collect Joel now,' Emma said. 'And we'll get out of your hair.'

'Don't be silly,' Jodi dismissed. 'Mrs McGinty's invited us up to the house for morning tea. She loves kids—and company.'

'We can stay, can't we, Emma?' Lauren pleaded.

How could she refuse the child? 'Well, I guess it would be rather rude if we didn't,' Emma gave in gracefully.

'Good.' Jodi looked well pleased. 'Let's round up young Joel.'

Lauren skipped ahead.

'You will let them come again, won't you, Emma?' Jodi asked as the two young women made their way slowly across to the barn. 'Lauren's little mishap was just that. I would never have put her on a pony that was unsafe.'

Emma managed a little smile. 'I'm not sure just how long the children will be staying with me but, while they are, I guess if you can manage the strain then I can too.'

CHAPTER NINE

EMMA was glad she'd had the distraction of the children's company throughout the day. But now it was almost nine o'clock and the long night stretched ahead of her.

She felt too restless to watch television, her thoughts too fragmented to read. And sleep was out of the question.

She wandered aimlessly about the kitchen. She could probably do some meal preparation for next week. Perhaps freeze some simple meals for the kids. When the firm rap sounded on her back door, her heart slammed into her ribcage with such force she had to gulp down her next breath.

It had to be Declan. No one else was likely to be banging on her kitchen door at this time of night. Like water draining out of a bath, the tension trickled out of her shoulders and the knots in her stomach began to loosen. Thank heaven he'd come. Now, she could apologise for her crazy reaction last night and they could get back on an even keel again. So simple when you thought about it.

Declan waited for Emma to answer the door. Physically, he was wiped. His eyes felt as if they'd been back-filled with fine sand sprinkled with wood ash and hisguts knitted into a tight uneasy series of knots. He lifted his shoulders in a huge controlling breath. Hell, would she even let him in?

In an agitated gesture, Emma wiped her hands down the sides of her jeans and went to open the door. She raised her gaze, looking out on to the lighted verandah. 'Declan…' Her voice shook and suddenly her limbs felt as though they were being held together by string. He looked dark and achingly familiar in his black sweater. His hair was mussed as though his fingers had run through it over and over and light stubble sprinkled his jaw and chin.

'This couldn't wait until surgery on Monday,' he said. 'May I come in?'

Emma held the door wide open.

Declan walked into the kitchen and then spun to face her. 'I thought, as you're temporary guardian of Tracey's children, you'd need to know how things went today.'

Emma felt the impact of his words right down in her gut. It wasn't what she'd expected to hear at all. And he was being so formal—as if they were medical partners and nothing more. Was that what he wanted? Had she ruined everything? She said the first thing that came into her head. 'Have you eaten?'

Declan rubbed his forehead with a long finger. 'Nev and I stopped for a bite on the way home. A coffee would be good, though–if you wouldn't mind,' he added, as if unsure of her response.

'Of course I don't mind. Sit down.'

'Kids in bed?' Declan dropped on to a chair at the head of the scrubbed pine table.

'Ages ago.' With her back towards him, Emma drew in a few calming breaths and set water to boil. She got down mugs and instant coffee and stood them on the bench. 'We had a very full day,' she said, shaking the contents of a packet of chocolate biscuits on to a plate.

'Oh, yes. How did the riding go?'

'A bit mixed.' She laughed jaggedly and filled him in. Then the jug boiled and she made the coffee, added milk and took it across to the table.

'Lauren's OK, though?' Declan took up his coffee mug and looked at her over its rim.

'Took it entirely in her stride. She wants to go back again and Jodi's happy to give her some riding lessons.'

'Good.' Declan drank his coffee slowly, looking into space, almost as if he'd run out of words.

A silence, awkward.

'How was Tracey, then?'

Declan brought his gaze up sharply. 'Things are still a bit iffy between her and Carolyn.'

'Well, they were never going to fall into each other's arms.'

'How naïve of me.' He gave a grunt of mirthless laughter. 'I was actually hoping they might have. I guess I'll never understand women.'

Emma recognized his response as a not too subtle dig at her own recent behaviour and swallowed any comeback she might have made. Instead, she'd stay entirely professional. 'How was Adam when he saw his mum?'

'A bit quiet. Tracey had some one-to-one time with him later in the day and they seemed much more in tune with each other by the end of it.'

'He's been a lost little boy,' Emma said quietly. 'So—has the family come up with any plan for the future—or even if there's to be one?'

'I'm not about to let Tracey slip through the cracks,' Declan said emphatically.

'You can't be all things to all people,' Emma reminded him.

After a long, assessing kind of look at her, Declan lifted his mug and drained the last of his coffee. 'I've arranged some joint counselling for the family. And Nev's come up with a kind of plan. He's going to try to persuade Carolyn to take a holiday with her sister at the Gold Coast.'

'So, Tracey could come back home without Carolyn peering over her shoulder?' Emma caught on quickly.

'It could work,' he justified.

'Small steps, then?'

'Better than none at all,' Declan said and got to his feet.

Emma swung upright after him. 'You'll keep me in the loop about Lauren and Joel, won't you?'

Declan scrubbed his hands across his face in a weary gesture. 'That goes without saying.' He moved towards the door. 'I'll get going, then.'

Emma's heart beat fast. If she didn't speak now, she had a terrible feeling the opportunity she sought would be lost for ever. 'I'm sorry about last night.'

Declan went very still. 'What part of it are you sorry about, Emma?'

Oh, dear God—what on earth was he thinking—that she regretted making love with him? Goosebumps ran up her backbone. 'Could we talk—properly?' Emma didn't miss his cautious look, nor the way he seemed to gather himself in.

'I guess an opportunity might present itself next week.'

'Next week?' Emma echoed stupidly. Then she thought— perhaps this is his way of breaking things off? Well, this time she intended fighting for what she believed in. And she believed in *them*. 'I—thought perhaps tomorrow?'

Declan felt the strength drain out of his legs. He'd been convinced it was never going to work between them. That Emma, for her own reasons, didn't want it to work. He swallowed deeply. 'You have the children.'

'I'll ask Moira to come over and stay with them. She won't mind…'

'OK.' Declan spread his hands in a shrug. 'Would you like to meet somewhere or—'

'No,' Emma cut in. 'I'll come to you. I should make it by afternoon.'

'Fine.' he nodded. 'Just one thing, Emma.'

'Yes?'

What could have passed for the flicker of a smile crossed his mouth. 'Don't bring food.'

Declan couldn't keep still. When would she get here? She hadn't specified a time. He'd been for a run, had a shower and a badly needed shave. 'For crying out loud, just get here…' he intoned softly. Already Emma Armitage had stirred such powerful feelings in him; she was so sweet and funny. Sexy.

But did she want a future with him? The thought that she might not made nerves tighten low in his belly. He stopped his train of thought.

It would be dusk soon. He slid a look at his watch and took a deep breath. He was on a knife-edge, his emotions seesawing from high to low and back. In the quiet still of late afternoon, he heard her car long before he saw it. His heart gave an extra thud as he hurried outside to wait for her.

Emma had steeled herself for a great deal of awkwardness when she and Declan faced each other. Little speeches, none of them right, ran through her head. And she had to face the fact that he hadn't seemed in any hurry for this conversation they had to have.

She drove slowly towards the cabin. She was going to her lover—wild for just the sight of him, the touch of him. Oh, Lord—her heart was hammering as she brought the car to a stop. Did he still want *her*?

Well, she'd never find out by sitting here. Throwing open the door of her car, she swung out.

Declan was standing there. Waiting.

'Hi,' she croaked.

'I thought you'd never get here.' His gaze snapped over her.

'Moira got held up.'

'Not literally?'

'No.' A ghost of a smile crossed her lips. 'Just a domestic drama.' She wanted to reach up and touch his newly shaven jaw, place her hands on his chest, but felt too held back by the air of tension running between them. She swallowed nervously. 'Are you OK?'

He gave a tight little smile. 'Dunno yet.'

'Oh—'

Declan saw the pitch and roll of emotion in her eyes. The uncertainty. Oh, hell. He didn't want to put her through the wringer like this. He spoke quietly into the stillness. 'Would you like a hug in the meantime?'

She nodded. 'Please…'

He closed the space between them in one swift move and gathered her in.

Emma felt herself melt into his arms, the familiar ache, the quivering in her stomach. She could have happily stayed there for ever.

'What are we going to do about this, Emma?' Declan asked, his voice a little rough around the edges. 'We seem to be going in circles.'

Emma's heart gave a sickening lurch. She pulled back, her hands creeping up to rest on his shoulders. 'The whole weekend's been manic. I've been wanting to talk but we haven't seemed able to connect.'

'No.'

'I never meant to hurt you, Declan.'

'In my heart of hearts, I knew that.' He lifted a hand, his knuckles brushing softly over her cheek.

'Thank you.' His kiss came seconds later, a long exquisite shiver of a kiss that twined through her body languidly like smoke haze. The tenderness and delicacy of the simple union of their lips left her shaky and she nestled into him, holding him closer.

When they finally pulled away, Declan kept his arms loosely around her. She slowly opened her eyes. They gleamed. But they asked him questions as well. 'Let's go in,' he said, his voice rough with emotion. His fingers slid down her arm, dragging through hers, and they made their way inside. 'Make yourself comfortable,' he said. 'Something to drink?'

'No, I'm fine, thanks.' Emma curled herself into the corner of the soft, cushiony settee.

Declan looked about him and then, because anything else would have seemed ridiculous, he parked beside her, stretching his arms along the back. He looked a question at her as much as to say, *Well, let's hear it.*

Very aware of him beside her, Emma bit gently at her bottom lip. He seemed ill at ease, although he was pretending not to. There was definitely an air of vulnerability about him. 'About what happened at the hospital—'

'When you all but cut me dead.'

She made a little gesture with her hand. 'None of this has been easy from the start, Declan. You landed on me out of nowhere. Took me over—'

'On the contrary. We agreed on a course of action for the practice.'

Her mind a whirlpool of jumbled thoughts and emotions, Emma said starkly, 'I just wonder if you'll stay, Declan.'

'That's not a decision for now.' His voice tightened and there was a long pause. 'You don't trust me at all, do you, Emma?'

'It's the circumstances we're in I don't trust. I see how frustrated you get with the shortcomings of working in a rural practice. Friday night with Agnes, for instance.'

'Guilty as charged.' His mouth pulled down. 'But that's nothing to do with my personal relationship with you.'

Emma's heart was pounding, uncertainty spreading to every part of her body. 'It has everything to do with it, Declan.' She blinked rapidly. 'If you walk away, then I'll have left myself open to hurt again.'

'Aren't you even willing to try? When we could have something good and true between us?'

She gave a bitter little laugh. 'I thought I had something good and true with Marcus.'

At his growl of dissent, Emma shook her head. 'I know it sounds pathetic but everything just imploded when I saw you and Rachel together. I was seeing Marcus and Bree again and I suppose I overreacted.'

'Just a bit.' Declan looked at her narrowly. 'How well do you know Rachel?'

She seemed surprised at the question. 'Professionally, quite well. Personally, I guess not that well.'

'So you don't know she's facing something of a personal crisis.'

Emma's eyes widened in alarm. 'Is she ill?'

'No. You're aware some time ago Rachel spent several ours of duty with Médicins Sans Frontières?'

'Doctors Without Borders—yes I knew that. She was a theatre nurse. Dad always said she was brilliant.'

Declan lifted a shoulder. 'Apparently, during her time abroad, Rachel had a long-term relationship with one of the surgeons, Ethan O'Rourke. They were planning to marry on their next leave. But it never happened because he was killed in some kind of tribal skirmish. Rachel got out and came home.'

'That's so sad.' Emma's hand went to her heart.

Declan continued, 'It was always Ethan's dream to have a properly equipped OR at the hospital where they worked. Now, it seems, his parents have gathered enough funds and support to make it happen. They want Rachel to go back and oversee its setting-up.'

Several wild thoughts juxtaposed in Emma's head. Her nerves tightened alarmingly. Had Rachel asked Declan to go with her? With his medical background, it would seem a feasible request. The implication struck her as painfully as fists.

'You said there was a problem?'

'Rachel doesn't want to go.'

'So, why did she need to speak to you about it?'

'She wanted an objective opinion.'

'I see…and what did you tell her?'

'I told her to follow her instincts.'

Emma nodded and felt relief sweep through her. 'Rachel's a strong person. She'll stand by whatever she decides. It will be the hospital's loss if she goes, though.'

'Another problem we don't need to solve just now.' Declan gave her a long look. 'Nothing's black and white, Emma. We're all just muddling along. But sometimes you have to take a chance. To trust someone other than yourself.'

'You're talking about us, aren't you?' She had a lump in her throat. 'I want to try—'

'But you're afraid?'

She nodded bleakly.

Oh, Emma…' He made a rough sound in his throat and opened his arms wide.

'Come here…'

On a little broken cry, she scooted up the settee and straight into his arms. They held each other tightly for a very long time, until Declan broke the silence with, 'Feel better now?'

She gave a shaky smile and touched a finger to the smooth skin at his throat where his shirt lay unbuttoned. 'You sound like my doctor.'

'I am your doctor,' he answered softly. 'If you want me to be?'

Her gaze faltered. 'I hate it when we're not friends.'

His fingers, blunt and strong, tipped her chin up gently so that she met his gaze. 'How long can you stay?'

He'd spoken so quietly, his voice so deep it made her shiver. 'Not as long as I'd like to,' she murmured, raising her hands, spreading her fingers to bracket his face. 'We could kiss and make up a bit, though…'

Their mouths sought each other's, then sipped and nipped and she heard a half growl escape from his throat as their kiss deepened. Was there time for what she really wanted? To make love again with him was what she really wanted. Needed.

Instead, she felt Declan pulling back, his fingers moving to twine in her hair at the back. The gentlest pressure brought her head up. His eyes were disturbingly intent as they looked into her face. 'Emma…' His throat worked as he swallowed. 'I want you. But not like this. Hurried and under pressure because you have to go. When we make love again, I want it to be long and leisurely. Slow. Very slow and with all the time in the world afterwards. You understand, don't you?'

'I suppose…' She felt her head drop a little. 'There will *be* a time, won't there?'

'I give you my word,' he said huskily, nudging a strand of her hair sideways, seeking the soft skin at her nape. 'Even if we have to close the surgery and fly the coop to accomplish it.'

'I can just see Moira's face if we did that!'

'I'm not so sure,' he countered with a lazy grin. 'Moira's a canny soul. I think she'd probably give us her tick of approval and reschedule all our appointments.'

On Monday morning, Declan popped his head into Emma's consulting room. 'Good morning.' His mouth tweaked at the corners. 'Sleep well?'

'Fine, thanks.'

'Good.' They exchanged a very private smile. 'Me too. Er...' He lifted a hand and pressed it to the back of his neck. 'Quick team meeting before surgery?'

'Now?'

'Please.'

'OK.' Emma left what she doing and went with him along to the staff kitchen.

'This is just to pull a few things together before the week gets away from us,' Declan explained to the assembled group.

'Before we start, Declan,' Moira said, 'what's the latest on Agnes? They won't tell me anything at the hospital except the standard response.'

'Sorry about that, Moira. I should have got back to you,' Declan apologized. 'Agnes has settled quite nicely. At this stage they don't think they'll have to operate. And I believe some family members from Brisbane arrived yesterday to be with her.'

'Oh, that is good news.' Moira picked up her cup of tea and held it against her chest. 'How long will she be in, do we know?'

'Not sure. I wouldn't think the hospital will be in any hurry to discharge her, though.'

'In that case, I'll send some flowers.'

'Better still, Moira, make the flowers from all of us and charge them to the practice,' Declan said. 'I think the place can stand the cost for one of our senior citizens.'

'That's a nice gesture,' Emma said quietly.

'I'm a nice guy,' Declan joked.

Emma laughed huskily, trying to hide the sudden leap in her pulse as his thigh brushed against hers. 'What else is on the agenda?' she got out quickly before her thoughts became entirely scrambled.

Declan sent her a wry smile. He knew what he'd *like* to be on the agenda. Instead, he snapped to attention. 'Cedric Dutton. I called round to see him, managed a good chat about things. He's OK now about you making a home visit, Libby. Just keep it low-key, hmm?'

The practice nurse made a small grimace. 'In other words, don't be a bossy cow.'

Declan grinned. 'I wouldn't have put it quite so bluntly. But he'll respond better if we all gentle him along. He's also agreed to try and socialize a bit. He thought the card morning at the seniors' club might be a start. He'll need transport, though. Ideas, anyone?'

'I'll have a word with Tiny Carruthers,' Moira said. 'He runs a minibus around to collect the older folk. There are a few with mobility problems. I'm sure he wouldn't mind adding Cedric to his list.'

'*Tiny* Carruthers?' Declan looked a question between the women. 'Is he quite fit himself, then?'

Emma chuckled. 'Perfectly. Tiny is six feet and used to play rugby.'

'I see…' Declan raised an eyebrow.

'He treats the older folk like they're the most important people in the world,' Moira enlarged. 'Cedric will be well looked after.'

'Good.' Declan nodded approval. 'I'll leave that in your capable hands, then, Moira. Now, as you know, I'm invited to the P&C meeting at the school tonight to put our case for the pool to be opened for the seniors' use. I wondered, Moira, whether you'd be free to come with me?'

'Me?' Moira looked flustered. 'What would you need me to do?'

'What you do best.' Declan tipped the older woman a re-assuring smile. 'Advocate for the seniors. I can cover the obvious health benefits that participating in physical activity brings. Like helping to strengthen bones and muscles and so reduce the possibility of falls and so on.'

'To say nothing of maintaining folk's independence and social connection,' Moira added, warming to her role. 'And water aerobics is so low-impact and lovely. It's such a shame the pool can't be put to use for the benefit of our older folk.'

'You've convinced me.' Looking pleased, Declan leaned back in his chair and folded his arms.

'Oh, heavens, I fell right into that, didn't I?' Moira looked a bit bemused. 'But I'm happy to do what I can.'

'Would you like me to swing by and give you a lift to the meeting?' Declan asked.

Moira flapped a hand in dismissal. 'You'd have to come in from the cabin and then detour to collect me.'

'Why go home at all after work?' Emma turned to Declan with a sudden idea. 'Stay and have dinner with me and the kids. Then you can leave from here for the meeting.'

He thought about it for one second. 'Thanks. Like me to cook?'

Remembering Friday night when he'd *cooked* for them, Emma felt her body engulfed in heat. But with the children around there'd be none of *that* happening tonight. She didn't know whether to feel glad or sorry. She lifted her gaze to his and for a second their eyes held and they were lost in a hush of silence, a stillness as profound as a mountain top at dawn. 'No need—' Emma blinked, lifting a hand to clutch the un-buttoned collar of her shirt. 'I'll pop a casserole in the slow-cooker at lunch time. If that's all right with you?'

His rather bemused smile began at his lips and moved to his eyes. 'I'll look forward to it. So, Moira—' he snapped back to attention '—I'll collect you and drop you home after the meeting.'

A few more matters regarding the practice were raised and settled.

'You going all right, Jodi?' Declan asked as the meeting broke up and people began standing and clattering their chairs back into place. 'Finding the job OK?'

'I love the work. It's so…interesting.'

'Perhaps you'll rethink your uni course.' Emma laughed. 'Switch to medicine.'

'Don't think so.' Jodi wrinkled her pert nose. 'I love my thoroughbreds too much.'

'I know it's difficult but try to avoid the temptation to scratch,' Emma told her first patient for the day. Shannon Gilmore had recently moved from North Queensland to settle in Bendemere's much cooler climate.

'Pardon me for saying the obvious, Doctor, but you don't have this wretched condition. Some days I could scratch myself to pieces.' The thirty-year-old's bottom lip quivered. 'I don't think the climate here suits me. I wish we'd never had to leave the north. And I don't think it's fair that the wife has to trundle along like so much baggage wherever the husband's job takes him.'

So, they were dealing with much more than her patient's eczema here. Emma's professional instincts sharpened and she prepared for a longer than usual consult. It was obvious Shannon had issues with alienation and resentment and probably sheer loneliness that were all adding to her stress levels and pushing the symptoms of her eczema into over-drive. Her doctor offering half-baked platitudes was not going to help matters. 'It must be difficult when you have your own career to think about,' she commiserated.

'I didn't have a structured career as such. But I had a nice little shop specialising in home décor. And clients willing to pay quite large sums for my expertise. I loved it…'

Emma thought. 'Is there a possibility you could start something like that here?'

Shannon's smile was brittle. 'If I hear that once more, I'll scream. I was living in the *tropics*, selling pieces in beautiful vibrant colours. Here, it's so cold all the time. Who wants to go out and shop? And the days never warm up.'

'Well, they do, actually.' Emma proffered a wry smile. 'But obviously not to the degree you're accustomed to.'

Shannon's shoulders hunched over.

'I understand things seem a bit bleak and insurmountable at the moment,' Emma said gently. 'But if we can't change that immediately, at least let's see what we can do for your eczema, shall we?'

'I didn't mean to come across as so pathetic and needy…' Shannon's little shrug was almost defensive.

Emma decided no follow-up comment was required. Instead, she said, 'First, I think we should consider the type of clothing you're wearing, Shannon. Overheating is a trigger for the eczema to flare up and the skin to start itching.'

'I just can't seem to get warm.' Shannon's fingers plucked at the bulky-knit jumper she was wearing.

'Anything synthetic is probably not a good choice for you at the moment. You'd be better wearing layers of lighter garments so your skin can breathe. Cotton clothing is good. Check out the shops in Toowoomba. You'll find they have a range of wonderful separates. I'm sure you'll find something to suit you. Now, on more practical matters, I imagine you know it's best to avoid soap and detergents?'

Shannon nodded. 'I use a non-perfumed moisturizer and I'm aware of the food allergy factor.'

'And stress,' Emma added gently.

'I guess…'

'You're obviously on the right track with your food.' Emma smiled. 'But you could try increasing your intake of vitamins A, E and C and fish oil supplements can help rebuild the skin. All that will take a little while to kick in so in the meantime I'll give you a script for a steroid cream as a short-term measure. That should get you back on track and don't hesitate to use a cold compress to help things along.'

'Thanks for this.' Shannon took the script and folded it into her bag. 'And for just listening, I guess…'

At the end of the surgery hours Emma popped her head into Declan's room and asked, 'Are you through for the day?'

He looked up from his computer, his eyes softening. 'One

more patient to see.' They exchanged a smile. 'I'll come through when I'm done, OK?'

'Fine. Lauren and I are making an apple crumble for dessert.' She fluttered a two-fingered wave. 'See you.'

Declan still had the smile on his face when he scooted his chair back and got to his feet. Rolling back his shoulders, he stretched. He had a few minutes before his last patient for the day was scheduled. He'd never read so much nor spent so much time on the Net than in the past weeks, he thought a bit ruefully. But there were so many areas where he'd had to refresh his knowledge to function effectively as a family practitioner. But he was getting there. Maybe there was hope for him yet.

CHAPTER TEN

DECLAN walked Moira safely to her door and then returned to his car. The meeting had gone well and he was upbeat about how his suggestions had been taken on board by the committee. It was a good outcome for the seniors. Very good.

Suddenly, he wanted to share his news with Emma. And it wasn't that late. She might still be up. He was only a few minutes from Kingsholme. He could cruise by and see whether her lights were on. Decision made, he started the motor and slid away from the kerb.

When he arrived at Kingsholme, Declan could see one solitary light on at the rear of the house. She was probably in the kitchen. Getting out of the car, he followed the path along the side of the building to the back verandah and mounted the steps. He gave a cursory knock and opened the kitchen door, calling gently, 'Emma? It's me.'

'Declan?' She spun round from the stove and frowned uncertainly. 'I didn't expect you.'

'Hi.' Slightly bemused, he stood with his back to the door and looked at her. She was dressed in polka-dot winter pyjamas, a cuddly dark blue dressing gown and fluffy socks. She looked adorable and he wanted to hold her for ever. 'I wanted to tell you about the meeting.'

She nodded vaguely. 'I've made some hot chocolate. It'll stretch to two.'

'Thanks.' He rubbed his arms briskly, watching as she

tipped the hot milk from the saucepan and filled the two mugs. 'It's cold out there.'

Taking their mugs, they sat at the kitchen table. Declan leaned forward eagerly. 'The committee have agreed to the seniors using the pool. They've even gone a step further and suggested having a huge fundraiser to have it heated.'

'Oh, good.'

'And Moira was impressive—in full flight,' he added with a chuckle. 'The committee didn't know what hit them. Even asked what more they could do for the older folk. I hope something comes of it—' He stopped abruptly. Emma was barely listening. Instead, she was gripping her mug like a lifeline and staring fixedly at the opposite wall. 'Hey…' he said gently, touching her arm to bring her out of her trance-like state. 'Are you all right?'

She looked at him blankly. 'Mum's here.'

A frown touched his eyes. 'Is that a problem?'

'It could be. I haven't told her about you. Only that I have a suitable partner for the practice.'

Declan's frown became more pronounced. 'What are you saying, Emma, that you don't want me to meet her?'

'Of course I want you to meet her!' Her gaze fluttered down and she hesitated. 'But when she hears your name—what if she…?'

'Connects the dots? Emma, we can't be held responsible for what our parents did. We don't even know if they did *anything* untoward. Do we?'

'No…' She swallowed heavily and foolish tears blurred her vision. 'I'd hate for her to be hurt, Declan.'

'Because of us and what we mean to each other? Emma, that's ridiculous.' He took her hands in his and gently chafed them. 'You're imagining wild scenarios that have no basis in fact. I'll meet your mum, OK?' he cajoled softly. 'And we'll go from there.'

She nodded mutely.

'Good.' He gave her fingers an approving squeeze. 'Now, drink your nightcap. It'll help you sleep.' Declan looked thoughtful as he lifted his own mug and took several deep mouthfuls of the hot chocolate. 'When did your mother arrive?'

'Just after you'd left for the meeting. She flew up today from Melbourne and hired a car at the Brisbane airport. She said she wanted to surprise me.'

Well, she'd certainly done that. Declan finished his drink. 'Is she just here for some family time or—'

'No,' Emma cut in and shook her head. 'There's an auction at one of the heritage homes in Toowoomba tomorrow. She's interested in bidding for a couple of paintings for her gallery. But I imagine she won't stay long. She'll want to get back to her business. We didn't have a chance to talk much. She was tired after the drive so she more or less had a shower and went off to bed.'

'I'll come in early, then.' Declan made up his mind. 'That way, I can at least meet her before she heads off about her day.'

Emma resisted the urge to lean closer and rest her head on his shoulder. Just. 'That might be best. I guess…'

'Emma, we can't keep walking on eggshells about this. Let's just take things as they come.'

'I'm sure you're right.' She drummed up her best and brightest smile.

He glanced at his watch. 'I should go and let you get some sleep.'

'And you as well.' She walked with him to the door. 'See you in the morning,' she said.

Declan cupped her face with both hands. 'I'll be here *early*.'

She gave a nod of understanding and agreement.

'It'll be all right, Emma.' His mouth brushed against hers. 'Trust me.'

The following morning, Emma felt the nerves in her stomach churning endlessly. She'd fed the children and now they'd gone to get dressed for school while she organized their lunches. Earlier, she'd heard her mother's alarm so she'd probably be up and dressed by now... Was Declan on his way in from the cabin? Oh, Lord...

'Morning, darling.'

'Oh—hi, Mum.' Emma's heart rate quickened as her mother came into the kitchen. 'Sleep all right?'

'Seemed a bit odd to be back in Andrew's and my old bedroom. But I slept well. I like the makeover, by the way.'

'It seemed time.' Emma was guarded. 'Now, what about some breakfast?'

'Just toast, thanks. Do you have leaf green tea?'

'China canister there on the shelf. Help yourself. I'll just finish packing the kids' lunches.' Emma's mouth flicked into a quick smile. 'You look lovely, by the way.' Dressed in her beautifully tailored black trousers and jacket, her mother looked Melbourne *chic* all the way. 'Your boots are *gorgeous*.'

'And comfortable. I expect to be doing a bit of running around today.'

Emma watched as her mother slid bread into the toaster. 'Are you after anything else beside the paintings?'

'The Kingsley estate was vast. There are some extremely delicate tapestries I might go after—if the price is right,' she added with a wry smile.

True to his word, Declan arrived early at Kingsholme. He unloaded his medical case in his consulting room and then made his way through to the living quarters. He heard muted conversation from the vicinity of the kitchen and guessed the voices belonged to Emma and her mother. His heart did a quick tango. He'd pretended to be calm about things for Emma's sake. But he was far from it. Mrs Armitage's reaction could ruin everything he and Emma had found. He hoped with all that was in him it wouldn't come to that.

Reaching the kitchen, he paused and then leant against the doorframe and poked his head in. Emma's mother was standing against the bench of cupboards, a delicate teacup in her hands. At least he supposed it was her mother. She looked like an older version of her daughter. Declan's gaze flicked discreetly and quickly over the slender-framed woman. She oozed style and sophistication in her dress and *very* good gold jewellery decorated her throat and hands. Hell, he hoped he'd measure up. He cleared his throat. 'Good morning.'

'Declan!' Her heart thumping, Emma turned, holding Lauren's lunch box like a shield against her chest. 'Come in. Um—this is my mother. Mum—' she smiled, her voice a bit breathless, earnest with her own need for things to go well '—this is Declan O'Malley, my practice partner.'

Emma's mother turned with a graceful movement and replaced her cup on its saucer and then held out her hand. 'Declan. How very nice to meet you.'

'Mrs Armitage.' Declan's handshake was firm. 'It's good to meet you too.'

'Oh, please. Call me Roz.' The older woman smiled. 'You've an early start this morning?'

'Most mornings,' Declan replied. 'But we don't mind, do we, Emma?' His wide-open gaze seemed natural and frank but it was telling Emma so much more. First hurdle over. It will be all right.

'It's like most jobs, I guess,' Emma said, getting into the spirit of the conversation. 'You get into a rhythm of sorts.'

Declan looked hopefully around the kitchen. 'Any tea going, guys?'

'I've just made a pot if you like green tea?' Roz offered.

'Sounds just the ticket,' Declan said diplomatically, even though he would have preferred Emma's strong brew first thing. As he poured himself a cup, he set out to be sociable. 'Emma tells me you have a busy day ahead, Roz.'

'Yes, and I should get going.' Emma's mother glanced at her watch. 'The paintings I want to bid for are up first thing. I shouldn't be too late home, though, darling,' she told Emma. 'Penny and Clive Bailleau are driving in from Munbilla and we're meeting up for lunch. After that, I'm pretty much done.'

'Oh, I'm glad you're seeing friends,' Emma said warmly. 'Give Penny and Clive my best.'

'I'll do that.' Roz rinsed her cup and placed it in the drainer.

Turning, she plucked a section of paper towel and dried her hands. 'And I thought I might pick up a treat for the children,' she said in a confidential undertone. 'What are they into?'

'Oh, that's so nice of you, Mum.' Emma's heart warmed.

Roz flapped a hand in dismissal. 'They've had a hard time, from what you said. And I'd like to do it anyway.'

'OK—' Emma thought for a second. 'Well, Lauren likes to read and she's keen to learn to ride, although she knows practically nothing about horses. Not sure about Joel…'

'He's mad about soccer,' Declan chimed in with a grin. 'At the moment, he's kicking a clapped-out piece of leather around the yard. I had it on my list to get him a decent soccer ball but now I'll leave it in your capable hands, Roz.'

'So—' Roz Armitage held up two crossed fingers '—the book shop and the sports shop, right? Now, I really must be on my way.'

'Take care on the roads.' Emma gave her mother a quick hug.

'And you two have a good day,' Roz said in reply and wrinkled her nose. 'If that's possible.'

'It is, Roz,' Declan quirked his mouth and drawled, 'even in medicine.'

Two hours later, Declan realized the rashness of that statement.

They had an emergency situation at the hospital. Students from a girls' school in Toowoomba were being brought in with suspected food poisoning. 'Apparently they're here in Bendemere on a school camp,' Moira told the doctors as they came together for a quick briefing. 'Both our ambulances have gone out and the teachers will bring the rest in the school bus.'

'The rest!' Declan's head pulled back. 'How many are we expecting?'

'Maybe in excess of ten?' Moira made a small grimace. 'They're from the upper grades, thirteen and upwards.'

'So at least we can expect some degree of cooperation and sensible answers,' he commented ruefully.

'Nursing backup might be a bit thin on the ground at the hospital,' Emma said. 'No doubt Rachel will call in casuals but apparently a few of the regular nurses are off with winter ills. Perhaps Libby could fill in and come with us?'

Declan nodded. 'Good idea. And Moira, do what you have to do to reorganize our patient list, please.'

'Anyone who is just waiting for repeats of their scripts could perhaps come back tomorrow,' Emma added. 'Whatever, we'll leave things in your capable hands.'

'Do we have any idea of the expected ETA?' Declan asked as they pulled in to the hospital car park.

'They won't be long,' Emma said. 'Camp Kookaburra is only about ten kilometres out.'

From the back seat of the car, Libby pondered, 'I wonder what they ate?'

Declan snorted. 'Something dodgy for breakfast, if they've all gone down so quickly.'

Within minutes the ambulances arrived, followed by the school bus.

Emma could see at once that the students were quite ill, some of them pale and sweaty. They were going to take some sorting out, that was certain.

Declan grimaced. 'Bang goes the rest of our morning surgery list.'

'Rural doctoring,' Emma reminded him.

'Got it.' Declan lifted a finger, acknowledging her point.

Talitha looked goggle-eyed at the volume of patients. 'We'll run out of cubicles! Where will we put them all?'

'We'll put some of them out on the verandah ward.' Rachel was in full flight in charge. 'And Tally, run and get bags or basins, please. They're bound to be still vomiting.'

Tally ran.

'Right, guys,' Declan came in authoritatively, 'Let's get some triage going, shall we?'

'Sorry I'm late.' Casual nurse Irene McCosker, fiftyish, arrived slightly breathless, still adjusting the belt on her uniform trousers. 'Jeff's off sick so I had to shoo the customers out and close the shop,' she explained.

Emma smiled at the older woman. 'Thanks so much for coming in at short notice, Irene. Perhaps, where you can, would you start taking names, please? And liaise with the accompanying teachers about letting the parents know. That would be a great help.'

'Certainly, Dr Armitage.' Irene looked pleased to be given responsibility.

'We should see the kids on stretchers first,' Emma said quietly to Declan. 'Would you like to team with Rachel? Then Libby and I can work together.'

His brow furrowed for a second. 'If you're sure?'

She nodded. 'Absolutely.' He'd said it was all about trust and so far he hadn't let her down.

Accompanied by Rachel, Declan went into the first cubicle. Their patient looked pale and clammy. Bending over the stretcher, Declan asked, 'What's your name, sweetheart?'

'Bronte Pearce.'

'And how old are you, Bronte?'

'Sixteen.'

'And when did you start feeling ill?'

'Soon after breakfast—' The youngster rocked her head restlessly from side to side and moaned softly.

'It'll be all right, honey.' Rachel smoothed the girl's long dark fringe away from her forehead. 'We'll get you feeling better soon.'

'Bronte,' Declan came in gently, 'I just need to feel your tummy.' His mouth compressed as he palpated. 'Right.' He stepped back and drew the sheet up. 'That's fine. Have you had any diarrhoea?'

'Some. Oh—help…' Her plea came out on a moan.

Noticing her patient's sudden pallor, Rachel reached for a

basin and helped her sit up. Then, exhausted from the bout of vomiting, Bronte fell back on the pillows. She blocked a tear with the palm of her hand. 'I feel awful,' she sniffed. 'And my little sister Sasha is so ill. She's only thirteen and she started her periods just yesterday…'

'It's OK, sweetie. Don't worry.' Rachel squeezed Bronte's hand. 'She'll be well looked after.'

'Someone's head should roll for this.' Grim-faced, Declan scribbled instructions on the chart. 'Put up ten milligrams of maxolon stat, please, Rachel. That should settle her tummy.'

'Lomotil for the diarrhoea?'

Declan nodded. 'Let's start with two orally and cut back to one after each bowel movement.' He frowned. 'She's dehydrating. I'd like her on four per cent glucose and one-fifth normal saline IV. Sips of water only. Could you take her blood sugar levels as well, please? Anything below three, I need to know. And, while you're doing that,' he added, replacing the chart, 'I'll just have a quick word with Emma.'

Declan found Emma in the next cubicle and beckoned her aside. 'Have you treated a child by the name of Sasha Pearce yet?'

'I've just sent her to the ward,' Emma confirmed. 'She was seriously dehydrated. She'll need to stay on a drip for some time yet. I'm recommending we keep her overnight.'

'How was she generally?'

'As you'd expect—scared and miserable. Is there a problem?' Emma queried.

'I've just seen her older sister, Bronte. She was concerned.'

And so are you, Emma decided. Declan really cared about these kids and that thought warmed her through and through. 'Tally's taken Sasha under her wing, Declan. Trust me, she'll be fine.'

'OK, thanks. I'll just relay that to Bronte.' He hesitated. 'Poor kid was pretty upset about her little sister's predicament.'

'The women's business?' Emma shot him a look as old as time. 'All taken care of.'

'Great. Thanks.' He swished back the curtains and disappeared.

They went on assessing and treating their juvenile patients for the next couple of hours, answering questions from anxious parents as they trickled in to check on their offspring. Several of the students appeared quite poorly and had to be admitted for observation but the majority were treated and allowed to go home.

'Did you get any joy from the Health Department?' Emma asked later, as they made their way out of the hospital to the car park.

'They've promised urgent action,' Declan said. 'Obviously, whatever they find will be sent for analysis. In the meantime, the camp has been cut short. Most of the kids will be home in their own beds by tonight.'

Moira had refused to overload the lists so the afternoon surgery finished in reasonable time. After his last patient had left, Declan went along to Emma's consulting room. He knocked and poked his head in. 'All done for the day?'

'Mmm.' She waved him in and swung off her chair as if her feet had wings. 'Hi...' She met his gaze, an almost shy smile playing over her lips. And Declan knew he'd crack wide open if he didn't kiss her.

He held out his arms and she flew into them, wrapping herself tightly around him and turning her face up for his kiss.

'Emma...' A gravelly sigh dragged itself up from the depths of his chest and his mouth took hers as if he were dying of thirst.

She shifted against him, each tiny movement a subtle invitation for him to hold her more tightly, more intimately.

And he did.

Heat exploded in him and he gave a strangled groan, her soft pleas driving him closer to the edge. For a split second he considered letting his natural instincts run wild and making love with her here in her office. To be inside her, to feel her legs wrapped round him, hear the sweet sounds of her climax…

But only for a second. Suddenly, the compulsion took flight. Somehow it seemed tacky and not worthy of her—of them.

But how he ached for her.

He found just enough control to break the kiss. 'Emma…' He pressed his forehead to hers. 'We have to slow down.'

'Yes, I know…' Her voice shook. 'But I wish—'

'Wish we didn't?' He gave a hard laugh. 'Opportunities are a bit unworkable at the moment.' He released her, then slid his hands down her arms to mesh her fingers with his. 'Our time will come,' he promised huskily.

'I suppose…yes.' She hung her head a little. 'Can you at least stay for dinner?'

'Nice thought, but no.' He leaned forward, brushing her mouth with his lips. 'You should have some quality time with your mother. Somehow, I think it's what you both need.'

She smiled unwillingly. 'Guru is your middle name now, is it?'

'Christopher, actually.' They looked at each other for a long moment and suddenly her eyes clouded. Declan shook his head. 'You're not still worrying about all that stuff regarding our respective parents, are you, Emma?'

'Perhaps a bit.'

He frowned. 'Why, for crying out loud? Roz was clearly very at ease when I met her.'

'I wonder—' Emma bit her lips together and hesitated. 'I mean—I hope Dad didn't deceive her. That would be too awful.'

'Emma, Emma.' Declan pulled her in close again, his patience clearly under strain. 'For your own sake, you have to let this go. None of it matters now. You do see that, don't you?'

'Yes, you're right. None of it matters.' Well, one part of her believed that. The logical, clear-thinking part. But underneath there was still a tiny doubt, niggling away like a bothersome pebble in a shoe.

But clearly Declan wanted to close the page, to put the discussion to rest once and for all. Deep down, she knew it was the best option. And yet… 'You're right,' she said again, as if she really meant it. 'None of it matters now.'

'Tell me again how you and Dad met.'

The children had long gone to bed and Emma and Roz, both dressed in their nightwear, were sitting in front of the fire. 'Darling, I've already told you several times, as I recall,' Roz said mildly.

'But not since I was about fourteen.' Emma filled their tiny glasses with a peach-flavoured liqueur. 'Now Dad's gone, it would be nice to hear it again,' Emma pleaded. 'And from the beginning, please.'

Roz gave a resigned kind of smile. 'We were both at Uni. I was doing fine arts. Andrew was doing medicine. I guess it was unlikely we would meet up at all, both doing very different disciplines. But there was a move on to close the crèche at the university.'

'Why?' Emma asked, more than a little interested.

'Oh, someone in a high place got a bee in his bonnet that babies and young children had no business being on campus.' Roz lifted a shoulder. 'Independently, both Andrew and I had read the flyers that were asking for numbers to rally to protest against the decision. And we both went along.'

'So you met waving banners.' Emma smiled, her chin parked on her upturned hand.

'Something like that.' Roz took a sip of her liqueur. 'As I remember, we were pretty outraged. We linked up and formed a committee and in time the idea to close the crèche was vetoed. In those days, most of the students who used the crèche were single mums. They really needed the facility.'

'So, you and Dad must have had very strong feelings about child welfare,' Emma pressed.

'We did.' Roz nodded her ash-blonde head. 'In fact, when the director at the crèche called for volunteers occasionally, we both went and helped out with the little ones. We both loved kids,' she added quietly.

'And yet you only had me.'

Roz responded to the question in her daughter's eyes with a tiny shrug of her shoulders. 'I didn't enjoy being pregnant,' she confessed. 'Andrew understood. But we delighted in you when you were born, Emma. So much.' She frowned a bit. 'You never felt...*unloved*, did you?'

'No, of course not.' Even as she said the words Emma felt the painful lurch in her heart. But, knowing what she did now, had that been the reason her father had drifted towards Anne O'Malley? A young widow with her little brood? He must have felt so *needed*. Would it be going too far to say even *fulfilled*? She swallowed deeply. 'Were you and Dad always happy together?'

'Yes, we were.' There was no hesitation in Roz's reply. 'It wasn't easy being married to a doctor, Emma. It took me a long time to realize the demands of Andrew's job. His patients always came first. I thought he was busy enough when he was at the Prince Alfred, but then, when he was offered tenure at John Bosco's, he got even busier. He was always very involved with his interns.' Roz gave a faintly wry smile. 'I guess in a way they became like his own kids.'

They were quiet for a while and then Emma said carefully, 'I sometimes wondered why you went off to Melbourne to open your gallery and left Dad here.'

'Yes...I suppose you did.' Roz sighed, slightly daunted by the need for explanation. 'Your dad thoroughly approved, you know, Emma. In fact, he suggested it. I'd put my own career on hold when we came here to Kingsholme. But I knew how much it meant to your father.'

'You never really settled here, though, did you?'

Roz laughed shortly. 'And I thought I hid it so well. It was different, that's all. I made a life, formed a few good friendships. I was managing. But suddenly, out of the blue, Andrew suggested the gallery idea. You'd returned to the practice.

Dad was quite sure you'd found your niche in rural medicine. And he was so proud to have you as his practice partner.'

'Yes, he told me that.' Emma looked down at her hands. 'But he missed *you*, Mum.'

'We missed one another,' Roz said patiently. 'But all along he'd planned to join me in Melbourne as soon as he'd found someone to replace him at Kingsholme. Someone he was sure would work well with you. Someone he could trust. He wanted to have it all lined up before he told you. Unfortunately, it didn't work out quite like that…'

'No…' Tears blurred Emma's vision and she reached for her mother's hand.

They stayed like that for some minutes more, both with a new sense of calm and acceptance. 'We should have talked like this a long time ago,' Emma said.

'My fault.' Roz looked a little sad. 'I had to grieve for Andrew on my own. He meant the world to me…'

Emma searched her mother's face. 'We should have grieved together.'

'Yes, I see that now. I do love you, darling.'

The reassurance flooded into Emma like warm sunshine parting a cloudy sky. 'I love you too, Mum.'

'Mum's under the impression Dad was still looking for a suitable practice partner for me when he died,' Emma told Declan the next day. They were sitting over a cuppa after surgery had finished.

'Maybe that's for the best,' Declan said. 'But *we* know Andrew tried his best to make sure both your and Roz's futures were assured when he was out of the picture.'

Emma gave a tiny shrug. 'Yes.'

Declan's jaw worked for a minute. 'If only I'd been able to fly out at the time Andrew first called me, instead of being banged up in a hospital rehab unit—'

'But you did come, Declan. You came as soon as you could. And Dad's wishes were fulfilled.'

'Did Roz get home all right?' he asked, changing the tenor of the conversation subtly.

'Yes. She rang about an hour ago. And you were right.' Emma felt a mix of emotions tumble around inside her. 'Mum and I did need to talk.' She stopped and bit down on her bottom lip. 'I think I've matched up all the pieces now.' And, if there was one small piece that still refused to go exactly where she wanted it to, well, so be it.

He smiled. 'I'm glad. By the way, I had some other news today about the Jones family. Carolyn has gone on holiday and Adam was discharged from hospital. For the present, he's staying with Tracey at the shelter.'

'Well, I guess that's progress of a sort.'

'I think we can assume that.' Declan moved restively in his chair. 'Just means you'll have Lauren and Joel for a bit longer, I guess.' And longer still until they could make love again...

CHAPTER ELEVEN

A WEEK later and the staff were on their lunch break before the afternoon clinic.

'Bendemere is hosting the schools' annual sports day tomorrow,' Emma said.

Declan looked up from his reading. 'Is it a big event?'

'All the schools from the neighbouring districts compete.' Jodi dipped into her mug of soup. 'It's a big deal. I was sports captain both years Bendemere won,' she added modestly.

'So, you want the day off tomorrow to go strut your stuff, do you?' Declan teased.

Jodi wrinkled her nose at him. 'I work at the supermarket tomorrow,' she reminded him.

'Lauren's race isn't until eleven.' Emma gave a tentative look around the faces. 'And, as she doesn't have her mum to cheer her on, I thought I might try to get across to the sports ground.'

'I'll cover your list,' Declan offered promptly. 'In fact, I might try to get along for Lauren's race myself. How are tomorrow's lists looking, Moira?'

'Fairly light,' Moira said. 'Most folk will be at the sports day.'

Declan lifted a hand and rubbed the back of his neck. 'Nev can't make it?'

'My guess is he would have used up all his family leave,' Moira said. 'I doubt he'd want to ask for a day off to go to his grandchildren's sports day.'

Emma looked at Declan. 'So, it's agreed I'll go?'

'No question.' Declan leaned back in his chair and folded his arms. 'What about Joel's events?'

'He's involved only in team events. I think he's more concerned about the food on the day,' Emma ended with a chuckle. Then she sobered. 'But I think it would make Lauren feel special if I was there for her.'

'Yes, it would,' Declan said softly. He wanted to lean forward and kiss her on the lips and tell her what a great job she was doing as a stand-in parent. Instead, he restrained himself and went back to his reading.

At a few minutes to eleven the next day, Emma took her place among the parents and supporters who were rapidly filling every space along the sides of the running track.

'Which one is your kiddie?' a friendly lady who looked like someone's nanna asked as she made room for Emma beside her.

'Over there.' Emma smiled, pointing to Lauren, her little face fierce in concentration as the children began to line up. 'Her mum can't be here so I'm standing in,' she felt compelled to add.

'That's my granddaughter, Taylor, beside her,' the older woman said.

She's at least a head taller than Lauren, Emma thought, her heart dropping. She'd been hoping like mad for Lauren to win. Even a small victory like winning a race would be magic for the child.

Emma felt strung tight, waiting for the starter's whistle to sound. So focused was she that it was a moment before she registered the tap on her shoulder. Spinning round, she took a quick breath of surprise. 'Declan! How did you manage to get here?'

'Easy.' He grinned. 'I booted the patients out of the waiting room and told them to come back tomorrow.'

Emma rolled her eyes.

'Moira and I juggled things. Several agreed to an after-

hours consult. I'll see them.' Moving closer, he rested hi
hand on Emma's shoulder. 'Am I here in time for Lauren'
race?'

'They're lining up now.' Emma flicked a hand. 'Lauren
seems like a little sprite next to some of the others.'

'I bet you she's a pint-size rocket.' Declan increased th
pressure on his hold. 'Look! They're off!' he yelled. 'Go
Lauren!'

The race, it seemed, took only seconds—seconds whe
they cheered themselves hoarse. Running like the wind, pac
for pace with her rival, Lauren finally pulled out a burst o
speed from somewhere within her slender little body and too
the lead, sprinting over the finishing line just centimetres i
front of her rival.

'She won! Lauren won!' Unable to contain her excitement
Emma grabbed at Declan and he whirled her around until sh
was breathless.

'Come on—' He grabbed her hand and together they bega
moving towards the finish line.

'Lauren!' Emma shrieked. 'Honey, over here!'

'Wait—' Declan hauled Emma to a halt beside him
'Look…' he said with something like disbelief in his voice.

Emma looked. 'Oh, my goodness,' she whispered and too
a shaky breath. 'It's Tracey… Oh, Declan!' she exclaime
softly. 'Lauren's wish has come true. She so wanted Tracey
to be here to watch her run.'

'Lauren's got her mum back,' he rejoined quietly, and thei
eyes linked in understanding.

Together they watched as Lauren threw herself into he
mother's arms. It was the hug of a lifetime. A hug that wen
on and on, mother and child clinging together and looking a
though they never wanted to be parted ever again.

Declan squeezed Emma's hand. 'Are we going over to say
hello?'

'Maybe we should. Unless…do you think we'd be intrud
ing?'

'No, I don't,' Declan said and he smiled. 'Come on.'

Lauren's little face lit up when she saw Emma. 'I won!' she said and her thousand-watt smile said it all.

'You did.' Emma held out her arms. 'Well done, sweetheart. You ran like the wind.'

Lauren allowed Emma a brief fierce hug and then she slipped back to her mother's side, tucking her skinny little arm through Tracey's very possessively.

Emma felt something crack inside her. Was it a feeling of loss? she wondered. But that was silly. She was never going to have Lauren indefinitely. She was back with her mother now and that was how it should be. But how she was going to miss that sweet child.

'Hello, Tracey.' Declan stuck out his hand. 'This is a real turn-up.' He grinned. 'You look great, by the way.'

'Thanks.' Tracey looked shyly between the two doctors. 'Marcella from the shelter drove me over. She's got Adam with her.'

'That's wonderful,' Emma said warmly. 'I'm so glad you managed to get here.'

Tracey held her daughter's hand tightly. 'I wouldn't have missed it. I would have got here somehow.'

'Are you back home with us now, Mum?' Lauren's big brown eyes asked the question neither Declan nor Emma had felt able to.

'Yes, baby, I am,' Tracey said softly and bent to press a kiss on her daughter's fair head. 'We'll all be back at Granddad's tonight.'

'You're going to miss them.' Practical as always, Moira was helping Emma pack up the children's clothes for their return home.

Emma blinked a bit, popping a pair of Lauren's jeans into the suitcase. 'Their place is with their mother now she's well. I was just the stopgap until things got back to normal.'

Moira kept folding. 'This house was made for children.'

'And maybe one day it will have some here permanently.' Ignoring Moira's not too subtle implication, Emma forced lightness into her voice. Already a gnawing kind of emptiness was beginning to surround her. But she'd get over it. She had to. 'Oh, Moira—hang on a tick before you close the case. I've something for Lauren. I'll just get it.' She came back with a jumper in the softest, purest wool. It was a happy poppy-red colour with a chain of daisies embroidered around the neckline.

'That's…lovely,' Moira said, but with a note of disquiet in her voice. 'But Emma, should you be spending so much money on the child?'

'It's a gift, nothing more, nothing less.' Emma folded the jumper neatly between some layers of tissue paper and placed it on top of the rest of the clothes. 'I thought Lauren might like to wear it when she goes riding. I want her to keep up her lessons.'

Moira sniffed. 'And who's paying for those riding lessons? You?'

Emma replaced the lid of the suitcase and zipped it shut. 'With respect, Moira, that's my business. Jodi and I have come to an arrangement.'

'You're just like your father.' Moira shook her head. 'Your heart overrules common sense sometimes. Let's just hope Tracey doesn't mess things up for those children again,' she added darkly.

'She won't.' Emma was firm. 'People have worked very hard with her and she's responded. For once, it's been a good outcome.'

'You're going to be at a loose end tonight.' It was late on the same day and Declan was grabbing a coffee before heading out to a house call.

'I suppose I will.' Emma looked up from giving the kitchen bench a quick tidy. 'Got any solutions?'

'I might.' Placing his mug carefully back on the counter top, he half turned to look at her. 'Come home with me.'

There was a moment's loaded silence. Emma blinked uncertainly and she realized what he was saying. She'd been

hinking only about the children's departure and how it would
affect her. She'd completely forgotten that, with their going,
her life was her own again. Her options were suddenly wide
open. 'I hadn't thought—'

'Well, I have.' He looked at his watch. 'I'm about to do this
house call, then I'll see the three after-hours patients. Should
be through by six-thirty. Put a few things together, hmm?
And something for work tomorrow.'

'All right.' She smiled, swallowing back a throatful of
emotions. 'I'll be ready.'

She hadn't been in his bedroom before.

It was almost spartan with a king-sized bed, books on the
bedside table, family photos in a fold-out frame, a set of
weights in the corner. And why was she even noticing?

Declan put her bag on the end table. 'Do you want to hang
anything?'

'Um—yes, please.' Emma slipped past him to hang her
work clothes in the wardrobe. She tried to swallow. Her mouth
had become so dry and her heart, with a mind of its own, had
gravitated to her throat. It seemed ages since they'd been
lovers. Perhaps she'd imagined more than the reality. Could
they possibly recapture what they'd found together? And, if
they couldn't—what then?

'Emma…'

'Declan, what if…?'

He shook his head, drawing her down to sit on the edge of
the bed. He stared at her for a moment. Then, lifting his hands,
he cupped her face. 'Emma, do you trust me?'

The catch in his voice told her everything she needed to
hear. 'Yes.'

'Oh, heavens! Look at the time!' Emma sprang upright and
then leaned down to tug Declan awake. 'Declan, get up!
We've only minutes to get to the surgery!'

He groaned. 'What's the hurry? They can't start without us.'

'But it'll look odd if we straggle in late. *And together.*'

'As if we care.' He reached up and pulled her back under the covers. 'I want to tell the world we're together.'

'Oh…' Emma felt her lips sigh apart. 'Really?'

He pulled her closer, nuzzling her throat, behind her ear then her throat again. 'Yes, really. What about you, Emma? Want to shout it to the tree tops?'

'It's all so new,' she offered, hardly knowing what her answer should be but tucking further into his closeness. His body felt deliciously warm, hard, expectant. Wonderful. All for her. 'Yes, oh, yes,' she said at last and turned her face to meet his mouth.

They tasted each other, taking it slowly, each press of their lips renewing their sense of wonder and delight. Emma closed her eyes and let it happen, letting her tongue tease him and her breath sigh over his face. She ran her hands along his torso, up the lightly tanned curve of his neck and into the dark soft strands of his hair.

And she didn't let herself think for one second that this commitment was anything but right. Right and perfect.

She opened her mouth wider on his, letting herself drown in his kiss, flinging her doubts into the air like a handful of sand in the wind.

Emma drifted through the morning surgery in a cocoon of dreamy recollection as memories of their lovemaking rolled over her. She felt as though someone had poured liquid sunshine over her bones. She was in love. In love with the most wonderful man in the world.

When, only seconds later, Declan rapped on the door and stuck his head in, she started up out of her reverie, snapping back to reality when he said starkly, 'We have the worst kind of emergency, Emma. Jodi's had a fall at the stables. It looks bad.'

'Oh, my God!' Emma's hand went to her mouth. 'How bad?'

He shook his head. 'Let's get out there. Every second counts.'

Declan looked strained as he took the emergency kit from Libby. 'Keep the hospital in the loop, please, Libs.' The nurse merely nodded.

Moira hovered, her face pale with shock. 'I know you want to come with us, Moira,' Declan said gently. 'But—'

'I'd be in the way.' Her mouth trembled. 'Take care of her, Declan. She's the dearest thing on earth to me.'

Emma wrapped an arm quickly around Moira's shoulders. 'We'll let you know the minute we have some details,' she promised.

'Do you have any more details about the accident?' Emma asked.

'Not much. Jodi was riding track with several others. Apparently, the horses were flat out in a time trial. The lead horse stumbled. Jodi was immediately behind.'

Emma sucked in her breath on a grimace. It would be a domino effect, resulting in a wild mix of riders, horses, limbs and bodies.

'Jodi's parents?' Declan's question took on the practicalities of the situation.

'Last I heard, they're away on holiday up north somewhere. She was staying with Moira.'

'Siblings?'

'One brother at Uni in Brisbane. Final year engineering.' Worst scenarios curled in a knot in Emma's stomach. Jodi's family would have to be summoned immediately.

When they arrived at the stables, they were out of the car and running. Jodi's cries of distress were endless. Heartbreaking. Emma ran faster.

Sarah McGinty was waiting. 'I tried to make her more comfortable,' she said. 'But I didn't dare move her. Patrick and James are away at the yearling sales. There's just me here.' She tightened her arms across her middle as if she was in pain herself. 'None of this should have happened…'

Emma placed a quick hand of sympathy on Sarah's forearm and squeezed.

The doctors worked seamlessly as a team, checking first

for any head or spinal injury. 'Stay with us, Jodi,' Declan said
gently. He slipped the oxygen mask into place. 'We'll have
you feeling better soon.'

And pigs might fly, he added silently, grimly.

Emma was doing her best to insert an IV. She shook her
head.

'Problem?' Declan snapped.

'Veins thready and constricted. OK,' she said with relief.
'I've got it. Normal saline going in now. What pain relief do
you want?'

'Spleen seems OK. We can give morphine. Let's make it
five milligrams, please. Anti-emetic ten. Both IV.'

'Jodi, sweetheart, we're giving you something for the pain
now.' Emma injected the drugs quickly. 'All done.'

'Thanks. I need to assess what's going on with her legs.'

Emma knew what had to be done. Grabbing the scissors
from the emergency pack, she slit Jodi's jodhpurs from ankle
to thigh, peeling back the layers of material. She bit hard on
her bottom lip at what lay revealed. Bone was protruding
from Jodi's thigh.

'Compound fracture to the right femur.' Declan was clini-
cally calm. 'I'd guess the horse in its fright has kicked out and
caught her legs.' His fingers ran gently along her shins.
'Multiple fractures to left tib and fib so both legs compromised. Let's get a doughnut dressing over that exposed bone,
please, and we'll splint both legs together for the transfer to
the ambulance.'

'For the best possible care, I think we should chopper her
straight through to the Royal Brisbane.' Emma's tone was unequivocal. 'She's going to need hours of surgery and follow-
up rehab.' She drew out her mobile phone. 'I'll put a call into
CareFlight. Ask them to meet us at the hospital. By the time
they get here, we should have Jodi stable enough to go.'

Two of the town's ambulance crew who had arrived barely
minutes behind the doctors moved in with the stretcher. Nick
Turner, the senior officer, looked stricken. 'I've known young
Jodi all her life…'

Declan's mouth drew in. This was no time to start hand-ringing. Their patient needed to be in the care of a surgeon nd fast. 'What's the situation with the other riders, Nick?'

'There were two lads. Both managed to roll out of the way f the horses. They're a bit shaken. No obvious injuries and ve've checked their neuro obs.' He shook his head. 'Poor little odi was caught in the middle of the scrum. Blasted nimals...'

Emma closed off her mobile. 'The base can't give us an TA on the chopper. It's presently evacuating injured from a notor pile-up on the Warrego Highway.'

Declan's expletive was muted. 'What now?'

Emma bit her lips together. Declan's face spoke volumes.

'We could take her by ambulance to Toowoomba and try nd get backup transport from there,' Nick said without much onviction. 'The road's still a bit dodgy in places from the torm but if we're careful...'

Declan shook his head. 'We can't put Jodi through that.'

'Then we'll wait on the chopper,' Emma said doggedly.

Declan's jaw tightened. God only knew what Jodi's circu-ation would be doing by the time the air ambulance got to nem. And they were wasting precious seconds messing about ere. Jodi's cry of distress sent a chill around the gathering.

'I'll check again with CareFlight.' Emma pulled out her nobile.

'Hold it,' Declan said clearly. 'I'll do the surgery here.'

Emma's eyes flew wide in alarm. Did Declan realize what e was suggesting? Surely he was placing their patient's life t risk if he didn't know for certain whether he had the stamina) complete the operation? Should she try to intervene and top him? 'Declan—'

In an abrupt movement, he drew her aside. 'I need you to ack me on this, Emma. It'll be a far better outcome for Jodi f she can have the surgery done here.'

But would it be the best outcome for *him*? Operating before e was ready could undo all the progress, both physically and motionally, that he'd made. And she knew if she dug her toes

in and refused to back him, he'd respect their profession[a]
partnership and stand aside and wait for the chopper. Bu
what of Jodi? Poor little injured Jodi. The wait would b
terrible. For all of them.

'Emma, listen…' he said, his jaw working. 'I can do this

Emma closed her eyes, praying for courage, because th[i]
was the hardest decision she'd ever had to make in her lif[e]
Her heart pounded. She thought of her father and what he'
want her to do. He'd tell her to trust her instincts. She close
her eyes for one second and then snapped them open. 'As lon[g]
as you're sure, I'll back you.'

'Thank you.' Declan already had his mobile phone in hi
hand. He punched a logged-in number and waited to be con
nected. 'Rachel? Declan. We're still at the stables. Th
chopper's a no-show. We're bringing Jodi in now. I'll do th
surgery. I'll have to pin and plate so I'll need all orthopaedi[c]
trays sterilized and ready.'

'Word of the RTA is all over the TV news,' Rachel sai[d]
'I've gone ahead and anticipated your request.'

'Brilliant—thanks.' Declan felt a huge weight begin t
slide from his shoulders. They could do this. 'What nursin[g]
backup can we manage?'

'Well, I'll scrub, of course, and I've got Dot here. She'[s]
theatre-savvy, even if she doesn't get much practice thes[e]
days.'

'Oliver Shackelton lined up to gas for us?'

'There we might have a slight problem.' Rachel sounde[d]
cautious. 'I called Oliver. He's had flu, and he's feeling to[o]
rocky to be in Theatre.'

'So, we don't have an anaesthetist?' Declan just resiste[d]
thumping his fist against his forehead in frustration. Wha
options did he have now to safely go ahead with Jodi'
surgery? 'Just give me a second here, Rachel.'

Beside him, Emma got the gist of the conversation an
wondered what unkind fate had singled her out today. She fe[lt]
as though her professional integrity had been pushed to th
limits. It wasn't fair. Emotion, real and powerful, churne[d]

nside her. Could she take this last step that would enable
Declan to operate? Could she afford not to? When did it
become obligation to speak up? Was it safer to just stand
aside and wait?

In her heart, she knew the decision had already been made
for her.

'Declan?'

Her fleeting touch in the small of his back had his gaze swi-
velling in her direction. He shrugged. 'Looks like we're
stuffed,' he said flatly. 'Oliver can't help.'

'But perhaps I can.' She looked unflinchingly at him. 'I did
my elective in anaesthesiology. I could probably manage. But
it will be a long op. I'll need Oliver's input on dosage for
longer-acting drugs. But if you think the whole thing's too
risky, I want you to pull out now.'

Declan shook his head. In his mind there were no doubts
left and only three words to be said. 'We'll go ahead.'

Emma could hardly believe how smoothly their little hospital
was coping with the emergency. She was still basking in a
sense of pride as she finished scrubbing. The sound of a door
swishing open sent her turning away from the basin and, by
the time Declan had begun scrubbing beside her, she was
drying her hands and asking sharply, 'You OK?'

'Yep.' He sent her an abrupt look from under his brows and
grinned. 'Glad I had that extra X-ray equipment installed,
though.'

'Even though we'll be paying for it for the rest of our
lives.'

'Oh, tut, Emma. We've managed so far, haven't we?'

She had to admit they had. And she knew they were batting
light conversation around because to get too serious now
would be more than either of them could cope with. The
decision to operate here had been made. They just had to
make sure they gave it their all.

'See you in there.' She turned and left the annexe and
crossed to the theatre. Rachel had prepared the anaesthetic

trolley perfectly and Emma felt a rush of adrenalin she hadn'
experienced for the longest time.

She'd do a brilliant job for Jodi.

They all would.

The surgery took almost seven hours. Hours when Emma fel
her skills were being tested mercilessly. Even though the
monitors indicated Jodi was handling the anaesthetic well
Emma knew she couldn't afford to relax her vigilance for
second. Time after time she raised her eyes to meet Declan's
wanting reassurance, wanting anything to tell her they'd don
the right thing. *I'm fine*, his look said, and he gave her th
merest nod.

'Thanks, team. Fantastic effort.' Declan inserted the last sutur
in Jodi's shin. He dressed the site with care and signalled fo
Emma to reverse the anaesthetic. 'How's our girl looking
Emma?'

'She's looking good,' Emma said.

'That's what I like to hear.' Above his mask, Declan's eye
crinkled with tired humour. 'OK, guys, would you mind fin
ishing up here?' He stepped back from the operating table
working his shoulders briefly. 'I don't want to keep Moir
waiting for news any longer than necessary.'

'I'm sure we don't mind at all.' Emma paused and the
added barely audibly, 'That was a fine piece of surgery
Declan.'

Declan's eyes met hers and held. 'You made it easy, D
Armitage.' With that, he turned on his heel and left the theatre

Declan answered the clamouring of his aching back with
long hot shower. The whole day had begun to take on a surrea
quality. The adrenalin rush he'd felt at the beginning of th
operation had disappeared, leaving him flat. He didn't dwe
on it. Instead, he dressed quickly and went to meet Emma a
the nurses' station.

At his approach, Emma looked up and smiled. She had

lot to smile about. Jodi was in Recovery and doing well. 'Apparently, there's some dinner for us in the canteen. Betty's made us her special Turkish lamb casserole,' she said.

He raised his brows in mock awe. 'We'd better have second helpings, then.'

'Did you get all your follow-up done?'

'I reassured Moira and left a few post-op instructions with the night sister. Jodi should be stable enough to make the transfer to the Royal late tomorrow. Her parents are flying back in the morning. They'll make their base in Brisbane for the next few days and see their daughter settled in.'

Emma nodded. She had a dozen questions for him, about him, but none she could ask. Not yet. And maybe she wouldn't have to ask them at all. Maybe, without her prompting, Declan would simply tell her what she wanted to know. Had to know.

They ate hungrily.

'Not half bad,' Declan said, finishing his meal and placing his cutlery neatly together on his dinner plate.

'And so sweet of Betty to have made it especially for us.' Emma sent him a half-smile. 'Word's got round pretty quickly that big things happened here today.'

'Is that so?'

Emma stood up. 'Cup of tea?'

'Sounds good.' He turned away as his mobile phone rang.

Emma placed their cups of tea on a tray, added some rosemary shortbread she'd raided from the nurses' cookie jar and began making her way back to their table. It was late and they were the only ones left in the hospital canteen. Although he hadn't said it, Declan must be feeling the strain of the day, she thought. The charcoal shadows around his eyes were a dead giveaway.

Well, they'd be home soon. She'd hold him all night, smooth away the tensions, pleasure herself with the hardness of his body and the careless male beauty of his nakedness. They'd made love only this morning but it already felt like a year ago.

Her breath felt fluttery.

'Drink up and we'll make tracks.' Declan's brow furrowed. 'I'll drop you home and then take off. I need to wind down a bit and I want to make a call to Scotland. Have a chat to Angus Menzies at St Mary's about today. Debrief, I guess.'

Why couldn't he debrief with *her*? A look of disbelief scorched Emma's gaze. Hell, she'd been there with him at the cutting edge. It was only because of her compliance that he'd been able to go ahead and perform the surgery at all. She couldn't believe he wouldn't want them to spend the night together. 'You could do all that from Kingsholme.'

Of course he could. But he knew that would mean Emma would want him, *expect* him, to stay the night. To make love with her. How could he tell her he doubted if he was physically capable? The hours spent in surgery had left him with a burning pain in his lower back, his legs feeling as if he'd run a marathon. It was too soon to know if it would be an ongoing problem for him. But hell, what if it was? He gathered the strands of his tattered pride, raising an eyebrow at her. 'I've got a bit to sort out. You know how it is.'

No, she didn't know at all. Her confidence in their new-found commitment dropped to the floor. And stayed there like an unwanted garment that didn't fit. Lifting a hand, she brushed an imaginary crumb from her bottom lip. 'I'm ready when you are, then.'

They made their way in silence to his car. When they arrived at Kingsholme, Declan walked her to the door. 'I thought we could meet up at the hospital in the morning. See Jodi together. Around eightish? Is that all right with you?'

'Fine.' Emma shrugged. 'I hope you get your debrief.'

'Mmm.' He leant and placed a swift little kiss on her mouth and then stepped back. 'Thanks for today,' he said abruptly then walked away.

The house felt cold and unlived-in. Emma shivered. She went from room to room, switching on the lights. She could have a fire. But why bother? The empty feeling inside her was terrible.

What was going on with Declan? Physically, he appeared to have coped with the long stint in the OR. But he hadn't en-lightened her about how he was feeling. Surely she deserved more than the cursory thanks he'd offered? Unless—Emma felt a river of alarm run down her spine. Was he intending to walk away now he had his career back? He'd said she had to trust him, but just now her trust was wearing very thin. Gossamer-thin and fragile.

The next morning, there was no sign of Declan when Emma arrived at the hospital. She decided to go and visit Jodi without him. He'd made the arrangements. It was up to him to keep them. Or let her know if he couldn't for some reason.

She found Jodi sitting up in bed, looking pale. Well, that was to be expected. The youngster had undergone major surgery. 'Hi, sweetie.' Emma pulled up a chair and sat down. 'How are you feeling?'

'I've been better.' Jodi pulled a sad little clown's face. 'I *so* cannot believe what happened.'

'They call them accidents, honey. All said and done, you were very fortunate.'

Jodi made a sound of disgust in her throat. 'The guys got off scot-free.'

'Except for getting the fright of their lives—and I think Mr McGinty will have a few hard words to say to them,' Emma predicted soberly.

Hell. Declan dragged a pair of jeans and a long-sleeved sweat-shirt out of the pile of clean laundry and dressed hurriedly. How on earth could he have slept in? He hadn't heard the alarm. Well, what did he expect? He'd spent most of night wide awake before sleep had finally claimed him around 4:00 a.m.

And he hadn't solved anything. He still felt caught in a sea of confusion. He felt bad about how he'd handled things with Emma last night. Or not handled them. With hindsight, he knew he should have told her how physically exhausted he'd felt. She would have understood. But then that would have opened another can of worms—should he have operated at all?

Now he was facing an even worse scenario. By the way he felt this morning—would he ever be able to operate again? Grabbing his jacket, phone and car keys, he stepped out into the chilly morning.

He wasn't surprised to see Emma's little four-by-four in the parking lot when he arrived at the hospital. He shook his head. She was always so reliable, did things by the book. Except for yesterday. His mouth twisted grimly. He knew that backing him to do the surgery had been a huge call for her. Right outside her comfort zone.

Entering the hospital, he flung a greeting at the nurse on duty at the station and made his way along the corridor to Jodi's room. Taking a deep controlling breath, he knocked and entered.

'Morning.' Both women looked up. Emma held his gaze for a second, then looked pointedly away. He winced inwardly. She was cheesed off with him and he didn't blame her. He picked up Jodi's chart and studied it. 'How's our star patient this morning?'

Jodi managed a half smile. 'I'm still here. I guess that's a plus.'

'A pretty big plus from where I'm standing.' Declan raised his dark head. 'And I dare say Emma feels the same. How's the pain this morning, Jodi?'

'Still hurts a bit.'

A lot, Declan interpreted, going on the night report. 'I'll up your pain relief. That should help.'

'Nan says I have to go to Royal Brisbane. Is that really necessary?'

''Fraid so.' Declan replaced the patient chart and pocketed his pen. 'We don't have the facilities to nurse you here, Jodi. Besides, you're going to need some specialized rehab to get your legs back in working order.'

Emma squeezed Jodi's hand. 'You're young and fit, Jodi. You'll be back with us before you know it.'

'And what *about* my legs?' Jodi's voice wobbled. 'How badly hurt were they? Will I be able to ride again? Can I have the truth, please…?'

Emma glanced at Declan, then snatched her gaze away as if it hurt her eyes. 'They're probably questions for your surgeon,' she said and held Jodi's hand tightly.

'I won't keep the truth from you, Jodi.' Declan slipped seamlessly into a role he knew so well. Dealing with the anxieties of post-surgery patients. 'Your legs were pretty badly knocked about.' At Jodi's little gasp of dismay, he lifted a staying hand and went on, 'But I've done this kind of operation dozens of times. You're back together.' He smiled then. 'And almost as good as new.'

'Oh—' Jodi gave a little mew of relief.

'If you work hard with your physio,' Declan promised, 'your fitness will return quite quickly.'

'And my legs… Will…will they look…gross?'

'Of course they won't!' Emma looked appalled. 'I won't regale you with the clinical details of the operation, but Declan did an amazing job. You'll find there'll be hardly any scarring at all.'

Jodi sent them a watery smile. 'Thanks.' She leaned back on her pillows, her look braver than before. 'And what about my job at the surgery?'

'Well, I don't know about that.' Declan rubbed his jaw as if considering a weighty problem. 'What do you think, Emma?'

Emma did her best to join in the light-heartedness for Jodi's sake. 'Oh, I think we can muddle along until you can come back to us, sweetheart.' She got to her feet. 'Now, we'll leave you in peace.'

'Nan said she'd be in a bit later on.' Jodi blocked a yawn. 'Are you both coming in to see me off on the chopper?'

'Wouldn't want to be anywhere else, would we?' Emma

placed a gentle hand on Jodi's shoulder. 'I'll check with the nurses' station about the ETA of the CareFlight chopper.' She fluttered a wave in Jodi's direction and made her way to the door. Declan followed closely behind.

Emma waited until they were outside the hospital before she asked, 'You do intend being here to see Jodi safely off, don't you, Declan?'

He shoved his hands into the back pockets of his jeans. 'I...need to talk to you about that. Could we go somewhere for a coffee?'

Emma sent him a speaking look. 'You mean you'll actually make time for me?'

He hunched his shoulders and scrubbed at a pebble with the toe of his shoe.

'Emma, this is very hard,' he said. And she could see in the strained expression in his face how much he meant it.

'It doesn't have to be, does it?' she countered, her throat tight. 'You could just talk to me.'

'I can't—not yet. A lot's happened over the last twenty-four hours. I need to find my own way through this. Please understand.'

Was he saying he couldn't share his thoughts with her? Or was it something deeper? Her mouth drooped. Whatever it was, she knew she couldn't push him any further. She glanced at her watch. 'Rina Kennedy is reopening the garden centre today. I promised I'd go along. They've incorporated a food court in the refurbishment. We could get a coffee there.'

'Fine,' he agreed quickly. 'I'll follow you.'

The garden centre was already buzzing. Quashing her immediate problems, Emma looked around her. The townsfolk had come out in droves to support the Kennedys. And it was looking lovely. Very upmarket.

Declan touched her arm. 'This looks like the coffee shop through here. Shall we get a table?'

Emma nodded, the well of emotion rising in her throat

threatening to choke her. When they were seated, she picked up the menu and made a pretence of studying it. 'Well, this is different,' she joked thinly. 'Fancy a wattle seed tea?'

Declan's mouth twisted in the parody of a smile. 'I'll stick to coffee, thanks. But don't let me stop you. What about some raisin toast to go with it?'

'I'll have a friand, I think.' She turned to catch the eye of the waitress and blinked. 'Oh, my goodness—there's Tracey! She must work here.' She was looking wonderful in her pristine white T-shirt and black pants covered by a dark green apron with the little shamrock embroidered on the front. Her hair was pulled neatly back and her smile was wide and welcoming as she approached their table.

They exchanged greetings and Tracey said, beaming, 'I've got a job here.'

'Congratulations,' Declan said warmly.

'From me as well,' Emma added. 'You're a star, Tracey.'

'I got the job off my own bat too,' Tracey said proudly. 'Mrs Kennedy is going to teach me the nursery side of things and I can do some college courses in Toowoomba and learn how to propagate plants and stuff.'

'That's brilliant.' Declan raised dark brows. 'I'm impressed.'

'Well, I've you to thank really, Dr O'Malley.' Tracey blushed. 'I mean you believed in me…'

Declan shook his head. 'You did all the hard work, Tracey.'

'Maybe…' She bit her lip. 'And Dr Armitage—you looked after my kids…' She stopped, embarrassed.

'It was a pleasure, Tracey.' Emma blinked a bit. 'They're wonderful kids. Are they here today?'

'Heck, no.' Tracey rolled her eyes. 'They're with Nev.'

'So, life is looking pretty good, then?' Declan asked.

Tracey nodded. 'And, best of all, I've been placed on the Defence Department's housing list. The kids and I should get our own place pretty soon. We'll be together again and Carolyn will get some peace at last. Anyway…' she huffed an embarrassed laugh and took out her order book '...what can I get you?'

There was an awkward silence after Tracey had gone.

'So, did you manage your debrief?' Emma's question had a sharp edge to it.

His look was guarded and cool. 'After a fashion.'

'Look, could we stop talking in riddles?' Emma threw caution to the winds and said what was uppermost on her mind. 'It hurt that you didn't want us to be together last night. What am I supposed to think now, Declan?'

'I hardly know what to think myself, Emma,' he said baldly. 'Yesterday changed everything.'

'You mean it's given you options you didn't have before, don't you?'

Declan's face was tightly drawn. 'I don't know yet. That's something I have to find out.'

The silence between them lengthened and became thicker.

'I need to ask a favour of you, Emma,' he said at last.

Her heart pounded uncomfortably. 'What do you need?'

'I need to be in Melbourne for a couple of days. I'll get a flight today from Brisbane and I should be back for surgery on Tuesday. If you could cover my patient list on Monday, I'd be grateful.'

She was hardly surprised at his request. It wasn't as though she hadn't conducted surgery countless times before on her own. It was obvious he was going to Melbourne to sort out what options were open to him. Maybe even get a new job operating now he knew he could. Well, she hoped he got what he wanted. He certainly didn't want *her*. She took a deep breath and pressed her palms down hard on the table. 'Go and do what you have to do, Declan. I'll manage.'

CHAPTER TWELVE

'MOIRA, streamline the patient lists as much as you can, please,' Emma said on Monday morning to the practice manager. 'I'm covering for Declan today.'

'Where *is* Declan?' Moira raised a questioning brow.

'Melbourne,' Emma said economically.

'He has family in Melbourne, doesn't he?'

'Yes.' Emma shrugged. And Declan was known there, had a network of professional contacts there. No doubt felt at home there. Enough to draw him back?

Her nerves tightened alarmingly. If he knew he could resume his chosen discipline, what on earth could entice him to stay in Bendemere?

The thought was painful. Almost impossible to bear. But Emma brought her fair head up determinedly. 'Don't worry about morning tea, Moira. I'll work straight through to lunch.'

Declan waited in the foyer of the lovely old building that contained within its hallowed architecture the professional rooms of the city's leading specialist doctors.

No one knew he was in Melbourne. No one apart from Emma and Matthew Levingston, one of Australia's top spinal consultants, who had agreed to see him first thing this morning as a professional favour. He hadn't wanted to tell his sisters he was in town. There would be too many questions— questions he didn't have answers to.

The lift arrived and Declan stepped inside. Even though he'd had only tea and toast for breakfast, it was sitting uneasily in his stomach. Breathing out a jagged breath, he pressed the button for the third floor.

Dr Levingston's receptionist, Jill Carter, was middle-aged and pleasant, her smile professionally in place as Declan approached the counter.

'Declan O'Malley.' His voice was clipped, strained. 'I have an appointment this morning.'

'Yes, Dr O'Malley. Dr Levingston is expecting you. Take a seat for a moment. He shouldn't be long.'

'Thanks.' Declan hesitated. 'Would you know if my notes arrived from Scotland? They were coming from St Mary's in Edinburgh.'

'Faxed through during the weekend. Doctor has them now.'

Declan nodded, relieved. That was the first hurdle over, then. He crossed to where a row of comfortable chairs were arranged along the wall and lowered himself into one of the cushioned seats. He stretched out his legs and looked at his watch for the umpteenth time. It was barely eight o'clock.

It seemed only seconds later when a side door opened and the consultant poked his head out. 'Declan. Come through, mate.'

The two men shook hands warmly. 'Thanks for seeing me at such short notice, Matt,' Declan said.

'Happy to do it.' The consultant's mouth twisted into a wry grin. 'Have to look after our own, don't we? Now, could I organize coffee?'

Declan's stomach protested. 'No—no, thanks. I'm fine.'

'Right, let's put you through your paces, then.'

Matthew's examination was painstaking, his questions, and Declan imagined there were a thousand of them, probing. 'OK,' he said finally. 'That's it for now. Anything you want clarified?'

'The residual pain I experienced after I'd been in Theatre?'

'Pretty normal. It would have helped if you'd been able to ease yourself back into work rather than go for a seven-hour marathon straight away,' he suggested dryly.

'I was faced with an emergency,' Declan said. 'Not much choice there.'

'Probably not.' Matthew's mouth pursed thoughtfully. 'You can get dressed now, Declan. Come back out when you're ready and we'll have a chat. It's looking good, by the way,' he added before pulling back the screen and returning to his desk.

Declan felt one layer of trepidation roll off him. One step at a time, though. That was all it could be until he knew…

'You appear to have healed particularly well,' said Matthew. 'Your spine is in good order.' He amplified the statement with technical language because he rightly guessed Declan would want the clinical assessment. 'Now, all that said, I'd like you to have an MRI before I can give you definitive answers.'

Declan gave a resigned grin. 'I was afraid you'd stick me with one of those.'

'You betcha. But, with the new technology, they're less onerous than they used to be.' Matthew picked up his phone and spoke briefly to his receptionist. 'Do the best you can,' he ended. 'Thanks.' He clipped the phone back on its cradle. 'There's normally a bit of a wait on these. How soon do you need to be back at your practice?'

In an instant Declan was transported back to Kingsholme, visualizing Emma beavering away through the morning's list, her fair head bent over the patients' notes. She probably hadn't had a moment to think of him. But he'd had the whole of the weekend to think of her. And she was filling his heart to overflowing. But his feelings were laced with vulnerability. Such vulnerability. He wasn't sure of her or her feelings for him. 'My partner is holding the fort but I'd like to get back as soon as possible.'

Matthew nodded, his hand reaching out as his phone pad lit discreetly. He leaned back in his chair, holding the receiver loosely and listened. 'OK, thanks, Jill. Excellent. We're in luck,' he said, replacing the handset. 'The imaging centre has a cancellation. How does ten-thirty sound?'

Although he wasn't particularly looking forward to the procedure, Declan nodded gratefully. 'Sounds good. Which centre do you use?'

'The new state-of-the-art set-up in St Kilda. Jill will give you the address. Then I'll need to see you again and discuss things.' Matthew pulled his diary open and studied it. 'I'm not in Theatre today so I could see you, let's see—around four this afternoon?' he suggested, sending a quizzical glance across his desk.

'I'll be here.' The two men stood and shook hands again.

'A word of advice, Declan,' Matthew said as he saw his patient out. 'Don't spend the day sweating about outcomes. I'll see you back here at four.'

Outside the building, Declan took a moment to get his bearings. He hardly remembered getting here this morning, so totally preoccupied as he'd been with the weight of his medical appointment. Now, he felt better, freer. The worst was over. His fitness hadn't lapsed and, whatever the outcome of the MRI, he knew now he could make a life for himself in medicine, even if it couldn't be permanently in the operating theatre. He'd enjoyed being a family practitioner more than he'd ever thought he would.

The feeling of optimism startled him, refreshed him. God, it felt good just be out in the world again, in a city he loved.

Suddenly he longed to share his news with someone who cared. He grimaced. Emma was out of the question. He had a lot of making up to do before he could expect her to listen to him. Both his sisters would be at work. Hailing a passing cab, he got in and gave the St Kilda address of the imaging centre. Then it came to him. There *was* someone he could talk to.

At the airport, Declan prowled past the ticketing booth yet again. He'd been waiting on standby for his flight to Brisbane. Several flights had been called but each time he'd missed out on a seat. Another flight was about to depart and he *had* to get on board if he was to have any chance of seeing Emma tonight.

He almost missed his name when it was called. Finally. Thank God. He looped his carry-on bag over his shoulder and strode swiftly down the covered walkway to the waiting aircraft.

Emma sat on the sofa in a kind of twilight daze. Earlier, she'd been for a run and on her return she'd showered and dressed in her track pants and fleecy top. She supposed she should go to bed but she knew she'd never sleep. She'd had one brief text message from Declan telling her he'd be back some time tonight. She wondered how late his flight had got in.

She should have swallowed her pride and texted back and insisted he stay the night in Brisbane. With the possibility of a fog always present, driving up that mountain road at night was fraught with risks.

When the knock sounded on the back door, she lifted her head sharply towards the sound, her heart swooping. Swallowing back a little cry of anguish, she half-ran, half-walked to the door. Reaching for the latch, she yanked it open.

Seeing him there, smiling, expectant, in one piece, when he'd envisaged all kinds of calamities, she felt suddenly overwhelmed by anger. 'What time do you call this, Declan? It's after midnight!'

The amber in her eyes glittered like fiery embers. She was beautiful and he suddenly realized he couldn't wait a moment longer to tell her how he felt about her. Feeling he was opening up his chest and showing her his heart, he said, 'I love you, Emma. I'm never letting you go.'

'Ooh—' Emma felt all the breath leave her body, a great jumble of emotions tumble around inside her. Was she dreaming? She stood frozen, love, hope and joy colliding in a great ball in her chest.

'Emma?' His eyes clouded. 'I'm freezing to death here. Did you hear what I said?'

She gave a frenzied little nod and found her voice. 'Come inside then, you crazy man.' She drew him inside to the warmth of the lounge room. And turned to him, eyes over bright. 'You must have been mad driving up the range at this time of night.'

'I must have been.' His eyes glinted and he reached for her and pulled her hard against him. 'Mad for the sight of you,' he said hoarsely. 'Do you love me too?'

Emma took a deep breath, feeling overwhelmed suddenly by recent events. 'Of course I love you.'

'Oh, thank God,' he whispered. 'Thank *you*,' he echoed, pressing kisses all over her face. 'I never want to be away from you again.'

They were words she'd longed to hear. But she wasn't letting him off the hook just yet. 'You owe me an explanation, Declan. I've been going slowly crazy wondering where your head was at for these past couple of days. Did I do something wrong—say something wrong?'

'No! It wasn't you—it was me. After Jodi's surgery, I was so preoccupied with my own problems, I wasn't thinking straight.'

'We *should* have debriefed,' she insisted. 'I needed it as much as you.'

'Yes, you did. I honestly didn't realize.' He frowned down into her face. 'I wasn't feeling all that great after Jodi's surgery,' he confessed, his voice a bit scratchy. 'But I didn't want to burden you. I'd pushed you to support me and I was afraid my career might be completely over—that you'd be forever lumbered with a practice partner—and a lover—who couldn't pull his weight…'

'Oh, my God—Declan!' Emma shook her head as if she couldn't believe his thought processes.

'I know, I know,' he admitted ruefully. 'It all sounds a bit pathetic and over-reactive now.'

'Shh.' She placed her fingers on his lips. 'It was a big deal for you. I should have understood that. I guess I was a bit selfish.'

'You're the least selfish person I know,' he countered.

Emma curled her fingers up around his neck. 'Are you terribly tired—or could we talk?'

The curve of her bottom through the soft stuff of her track pants felt good tucked into his palms and he shook his head. 'I'll never be too tired for you, Emma.'

They stoked up the fire and fell on to the sofa in a tight tangle of arms and legs, her cheek pressed against his chest so that she could hear the steady rhythm of his heart. 'So—' she paused and reached up to touch his face, stroking the dark shadows around his eyes with gentle fingers '—what did you do in Melbourne?'

His brain fizzed with technical information but he kept it simple, telling her about his medical appointments but leaving nothing out.

'And what did Dr Levingston say when you went back to see him?' She almost held her breath for his answer.

'That I'm fully recovered.' He looked suddenly youthful, eager. 'I can operate again without fearing I'll fall over.'

'Oh, Declan!' Emma's pulse trebled before she could put the brakes on. 'I'm so happy for you,' she said, but thinking also what this new state of affairs could mean to them personally, to their practice, if he wanted to leave… 'It's going to change things here, isn't it?'

'Only if it's what we both want.' He looked down at her, his face unsmiling, deep in concentration. 'I had plenty of time to think while I was waiting for a flight home. I came up with a couple of possibilities.'

'OK…' Emma felt a hard-edged little lump that lodged somewhere in her chest. 'Tell me.'

'Well, we could leave things as they are,' he said slowly. 'I'm sure I could schedule enough orthopaedic work in Toowoomba to keep my hand in, as well as pulling my weight here in the practice.'

Emma looked doubtful. 'Would that be fulfilling enough for you, though?'

'Yes,' he said without hesitation. 'If that's what you want too. I've learned a lot here. Being a doctor in a rural practice carries clout, enables you to get things done for people. Good things. Necessary things. It's a great feeling.'

Oh, she was so glad he felt like that. 'That's what I think too.'

He smiled. 'Yes. I knew that.'

'And we could open up the OR here and do basic procedures, like Dad did,' Emma expanded. 'Rachel's staying, by the way. I talked to her yesterday.'

'That's good. She's needed here.'

Emma noticed he'd gone quiet. He looked tired, she thought. And a little strained. It made her love him more. Made her want to smooth out those lines around his eyes and mouth with her fingers, and with her lips… They'd get to that. Later. 'What was the other possibility you came up with then?'

'Ah!' There was life in his face again. 'I thought we could lease out the practice for a year and go and live in Melbourne.'

'Melbourne?' This was right out of left field. Emma wriggled upright. 'What would we do there?'

'I could go back to the OR full-time, be part of a surgical team again.'

'I see.' A tiny frown came to rest between her brows. 'And what would I do?'

'You, my love, could get a place in an anaesthetist training programme, upgrade your skills so you could be my gas woman when we come back to Kingsholme.'

She chuckled. 'Your gas woman? I like the sound of it, though. But would I get into a programme? I imagine places are at a premium.'

'I know a few faces,' he said modestly. 'And I imagine if you used your dad's name in the right places, doors would open.'

Emma digested all that. The idea appealed to her. Quite a lot, actually. 'I think I'd really, really like to do that,' she said quietly. 'But we'd need to get someone of calibre for Kingsholme.'

'We would. If we offered a year's tenure, we'd be sure to get quality applicants.'

'And we *will* come back to Kingsholme eventually, won't we?'

'Of course we will,' he promised. 'We'd want to raise our kids here, wouldn't we?'

'Oh, yes… I'd love to fill the house with our children.' He looked startled and she wrinkled her nose and compromised, 'With two or three, then.'

'That's manageable.' He sliced her a grin and then sobered. 'You've been bowed down under tremendous pressure for a long time now, Emma. A year away will be good for you to do something for yourself, be a student again.'

She rolled her eyes at him. 'I'll probably end up with some pedantic authoritarian boss who'll yell at me.'

'Yell back.' Declan ran the tip of his finger down her straight little nose. 'You're a fully qualified doctor, not some poor intern struggling for approval.'

'Mmm.' She settled herself more comfortably in his arms. 'It's pretty exciting to think we could do something like this, isn't it, Declan?'

'I think so.' He paused and rested his chin on the top of her head. 'I had lunch with Roz while I was in Melbourne.'

Emma twisted to look at him. 'You had lunch with my mother! Why?'

'I was at a loose end. Felt the need for family but Erinn and Katie were at work. Then I thought of your mum and it just seemed to fit. If I couldn't have you with me, then I had the next best thing. Roz was brilliant. We got on like a house on fire. We talked about you a lot.'

'Did you tell her why you were in Melbourne?'

'Yes. She was sympathetic, practical. Talked me up. I also told her I was in love with you.'

'You did?' Emma laughed. 'What did she say?'

'Said she'd gathered how things were between us when she stayed here recently. She approves, by the way.'

Emma gave him a quick intense glance. He'd taken her breath away.

'And she gave me something for you as well,' Declan said. 'A photo album she thought you'd like to have. It's in the car.'

'Oh, Lord,' Emma groaned. 'Not nude baby shots—please?'

His head went back in a laugh. 'One or two. But mostly they're of you and your parents from when you were tiny until your teens. Your parents had a happy marriage, Emma. You can't fake the kind of warmth I saw in those snapshots.'

'I'd come to that conclusion myself,' she said softly, drawing closer to him. 'But it was sweet of Mum to send the album.' And put her last remaining fears to rest. Emma wanted to say it but her heart was so full she couldn't find the words and anyway he didn't give her time.

'Will you marry me, Emma?'

The words were bliss to her ears. She hesitated and then said, 'Yes, Declan, I'll marry you. But not yet.'

His dark brows shot up in question.

'I want us to do some old-fashioned courting first.'

He reached out and brought her chin up gently, and his eyes when they looked into hers were lit with devilment. 'You want me to *court* you?'

'Yes, please.'

'Like with flowers and presents and…love notes?'

'All of those.'

'And dinners out?'

She looked dreamily at him. 'And dinners in.'

'I can do that.' He kissed her very sweetly, very tenderly. 'And when I've done everything to your satisfaction, you'll become my bride?'

'Yes, Declan…' Her voice broke on a whisper as she looked up at him and saw the soft sheen of love in his eyes. 'Then I'll become your bride.'

MEDICAL™ 2-in-1

Coming next month
WISHING FOR A MIRACLE
by Alison Roberts

Mac MacCulloch and Julia Bennett make the perfect team. But after an illness left Julia unable to have children, she stopped wishing for a miracle. Yet Mac's wish is standing right in front of him – Julia...and whatever the future may hold.

THE MARRY-ME WISH
by Alison Roberts

Nine months pregnant with her sister's twins, paediatric surgeon Anne Bennett bumps into ex-love Dr David Earnshaw! When the babies are born, learning to live without them is harder than Anne expected – and she soon discovers that she needs David more than ever...

PRINCE CHARMING OF HARLEY STREET
by Anne Fraser

Temporary nurse Rose Taylor is amazed when her playboy boss, Dr Jonathan Cavendish, expresses an interest! Swept off her feet, shy Rose realises she's misjudged this caring man but when her contract ends she knows she *has* to walk away...

THE HEART DOCTOR AND THE BABY
by Lynne Marshall

When Dr Jon Becker agrees to father his friend René Munro's baby, he's determined to support her...but his attraction to the radiantly pregnant René takes him by surprise! Jon's got used to the idea of becoming a father – is becoming her husband the next step?

On sale 6th August 2010

Available at WHSmith, Tesco, ASDA, Eason and all good bookshops.
For full Mills & Boon range including eBooks visit
www.millsandboon.co.uk

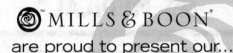

2 FREE BOOKS
AND A SURPRISE GIFT

We would like to take this opportunity to thank you for reading thi
Mills & Boon® book by offering you the chance to take TWO mor
specially selected books from the Medical™ series absolutely FREE
We're also making this offer to introduce you to the benefits of th
Mills & Boon® Book Club™—

- **FREE home delivery**
- **FREE gifts and competitions**
- **FREE monthly Newsletter**
- **Exclusive Mills & Boon Book Club offers**
- **Books available before they're in the shops**

Accepting these FREE books and gift places you under no obliga
tion to buy, you may cancel at any time, even after receiving your fre
books. Simply complete your details below and return the entire pag
to the address below. You don't even need a stamp!

YES Please send me 2 free Medical books and a surprise gift.
understand that unless you hear from me, I will receive 5 superb nev
stories every month including two 2-in-1 books priced at £4.9
each and a single book priced at £3.19, postage and packing free.
am under no obligation to purchase any books and may cancel m
subscription at any time. The free books and gift will be mine to kee
in any case.

Ms/Mrs/Miss/Mr _____ Initials _____

Surname _____

Address _____

_____

_____ Postcode _____

E-mail _____

Send this whole page to: Mills & Boon Book Club, Free Book Offe
FREEPOST NAT 10298, Richmond, TW9 1BR